Off the Menu

Off the Menu

*Asian and Asian North American Women's
Religion and Theology*

Rita Nakashima Brock
Jung Ha Kim
Kwok Pui-lan
Seung Ai Yang

EDITORS

Westminster John Knox Press
LOUISVILLE • LONDON

Except as otherwise indicated, Scripture quotations from the New Revised Standard Version of the Bible are copyright (c) 1989 by the Division of Christian Education of the National Council of the Churches of Christ in the U.S.A. and are used by permission.

Chapter 3 is an updated version of an article that originally appeared as Gale A. Yee, "'She Stood in Tears amid the Alien Corn': Ruth, the Perpetual Foreigner and Model Minority," in *They Were All Together in One Place? Toward Minority Biblical Criticism*, ed. Randall C. Bailey, Tat-siong Benny Liew, and Fernando F. Segovia. Semeia Studies 57 (Atlanta: Society of Biblical Literature, forthcoming); reprinted with the permission of the Society of Biblical Literature.

Chapter 4 is an updated version of an article that originally appeared as Jung Ha Kim, "Sources outside of Europe," in *Spirituality and the Secular Quest*, ed. Peter H. Van Ness (New York: Crossroad, 1996), 53–71; reprinted with the permission of Crossroad Publishing Co.

Portions of chapter 6 first appeared in Jane Naomi Iwamura, "Homage to Ancestors: Exploring the Horizons of Asian American Religious Identity," *Amerasia Journal* 22, no. 1 (1996): 162–67; reprinted with the permission of the University of Southern California, Los Angeles.

Portions of chapter 7 first appeared in Rita Nakashima Brock, "Interstitial Integrity: Reflections toward an Asian American Women's Theology," in *Introduction to Christian Theology: Contemporary North American Perspectives*, ed. Roger A. Badham (Louisville, KY: Westminster John Knox Press, 1997), 183–96; reprinted with the permission of Westminster John Knox Press.

Chapter 14 is an updated version of an article that originally appeared as Seung Ai Yang, "Jesus' Saying on Divorce: A Korean Perspective," *Bible Today* 35, no. 1 (1997): 49–54; reprinted with the permission of the author.

Chapter 15 is an updated version of an article that originally appeared as Rose Wu, "A Story of Its Own Name: Hong Kong's *Tongzhi* Culture and Movement," in *Other Voices, Other Worlds: The Global Church Speaks Out on Homosexuality*, ed. Terry Brown (New York: Church Publishing, 2006), 40–57; reprinted with the permission of Church Publishing.

Susan Mukai's poem in *Rising Waters* 2 (Santa Cruz: Asian American Studies Planning Group, University of California at Santa Cruz, 1977), n.p.; reprinted with the permission of the author.

Book design by Sharon Adams
Cover design by Jennifer K. Cox

First edition
Published by Westminster John Knox Press
Louisville, Kentucky

This book is printed on acid-free paper that meets the American National Standards Institute Z39.48 standard. ∞

PRINTED IN THE UNITED STATES OF AMERICA

07 08 09 10 11 12 13 14 15 16 — 10 9 8 7 6 5 4 3 2 1

Library of Congress Cataloging-in-Publication Data
Off the menu : Asian and Asian North American women's religion and theology / Rita Nakashima Brock . . . [et al.], editor. — 1st ed.
p. cm.
Includes bibliographical references and index.
ISBN 978-0-664-23140-8 (alk. paper)
1. Asian American women–Religion.   2. Feminist theology.   3. Women—Asia—Religious life. I. Brock, Rita Nakashima.
BR563.A82034   2007
230.082'095—dc22
2007006716

In Memoriam Suzette H. Loh (1961–2006)
Trustee, The Sister Fund

To the women of
Pacific, Asian, and North American Asian Women
in Theology and Ministry
(PANAAWTM)
and
with special thanks to
Letty M. Russell and
J. Shannon Clarkson

Contents

Acknowledgments

We are deeply grateful to Letty M. Russell and J. Shannon Clarkson for coordinating and raising funds for Pacific, Asian, and North American Asian Women in Theology and Ministry (PANAAWTM) during its first thirteen years. They have been inspiring role models and mentors, compassionate friends, and devoted white allies for two generations of Asian and North American Asian feminist theologians and scholars in religion.

This book would not have been possible without support from a fund established by The Sister Fund in honor of Suzette H. Loh, a Chinese American trustee of the fund. Thirteen years ago Helen LaKelly Hunt began this foundation, which supports fullness of life for women and girls. Loh was a trustee and a vital part of its success. She was a partner at Eisner LLP, one of the twenty largest regional accounting and advisory firms in the country. She married Antonio Lee, a childhood sweetheart, and together they raised two sons, Theodore and Thomas. She was diagnosed with breast cancer and passed away on February 1, 2006; she would have been forty-five on her next birthday. At her funeral her father spoke lovingly of "the brightest pearl in his palm," his Suzette. She was a bright pearl in many lives.

At her passing, her family decided that any funds for her memory be sent to The Sister Fund. Donations came from many sources, including the PTA where Suzette's sons attended school and companies that credited their success to her expert guidance. With the donations, The Sister Fund chose to honor her memory by supporting the publication and distribution of this anthology of Asian women's theology. Helen LaKelly Hunt offered tribute to Suzette's life by noting,

Those who knew Suzette Loh consider her to be one of the most remarkable women we have ever met. Her wisdom guided my family in ways for which we will forever be grateful. Her patience, courage, and tenacity were beyond compare. As she became ill, her gentle strength became a testimony to her family, friends, and colleagues. She just went on being the mother, advisor, friend, professional, daughter, and exemplary human being we had always known her to be. Her brilliance never faded.

On behalf of Tony and Suzette's dear family, her sons Teddy and Tommy, her closest colleagues and friends, we are pleased to support this anthology in tribute to her amazing spirit. The women who contributed to this anthology write of a presence to the divine that Suzette's life embodied. Suzette's spirit will continue to live on in those of us who were favored to know her.

We want to thank The Foundation for Theological Education in South East Asia and the Lilly Theological Research Grants of The Association of Theological Schools in the United States and Canada for providing additional funding for the book project. Over the years many churches have given generous support for our network, including the Christian Church (Disciples of Christ), the Episcopal Church, the Evangelical Lutheran Church in America, the Presbyterian Church (U.S.A.), the United Church of Christ, the United Methodist Church, The United Church of Canada, and The Presbyterian Church in Canada. We want to acknowledge the long-term support from The Foundation for Theological Education in South East Asia and from the Institute for Leadership Development and Study of Pacific and Asian North American Religion (PANA) at Pacific School of Religion. Many seminaries and divinity schools in the United States and in Canada have hosted our annual conferences, and we want to thank the administrators, faculty, staff, and students of these institutions for their support and for sharing our vision.

We are grateful to the contributors to this anthology for their insights, collaboration, and friendship. They have worked conscientiously under a tight schedule to make the editing and production processes as smooth as possible. Grateful acknowledgment is due to our editor, Jon Berquist, at Westminster John Knox Press, who saw the significance of our work from the beginning, and to the editorial staff of the press. The book is greatly improved because of the superb advice and comments we received from Christina Robb, a Pulitzer Prize–winning reporter and writer. Rosemarie Buxton, a teacher of creative and nonfiction writing, helped with editing and preparing the bibliography, and we are deeply indebted to her for her prompt and committed work for us. We also thank Toni Mortimer for her meticulous professional editing, which made the book more readable and the details more consistent. Paula K. R. Arai, an early member of PANAAWTM, made valuable suggestions for the selected resources.

As coeditors, we thank one another for sisterhood and comradeship throughout our bringing this groundbreaking volume to fruition. We cherish our many years of friendship and celebrate with joy and pride our work to introduce to a wider public the conversations that have taken place at PANAAWTM.

Introduction

In the fall of 1984 when the leaves had already started to change colors in New England, thirteen Asian and Asian North American women gathered at the home of Professor Letty M. Russell of Yale University. They were predominantly from Asia and enrolled in graduate theological institutions or working in ministries in the United States. They discussed their common interests and explored the possibility of forming a network. None among them could have imagined that this small network would continue to grow and flourish for twenty-some years. It has provided support and stimulated conversations among two generations of ministers, activists, scholars in religion, and community leaders.

This network, now called the Pacific, Asian, and North American Asian Women in Theology and Ministry (PANAAWTM), has generated this anthology. It showcases current Asian and Asian North American women's theological and religious thinking and indicates directions for future scholarship. It charts a fresh field of interdisciplinary works by Asian North American women theologians, biblical scholars, ethicists, religious educators, and activists. Emerging out of two decades of dialogue, the book includes pioneers in the field as well as promising new scholars from a variety of cultural and geographical backgrounds. It engages current issues in the academy, such as globalization, postcolonialism, and postmodernism, as well as broadening religious imagination through paradigms of cross-cultural and intergenerational interactions.

Since its inception, PANAAWTM members have recognized the complex historical, cultural, linguistic, and class backgrounds among us. Early on we became keenly aware that the cultural heritages, struggles, and intellectual traditions of Asian and Asian North American women are diverse, although we may look similar from the outside. This was brought home to us when we had a cultural evening in one of our early conferences. After a young woman demonstrated a traditional Thai dance, moving her fingers elegantly in all directions, the Asian American members rose from their chairs and boogied to the rhythms of rock music. We have learned much about our differences and similarities. Most Asian American women are concerned with racism, while many Asian women focus on the impacts of colonialism. We share concerns about the oppression of women, militarism, and the United States as a superpower, although we approach these issues in different ways.[1] Our divergent social locations and life experiences enable us to look at our intertwined histories from numerous vantage points and to examine the current discussions of empire and globalization from multiple subject positions—as insider, outsider, insider without, and outsider within.

Although the dominant white culture views Asian women as stereotypically gentle, submissive, and forever foreign, Asian women share neither a common language nor a unifying culture. In fact, some of the Asian countries warred against one another just a generation ago, and Japan colonized both Korea and Taiwan in the first half of the twentieth century. Hindu culture in South Asia is radically different from the Confucian heritage in East Asia, the Muslim traditions in Indonesia and other Southeast Asian countries, and ethnic subgroups such as the Hmong. The Philippines shares a colonial history and culture more similar to that of Latin America than that of her Asian neighbors. While countries on the so-called Pacific Rim have developed phenomenally since the 1970s, many Asian people continue to live in abject poverty and suffer from malnutrition, poor sanitation, and the lack of safe drinking water. Just as there is no unified "Asia" but many "Asias," depending on our interpretive frameworks and choices of focus, it is important to bear in mind that ideas of gender and the status of women vary from country to country and ethnicity to ethnicity.

Because of such diversity it has taken time as well as patience for us to engage one another in PANAAWTM and to promote solidarity across differences. From the beginning we chose to include not only those in the academy but also those working in churches, faith communities, and other social ministries. We have welcomed members who fight to end domestic violence, advocate for gay and lesbian families, work against racism, struggle for women's rights, and raise faith voices in the public square. These members and their commitments have helped us remain grounded as a grassroots movement and prevented our metamorphosis into another elite club in the ivory tower.

As the group has grown, its name has been changed several times to reflect its commitment to remain inclusive and welcoming.[2] Our first conference, held in 1985, was convened under the name Asian Women Theologians, which was expanded to Asian and Asian American Women Theologians the following year to recognize the presence of Asian American members. Then the word "Ministry" was added in 1991 to reflect the fact that not every member identifies as a theologian or intends to work in an academic setting. Our gatherings have included women belonging to the Jewish, Muslim, Hindu, Buddhist, and Shinto traditions, although we are predominantly affiliated with Christianity. In 1996 we expanded our name once again to Pacific, Asian, and North American Asian Women in Theology and Ministry because our Canadian sisters drew our attention to the fact that "American" did not include women from Canada. We have learned to say "North American" and not simply "American" when referring to people from Canada and the United States.

Although PANAAWTM is a small grassroots movement, it has left indelible marks on the work of the academy. The network organized the first panel on Asian feminist theology at the 1986 annual meeting of the American Academy of Religion (AAR), and the papers were subsequently published in the *Journal of Feminist Studies in Religion*.[3] This program then led to the first panel specifically on Asian American women at the AAR, from which its PANAAWTM participants created the Asian North American Religion, Society, and Culture Group, an ongoing, successful program unit of the AAR that has been cochaired by a number of our members. Out of this program unit the first Consultation on Asian North American Theologies was held in 2002 in Toronto, organized by Rita Nakashima Brock. In addition, Jane Naomi Iwamura was instrumental in starting the Asian Pacific Americans and Religion Research Initiative (APARRI), which continues to hold a conference every summer. Our members have also maintained contacts with various theological networks and institutions, such as the Institute for Leadership Development and Study of Pacific and Asian North American Religion (PANA) at Pacific School of Religion, the Congress of Asian Theologians, and the Ecumenical Association of Third World Theologians (EATWOT). Jung Ha Kim has served as a coordinator of the U.S. minorities group of EATWOT. Lai Ling Elizabeth Ngan is currently cochair of the Asian and Asian American Hermeneutics Group of the Society of Biblical Literature. Gale A. Yee was the president of the Ethnic Chinese Biblical Colloquium and one if its founding members, and Mary F. Foskett is its current president. Seung Ai Yang is a founding member of the Korean Biblical

Colloquium and has served as executive director. In addition to making contributions in religious studies and theological education, participants have served in churches, religious organizations, denominational offices, social service agencies, and other nonprofit organizations across North America and in Asia as ordained ministers and lay leaders.

As we celebrated our twentieth anniversary in 2005, we began to dream of publishing an anthology to mark this significant milestone. We were encouraged by the example of black women scholars in religion, who were planning the volume *Deeper Shades of Purple*, which commemorates two decades of their scholarship. Their movement adopted the term "womanist" in 1985.[4] We recall with fondness and gratitude that the womanist scholars Katie Geneva Cannon and Joan Martin, the *mujerista* (*mujer* is Spanish for woman) ethicist Ada María Isasi-Díaz, and the Latin American theologian Elsa Tamez participated in early conferences. They supported us and shared their insights in organizing a movement while we were still finding our way. We have all continued to be part of ever-expanding networks that include Native American, Middle Eastern, and Pacific Islander women. This interconnected, mutually supportive community continues to generate important conversations and further all our work, both within and across racial and ethnic groups, as chapters in this volume demonstrate.

While we continue to celebrate PANAAWTM accomplishments and networking of the past twenty years, all done by volunteers and teamwork, this book is born of the same collaborative and community-building spirit as we look to the future. The labors of creation have been as important to us as the outcome. The contributors met and discussed every aspect of the production of the book, from the inception of an essay idea to the image on the cover. In the summer of 2005 we gathered at Union Theological Seminary in New York to brainstorm ideas for the title and contents of the book. We are grateful for the input of Su Yon Pak (Korean American) and Damayanthi Niles (Indian), although they were not able to contribute to the book because of other commitments. In addition, Mary Foskett (a Chinese American adoptee) had planned to contribute but became unable to do so.

As the book chapters took shape, we met again. In spring 2006 we gathered during the annual PANAAWTM conference to share progress reports, present working chapters, and receive feedback. Later in the summer we met again to discuss drafts, structure each chapter, and organize the sections of the book. We took delight in imagining the cover and struggled to find the right title and subtitle. These meetings were marked by frequent laughter and jokes, told over Chinese buffet, Korean *kim-chee*, Americanized sushi, and Greek American food. Through these gatherings we were able to get to know one another more deeply and understand the passions that sustain each of us as scholars. We believe that the book achieves its coherence because our friendly and intense mutual probing has resulted in a more engaging, interconnected anthology.

The title of the book, *Off the Menu*, came to us when we were exploring various metaphors that bind our work together. Food came immediately to mind, as this is such an important part of the inter-Asian culture we have been constructing together and that characterizes many of our social functions. Indeed, one of the things that we are unable to do without during all our gatherings is a variety of Asian and Asian American foods. As we talked about preparing, cooking, eating, and sharing food, we also shared our experiences of going to Asian restaurants in North America. When Asians go to Asian restaurants, the waiters often advise us not to order from the menu, because these dishes are meant to satisfy the Western palate. They tell us that the kitchen can prepare "authentic" Asian dishes "off the menu." In some Chinese and Korean restaurants we are provided with two menus, one in English and the other in Chinese or Korean. Needless to say, these menus offer dissimilar dishes. In some Indian restaurants, while the menu is in English, Asian patrons can ask for hotter spices or different vegetables in the dish.

"Off the Menu" has meanings that are more complex for many Asian Americans, those who do not speak Asian languages and may have grown up eating pizza, pot roast, chop suey, and spaghetti. Asian Americans adopted by Euro-Americans may be completely unfamiliar with Asian foods or know only the American, made-up versions. One of our Japanese American PANAAWTM members ate lunch once in a Chinese restaurant with another Japanese American, a noted filmmaker, and a white, male scholar of East Asian studies. The only speaker of Chinese was the white male, who ordered off the menu, while the two Asian American women wondered what would arrive at the table for lunch. Every time the waiter responded to the man's Chinese, he looked at the two women for approval, as if to confirm that the white man knew what he was doing. Asian Americans who eat out in Asian restaurants in mixed groups are often called on by their non-Asian friends to provide insider knowledge for food off the menu, whether or not they have such knowledge. If we offer tips, we reinforce a major form of racism against Asian Americans as perpetual outsiders. If we say we do not have such knowledge, our friends are often surprised and baffled or suspect that we are withholding information.

We intend with *Off the Menu* to identify how the analogy to food signifies a commonly created new social culture that characterizes our time with one another and to raise questions about cultural authenticity in a globalized world. Who is the insider and who is the outsider within a given culture? Given the diversity of the contributors, are Asians more "authentically" Asian than Asian North Americans? Are second- or third-generation Americans more authentically "American" than first-generation immigrants? Are those adopted from Asia into Euro-American families more "Asian" than third-generation Asian Americans or less Asian because their predominant family culture is Anglo? As readers peruse the book, they will find that the chapters serve as a prism reflecting the many perspectives of Asian and Asian North American women as they seek to address such questions. These diverse essays reveal why there is no set menu for PANAAWTM theology and religion. Instead, each writer joins the discussion at her own entry point. Hence each essay has its own integrity, and there is no necessary order in which the chapters must be read. Some may want to finish the appetizers before sampling the main dishes, but others may choose to start with dessert.

The "menu" in the title can also be understood metaphorically to mean a program, schemata, curriculum, or body of knowledge. We agree with Stacey M. Floyd-Thomas, editor of *Deeper Shades of Purple*, that the academic study of theology and religion has been defined predominantly by white experiences and has served white interests and male egos.[5] The experiences and realities of racial minority women have not been perceived as sources for theological and religious inquiry. The works of Asian and Asian North American women have seldom been included in course syllabi or discussed as a serious body of scholarship. This neglect is unwarranted, for the Asia Pacific region occupies a crucial position in the realignment of geopolitics of the world. Asians and Asian North Americans play pivotal roles in transnational relationships across the Pacific.

Off the Menu is our transgression of the white religious curriculum, with its rigid cultural and disciplinary boundaries and its narrow frames of mind. We invite readers to enter into different cultural worlds, to listen to "newer" voices that are shaping religious discourse, and to expand ways to think about and experience what is sacred in life. In moving beyond Eurocentric and binary-oppositional ways of conceptualizing the field, we offer fresh insights for disrupting old habits of thought and for discovering unexpected ways to savor and integrate human understandings of each other and God.

We transgress disciplinary boundaries because the conventional menu of fields of expertise does not serve our purposes. We have sought, instead, the common themes arising from the chapters and have structured the book more organically to reflect the interdisciplinarity of the essays. We also do not separate the work of Asian authors from that of the Asian North American contributors because we believe that in our globalized world we must disrupt a strict demarcation based on geography or the imaginary construct of "continent." Such an area-studies model, emerging from the Cold War era, is now inadequate to analyze the complexity of our intersected world.

We note that Asian North Americans have been oppressed as racial minorities and treated as forever foreign throughout the history of North America. We do not intend simply to erase all demarcations between Asians and Asian North Americans, but rather, we choose to analyze both racism and colonialism within a more complex framework of contemporary globalization. We believe that this interweaving of distinct perspectives from Asian and Asian North American women illuminates issues and theological questions in meaningful ways. The imperialist tendency to set Asia and North America in terms of sharp separations divides us, whereas we work together to note our distinctions as well as our common commitments. Our two decades of collaboration have helped us understand more clearly where we find common ground and where we can offer mutual support when we differ. This book reflects our clear vision that, although we may be unlike, we are engaged in a joint struggle for justice. Through years of community building among the diverse women of PANAAWTM, we have made a conscious decision to present all sections of this book as they have emerged in our conversations and grouped the various chapters by shared themes.

The book is divided into four parts. Part 1, "History and Identity," provides the history, background, and concerns of Asian and Asian North American women. At the same time, it interrogates the creation and meanings of these identities as they have evolved through the history of colonialism and racism. In offering a complex, multisided look at questions of definitions and identities, it opens ways to think more creatively and carefully about how we conceptualize identities in a changing, globalized world.

The second part, "Reinventing Spiritual Traditions," analyzes how Asian and Asian North American women have critically reassessed and reinvented our spiritual traditions. The essays rethink key categories in Christian theology and in the study of religion. Each offers examples of how Asian and Asian North American women imaginatively interweave and redesign Asian cultural ways of enacting and reflecting on religion.

Part 3, "Reorienting We-Self," addresses the ways many Asian and Asian North American communities offer a critique of the individualism that characterizes Euro-American theories of self. Alan Roland uses the term "we-self" to indicate the significance of the family and community within Indian culture, which is also evident within other Asian communities.[6] In highlighting social understandings of self, family, community, and society, these essays discuss both the possibilities for a more social and relational understanding of self and the liabilities such an understanding poses for women and oppressed minorities within these cultural frameworks.

The final part, "Embodied Agency," offers essays that consider how Asian and Asian North American women live out their commitments to justice and work for social change. As each essay shows, our work takes on many dimensions, attuned to specific locations and issues as well as to the global implications of such work.

Since we have so many cultures, languages, and generations represented in one volume, we have sought to make transliterations of Asian terms as uniform as possible to assist those unfamiliar with these languages. For Chinese, we follow the pinyin system, except for terms long familiar in the Western world, such as Taoism and tai chi. For Korean, we use a modified form of the McCune-Reischauer system, except certain terms that a particular author has already used in published work, such as *jeong*.

This anthology is the beginning of many works to come. Other voices we hope to add in future books include women from other Asian ethnic groups, such as the Hmong. We hope to include women from the Pacific Islands, such as Fiji and New Zealand; from Southwest Asia, such as Iran and Pakistan; and Asian North Americans who trace their ethnicity from such backgrounds. In addition, we will include work by Asians adopted by non-Asian families, a growing aspect of Asian America. This first, landmark book reflects the current membership of PANAAWTM, and it is a first taste of what is yet to emerge from the menus we continue to create for ourselves.

Notes

1. See Kwok Pui-lan, "Diversity within Us: The Challenge of Community among Asian and Asian-American Women," *In God's Image* 15, no. 1 (1996): 51–53.
2. For the history of PANAAWTM, refer to Kwok Pui-lan and Rachel A. R. Bundang, "PANAAWTM Lives!" *Journal of Feminist Studies in Religion* 21, no. 2 (2005): 147–58.
3. See the special section on Asian and Asian American women in the *Journal of Feminist Studies in Religion* 3, no. 2 (1987): 103–50.

4. Stacey M. Floyd-Thomas, ed., *Deeper Shades of Purple: Womanism in Religion and Society* (New York: New York University Press, 2006).

5. Ibid., 2.

6. Alan Roland, *In Search of Self in India and Japan: Toward a Cross-Cultural Psychology* (Princeton, NJ: Princeton University Press, 1988).

Part 1

History and Identity

Chapter One

Fishing the Asia Pacific

Transnationalism and Feminist Theology

Kwok Pui-lan

A young Filipina was sexually assaulted by a U.S. marine in a van, while three other marines watched and cheered him on. The twenty-three-year-old woman, identified with the pseudonym Nicole, met the marine at a bar on the former U.S. naval base at Subic Bay, near Olongapo City, about ninety kilometers northwest of Manila. According to the doctor who examined her, she suffered from bruises on her arms, legs, and genital area, injuries consistent with rape.

The incident took place in November 2005, when the marines went for a night out after two weeks' counterterrorism exercises with Filipino troops. They belonged to a marine expeditionary force stationed in Okinawa, which hosted most of the fifty thousand U.S. troops in Japan. When the charge surfaced, the U.S. government refused to turn over the marines, citing provisions of a Visiting Forces Agreement between the two countries. The marines were placed under custody in the American Embassy in Manila.

During the trial the accused marine admitted that he had had sexual intercourse with Nicole, but he declared that he was innocent and the sex was consensual. But according to a witness, Nicole was offered money to drop the charges hours after the alleged attack occurred. The case sparked anti-American protest in the former U.S. colony, as feminist and civic groups mobilized to bring justice for Nicole. Some protesters and even legislators demanded the revocation of the country's security pact signed with the United States. Others countered that the rape case has blemished the joint military exercises aimed at weakening al Qaeda–linked militants in the southern Philippines.

I heard about Nicole from a Christian women's group when I visited Manila to discuss feminist theology. On leaving, the women asked me to bring the case to the attention of the American public and try to find ways for American women to express solidarity with Filipino women's struggles. After my return to the United States, they continued to update me via the Internet on the case as well as other human rights violations. Filipino feminist theologians have been in the forefront in the struggles for social justice and the empowerment of women. Solidarity among women across national and geographical boundaries in our globalized age is an urgent issue, demanding critical attention from feminist theologians.

Nicole's case is not an isolated incident. It must be placed in the long, contentious relationship between Asia and the United States. For before it emerged as a market for U.S. global capital, Asia was seen as a war zone.[1] Beginning with the Spanish American War over the destiny of the Philippines, the United States has fought successive wars in Asia. During the Cold War the United States pursued a containment policy against China and the former Soviet Union. Today U.S. hegemony in the region is maintained by the strategic deployment of American forces throughout the Pacific. The United States signed bilateral security pacts with Asian nations, creating a vast network of political influences, comparable to a solar system with the United States at the center. In America's so-called global war against terrorism and campaign against "the axis of evil," the collaboration of Asian allies becomes even more crucial.

Geopolitical conflicts with Asia always touch a raw nerve in the American psyche. The popular myth of the "yellow peril" surfaces again and again whenever the United States has tensions with Asian countries. The "Orient" has been constructed as barbaric, exotic, alien, and racially different from and inferior to the "West," in what Edward W. Said has called "Orientalism."[2] American Orientalism puts Asian Americans in a double bind—although they are Americans, they are perceived as perpetual foreigners, whose loyalty is suspect and who can never be fully assimilated. As such, Asian Americans become easy targets and scapegoats during national crises, as the internment of nearly one hundred and twenty thousand Japanese Americans during World War II clearly reminds us. Transnational relations have direct bearings on the racial formation on the U.S. home front. As Lisa Lowe comments,

> During the crises of national identity that occurred in periods of U.S. war in Asia—with the Philippines (1898–1910), against Japan (1941–45), in Korea (1950–53), and in Vietnam—American Orientalism displaced U.S. expansionist interests onto racialized figurations of Asian workers within the national space. . . . On the one hand, Asian

states have become prominent as external rivals in overseas imperial war and in the global economy, and on the other, Asian immigrants are still a necessary racialized labor force within the domestic national economy.[3]

Lowe's astute observations point to the necessity of a transnational analysis of the intersections of race, labor, state, and gender in the age of global economy. To bring justice to Nicole we would need a transnational scrutiny because of the complex configuration of powers in the case (the deployment of American troops involving three governments, the service industry surrounding military bases, the judicial systems and the bilateral agreements, the war against terrorism, grassroots people's movements, and women's international networks). It would have been simplistic to interpret her rape as another example of male violence or male domination over women. The rape of Nicole is an inscription on a Filipina's flesh and blood of the forces of transnational capital, masculinist military power, corruption of national government, and American imperialistic interests in the Asia Pacific. The case points to how globalization, supported by military and political might, has changed the configuration of social, economic, political, and juridical powers in the world. While globalization is a worldwide phenomenon, this chapter uses the Asia Pacific region as a critical lens to articulate the challenges of transnationalism to feminist theology. Since I am using "Asia Pacific" as a framework to explore some of the critical issues that Asian and Asian North American feminist theologians might address together, I begin with an analysis of the discourses on the Asia Pacific and critical interventions that feminist scholars and theologians on both sides of the Pacific have offered.

Conceptualizing the Asia Pacific Region and Feminist Voices

"Asia Pacific" is a contested term, and, as Rob Wilson says, it needs to be "situated and unpacked from within distinct cultural-political trajectories to disclose what this signifier stands for in its present ambivalent implications."[4] Following Arif Dirlik, I adopt a world system approach to interpret the Asia Pacific as a regional formation, developed as a result of European and American capitalist expansion.[5] The Pacific region, as we have come to know it, was an invention of Europe. Christopher Columbus's original intention to go to India linked Asia with the "newly discovered" Pacific. Columbus thought that he had found the fabulous East, the earthly paradise, and its peoples were Asians—the "Indians."[6] The Pacific emerged in the European consciousness as an extension of the conquest of the Americas. The Pacific was called a Spanish lake during the sixteenth and seventeenth centuries, and an English lake from the eighteenth to nineteenth centuries. With the rise of the United States in the late nineteenth century, it has been renamed an American lake. Although the peoples living in the region have their diverse cultures and ways of life, it was the Euro-American powers that invented the regional structure both economically and ideologically to serve their capitalist interests.

The domination of Western powers in the Asia Pacific has not been unchallenged. After the modernization of Japan, the Japanese government attempted to create a Greater East Asian Coprosperity Sphere in the early twentieth century through the colonization of Korea and Taiwan and brutal military aggression in other Asian countries. The United States reasserted its power by joining World War II after the attack on Pearl Harbor and remodeled Japan in the postwar era under American tutelage, including drafting the Japanese Constitution. Since the 1970s the rapid economic growth of the Asian dragons (South Korea, Hong Kong, Taiwan, and Singapore) and the cultural assertion of an Asian way to modernization have highlighted the Asian contributions in redefining the region as Asia Pacific. The Asia Pacific regional formation affects women's lives differently than those of men, and feminists have sought to disrupt a unified, seamless, and cooperative myth of coprosperity.

The discourse on the Asia Pacific in the academy and mass media has undergone several shifts since World War II, but the influences from the area-studies model remain strong. During the Cold War, area studies were set up in American colleges and universities to provide information about the enemy countries and other strategic regions. Asia was divided into the subregions of East Asia, Southeast Asia, and South Asia, and the countries in the Pacific were left out of this purview. Although designated as subregions, the focus was on national entities. For example, "East Asia" means the study of Japan, Korea, and China. Scholars went into the field to observe and represent "native" culture, as if East Asia were a unified and bounded unit. This research produced a theory of knowledge of the non-Western world based on the authority and authenticity of indigenous experience and the asymmetrical relation between the researcher and the so-called native informants.[7]

Early feminist literary and theological writings presented images of the Asia Pacific that challenged fixed boundaries of nation and the homogeneity of culture. For example, Maxine Hong Kingston's *Woman Warrior* (1976)[8] created a genderized and racialized narrative of Chinese immigrants for whom crossing the Asia Pacific had become "a space of fractures, disjunctures, traumas, confusion, and disappointments."[9] In *Compassionate and Free* (1979), the first book on Asian feminist theology, Marianne Katoppo describes in detail the cultural, ethnic, and religious diversity in her country, Indonesia, and the ways women are situated as the Other in Christian, familial, and national narratives.[10] From the beginning, Asian American feminist theologians have also emphasized their multicultural context and their in-between social location.[11] These feminist writings disrupt homogeneous national tales by including race, ethnicity, gender, and class in their analysis of the female subject.

Since the mid-1970s, the discourse on the Pacific Rim caught public attention when the newly industrialized Asian countries began their economic takeoffs, following Japan's phenomenal success. Commentators and the media soon predicted that the twenty-first century would be a "Pacific" century. The success of the East and Southeast Asian countries was hailed as a model for the "underdeveloped" world, just as Asian Americans were held up as a "model minority." The Pacific Rim discourse had great appeal for the capitalist managers in North America who saw the benefit of Asia being successfully integrated into the capitalist economy. In Asia, politicians and scholars also seized the opportunity to reassert their cultural identity and argued for a Pacific way of development. In particular, Neo-Confucianism was revived from Japan all the way to Singapore as the characteristic feature of this Asian way of modernization. The devastating 1997 Asian economic crisis, which brought several Asian countries to the brink of bankruptcy, sent a cautionary signal to any overheated and celebratory "Rimspeak."

While Asian politicians boasted about the prosperity of the Rim, Asian feminist theologians contested that the majority of the Asian people were poor and the economic development in Asia was grossly uneven. The so-called Asian miracle was built on the availability of cheap female labor, unsafe and unhealthy working conditions, and inadequate labor protection. I have articulated the ways Neo-Confucianism, patriarchy, and capitalism have formed an "unholy trinity" to oppress women.[12] While Asian women were increasingly absorbed into the labor force in the newly industrialized Asian countries, a growing number of Asian immigrant women arrived to work in the garment and other light industries in the United States, following the change of the Immigration Act of 1965, which lifted the national quotas for Asians. Activists and scholars have paid attention to the struggles of these Asian immigrant females whose work in the sweatshops and other low-paid jobs has bolstered the American economy.[13]

The economic development of some of the Southeast Asian countries depended also on the exploitation of sexual labor of women. During the Vietnam War, Southeast Asia provided places of "rest and recreation" for American soldiers, and a vibrant sex industry developed around the military bases and large urban centers. The rape of Nicole reflects both the socialization of men to use sex for dominance and the subtext that Asian women's flesh is available for the taking.[14] The sex industry has been crucial to the economic development of countries such as the Philippines and Thailand, not only because of money made on their own soil but also in the funds that women trafficked for sex work in other countries have sent home. Some of these trafficked women and children were brought to the United States through an international ring of organized criminal activities.

Since the end of the Cold War, discourses on the Asia Pacific have taken different directions. On the one hand, the forum of Asian Pacific Economic Cooperation, formed in Canberra in 1989, promotes an image of the Asia Pacific as having open borders, regional coherence, shared direction, and transnational globalization. On the other hand, the rapid rise of the Chinese economy and the huge trade deficit between China and the United States have made Samuel P. Huntington's prediction of a "clash of civilizations" plausible to many people. Huntington has surmised that the conflict in the future would not be a clash of ideologies but, rather, a clash of civilizations. Not surprisingly, he predicts that a major fault line will be drawn between the Western and the Sinic worlds.[15] While many have criticized Huntington's concept of civilization as bound and essentialist (much based on the area-studies model), I underscore how globalization has produced new discourses about the Asia Pacific through a rehashing of old myths and the addition of new fantasies.

Globalization and transnationalism require feminists to use fresh conceptual frameworks and mental constructs to analyze the Asia Pacific. While transnational processes have occurred since the formation of nation-states, transnationalism as a contemporary phenomenon is largely associated with flexibility and globalization. Michael Chang refers to transnationalism as "the movement across national borders of human beings, capital, and the cultural and social ideas and practices that come with both people and money."[16] In the course of constant transnational flow of capital, labor, and ideas, basic categories such as gender, race, ethnicity, nation, and citizenship are being rearticulated. For example, we can no longer separate the study of a nation without taking into consideration the phenomena of migrancy and diaspora. The large number of female migrant workers from the Philippines, Thailand, Indonesia, and Sri Lanka working overseas changes the shape of the international division of labor as well as gender relationships both in the home and the receiving countries.

Feminist theorists and theologians have grappled with the challenges of globalization in various ways. The anthropologist Aihwa Ong articulates the concept of flexible citizenship to describe how individuals and governments develop a flexible notion of citizenship and sovereignty to accommodate capital accumulation and people's mobility.[17] Assimilation is no longer the only route open for immigrants who can maintain transnational loyalties and relations via travel and communication networks. Using a transnational methodology, Lowe studies immigration, nationhood, and the racialized feminization of labor.[18] In theological circles Wai-Ching Angela Wong has questioned whether a binary construction of "Asia" and the "West" from an anti-imperial stance would be adequate in the globalized world.[19] Likewise, Nami Kim challenges the use of the unifying category "Asia," argues that Asian feminist theology should go beyond speaking for or to "Asian" women, and tells us that, instead, it should be rearticulated as a critical, global feminist theology.[20] Employing a postcolonial lens, I have suggested a diasporic imagination for interpreting the Bible and developing an intercultural feminist theological framework.[21]

A transnational analysis will help us see Asia and America not as two separate entities but as ones that are constantly influencing each other within the broader regional formation of the Asia Pacific. There are different existing models to help us conceptualize how "Asia" and "America" are mutually inscribed. Paul Gilroy's study of the so-called black Atlantic comes easily to mind.[22] He uses the images of ships and sea voyages crisscrossing the Atlantic to describe black culture as multiply centered and diasporic in the Atlantic space, which transcends the narrow confines of ethnicity and nationality. In so doing, Gilroy transgresses the disciplinary boundaries of black, American, Caribbean, and British studies, as well as debunks the rigid notions of Afrocentrism and Eurocentrism. With an expansive imagination Gilroy describes black Atlantic culture with multiple points of entries and polyrhythmic beats, following not a single linear pattern but constantly improvising. Gilroy's work stimulates us to think about the multiple linkages of the Asia Pacific in critically new ways, even though we might not want to call it a "yellow Pacific" because of the residual fear of the "yellow peril." In popular consciousness a "black Atlantic" and a "yellow Pacific" have drastically different connotations because, unlike the black people in the Atlantic, Asian peoples have much more power to contest Euro-American economic and political power, and China is poised to become a major threat to U.S. hegemony.

In postcolonial discourse Said has used the counterpoint in Western classical music to develop his contrapuntal reading, which looks at metropolitan history and histories of the colonies as overlapped and intertwined.[23] If we analyze the history and cultures of any Asian nation, we will see how much they have been restructured to fit into the model of U.S. hegemony in the region. Although Said is not primarily interested in racial minority issues, we can use insights from his contrapuntal reading to unpack racialized and genderized migration patterns in the Americas and to understand how Asian Pacific peoples have contributed to the shaping of the national cultures, although such contributions are often relegated to the margins of metropolitan history or remain silenced and exempt from history.

Developing Transnational Feminist Theologies in the Asia Pacific

If we use transnationalism as a critical lens, we will see that Asian and Asian North American feminist theologians have only recently begun to probe the perimeters and chart the issues of globalization. While we have done more work on how colonialism has affected the church and the lives of women, we have yet to develop substantial theological thinking on how globalization is reshaping the Asia Pacific. As Michael Hardt and Antonio Negri have observed, the old form of colonialism, based on the sovereignty of the nation-state, has given way to a new global form called "the Empire," which is composed of decentered and deterritorialized as well as complex and expansive networks of power, with multiple centers and margins. They write, "Empire manages hybrid identities, flexible hierarchies, and plural exchanges through modulating networks of command."[24]

The Asia Pacific region plays critical roles in the development of Empire, in terms of capital and technology transfer, sharing of managerial know-how, outsourcing of manufacturing and service industries, migrant workers across the region, and so forth. No matter how differently we may assess the impact of globalization, we have to realize that the "natives" are no longer on the outside, as once imagined, but are "subjected to the same political-economic processes and structures that all of us encounter in our everyday lives, everywhere and anywhere."[25] Asians and Asian North Americans are strategically located in the interstices of some of these immense transnational networks, whether they work in the Silicon Valley or in the financial districts of Seoul, Hong Kong, or Tokyo. A critical scrutiny of their experiences will help us look at Empire from many vantage points, and not just that of U.S. dominance but also the keen competition from China and Japan. In the following pages I will discuss three areas to which feminist theology will need to attend: economic and social formation, cultural difference, and power and resistance in the age of transnationalism.

Transnational feminist theology in the Asia Pacific has to pay more attention to economics and social formation and to the question that the anthropologist Arjun Appadurai has asked: "What is the hidden dowry of globalization?"[26] Although Appadurai may not have intended it this way, the genderized and sexualized nature of dowry brings into sharp relief the collateral that the majority of the world's women and their families must pay to the deregulation of the market, the unfettered chase for consumer goods, the commodification of sex and culture, the privatization of public services, and the structural adjustment that the international financial and monetary agencies impose. And we have to ask what roles religious and cultural ideologies have played to justify the unequal burden on the vast number of women.

If Calvinistic ethics served as the religious backdrop for the rise of capitalism, as Max Weber claimed,[27] today's economic globalization is promoted by the Christian Right, made up of religious fundamentalists and evangelicals of various stripes. These televangelists, conservative pundits, and Web-savvy leaders exert a huge influence in the Asia Pacific through megachurches, the mass media, and other transnational networks. They promote a gospel of prosperity, individual salvation, family values, and economic success as the sign of God's grace. A substantial number of Asian and Asian American professionals in the Asia Pacific, many of whom occupy key positions in economic globalization, are conjoined in their subscription to this gospel of upward social mobility. They can be found among those waking up at 5:00 a.m. to attend morning prayers in Seoul, speaking in tongues in charismatic worship in Singapore, or devoting time to organize cell groups of ethnic churches in the United States. The Asian American ethnic churches are mostly conservative in their worldview, patriarchal in their leadership, and dedicated to providing services for displaced immigrants rather than challenging racism and the status quo.

Fundamentalist Christianity is not the only religion competing for hegemony in globalization. As we have seen, Neo-Confucianism has been revived in the Pacific Rim discourse. If Weber dismissed Chinese religion as stagnant and lacking progress in his comparative study of world cultures,[28] Asian scholars today proudly point to the fact that Confucianism provides the religious motivation for economic growth equivalent to Calvinism in the West. They insist that Asian people have found their own way of development and need not adopt a wholesale Westernization in order to be modernized. Confucianism, they claim, is making a critical contribution to world civilization by offering an alternative model of modernization.[29] In the United States the argument that Asian peoples have strong family support and cultural values has also drawn from the Confucian background of the East Asians, the largest group among Asian Americans.

If women do not fare well in fundamentalist Christianity, they are also discriminated against in Confucian ethics. In the discussion of "Asian values," the emphases have been on Confucian familism and on human relatedness. Asian communitarian ethics is seen as superior to Western individualism. The theologian Nam-Soon Kang cautions against such binary constructs and points to the patriarchal domination in the Confucian family and social relations. She articulates the contradiction that while South Korea marches forward toward modernization, the Asian values discourse "freezes women in the patriarchal past, the traditional images, and the pre-modern reality."[30] And she has discussed how Confucian familism has cast its huge influence in the construction of patriarchal Korean Christianity in its religious leadership, theology, and theological education.

Fundamentalist Christianity and the Confucian revival have several things in common. In the United States the Christian Right has exerted tremendous influence in politics, and it is part of the neoconservative force supporting big business and tax cuts for the rich. From Japan to Singapore the so-called Asian way of modernization developed under strong leadership (or intervention) from the state, resulting in a small group of politicians and business leaders wielding enormous power. Both fundamentalist Christianity and the Confucian revival support modern globalization, and yet they claim their moral authority by assuming a countercultural and countermodern stance. To bolster their conservative political agenda both appeal to a "traditional" patriarchal morality and condemn feminism and homosexuality as antifamily ideologies. To various degrees both subscribe to the conservative moral worldview and, as George Lakoff describes, both are (1) promoting strict father morality; (2) promoting self-discipline, responsibility, and self-reliance; (3) upholding the morality of reward and punishment; (4) protecting moral people from external evils; and (5) upholding the existing moral order.[31] It is evident that controlling women and their sexuality is a central component of the family values ideology, which consolidates patriarchal control in the public and private realms. I would name this temporal lag, or what Kang has sarcastically called "freez[ing] women in . . . the pre-modern reality," as the hidden dowry of globalization.

While Confucianism was rearticulated to serve the capitalist cause, other religiocultural elements in the Asia Pacific have been used to construct counterhegemonic discourses. I compare here the work of Kathryn Tanner and Aruna Gnanadason, because both address the economic and ecological consequences of runaway capitalism. Tanner, a university professor in the United States, notes that several Western scholars have found gift exchange in non-Western societies, especially in the Asia Pacific, as an alternative to the commodity exchange that defines modern capitalism. Some of these writings tend to romanticize the gift exchange and the human relatedness in Asia Pacific societies. After offering an assessment of gift exchange, Tanner proceeds to develop an economy of grace, based on the unconditional and universal giving of God. Out of joyfulness and gratitude for God's free gifts, human beings also give to others. She offers the image of a noncompetitive community of mutual benefit as an alternative to the cutthroat capitalist competition.[32]

With good intention, Tanner and the British theologian John Milbank articulate an alternative social imaginary and look for inspiration to the marginal spaces that they consider to be less absorbed into the capitalist economy.[33] Not being an expert of these marginal spaces and cultures, Milbank relies on anthropological accounts, often without some serious questioning of the ways that scholars, such as Marcel Mauss and Bronislaw Malinowski, had represented the "primitive" societies in the Pacific. Just as anthropologists and social scientists draw raw data from the field to develop their grand theories, such as reciprocity and gift economies, theologians extract from these theories ideas and concepts—in this case, gift exchange—to construct their grand ideas about God. From the localized ideas of gift exchange, Tanner develops the doctrine of God as the perfect giver, whose love is unconditional and universal and does not depend on human beings. In so doing, Tanner superimposes the Christian model of self-sacrifice onto a more generous and reciprocal model of gift exchange in non-Western societies.[34] This understanding of God and the sacrificial love on the cross can now be universalized, context free, ready to be adopted not only in the American churches but also circled back to places in the Asia Pacific.

Aruna Gnanadason is from India and currently serves as the coordinator for Justice, Peace, and Creation of the World Council of Churches. Instead of focusing on gift exchange, she begins with elaborating the traditions of "prudent care" of the earth, a practice found in several areas where indigenous peoples live in India. She highlights human beings' relationship with the earth—not just human relatedness through gift exchange. By so doing, Gnanadason shifts the traditional understanding of grace coming purely from divine power to a relational power that motivates us to love the earth and work for justice.[35] She articulates the concept of brown grace, which stands for the traditions of prudent care—"of people who live in closest proximity to the earth and who give to the land its integrity."[36] Contrasted with Tanner's anthropomorphic God as the self-giver, a metaphor based on the cross, Gnanadason points to the earth as the body of God, a metaphor of God who transforms the earth with grace. Their differing approaches can be attributed to their adherence to different theological frameworks: Tanner from a postliberal tradition and Gnanadason from an ecofeminist perspective. But I emphasize that both use Asia Pacific resources, and by staying close to the context, Gnanadason respects peoples' stories and describes how theological ideas are contested, modified, and rearticulated through concrete struggles. Tanner's theological economy of grace sounds a bit too utopian, and her discussion of noncompetitive community is hard to put into practice in the face of grinding competitive economic forces.

The above discussion has already drawn us into the deep waters of identity, cultural difference, and cultural politics, issues that have been discussed widely in Asian and Asian North American feminist theology. The cultural critic Rey Chow has coined the term "the difference revolution"[37] to describe the preoccupation with difference in critical theory, cultural studies, literary criticism, and cognate fields resulting from poststructuralism. She cautions that the self-referential discourse on difference, focusing on language and texts, could be academically avant-garde but politically conservative, if the material and sociopolitical dimensions are foreclosed or overlooked.[38] The articulation of so-called Asian values, as we have seen, can create a competing cultural discourse, yet the notion is used to serve conservative political and economic agendas.

How do we understand the terms "Asian" and "Asian American" at a time when some feminists have cautioned against "mapping politics and identities geographically or culturally"[39] because of the tendency to homogenize regions and cultures as bounded units? Why is it that Asian, African, Latin American, African American, Hispanic and Latina feminist and womanist theologians have refused to drop these modifiers in order to differentiate their work from the "unmarked" feminist theology produced by some European and American white women? By using these cultural, racial, and geographical modifiers, these feminist and womanist theologians claim that they speak to the world from a particular social and cultural context, and they want to specify their positionality in relation to other theological projects and discourses. They challenge that European and Euro-American feminist scholars also speak from particular vantage points, although the latter have a tendency to leave their positions unmarked as a tactic to universalize their experiences and theology.

In claiming their cultural differences these marginalized and minoritized feminist and womanist theologians have learned to avoid a binary construction of the West and the Other, on the one hand, and essentializing Asian, black, Latina, and so forth, on the other.[40] At the same time, they know from their involvements in social movements and struggles that the fine splitting of differences will not serve the political cause of mobilizing women to form coalitions. They criticize the postmodern play on the indetermination of meanings and difference and insist that the social and political must not be left out in the definition of culture and the theorization of cultural difference.[41] The historian Harry D. Harootunian articulates this clearly: "The politics of identity based on enunciation of cultural difference is not the same as political identity whose formation depends less on declarations of differences than on some recognition of equivalences."[42] These dynamics are evident when Asian Americans used the term "Asian American" during the civil rights era to denote a plurality of Asian peoples of diverse cultures, histories, and languages in the United States.

In the globalized world we will need a new imagination to conceptualize geographies, cultures, and peoples. Appadurai suggests that we shift away from "trait" geographies, which are the legacy of the areas-studies model, to what he calls "process" geographies. He argues that area studies tended to

> mistake a particular configuration of apparent stabilities for permanent associations between space, territory, and cultural organization. These apparent stabilities are themselves largely artifacts of the specific trait-based idea of "culture" areas, a recent Western cartography of large civilizational landmasses associated with different relationships to "Europe" (itself a complex historical and cultural emergent), and a Cold War–based geography of fear and competition.[43]

His process geographies see human organization not as static but as always on the move, with action and interaction—trade, travel, warfare, colonization, proselytization, and the like.[44] While the trait model most often speaks from the center, from the male elite point of view, the process model allows room for feminists to imagine the marginalized, the migrant, and new social subjects that are being formed.

Additionally, this process model helps us to theorize authenticity, hybridity, and heterogeneity among Asians and Asian North Americans in newly fashioned ways. Emerging in the late 1970s, Asian feminist theologians were concerned with finding out what is "unique" about Asia and what could be said of a distinctive Asian feminist methodology.[45] The use of Asian religiocultural resources was encouraged, such as folklore, stories, legends, songs, and peoples' popular religions. As Wong has commented, "This emphasis on the 'Asian-ness' of doing theology in Asia is echoed by what postcolonial discussion calls a 'fictional' return (of the colonized) to one's indigenous history and culture."[46] The search for "Asian-ness" can easily fall into the trap of the trait model of areas studies, when theologians characterize the essential features of Asia as poverty and religious diversity.[47] But the search for the past needs not be a self-Orientalizing exercise if it is consciously done as a process to suture a broken historical and cultural memory that has been repressed and disrupted by colonialism, in order to point to the contradictions of historical trajectories of modernity and contest the "McDonaldization" of the world.

If Asian feminist theologians have a tendency to return in time in order to find out what is "authentically Asian," their Asian North American counterparts look to space to create their new fluidly global identities. Many use spatial metaphors to describe and elaborate their hyphenated and hybrid identities, including the in-between space, the third space, the interstices, the imaginary homeland, and a notion of deterritorialized panethnicity.[48] The Japanese American theologian Rita Nakashima Brock has coined the term "interstitial integrity" to describe the need to balance multiple dimensions of the self in the fluid yet unsettling spaces. She writes, "Interstitial refers to the places in between, which are real places, like the strong connective tissues between organs in the body that link the parts. . . . Integrity is closely related to integration, to acts of connecting many disparate things by holding them together."[49] Because of racism the margins and the in-between spaces become sites for Asian North Americans to create cultural productions that both resist the white dominant culture and allow them to reinvent themselves.

It would be difficult to create a meaningful dialogue if Asian feminists emphasize their Asianness while Asian North American women claim their rights to be Americans and Canadians and downplay the connection with Asia in order to avoid being labeled perpetual foreigners. But if we can see cultures, nations, and geographies not in terms of reified traits but as process, we will see that heterogeneity and competing positionalities are part and parcel of globalization. The need to return to what is "authentically Asian" is the result of a globalized culture, in which one is made to feel alienated and diasporic even at home. While the global increasingly impinges on local places, hybridization is a phenomenon in North America as well as in many Asian cities. As Michael Chang says, "Transnationalism has also brought an unprecedented hybridity within this global culture. . . . [G]lobal capitalism is digested at the 'local' level, imprinting it with a hybrid mix of Western and 'local' cultural practices and views."[50] In fact, Wong, writing from the cosmopolitan city of Hong Kong, proposes using the language of hybridity, instead of a binary opposition of "Asia and the West," as a new strategy of doing Asian feminist theology.[51]

The flexibility and innovation associated with the fluidly global can also be symptomatic of a highly adaptive global culture, which has a tendency to commodify and aestheticize ethnic differences for commercial gain. In the name of diversity and multiculturalism, different cultural elements have been brought together superficially and selectively, disregarding context and history, as in a sprawling buffet of multiethnic food. To guard against such commodification of ethnic difference, one must go beyond a superficial embrace of hybridity and the in-between spaces to find out the ways in which the material history of racial dynamics is inscribed in such spaces. Lowe reminds us that the "difference" of Asian American cultural forms is not "a matter of mere technical innovation that we might find in aestheticist texts that are critical of traditional forms and of mass culture but reside in racial formation as *the material trace of history*."[52]

Speaking within Asia and in between Asia and North America, feminist theologians of Asian descent occupy different positions, sometimes mutually reinforcing and other times contesting, in the vast flow of ideas, peoples, cultures, and histories of the transnational Asia Pacific. They will start from disparate points, plot various trajectories, and mold distinct shapes and spaces for their cultural matrices and theological interstices. Their feminist theologies are heterogeneous not only because of cultural difference but also because of material inequities and the historical and political vicissitudes in the Asia Pacific. Yet for more than two decades some of them have found one another and established dialogical relations within, between, and among cultures, ethnicities, and nations along the many shores of the ocean. These conversations are held despite the fact that some of their countries have been at war with one another and some have colonized others. Out of these mutual probings and learnings, as well as debates and criticism, they contribute to the theological discourse by offering a wide range of possibilities for imagining new social life, cultural forms, subject positions, and theological sensibilities in contesting the overdetermination of global capital and consumerist culture. They also point to the heterogeneity of the construction of time and space and the changing multiple subject positions they occupy as they continuously renegotiate the meanings of "Asian" and "Asian North American" in a world in flux.[53] Together they are creating feminist theologies that disrupt the dominant forms of theological discourses emerging from nationalist, imperialist, and Euro-American feminist traditions.

I conclude by elaborating Appadurai's concept of grassroots globalization, or globalization from below,[54] in the Asia Pacific theological context. By "grassroots globalization" he refers to the work of the nongovernmental organizations, the transnational advocacy networks, public intellectuals, and socially concerned academics. In the theological context the challenge is to reconceptualize power, especially divine power, from below and not from above. Historically the images for divine power, such as father, warrior, and king, portray a God situated at the apex of power. Even the masculinist image of Jesus as the liberator portrays him as having the enormous power of intervening in history and liberating humankind from structural oppression. What would divine power look like if we speak of a theology from below and not a theology from above?

One of the images I suggest is a God of the interstices. The interstice is the space where different cultural currents, flows of people, and streams of ideas collide and coalesce. The feminist theologian Catherine Keller has raised the question of whether the interstitial will help to confront the imperial.[55] I posit that the imperial is not totalized, for it produces contradictions, disjunctures, and competing interests. Said has added, "Every situation also contains a contest between a powerful system of interests, on the one hand, and, on the other, less powerful interests threatened with frustration, silence, incorporation, or extinction by the powerful."[56] The interstice is where such kinds of competing interests and powers occur most clearly, and the task of theologians as public intellectuals is to reveal and elucidate this contest. We can no longer focus our resistance as citizens of one nation against another nation, as in the older form of nationalist struggle against colonialism, but we have to look toward "those institutions, spaces, borders, and processes that are the interstitial sites of the social formation in which the national intersects with the international."[57] It is in these interstitial sites where cultural hybridity occurs, and new social subjects are formed because the boundaries of nation-state, citizenship, race, gender, and culture are being redrawn and rethought. If we imagine divine power not as hierarchical, unilateral, and unidirectional but rather in the form of a matrix, then the interstices are the nodal power connections where something clever and creative can occur.

The young woman Nicole and her family courageously brought her case against the military of the greatest superpower the world has ever seen. Her story reminds us of other incidents of rape, sexual abuse, and torture of women committed by American servicemen in Okinawa and Iraq. Confronting the powers in Manila and Washington, D.C., Nicole is like a small David facing a gigantic Goliath. Yet she cannot be silenced because her case has been brought to the attention of the international civil society through the media, the Internet, grassroots organizations, and Christian women's networks.[58] In the mobilization of transnational networks that stand in solidarity with her and with other victims of violence, war, and oppression, we see the grace of God—divine interstitial power at work. Such a power is energizing and enabling, because it rejoices in creating "synergetic relations,"[59] readjusts and shifts to find new strength, and discovers hope in the densely woven web of life that sustains us all.

Notes

1. For a discussion of various wars of the United States in Asia, see Philip West, Steven I. Levine, and Jackie Hiltz, eds., *America's Wars in Asia: A Cultural Approach to History and Memory* (Armonk, NY: M. E. Sharpe, 1998).
2. Edward W. Said, *Orientalism* (New York: Vintage, 1979).
3. Lisa Lowe, *Immigrant Acts: On Asian American Cultural Politics* (Durham, NC: Duke University Press, 1996), 5.
4. Rob Wilson, "Imagining 'Asia-Pacific' Today: Forgetting Colonialism in the Magical Free Markets of the American Pacific," in *Learning Places: The Afterlives of Area Studies*, ed. Masao Miyoshi and H. D. Harootunian (Durham, NC: Duke University Press, 2002), 234.
5. Arif Dirlik, "The Asia Pacific Idea," in *What Is in a Rim? Critical Perspectives on the Pacific Region Idea*, ed. Arif Dirlik, 2nd ed. (Lanham, MD: Rowman & Littlefield, 1998), 15–36.
6. Gary Y. Okihiro, *Margins and Mainstreams: Asians in American History and Culture* (Seattle: University of Washington Press, 1994), 16.
7. Harry D. Harootunian, *History's Disquiet: Modernity, Cultural Practice, and the Question of Everyday Life* (New York: Columbia University Press, 2000), 25–58; Rey Chow, "Theory, Area Studies, Cultural Studies: Issues of Pedagogy in Multiculturalism," in *Ethics after Idealism: Theory, Culture, Ethnicity, Reading* (Bloomington: Indiana University Press, 1998), 1–13.
8. Maxine Hong Kingston, *The Woman Warrior: Memoirs of a Girlhood among Ghosts* (New York: Knopf, 1976).

9. Wilson, "Imagining 'Asia-Pacific' Today," 233.

10. Marianne Katoppo, *Compassionate and Free: An Asian Woman's Theology* (Geneva: World Council of Churches, 1979).

11. Naomi Southard and Rita Nakashima Brock, "The Other Half of the Basket: Asian American Women and the Search for a Theological Home," *Journal of Feminist Studies in Religion* 3, no. 2 (1987): 137–39.

12. Kwok Pui-lan, "Business Ethics in the Economic Development of Asia: A Feminist Analysis," *Asia Journal of Theology* 9 (1995): 133–45.

13. Chalsa M. Loo, "Slaying Demons with a Sewing Needle: Gender Differences and Women's Status," in *Chinatown: Most Time, Hard Time* (New York: Praeger, 1991), 189–210; Miriam Ching Louie, "Immigrant Asian Women in Bay Area Garment Sweatshops: 'After Sewing, Laundry, Cleaning and Cooking, I Have No Breath Left to Sing,'" *Ameriasia Journal* 18 (1992): 1–26; Miriam Ching Louie, *Sweatshop Warriors: Immigrant Women Workers Take on Global Factory* (Cambridge, MA: South End Press, 2001). See also Saskia Sassen, "Notes on the Incorporation of Third World Women into Wage Labor through Immigration and Offshore Production," in *Globalization and Its Discontent* (New York: New Press, 1998), 111–31.

14. See Mary John Mananzan, "Sexual Exploitation of Women in a Third World Setting," in *Essays on Women*, rev. ed., ed. Mary John Mananzan (Manila: Institute of Women's Studies, St. Scholastica's College, 1991), 104–12; and Nantawan Boonprasat Lewis's chapter in this volume.

15. Samuel P. Huntington, *The Clash of Civilizations and the Remaking of World Order* (New York: Simon & Schuster, 1996).

16. Michael Chang, *Racial Politics in an Era of Transnational Citizenship: The 1996 "Asian Donorgate" Controversy in Perspective* (Lanham, MD: Lexington Books, 2004), xiii.

17. Aihwa Ong, *Flexible Citizenship: The Cultural Logic of Transnationality* (Durham, NC: Duke University Press, 1999).

18. Lowe, *Immigrant Acts*.

19. Wai-Ching Angela Wong, *"The Poor Woman": A Critical Analysis of Asian Theology and Contemporary Chinese Fiction by Women* (New York: Peter Lang, 2002).

20. Nami Kim, "'My/Our' Comfort *Not* at the Expense of 'Somebody Else's,'" *Journal of Feminist Studies in Religion* 21, no. 2 (2005): 75–94.

21. Kwok Pui-lan, *Postcolonial Imagination and Feminist Theology* (Louisville, KY: Westminster John Knox Press, 2005).

22. Paul Gilroy, *The Black Atlantic: Modernity and Double Consciousness* (Cambridge, MA: Harvard University Press, 1993).

23. Edward W. Said, *Culture and Imperialism* (New York: Knopf, 1994), 51.

24. Michael Hardt and Antonio Negri, *Empire* (Cambridge, MA: Harvard University Press, 2000), xii–xiii.

25. Harootunian, *History's Disquiet*, 41.

26. Arjun Appadurai, "Grassroots Globalization and the Research Imagination," in *Globalization*, ed. Arjun Appadurai (Durham, NC: Duke University Press, 2001), 2; see also the discussion in Elizabeth A. Castelli, "Globalization, Transnational Feminisms, and the Future of Biblical Critique," in *Feminist New Testament Studies: Global and Future Perspectives*, ed. Kathleen O'Brien Wicker, Althea Spencer Miller, and Musa W. Dube (New York: Palgrave Macmillan, 2005), 68.

27. Max Weber, *The Protestant Ethic and the Spirit of Capitalism*, trans. Talcott Parsons (New York: Scribner's, 1958).

28. Max Weber, *The Religion of China: Confucianism and Taoism*, trans. Hans H. Gerth (New York: Macmillan, 1964). The original in German was published in 1915. For a critique of Weber's view, see C. K. Yang's introduction to this 1964 edition, xiii–xliii.

29. Tu Wei-ming, *Confucian Ethics Today: The Singapore Challenge* (Singapore: Federal Publications, 1984); see also his article "Cultural China: The Periphery as the Center," *Daedalus* 120, no. 2 (1991): 1–32; Arif Dirlik, "Confucius in the Borderlands: Global Capitalism and the Reinvention of Confucianism," *boundary 2* 22, no. 3 (1995): 229–73.

30. Nam-Soon Kang, "Confucian Familism and Its Social/Religious Embodiment in Christianity: Reconsidering the Family Discourse from a Feminist Perspective," *Asia Journal of Theology* 18 (2004): 171.

31. George Lakoff, *Moral Politics: How Liberals and Conservatives Think*, 2nd ed. (Chicago: University of Chicago Press, 2002), 166–67.

32. Kathryn Tanner, *Economy of Grace* (Minneapolis: Fortress Press, 2005).

33. John Milbank's work on gift exchange has been cited by Tanner and other scholars; see John Milbank, "Can a Gift Be Given?" *Modern Theology* 11, no. 1 (1995): 119–61; John Milbank, *Being Reconciled: Ontology and Pardon* (London: Routledge, 2003). See also Marion Grau, "'We Must Give Ourselves to Voyaging': Regifting the Theological Present," in *Interpreting the Postmodern: Responses to "Radical Orthodoxy,"* ed. Rosemary Radford Ruether and Marion Grau (New York: T. & T. Clark, 2006), 141–60.

34. I thank Rita Nakashima Brock for her input on the gift-exchange model.

35. Aruna Gnanadason, *Listen to the Women! Listen to the Earth!* (Geneva: World Council of Churches, 2005), 90–91.

36. Ibid., 96.

37. Rey Chow, "The Secrets of Ethnic Abjection," in *The Protestant Ethnic and the Spirit of Capitalism* (New York: Columbia University Press, 2002), 128.

38. Rey Chow, "The Interruption of Referentiality; or, Poststructuralism's Outside," in *The Age of the World Target: Self-Referentiality in War, Theory, and Comparative Work* (Durham, NC: Duke University Press, 2006), 45–69.

39. Castelli, "Globalization, Transnational Feminisms, and the Future of Biblical Critique," 70.

40. Theologians and ethicists from these groups have debated vigorously about how they use these terms to designate themselves. See Kwok Pui-lan and Rachel A. R. Bundang, "PANAAWTM Lives!" *Journal of Feminist Studies in Religion* 21, no. 2 (2005): 147–58; the roundtable discussion "Must I Be Womanist?" *Journal of Feminist Studies in Religion* 22, no. 1 (2006): 85–134; and Michelle A. González, "'One Is Not Born a Latina, One Becomes One': The Construction of Latina Feminist Theologian in Latino/a Theology," *Journal of Hispanic/Latino Theology* 10, no. 3 (2002): 5–30.

41. Ivone Gebara, *Longing for Running Water: Ecofeminism and Liberation* (Minneapolis: Fortress Press, 1999), 12–13; Karen Baker-Fletcher, "The Erotic in Contemporary Black Women's Writings," in *Loving the Body: Black Religious Studies and the Erotic*, ed. Anthony B. Pinn and Dwight N. Hopkins (New York: Palgrave Macmillan, 2004), 199–200; Kwok, *Postcolonial Imagination and Feminist Theology*, 128–37.

42. Harootunian, *History's Disquiet*, 46.

43. Appadurai, "Grassroots Globalization," 8.

44. Ibid., 7–8.
45. Virginia Fabella, "A Common Methodology for Diverse Christologies?" in *With Passion and Compassion: Third World Women Doing Theology*, ed. Virginia Fabella and Mercy Amba Oduyoye (Maryknoll, NY: Orbis Books, 1990), 108–17.
46. Wai-Ching Angela Wong, "Asian Theology in a Changing Asia: Towards an Asian Theological Agenda for the Twenty-first Century," *CTC Bulletin*, Special Supplement 1 (1997): 33.
47. This formulation of the uniqueness of Asia was first presented by Aloysius Pieris in "Towards an Asian Theology of Liberation: Some Religio-cultural Guidelines," in *Asian's Struggle for Full Humanity*, ed. Virginia Fabella (Maryknoll, NY: Orbis Books, 1980), 75–76. Many Asian theologians have subsequently followed his characterization.
48. See the discussion of hybridity and interstitial third space in Wonhee Anne Joh, *Heart of the Cross: A Postcolonial Christology* (Louisville, KY: Westminster John Knox Press, 2006), 53–66.
49. Rita Nakashima Brock, "Interstitial Integrity: Reflections toward an Asian American Woman's Theology," in *Introduction to Theology*, ed. Roger A. Badham (Louisville, KY: Westminster John Knox Press, 1998), 190.
50. Chang, *Racial Politics in an Era of Transnational Citizenship*, xiii.
51. Wong, "Asian Theology in a Changing Asia," 37–39.
52. Lowe, *Immigrant Acts*, 30, emphasis added.
53. I benefit from the work of Ella Shohat in conceptualizing these complex phenomena. See Ella Shohat, "Area Studies, Gender Studies, and the Cartographies of Knowledge," *Social Text* 72 (Fall 2002): 67–78.
54. Appadurai, "Grassroots Globalization," 16.
55. Catherine Keller, *God and Power: Counter-Apocalyptic Journeys* (Minneapolis: Fortress Press, 2005), 116.
56. Edward W. Said, *Humanism and Democratic Criticism* (New York: Columbia University Press, 2004), 135.
57. Lowe, *Immigrant Acts*, 172.
58. Nicole won the case against Lance Corporal Daniel Smith, who was convicted and sentenced to forty years in prison by a Philippine court in December 2006. The three other marines were acquitted of complicity. Smith has appealed his conviction.
59. Shohat, "Area Studies," 78.

Chapter Two

The "Indigestible" Asian

The Unifying Term "Asian" in Theological Discourse

Nami Kim

Identifying the Contours of the Problem

The categorical and representational term "Asian" has been used by Christian theologians to describe a theology that aspires to be relevant and liberative to people and their lives in an Asian context. "Asian" and "Asianness" are keywords that distinguish and differentiate Asian theology,[1] including Asian feminist theology,[2] from other theologies, such as Western (Euro-American) theology. The term "Asian" is often expressed in phrases such as "Asian way," "Asian sense," "Asian reality," "Asian context," and "Asian method" to signify the context, relevance, and characteristics of the works. While Asian feminist theology began with the critique of sexism and the lack of attention given to Asian women's experiences and perspective in Asian churches as well as in theological circles, it has been in accord with Asian theology with regard to the use of the terms "Asian" and "Asianness." Asian feminist theology from the 1980s to the mid-1990s adopted and reiterated much of Asian theology's way of using the unifying term "Asian." What is it, then, that theologians claim as Asian? Does "Asian" simply refer to the non-Western or anti-Western? Is the term "Asian" used as a cultural category or as a racial or ethnic category? When and how do theologians employ "Asian" or "Asianness" to underscore the distinctiveness of Asian theology?

This chapter examines the ways in which the unifying term "Asian" has been used in Asian theology through the genealogical study of the term. Genealogy is understood here as the "first step of problematization" through the interrogation of "the past from the vantage point of the needs and perplexities of the present situation."[3] A genealogical study of the

23

terms "Asian" and "Asianness" stems from the present need to respond to the conditions of life in and across the Asia Pacific region[4] under the rapidly changing context of globalization. A critical examination of the terms "Asian" and "Asianness," however, does not necessarily mean either the abandonment of the terms or the refutation of all prior Asian theological projects.[5] A genealogical study will reveal that the unifying term "Asian" emerged within the context of Japan's nationalism and colonialism in response to Western colonialism in the late nineteenth and early twentieth centuries. Japan's use of the term "Asian" as a unifying racial, cultural, and political entity was later employed at the Bandung Conference, which signaled the advent of the "third world," and it was the Bandung Conference that greatly influenced theological development in Asia and the Ecumenical Association of Third World Theologians (EATWOT).

I argue that the terms "Asian" and "Asianness" in their current categorical and representational usages in theological discourse are inadequate for a pertinent and liberative feminist theology in the face of increasing forces of globalization that compel us to rethink national borders, citizenship, identity, and community. When "Asian" identity is used as the primary mark of difference, disputes and differences within Asia are depoliticized and erased, obscuring the reality of historical changes and political contestations. Current transnational market economies, cultural exchanges, political interventions, and military expansions further illustrate how difficult it is to retain the unifying category of Asian. The Asian North American theorist Laura Hyun Yi Kang drives home the point when she casts doubt on the so-called shared Asian designation: "The growing numbers of male tourists from South Korea, Taiwan, Singapore, and Hong Kong attest to how the contours of transnational sex tourism unsettle any sense of their shared 'Asian' designation with the Thai and Filipina sex workers."[6]

After briefly mentioning my own social location in examining the unifying term "Asian," I will look at the history of the emergence of the terms "Asian" and "Asianness." This will be followed by a brief discussion of the usages of the terms in various phases of Asian theology. I will conclude this chapter by suggesting a strategic use of the term "Asian" and its implications for doing theology.

Where I Come from and Where I Stand: Self-referentiality

Having grown up in a place where people are still haunted by and are suffering from the unresolved legacy of Japan's colonialism, I became aware of the danger of pan-Asianism rooted in the history of multiple colonialisms (for example, those of Japan and Europe as well as the neocolonialism of the United States in Asia). This background has allowed me to see the risk of reinscribing colonial discourses in addition to the regionalization of theological and religious discourses when "Asian" identity is used as the primary mark of difference. At the same time, my outsider-within location in the United States—as a foreign visitor from Asia who came to the United States and later as a resident Korean in the United States who has become part of the Asian North American community—has pressed me to reconsider categorical identities from a new perspective. As an outsider within the United States, I live with the disadvantages of being neither/nor since I am often considered too Americanized to have an "authentic" Asian view yet am regarded as an international or foreigner who can be deported to my country of origin at any given time. Also, as a speaker of nonstandard English—for example, broken English, or "Konglish"—I am marked not only by gender, race, ethnicity, class, and sexuality but also by language in a context of the U.S. academy, where the standard English speaker is valued. At the same time, however, I am aware that there are other aspects of being an outsider within, which are often unspoken. There are certain privileges that an outsider within enjoys in comparison to those who live in the so-called third world, those who do not have access to the resources that an outsider within has.

Leslie Bow's question illustrates this dynamic when she asks what it means for "Asian theorists like Trinh T. Minh-ha and Gayatri Chakravorty Spivak to identify [themselves] as third world cultural critics rather than as Asian Americanists."[7] Bow challenges the politics "inherent in leaving unmarked one's identification with the United States as a first world power, while at the same time benefiting from its resources."[8] She further maintains that "it is a seductive positioning—at once to claim an outsider's position to lend credibility to one's first world critique, and to mark one's distance from U.S. 'colonized minorities.'"[9] This issue requires a more nuanced analysis, since identifying oneself as Asian American is not simply a matter of having U.S. citizenship, as the immigration history of Asian North Americans has demonstrated.[10] The issue of self-referentiality is a complicated matter, especially in light of changing patterns of transnational (im)migration. Nonetheless, Bow's argument compels us to think about the effects of taking "Asia" or the "third world"—often used interchangeably—as the only reference point from which one defines one's social location. An effect of this dynamic is the reinscription of the binary opposition between Asia and North America, or the first world, erasing power differentials within both Asia and North America. Another effect is a claim of epistemological privilege based on this binary opposition—that is, being an Asian or a non-Western automatically guarantees a better knowledge or perspective of the world. Here I do not claim that one should include all the reference points in self-designation. Rather, I highlight that Bow has cautioned one to be critical of one's social location, or what Arif Dirlik calls the critique of self-referentiality[11] in the web of power, and to be responsible for one's work: to be accountable to those with whom I speak. Self-critique of one's social location helps one to avoid the danger of ranking disadvantages or oppressions among those of us who have been marginalized by allowing us to see the interconnectedness in the complex web of power and to realize that the goal is not to fight for a limited access to power but rather to struggle collectively to dismantle the dominant power structure that constantly seeks to divide and conquer us.

As an outsider within the United States, I also began to realize the political necessity of using the category of Asian in forming alliances in the midst of the ongoing discrimination against Asian North Americans through prejudices and biases in U.S. political, economic, cultural, and religious contexts. Hence, finding ways in which feminist theological discourse can use the term "Asian" without reinscribing the dominant racist, nationalist, and colonialist constructions of "Asian" identity has become one of my tasks.

Emergence of the Unifying Terms "Asian" and "Asianness": From the Rise of Japanese Colonialism to the Bandung Conference

"Asian,"[12] as a categorical and representational term, is neither self-evident nor value free. Often used interchangeably with "Eastern" or "Oriental," "Asian" epitomized the Otherness oscillating between the two seemingly contradictory representations—for example, "the origin of all civilizations" and "the womb of the world," on the one hand, and "barbaric," "uncivilized," and/or "primitive," on the other hand—in the Orientalist discourse.[13] The term "Asian" was also used to refer to attributes such as "yellow, melancholy, rigid, black hair, dark eyes, severe, haughty, covetous, covered with loose garments, governed by opinions."[14] Concerning the term "Asian," the philosopher Yoko Arisaka states,

"Asian" is supposed to be a racial, ethnic, or cultural category indicating in some vague sense "non-white." (The color of choices is yellow or brown, to which are added physical features involving short stature, slanted eyes, and straight, black hair.) "Asian" is also "non-Christian," which may mean innocuously Buddhist or Hindu. But often, "Asian" means "heathen," "barbaric," or "evil." "Asian" is also "non-western," which is to say "eastern" or "oriental" (with the sense of distance, opacity, insignificance, or at best, exoticism).[15]

With the resurgence of anticolonial nationalist movements in Asia from the late nineteenth century through the early twentieth century, the category "Asian," not as a signifier of inferiority or exotic Other but as an oppositional identity, came into use.[16] K. M. Panikkar (1895–1963), prominent Indian historian and diplomat, argued in his *Asia and Western Dominance* that it was the European nations' emphasis on their solidarity and their Europeanness that gave rise to a common feeling of Asianness in their dealing with Asian countries.[17] Panikkar drew his argument regarding the oneness of Asia and Asianness from the work of Kakuzo Okakura (1863–1913).[18] In his book *The Ideals of the East*, Okakura claimed that "Asia is one" and the "Asiatic races form a single mighty web."[19] He maintained that it was Japan that realized "the unity-in-complexity with a special clearness" and that Japan was "the real repository of the trust of Asiatic thought and culture."[20] Okakura further asserted that the history of Japanese art became the history of "Asiatic ideals."[21] As Panikkar demonstrated, Okakura employed the term "Asian" to signify a racial and cultural unity, which was deemed no longer inferior to the West (read, Europeanness). Joseph Kitagawa, in *The Christian Tradition: Beyond Its European Captivity*, also points out Panikkar's observance of the emergence of "Asianness" along with political and cultural nationalism in Asia.[22]

Drawing on Okakura almost a century later, the theologian Wai-Ching Angela Wong asserts, "[This] Asianness, as a collective of the growing nationalisms in various countries in Asia, was primarily produced by Asians' reaction to the 'unified aggression' of the Europeans."[23] She maintains that this "emerging shared identity of a common 'Asianness' is a result of a general rise of nationalism in the former colonized territories in the region."[24] In relation to theology, Wong claims that it is "the very history of colonialism which discursively gave rise to the conception of a contextual theology of a vaguely 'unifying Asia.'"[25]

What Panikkar and Wong do not address, however, is that the rhetoric of "oneness of Asia" or "Asianness" was used by Japan's nationalists and later by Japan's colonial powers as an ideological justification for colonizing other neighboring countries in Asia from 1895 until 1945, rather than these terms being used to bring justice and peace to people and to the regions that had been devastated by Western colonial exploitation. To put it differently, the unifying category "Asian," which was employed by anti-colonial nationalists who opposed Western colonialism, was used by Japan's political powers to justify their imperial aggression in various regions of Asia. Under the slogans Pan-Asianism and the Greater East Asian Coprosperity Sphere, Japan used the rhetoric that it should "save" and "liberate" Asia from the Western aggressors and emphasized racial and cultural affinities as "Asian" under Japan's rule. Although some anticolonial nationalists expressed similar thoughts,[26] the idea of pan-Asianism, or the unity of Asia, began to be actualized by Japan as a colonial policy imbued with its imperial ambition in the midst of Western colonial encroachment on the various regions in Asia and was manifested throughout Japan's colonial expansion until the end of World War II.

Pan-Asianism, which was Japan's colonial policy, professed racial and cultural affinities between the Japanese and other peoples in Asia as well as the unity of all people in Asia. When Japan came to control most of the Southeast Asia region and the Pacific Rim by mid-1942, the region became part of Japan's Greater East Asian Coprosperity Sphere, which expressed the idea of a politically and economically integrated Asia free from Western colonialism. Japan sought to create "a new Asian order" and bring about "a spiritual regeneration of Asia under Japanese leadership."[27] Both pan-Asianism and the Greater East Asian Coprosperity Sphere were carried out by Japan's colonial power for the purpose of expanding and increasing Japan's economic and political dominance in Asia at the expense of other colonized people. In this way, "Asian" did not refer to a simple geographical location but was instead a racial and cultural category. It was also a political category that signified anti-Western. While "Asian" was employed as an opposing category to "Western," it meant, by no means, that all Asians were considered or treated as equal. It is startling to see that many black political (male) leaders and intellectuals in the United States in the early twentieth century hailed Japan as a role model or a great challenge to white supremacy, and many rejoiced with the news that Japan defeated Russia in the Russo-Japanese War of 1904–5.[28]

Japan's ambition to create "a new Asian order," according to Clive Christie, was expressed most clearly when an Assembly of Greater East Asian Nations met in Tokyo under the leadership of Japan in November 1943.[29] Burma, the Philippines, the Japanese-occupied states of China and Manchukuo, and Thailand also participated in the meeting. The "supreme leader" of Burma, Dr. Ba Maw, made the point that with the help of the new order created by Japan, "Asians," who had lost an "instinctive sense of affiliation," could once again "discover" one another.[30] The principles of coexistence, cooperation, and coprosperity were pronounced in the meeting by Jose Laurel, president of the Philippines at the time. Christie asserts that the formula of coexistence, cooperation, and coprosperity reflects the balance between the two main themes that were highlighted by the Tokyo meeting: (1) "respect for each other's independence, culture and political development"; and (2) "an attempt to define the principles underlying the new Asian order."[31] The long-term goal of Japanese policy, according to John W. Dower, was to create "an inseparable economic relationship between the Yamato race, the leader of the East Asia Cooperative Body, and other member peoples," whereby Japan would hold the key to the existence of all the races of East Asia.[32] This was also the time when anti-Asian sentiment intensified in the United States, drastically so after Japan's attack on the American naval base at Pearl Harbor in Hawaii in 1941. Orientalist caricatures of the yellow peril and of Asian peoples as villains persisted to the extent that Japanese Americans were considered an enemy of the United States, resulting in the internment of Japanese Americans until the end of World War II.[33]

Not only the sentiments but also the principles of coexistence, cooperation, and coprosperity were still in use at the Bandung Conference, even after the defeat of Japan. Signaling the emergence of the third world, the Bandung Conference, or what was called the Asian-African Conference, was held in Bandung, Indonesia, April 18–25, 1955. The leaders of twenty-nine independent Asian and African nations participated in this conference, which Indonesia hosted and Burma, India, Pakistan, and Ceylon (now Sri Lanka) cosponsored.[34]

According to Richard Wright, an African American journalist who observed the conference, the Bandung Conference was an indictment of Western racialism, which promoted the racial superiority of white Westerners and was the cornerstone of Western justification for colonial exploitation.[35] Wright informed readers of his 1956 *The Color Curtain* that the Bandung Conference stressed economic cooperation among the Asian and African powers. Likewise, Chitta Biswas, in his reflection on the thirteenth anniversary of the Bandung Conference, stated that the most important, concrete idea of the conference was the question of the "general desire for economic cooperation among the participating countries on the basis of mutual interest and respect for national sovereignty."[36]

Christie argues that the reason the Bandung Conference could be seen as the pan-Asian successor to the Assembly of Greater East Asian Nations held in Tokyo in 1943 was that Asian states dominated the conference, since most of the African states, including several in northern Africa, had yet to achieve independence.[37] Moreover, the conference stressed economic cooperation among participating countries, which was also the focal point of the Tokyo meeting. Kang supports this view, saying that "economic cooperation" was the strategy by which Japan "sought to make Asia the offshore base of Japanese capitalist expansion," which continued after World War II.[38] Kang further points out that the Japanese transnational corporations (TNCs) moved into the free trade zones (FTZs) before American and European corporations in Asia and that the TNCs' investments were especially extensive in former colonies, such as Taiwan and South Korea.[39]

On a cultural level the Bandung Conference represented anticolonial nationalists' summons for the renewal of traditional cultures and religions, for it called for a renewal, in the "context of the modern world," of the ancient Asian and African cultures and religions that have been interrupted during the past centuries.[40]

Nonetheless, the Bandung Conference was significant in terms of influencing further theological development at the East Asian Christian Conference (EACC), the Christian Conference of Asia (CCA), and the Ecumenical Association of Third World Theologians (EATWOT). Franklyn J. Balasundaram, who has actively participated in EATWOT in Asia, credits the Bandung Conference for its significant influence on the EACC and its influence on EATWOT. Balasundaram captures well the significance of Bandung:

> The Bandung Conference gave a sense of inter-regional solidarity not only to Asia, but also to the Third World. Bandung was a movement in the sense that it not only affected the social, political, religious, cultural and economics of Asian countries, but also created, to quote Wiedenmann, a movement in the theological history that even now is at work and the whole theological direction in the Third World came to be named after it. In other words, in the given colonial and post-colonial experience of the nations in Asia, Bandung highlighted the challenges from the Asian context to theology.[41]

Defining the Bandung Conference as a "meeting of the rejected, the underdogs," and a kind of "judgment upon the Western World," Balasundaram asserts that the Bandung Conference symbolized the self-discovery of nations within Asia.[42] Furthermore, he recapitulates the historical importance of the Bandung Conference for Christianity in Asia, stating, "In the post-independence era, the churches of different confessions had to come together to reflect as to how they could make the gospel relevant to the Asian context. The Bandung Conference provided necessary motivation in this context."[43] Referring to the EACC,[44] Balasundaram writes, "The conference recognized that the Asian revolution was a total one, affecting not only politics and economics, but also involving the reformation of culture and religion as well. [The] Bandung Conference, held two years earlier, influenced very much the content of the conference."[45]

This is the historical context of Western colonialism and the emerging anticolonial nationalisms in Asia headed by Japan's nationalism that gave rise to the discursive construction of "Asian" as a unifying force in contrast to another entity, "Western." "Asian" as a racial, cultural, economic, and political category continued to be used during the Bandung Conference. It is ironic, however, that while "Asian" at the Bandung Conference signified "anti-Western" (read, anti–white European) in terms of race, culture, and religion, it was not anti-Western with regard to the desire for economic development. Drawing from Partha Chatterjee, the postcolonial feminist theorist Meyda Yeğenoğlu contends that anticolonial nationalist thought is "selective about what it takes from Western rational thought," rather than being a duplication of Orientalist discourse, which is often a critique leveled against a nationalist framework.[46]

In addressing the question of what to take from the West and what to reject, the distinction between the material and the spiritual spheres provides a useful framework of selection for anticolonial nationalists.[47] According to this distinction, the material sphere is the site in which nationalists need to embrace the knowledge of the superior techniques of the West in order to defeat colonialism.[48] It is in the spiritual sphere where the anticolonial nationalist project protects the "inner side" of Asia and leaves it uncontaminated by the West. This inner side is identified as "authentic" or "truly" Asian and is thus distinct from the Western realm. However, in the process of constructing anticolonial nationalist political identity, anticolonial nationalists often contrasted the indigenous culture and values to those of Western culture, calling for the return to the traditional roles, practices, and values for colonized women.[49] The postcolonial feminist Uma Narayan argues that a return to the traditional values and practices confined women to traditional gender roles, and such a return was what anticolonial nationalists considered to be the best way of preserving national identity and cultural pride. Also, economic concern for anticolonial nationalists in building an economically strong Asia often represented and served the interests of nationalist male elites at the expense of women and underprivileged people within its national borders.

Despite the inextricable relationship between the unifying term "Asian" and Japan's colonialism, Japan's colonialist use of pan-Asianism and the unity of Asia was rarely questioned or discussed in Asian theology. Japan's colonialism became a forgotten history, at least, in the usages of the unifying term "Asian" in theological discourse. Instead, it remained buried behind the Western colonial legacy. Although the way "Asian" has been used in Asian theology is not identical with the employment of "Asian" in Japan's colonial policy, the unifying term became the cornerstone through which Asian theology claimed its distinctiveness from the nation-building stage to the present.

"Asian" in Asian Theology during the Nation-Building Stage

M. M. Thomas's *The Christian Response to the Asian Revolution*[50] illustrates how the term "Asian" was used in the development of theology during the nation-building stage. In his theological work, it is most clearly expressed in his use of the phrase "Asian revolution." Despite Thomas's awareness · of the cultural, political, ideological, and social plurality in Asia, he has asserted that the use "Asian revolution" in the singular was justified because "Asian nationalism," deemed to be the bearer of the Asian revolution, has always sought to interpret its mission in relation to the Western impact on Asia.[51] In other words, for Thomas, the Asian revolution could not be understood apart from the impact of the West on Asia.[52] The Asian revolution, components of which derive from various forms of nationalism,[53] opened up ways for extending God's salvific work that were manifested through Jesus Christ, making it relevant beyond the Western realm. While the Asian revolution could not be understood apart from Western influence on Asia, Thomas wrote that the Asian revolution "broke the too close identification of the gospel with Western culture and Western imperialism and brought the awareness of the transcendence of the gospel over all cultures."[54] In this sense, for Thomas, the Asian revolution broadened the influence of Christianity beyond Western culture, instead of rejecting Christianity. Thomas posited that through the Asian revolution, Christianity could expand its impact, moving "transcendentally" to other cultures (for example, Asia).

While agreeing with many other nationalists on the necessity to transform and reform the age-old religions and cultures of Asia, Thomas argued for the relevance of Christianity in the context of Asian revolution, which made him different from the majority of nationalists, who often equated Christianity with Western colonialism. Unlike nationalists who did not appreciate the spiritual or nonmaterial aspects of Western culture, Thomas sought to embrace an element attached to its spiritual realm, that is, Christianity. What Thomas challenged was the Western Christendom that has been associated with Western imperialism. In order to unfetter Christianity from being associated with Western imperialism, Thomas attempted to separate the so-called core Christian message from Western culture and its political practice. Thomas's work was different from that of many non-Christian nationalists because he emphasized the significance of Jesus Christ as well as the relevance of Christianity in the process of Asian revolution. For him, the humanity of Jesus Christ exemplifies an ideal human being, and this can be separated from Western culture. He insisted that the core message of Christianity is different from the Christianized Western cultural hegemony, and it can be transferred to other contexts, such as an Asian context. Only through this process of separation between the core message of Christianity and its culture could Thomas argue for the relevance of Christianity during the nation-building process in Asia. He also carefully inverted the linkage between Christianity and Western social progress. That is, while Westerners (read, Christians) believed that God had worked through Western imperial expansion as a way to come closer to God's reign, Thomas argued that God also worked in the Asian revolution.

Challenging the links between Christianity and Western imperialism, Thomas produced a nationalist discourse of Christian theology in which a distinctive identity of Asia was constructed in contrast to that of the West. For him, theology that was relevant to the Asian reality was not and could not be a Western theology of Western Christendom. Instead, such a theology was an Asian theology that was emerging in the midst of the nation-building process. Asian theology during this period, unlike Western (Euro-American) theology, strove to respond to the Asian reality, seeking to understand God's purpose in it, since God is not just a God of the West but also a God of Asia.

Hence the term "Asian" in Thomas's theology did not necessarily signify anti-Western. It was used in a way that was complementary to the term "Western" rather than simply oppositional or hostile, since the Asian revolution did not indicate a closure of theological justification for God's working in the West. "Asian" signified the expansion of the Christian message beyond the confines of the West. It referred to the realm beyond the West, both culturally and theologically. The term "Asian" indicated a new opportunity through which God could expand God's salvific work and signified a newly fashioned realm in which Christianity could be relevant and legitimized beyond a limited realm, that is, the Western context.

One major difference that distinguished Thomas's and subsequent Asian theological discourses is that the term "Asian" rarely referred to a people's racial identity whereas it carried a racial ethnic connotation—for example, Asiatic race, yellow, brown—in Orientalist discourse, in Japan's colonialist slogan of pan-Asianism, as well as at the Bandung Conference. In other words, "Asian" was not used to signify a racial or ethnic category in Asian theological discourses not only because Asian theologians were aware of racial ethnic plurality in Asia but also because many Asian theologians adopted, albeit differently, anticolonial nationalists' distinction between the material sphere and the spiritual sphere, often using the term "Asian" to refer to the spiritual realm. The Bandung Conference, the EACC (later Christian Conference of Asia), and EATWOT Asian conferences, especially the first Asian theological conference held at Wennappuwa, Sri Lanka, in 1979, shared their emphases on both political and economic independence from Western domination as well as cultural and religious distinctiveness from the West. Such common ground among these conferences provides a crucial clue as to how Asian theology used "Asian" as a distinctive mark that differentiates Asian theology not only from the dominant Euro-American theology but also from other third-world theologies.

"Asian" in Asian Theology: From EATWOT to the Present

In Asian theology from the beginning of EATWOT Asian conferences (1979) to the present, the term "Asian" has evolved in connection with the themes of poverty and religion. The work of Aloysius Pieris is illustrative of this. Pieris, a Jesuit and Buddhist scholar in Sri Lanka, is one of the leading theologians who have vigorously articulated an Asianness and Asian identity of Asian theology that differs not only from dominant Euro-American theology but also from Latin American liberation theology.[55] In his work the "Asian reality," which is the "matrix" of Asian theology, is constituted by the "religiousness of the poor and the poverty of the religious masses."[56] Western neocolonialism is identified as the root cause of poverty in Asia. This is also deemed to be the case for other third-world contexts. In terms of poverty, "Asian" is considered synonymous with the term "third world." While the problem of poverty is understood as a shared condition of all third-world contexts, including Asia, three characteristics, according to Pieris, distinguish the Asian context from other third-world contexts: (1) linguistic heterogeneity, (2) the coexistence of metacosmic religion and the cosmic religion of the peasant people, and (3) the existence of non-Christian soteriologies. While these three characteristics, along with third worldness, constitute Asian reality, what renders Asian theology Asian is not just a third-world context but also the plurality of religions and the heterogeneity of language. Although Asian reality is conceptualized in terms of poverty and religion, only religion becomes a defining factor that characterizes Asianness and Asian identity.

An articulation of Asianness through the themes of religion and poverty is also found in some Asian feminist theologians' work. While Asian women theologians have been critical of sexism and the absence of Asian women's experiences and perspectives in Asian theology, the use of the unitary term "Asian" in the work of theologians who have been actively involved in or influenced by EATWOT, such as that of Virginia Fabella, Sun Ai Lee Park, and Chung Hyun Kyung, resonates with the work of Pieris and other EATWOT Asian theological discourses.

For instance, an articulation of Asianness through the themes of religion and poverty is also found in the collection of theological essays *We Dare to Dream: Doing Theology as Asian Women*, edited by Virginia Fabella and Sun Ai Lee Park.[57] The premise of doing theology as Asians and as women is a thread running through the collected essays. In their introduction, the editors begin by stating, "More recently, Christian women have become aware that without their distinctive voices as Asians and as women, the emerging theologies in Asia cannot be liberating or relevant, not for themselves or for the Church or society at large."[58] Like other Asian theologians, these Asian feminist theologians are primarily concerned with theology that is relevant to the Asian context, which, according to Fabella and Park, is marked by poverty and is dominated by patriarchal institutions, on the one hand, and characterized by the diversity of religions and cultures, on the other hand. As in other Asian theology, the Asian context in Asian feminist theology is two-pronged: that is, it includes both the socioeconomic and the religiocultural contexts. While Asia is regarded as a part of the third world in terms of the socioeconomic context, only religion and tradition represent a distinctive Asianness.

The essay in *We Dare to Dream* titled "Final Statement: Asian Church Women Speak" (Manila, Philippines, Nov. 21–30, 1985) drives home the point, as the following excerpt demonstrates: "We did not delve deeply enough into other important facets of our Asian roots—the great Asian religions and traditions that have shaped our Asianness."[59] In "A Common

Methodology for Diverse Christologies" Virginia Fabella states, "What distinguishes Asia from the rest of the Third World is its religious, cultural, and linguistic pluralism. Asia has at least seven major linguistic zones, more than any other continent can claim. It is the birthplace of all the great world religions and, with the exception of Christianity and Judaism, it is the home of most of their adherents."[60] This statement resonates with the unique characteristics of the Asian context that Pieris articulated, that is, linguistic heterogeneity and the existence of non-Christian soteriologies (metacosmic religions).

A similar example can be found in Chung Hyun Kyung's[61] landmark *Struggle to Be the Sun Again: Introducing Asian Women's Theology*. Addressing the social context of Asian women's theology, Chung claims that "Asian women's theology" is "very Third World," "very Asian," and "very women."[62] For her, "Third World–ness" refers to the everyday reality marked by poverty and oppression that colonialism, neocolonialism, militarism, and dictatorship have caused.[63] She writes, "Together with Asian male liberation theology, Asian women's theology is derived from this Third World reality of poverty and oppression."[64] Quoting Virginia Fabella and Aloysius Pieris, Chung states,

> Asian women's theology is also "very Asian." It embraces many different people and rich religious, cultural, and linguistic heritages. Asia encompasses 58 percent of the world's population and Asian women comprise one quarter of the world's people. Asia is also the birthplace of all the great world religions. Christians in Asia are less than 3 percent of the population. The majority of Asians are Buddhists, Hindus, Muslims, Taoists, or Confucianists. Asia, therefore, is a non-Christian continent. Asian women's theology seeks to articulate the meaning of the Christian message "through the sources within its [Asia's] own millennia-old culture, and all the living faiths of its neighbours."[65]

While "third worldness" indicates the material dimension of Asia marked with poverty and exploitation, "Asianness" stands for the plurality and greatness of religion, culture, and language, as well as referring to non-Christian spiritual heritages and traditions.

Poverty and oppression have characterized Asia's third worldness, whereas Asia's religious and cultural traditions have represented the spiritual sphere, where all the timeless values are kept intact and the world's major religious and cultural heritages originated and were maintained. Furthermore, only the latter understanding of "Asian," that is, Asian as a spiritual sphere, was designated as "truly" or "authentic" Asian, which differentiated it not only from the West but also from other third-world regions. What has distinguished Asian theology from other theologies has been, in fact, religions, traditions, and cultures. In other words, "Asian" could be understood as another name for "non-Christianity," which was often used interchangeably with "non-Western."

Strategic Use of the Term "Asian"?

What are the ways, then, in which feminist theologians can define and reclaim "Asian" and "Asianness" that are not confined to the binary oppositions between the East and the West, oppressed and oppressor, harmonious and confrontational, and non-Christian and Christian, nor confined to the spiritual realm? Drawing from Spivak's notion of strategic essentialism, I propose that the term "Asian" be used strategically.[66] By "strategic use," Spivak means a "persistent critique" with the acknowledgment of "the unavoidable usefulness of something that is very dangerous" and the awareness of "the dangerousness of what one must use."[67]

One of the notable examples of the strategic applications of the term "Asian" is its political use by Asian North Americans within the context of the struggle against racist oppression and the dominant usage of Asian as a racial, ethnic category. On the one hand, Asian North American theorists and activists have persistently critiqued the essentialized racist use of the term "Asian" as it has been used against Asian North Americans. On the other hand, keenly acknowledging the danger of using the term "Asian," they have attempted to conceptualize Asian not as an already-constituted racial ethnic entity but as a political denominator that binds a group of people together based on the common history of oppression and struggle in the United States as well as struggle against American imperialism in Asia.[68] The term "Asian" when used by Asian North Americans in the United States signifies the political struggle and resistance against racism. Yet since such struggle is neither static nor complete, ongoing examination of the effectiveness of using the term "Asian" as a political and social category is necessary, especially in light of the changing demographics of migrations from Asia—for example, immigrants from Southeast Asia and other affluent, new immigrants and migrants—that challenge the Asian North American as a "unified subject of resistance."[69]

The strategic use of the term "Asian" also implies a critical examination of the tendency to use it primarily as a religious and cultural category—that is, non-Christian—in theological discourse.[70] Defining "authentic

Asian" in terms of traditional cultures and religions is problematic because it essentializes the term "Asian" as a static and ahistorical entity. Feminist theology needs to move beyond a portrayal of Asian religions and cultures as relatively unchanging practices and beliefs, transcending time and space. Along with this, it is necessary to reconsider how to understand "Asian religions" in the global context, because transnational (im)migration, which continues to take place all over the world in different forms, whether voluntarily or involuntarily, has always accompanied changes in the religious landscape.[71] A pressing question is, Would it be accurate to describe these religions as Asian based only on their geographical origin or association? Although the majority of people whose identities have been shaped by these religions still reside in Asia, confining these religions to Asia reinscribes the binary opposition between the East (read, religions except Christianity) and the West (read, Christianity). For the same reason, it is questionable to define Christianity as a Western religion, because the West, especially Europe, is no longer the home of the majority of Christians; and the fastest growing religion in various parts of Asia is Christianity, particularly theologically and politically conservative forms of Christianity. As Russell T. McCutcheon puts it in his *Critics Not Caretakers: Redescribing the Public Study of Religion*, the "traditional West/East division," whether to categorize religions or the history of the world, has "little use for contemporary scholars."[72]

With the rapidly expanding global capitalism in Asia[73] that is often morally justified under a banner called Asian values, as well as with the increasing complexity and diversity within Asian North American communities due to the changing patterns and dynamics of transnational migration, the term "Asian" requires an ongoing scrutiny as to how and why it is used and to whom it refers. Noticing the changing and multiple "Asias," Kwok Pui-lan pays attention to the growing uneven economic development in Asia and the subsequent disparity among women, thereby alluding to a possibility of conceptualizing "Asian" not in terms of binary opposition to the monolithic category "Western" but in terms of the complex interactions within, between, and across national borders under a transnational capitalist market economy.[74] In this sense, it is problematic to categorize one's theological work as Asian only because she or he can be categorized as Asian by the standard of the dominant group. Accordingly, there is no automatic connection between being an Asian woman and doing Asian feminist theology. Claiming oneself as an Asian feminist theologian is not based on one's being a woman or being Asian. Rather, identifying oneself as an Asian feminist theologian means that one is willing to engage in a strategic use of the term "Asian" while simultaneously doing theology from a feminist perspective. Asian feminist theology, then, can be claimed and articulated by those who want to participate in an "imagined community" of struggle,[75] not because she or he is seen as Asian through her or his country of origin or through racial ethnic affiliation but because she or he is willing to engage in a critical theological discourse that unceasingly challenges the dominant racist, nationalist, and colonial discourse, and that, simultaneously, can provide a theological vision for a better and just world.

Feminist theology that aspires to be critical, relevant, liberative, and empowering needs to take into account the changing contours of the usefulness and the dangerousness of the term "Asian" in its theological reflection. Since "Asian" is not a kind of category that can be simply discarded, it is theologians' ongoing task to wrestle with its "strategic use," acknowledging its "unavoidable usefulness" and being aware of its "dangerousness."[76]

Notes

1. By "Asian theology" I indicate an already-established theological corpus and movement. By "Asian theologian(s)" I refer to those who have identified themselves as Asian theologians through either their writings or institutional affiliations, such as East Asian Christian Conference (EACC) or Ecumenical Association of Third World Theologians (EATWOT). This chapter, however, is limited in its scope, for it discusses only several stages of theological development. Yet it certainly has implications for those who continue to work as "Asian" theologians and who search for what it means to do "Asian" theology in the early twenty-first century.

2. By "Asian feminist theology" I refer to an already-existing Christian women's and feminist theological corpus and movement in and from Asia.

3. Jan Goldstein, ed., *Foucault and the Writing of History* (Malden, MA: Blackwell, 1994), 14.

4. Rob Wilson traces a genealogy of the term "Asia Pacific" in his article "Imagining 'Asia-Pacific' Today: Forgetting Colonialism in the Magical Free Markets of the American Pacific," in *Learning Places: The Afterlives of Area Studies*, ed. Masao Miyoshi and H. D. Harootunian (Durham, NC: Duke University Press, 2002).

5. Part of this and the following paragraphs appeared in my article "'My/Our' Comfort *Not* at the Expense of 'Somebody Else's': Toward a Critical Global Feminist Theology," *Journal of Feminist Studies in Religion* 21, no. 2 (2005): 75–94.

6. Laura Hyun Yi Kang, *Compositional Subjects: Enfiguring Asian/American Women* (Durham, NC: Duke University Press, 2002), 185. I also talk about this in the roundtable discussion in *Journal of Feminist Studies in Religion* 21, no. 1 (2005): 137–41.

7. Leslie Bow, "For Every Gesture of Loyalty, There Doesn't Have to Be a Betrayal: Asian American Criticism and the Politics of Locality," in *Who Can Speak: Authority and Critical Identity*, ed. Judith Roof and Robyn Wiegman (Urbana: University of Illinois Press, 1995), 46. Part of the following section first appeared in my contribution to the roundtable discussion in the *JFSR* 21, no. 1 (2005): 137–38.

8. Ibid., 146.

9. Ibid.

10. See Rita Nakashima Brock and Nami Kim, "Asian American Protestant Women: Roles and Contributions in Religion," in *Encyclopedia of Women and Religion in North America*, ed. Rosemary Radford Ruether and Rosemary Keller (Bloomington: Indiana University Press, 2006).

11. See Arif Dirlik, "The Postcolonial Aura: Third World Criticism in the Age of Global Capitalism," *Critical Inquiry* 20, no. 2 (1994): 328–56.

12. See Demetrius J. Georgacas, "The Name Asia for the Continent: Its History and Origin," *Names: Journal of the American Name Society* 17, no. 1 (1969): 10–33.

13. Meyda Yeğenoğlu maintains that the East/Orient is "pushed back in time and constructed as primitive or backward" in contrast to the West. In other words, Asia/ East/Orient, wrestling with the time lag, often signified a racially, socially, culturally, and politically inferior counterpart of the "civilized" West. See Meyda Yeğenoğlu, *Colonial Fantasies: Toward a Feminist Reading of Orientalism* (Cambridge: Cambridge University Press, 1998), 6.

14. See Carolus Linneaus, *Systema Naturae* (Stockholm: Impensis Laurentii Salvii, 1758–59).

15. Yoko Arisaka, "Asian Women: Invisibility, Locations, and Claims of Philosophy," in *Women of Color and Philosophy: A Critical Reader*, ed. Naomi Zack (Malden, MA: Blackwell, 2000), 211. Also see Yen Le Espiritu, *Asian American Panethnicity: Bridging Institutions and Identities* (Philadelphia: Temple University Press, 1992), 6.

16. Part of the following section first appeared in my contribution to the roundtable discussion in the *JFSR* 21, no. 1 (2005): 139–40.

17. K. M. Panikkar, *Asia and Western Dominance: A Survey of the Vasco da Gama Epoch of Asian History, 1498–1945* (New York: Day, 1954), 494.

18. According to the publishers' preface to Kakuzo Okakura's *Awakening of Japan*, written in 1905, Okakura was one of the "promoters of the reactionary movement against the wholesale introduction of Western art and manners," and the movement was carried on by the "starting of periodicals and clubs devoted to the preservation of the old life of Japan." See Kakuzo Okakura, *Awakening of Japan* (New York: Century Co., 1905), x.

19. Kakuzo Okakura, *The Ideals of the East: With Special Reference to the Art of Japan* (New York: E. P. Dutton Co., 1904), 1, 2.

20. Ibid., 1, 5.

21. Ibid., 8.

22. Joseph Kitagawa, *The Christian Tradition: Beyond Its European Captivity* (Philadelphia: Trinity Press International, 1992), 29.

23. Wai-Ching Angela Wong, "'The Poor Woman': A Critical Analysis of Asian Theology and Contemporary Chinese Fiction by Women" (Ph.D. diss., University of Chicago, 1997), 31. Wong's dissertation was published as *"The Poor Woman": A Critical Analysis of Asian Theology and Contemporary Chinese Fiction by Women* (New York: Peter Lang, 2002).

24. Ibid., 32.

25. Ibid., 31.

26. For example, Clive J. Christie notes that the Vietnamese writer and patriot Phan Boi Chau (1867–1940), who was born into a Mandarin family, turned his hopes during the decade before World War I to "the creation of some kind of 'Pan-Asian' anticolonial alliance," believing that the alliance would ultimately generate "an irresistible Pan-Asian force that would drive the West out of Asia altogether." See Clive J. Christie, *Ideology and*

Revolution in Southeast Asia, 1900–1980: Political Ideas of the Anticolonial Era (Richmond, Surrey: Curzon, 2001), 20–21. Bung Karno of Indonesia also said that Chau introduced the idea of pan-Asianism. See Roeslan Abdulgani, *The Bandung Connection: The Asia-Africa Conference in Bandung in 1955*, trans. Molly Bondan (Singapore: Gunung Agung, 1981), 46; and Sun Yat-sen, *His Political and Social Ideals*, comp., trans., and annot. Leonard Shihlien Hsu (Los Angeles: University of Southern California Press, 1933).

27. Christie, *Ideology and Revolution in Southeast Asia*, 79.

28. See Gerald Horne, "Tokyo Bound: African Americans and Japan Confront White Supremacy," *Souls: A Critical Journal of Black Politics, Culture, and Society* 2, no. 2 (2001): 17–29.

29. Christie, *Ideology and Revolution in Southeast* Asia, 79.

30. Burma and the Philippines had been given "independency" by Japan in 1943. See Ba Maw, *Breakthrough in Burma: Memoirs of a Revolution, 1939–1946* (New Haven, CT: Yale University Press, 1968), 343–44, quoted in Christie, *Ideology and Revolution in Southeast Asia*, 80.

31. Ba Maw, *Breakthrough in Burma*, 340–41, quoted in Christie, *Ideology and Revolution in Southeast Asia*, 80.

32. John W. Dower, *War without Mercy: Race and Power in the Pacific War* (New York: Pantheon Books, 1986), 290.

33. See Espiritu, *Asian American Panethnicity*. Also see Gale A. Yee's chapter in this volume.

34. Originally thirty countries, which constituted half of the independent countries throughout the world at the time, were invited, but the Central African Federation decided not to attend. Taiwan, South Korea, and North Korea were not invited to attend the conference. See Abdulgani, *Bandung Connection*.

35. Richard Wright, *The Color Curtain: A Report on the Bandung Conference* (Cleveland: World Publishing Co., 1956), 151–53.

36. Chitta Biswas, *The Relevance of Bandung: Thirteenth Anniversary of the Bandung Conference* (Cairo, Egypt: The Permanent Secretariat of Afro-Asian People's Solidarity, 1985), 19.

37. Christie, *Ideology and Revolution in Southeast Asia*, 131. Richard Wright observed at the Bandung Conference that one Australian journalist commented bitterly, "Bandung means that Japan really won the war in the Pacific" (*Color Curtain*, 127).

38. Kang, *Compositional Subjects*, 184.

39. Ibid., 184–85. The so-called intracontinental industrial restructuring continues as factories have been relocated to Southeast and South Asian countries from East Asian countries.

40. Wright, *Color Curtain*, 204.

41. Franklyn J. Balasundaram, *EATWOT in Asia: Towards a Relevant Theology* (Bangalore: Asian Trading Corporation, 1993), 113.

42. Ibid., 112, 115.

43. Ibid., 111.

44. Balasundaram was referring to the second EACC meeting held in Prapat, Indonesia, March 17–26, 1957. EACC's first meeting was held in 1949, and the official inauguration took place in 1959.

45. Balasundaram, *EATWOT in Asia*, 117.

46. Partha Chatterjee, *Nationalist Thought and the Colonial World: A Derivative Discourse* (London: Zed Books, 1986), 38, quoted in Meyda Yeğenoğlu, *Colonial Fantasies*, 124. See Uma Narayan, *Dislocating Cultures: Identities, Traditions, and Third World Feminism* (New York:

Routledge, 1997), chap. 1, in which she talks about the selective labeling of certain changes and not others as symptoms of "Westernization" and selective appropriations of modernity by nationalists.

47. Yeğenoğlu, *Colonial Fantasies*, 124.

48. Ibid.

49. See Narayan, *Dislocating Cultures*, 14; and Leila Ahmed, *Women and Gender in Islam* (New Haven, CT: Yale University Press, 1992). Narayan and Ahmed maintain that both colonial and anticolonial nationalists have played their ideological part in the construction of women's gender roles in surprisingly similar ways.

50. In this book Thomas articulates the relevance of Christianity in the midst of the nation-building process that was taking place in various countries in Asia. The book is an outcome of a lecture series that Thomas presented primarily to a Christian audience in England, many of whom believed that the Western imperial expansion, along with mission activities, was an effort to expand Christendom and wondered how to respond to what Thomas called "the Asian revolution" as a responsible Western Christian (*The Christian Response to the Asian Revolution* [London: SCM Press, 1966]). See also M. M. Thomas, *Man and the Universe of Faiths* (Madras: Christian Literature Society, 1975); M. M. Thomas, *Response to Tyranny: Writings between July 1975 and February 1977* (New Delhi: Forum for Christian Concern for People's Struggle, 1979); and M. M. Thomas and Paul E. Converse, *Revolution and Redemption* (New York: Friendship Press, 1955).

51. Thomas, *Christian Response to the Asian Revolution*, 9.

52. Ibid., 9. John England also talks about the impact of the West on Asia in the volume he edited with Alan Torrance, *Doing Theology with the Spirit's Movement in Asia* (Singapore: Association for Theological Education in South East Asia, 1991).

53. According to Thomas, the first interpretation of nationalism sees its mission as the "instrument of Western democratic humanism," and it represents the Asian leaders' understanding of nationalism. The first interpretation sees the mission of Asian nationalism as a continuation of the mission of Western imperialism, that is, Asian nationalism as a friend and ally of imperialism (Thomas, *Christian Response to the Asian Revolution*, 10). The second interpretation, which is the dominant view of Asia's left-wing nationalists, considers nationalism as "the instrument of technological development and economic productivity in Asia" (9). As Thomas repeatedly points out, the emphasis is not on Western human values but on Western technology. The third interpretation of nationalism is understood as the "search for unique Asian selfhood or Asian personality" (9).

54. Ibid., 33.

55. See Aloysius Pieris, *Asian Theology of Liberation* (Maryknoll, NY: Orbis Books, 1989).

56. Ibid., 113.

57. Virginia Fabella is a Maryknoll sister in the Philippines. Sun Ai Lee Park, originally from South Korea, is the founder of the journal *In God's Image*.

58. Virginia Fabella and Sun Ai Lee Park, "Introduction," in *We Dare to Dream: Doing Theology as Asian Women*, ed. Virginia Fabella and Sun Ai Lee Park (Maryknoll, NY: Orbis Books, 1989), vii.

59. Fabella, "Final Statement: Asian Church Women Speak" (Manila, Philippines, November 21–30, 1985), in *We Dare to Dream*, 147.

60. Virginia Fabella, "A Common Methodology for Diverse Christologies," in *With Passion and Compassion: Third World Women Doing Theology*, ed. Virginia Fabella and Mercy Amba Oduyoye (Maryknoll, NY: Orbis Books, 1988), 109.

61. Chung Hyun Kyung is a theologian from South Korea. She currently teaches at Union Theological Seminary in New York.

62. Chung Hyun Kyung, *Struggle to Be the Sun Again: Introducing Asian Women's Theology* (Maryknoll, NY: Orbis, 1990), 23–24.

63. Ibid., 23.

64. Ibid.

65. Ibid., 23–24.

66. Portions of this and the following paragraphs first appeared in my article "'My/Our' Comfort," 78–82.

67. Gayatri Spivak, with Ellen Rooney, "In a Word," *Differences: A Journal of Feminist Cultural Studies* 1, no. 2 (1989): 129.

68. See Lisa Lowe, "Heterogeneity, Hybridity, Multiplicity: Making Asian American Differences," *Diaspora* 1, no. 1 (1991): 24–44; Espiritu, *Asian American Panethnicity*; and Kang, *Compositional Subjects*.

69. Inderpal Grewal, *Transnational America: Feminisms, Diasporas, Neoliberalisms* (Durham, NC: Duke University Press, 2005), 60. See also Aihwa Ong, *Flexible Citizenship: The Cultural Logics of Transnationality* (Durham, NC: Duke University Press, 2005), 96–103. Ong discusses how the arrival of affluent immigrants from Asia restructures the "ethnic landscape" in the United States.

70. Part of this and the following paragraphs appeared in my article "'My/Our' Comfort," 78–82.

71. See Diana L. Eck, *A New Religious America: How a "Christian Country" Has Become the World's Most Religiously Diverse Nation* (San Francisco: HarperSanFrancisco, 2001), 3.

72. Russell T. McCutcheon, *Critics Not Caretakers: Redescribing the Public Study of Religion* (Albany: State University of New York Press, 2001), 223.

73. Aihwa Ong discusses how global capitalism in Asia is linked to new cultural representations of "Chineseness" rather than "Japaneseness" in relation to transnational Asian capitalism (*Flexible Citizenship*, 7).

74. See Kwok Pui-lan, *Introducing Asian Feminist Theology* (Cleveland: Pilgrim Press, 2001).

75. See Chandra T. Mohanty, "Introduction: Cartographies of Struggle," in *Third World Women and the Politics of Feminism*, ed. Chandra T. Mohanty, Ann Russo, and Lourdes Torres (Bloomington: Indiana University Press, 1991), 4. In her keynote speech at the Consultation on Asian Pacific North American Theologies at the annual meeting of the American Academy of Religion held in Toronto in 2002, Kwok Pui-lan also mentioned that "Asian" signifies an "imagined community." See also Benedict Anderson, *Imagined Communities: Reflections on the Origin and Spread of Nationalism* (London: Verso, 1983).

76. Spivak, with Rooney, "In a Word," 129.

Chapter Three

"She Stood in Tears amid the Alien Corn"

Ruth, the Perpetual Foreigner and Model Minority

Gale A. Yee

One of the joys of reading a biblical text from my own social location was learning about the history of my people here in the States. I immersed myself into the vast field of Asian American Studies. Even as it was an immensely satisfying experience, especially as I inserted my family's story into the larger narrative of the Chinese in America, it was also sobering. Our immigration history is one of bitter hardship and oppression.

As I looked for a biblical text to explore through Asian American eyes, I found one that readily lent itself to such a reading. One can safely say that, of the books of the Hebrew Bible, the book of Ruth has captured the attention of many scholars interested in feminist and multicultural interpretations of the text. The book conjoins issues of gender, sexuality, race/ethnicity, immigration, nationality, assimilation, and class in tantalizing ways that allow different folk to read their own stories into the multivalent narrative of Ruth and Naomi. It is particularly apt for the purposes of this volume that the book of Ruth is the only biblical text bearing the name of a female Gentile,[1] a non-Jew, and a foreigner. The multicultural perspectives on the book of Ruth are a veritable global village: African South African female, South African Indian female, Batswana female, Kenyan female, Mexican American male, Costa Rican female, Cuban American male, Hindu Indo-Guyanese female, Latin American female, Brazilian male, Palestinian female, Hong Kong Chinese male and

This article is a slightly modified reprinting of "'She Stood in Tears amid the Alien Corn': Ruth, the Perpetual Foreigner and Model Minority," in *They Were All Together in One Place? Toward Minority Biblical Criticism*, ed. Randall C. Bailey, Tat-siong Benny Liew, and Fernando F. Segovia, Semeia Studies 57 (Atlanta: Society of Biblical Literature, forthcoming).

female, Taiwanese female, mainland (PRC) Chinese female, Thai and Philippine females, Myanmar female, New Zealand Pakeha (non-Maori) female, Native American female, African American womanist, European female immigrants, German rural women, Eastern European foreign workers in Israel, and African women suffering from HIV/AIDS.[2]

In this chapter I enter into this global conversation by reading the book of Ruth as an Asian American biblical scholar of Chinese descent. I argue that the construction of Asian Americans historically as the "perpetual foreigner" and "model minority" can shed light on the various, often conflicting, interpretations and readings about Ruth the Moabite. The portrayal of Ruth as the model émigré is similar to the construction of Asian Americans as the model minority. Their depictions in both cases are used for propagandistic purposes, casting them simultaneously as the perpetual foreigner in the lands in which they live.

The Asian American as the Perpetual Foreigner

Asian American racialization involves two specific and related stereotypical configurations. The first is that of the perpetual foreigner, which lurks behind the seemingly harmless question white people constantly ask Asian Americans: "Where are you from?"[3] Notice that this question is usually not asked of African Americans. When I tell whites that I am from Chicago, they are not satisfied. Predictably, they follow up with "Where are you really from?" Sometimes I inform them directly that I am a Chinese American. At other times I cheekily play with and deflect their interrogation: I now live in Boston; I was born in Ohio; and I have lived in Canada and in Minnesota. The dance of the seven veils performed by white America to uncover my ethnicity is symptomatic of their assumption that I do not really belong in this country.

Asian American intellectuals have criticized the U.S. discourse on race as being circumscribed by the conflicts between blacks and whites.[4] They point out that in the black/white binary, the experiences of Asian Americans (as well as Latino/a and Arab Americans) fall through the cracks, since racial bigotry can vary qualitatively among different racial and ethnic groups. Asian Americans experience the process of racialization differently than African Americans.[5] Although both groups have suffered horrendously under white racism, the markers for determining the Other rest on different axes. For African Americans the axis is color, white versus black. For Asian (and Latino/a and Arab) Americans it is citizenship, American versus foreigner.[6]

Because of the focus on racial color (being black), as well as a shared history of slavery, African Americans do not identify themselves by their national origins, such as Nigerian American or Ghanan American, and much less by their African tribal origins, such as Mandingo American or Ashanti American.[7] In contrast, Asian Americans hail from ethnically and culturally distinct Asian nations and have different immigration histories to and ethnic conflicts with white America. They therefore consistently describe themselves in terms of their national or ethnic origins: Chinese American, Japanese American, Korean American, and so forth. With respect to citizenship in the United States these ethnic demarcations have often been a matter of great importance in the conflicted history of U.S.-Asian relations. During World War II Chinese Americans consciously distinguished themselves from Japanese Americans to prevent being interred with them.

Institutional and cultural racism found in the legal system, government policy, and so forth has traditionally constructed what it means to be American and hold power in terms of white, male, European descent—particularly Anglo-Saxon Protestant descent—to the exclusion of other groups. After long and difficult struggles women and blacks were enfranchised as American citizens with the right to vote. Evinced by the ubiquitous experience of being asked, "Where are you from?" Asian Americans have not been fully assimilated into the collective consciousness of what it means to be American.[8] Even though many, like my family, have been here for generations, the perception of being aliens in their own land is one that Asian Americans find difficult to shake off. They continue to be seen as more Asian than American.

The notion of Asian Americans as the perpetual foreigner intensified during certain overlapping periods of economic, military, and political conflicts in U.S.-Asia relations. The U.S. government and businesses exploited Chinese peasants as cheap labor at various points of American history (for example, for building the transcontinental railroad, to replace blacks on southern plantations after emancipation, and as strikebreakers for New England textile mills).[9] Incensed by the competition, however, whites violently harassed and oftentimes killed Chinese laborers and their families. They eventually lobbied Congress to pass the Chinese Exclusion Act in 1882, barring Chinese from entering the United States and becoming citizens. This act was not repealed until December 17, 1943, when the United States wanted the Chinese as allies during World War II against Japanese aggression. Nevertheless, Chinese Americans were still racialized as the foreign Asian enemy. Collapsing diverse Asian groups into the foreign

Other, white Americans did not always distinguish Chinese Americans from the Japanese (during WWII), the Koreans (during the Korean War), and Vietnamese (during the Vietnam War). In 1982 the economic down-turn in the Detroit, Michigan, automobile industry fueled the rage of two white men who killed the Chinese American Vincent Chin, scapegoating Chin as one of the Japanese automobile makers who cost them their jobs.[10] During the Cold War the United States recruited Chinese scientists and engineers to strengthen American defense systems, only to nurse suspicions later that some Chinese were passing nuclear secrets to mainland China. The unfounded accusations against the Taiwanese American Wen Ho Lee during the late 1990s continued to demonstrate that simply looking like the enemy means that you are.[11] The Chinese American architect Maya Lin, who won the national contest to design the Vietnam Memorial, was con-demned as a "gook" (a derogatory term for the Vietnamese) by U.S. veter-ans. Chinese American identity is thus inescapably linked with other Asian ethnic and national identities for whom it is mistaken.

The perpetual-foreigner syndrome takes on a different permutation nowadays in the politics of U.S. multiculturalism, which "in its reliance on symbolic representations of diversity, only serves to oversimplify and essen-tialize the diversity of racial/ethnic groups in the United States."[12] Chinese Americans are expected to put their Chinese "culture" on display. This cul-ture becomes objectified and measurable, taking the form, for example, of speaking and writing Chinese, using chopsticks, immersing oneself in *The Analects* by Confucius, celebrating Chinese New Year, enjoying Jackie Chan movies, and, perhaps, even taking kung fu lessons.[13] Chinese American females might feel compelled to "go native" and slip their heftier American bodies into *cheongsams*, those form-fitting Suzie Wong–type dresses with the slit up the side.

When such traits of Chineseness become essentialized as visible hall-marks of authenticity, Chinese Americans are put in a double bind. As perpetual foreigners, they are tagged as not being American enough. Alternatively, they are expected to exhibit on demand their knowledge and culture of China, about which many, whose families have lived in the United States for generations, know little. The commodification of Chi-nese identity in U.S. multicultural politics presumes that this identity is out there, just waiting to be discovered. When placed on a continuum of being more or less authentically Chinese, many American-born Chinese sometimes experience an ambivalence in the presence of those who seem to be "more" Chinese (for example, those who have a Chinese accent or have recently come from China).

While on the one hand Chinese Americans, under assimilationist models, should identify with their U.S. roots, the realities of racial politics cause them to remain perpetual foreigners. Chinese Americans have always been told that "home" is in the United States but that their "roots," and therefore a missing piece of their identity, is somewhere in China.[14]

Eventually some American-born Chinese, such as myself, might actually visit China to find the missing piece that will ostensibly transform one into an "authentic" Chinese. Actually finding that piece is another matter. Although the stigma of perpetual foreigner assumes that I do not belong in the United States, I discovered that I did not belong in China either, as my recent yearlong experience teaching in Hong Kong starkly revealed.[15] I faced several challenges during my time in Hong Kong that I did not have to face in my twenty years of undergraduate and graduate teaching in the United States. First were the obvious personal and cultural dislocations I experienced as a Chinese American who had never been west of San Francisco, California, going ashore in a Hong Kong Chinese context. (Asian Americans often refer to newly arrived immigrant Asians as FOBs or Fresh off the Boats. In a sense I was the FOB counterpart in Hong Kong, although it would be more accurate to say that I was a FOP, Fresh off the Plane.) Second was a linguistic dislocation since my three weeks of Mandarin study (which was not good to begin with) were completely forgotten in the largely Cantonese-speaking culture. I taught in English, a dislocation for my students. There was also a gender dislocation. The Department of Religion at the Chinese University of Hong Kong was primarily composed of men. Only one other female colleague, untenured, taught in the department, while more than half of the faculty at my home institution, the Episcopal Divinity School, are female, and all are tenured. Finally, there were what I can only describe as ideological dislocations in that I came as a feminist with strong social views on racism, class exploitation, American imperialism and colonialism, and fundamentalistic readings of biblical text. All of these strong positions are formed by and in reaction to my U.S. context. For a third-generation Chinese American who grew up in the urban slums of Chicago's South Side,[16] Asian forms of theologizing, such as Waterbuffalo Theology,[17] seemed to come from another planet and were just as alien. Minimally knowing the language, the history, and the culture in Hong Kong made me like Ruth the Moabite, a woman who "stood in tears amid the alien corn" (John Keats, "Ode to a Nightingale"). My experience of being a foreigner both in the United States and in China is typical of many

American-born Chinese who visit China in search of their "roots." Just as Chinese Americans are not American enough for whites in the United States, they are not culturally Chinese enough with respect to China.[18]

The Asian American as the Model Minority

Besides being pigeonholed as the perpetual foreigner, Asian Americans simultaneously labor under the model-minority stereotype.[19] After a century of blatant racial discrimination and slander,[20] Asian Americans are singled out as a group that has successfully assimilated into American society, becoming financially well off and achieving the American Dream. This stereotype is often part and parcel of those essentialist traits that "real" Chinese individuals are assumed to have. Traditional Chinese values and attributes are said to include respect for elders, strong family ties, intellectual giftedness, hard-work ethic, focus on higher education and a striving to achieve, mathematical and scientific ability, and so forth.

My experiences as a model minority were much more conflicted. For example, when my family moved from the inner city to a white neighborhood, the Catholic grade school I attended had "homogeneous" groupings. In descending order, Group 1 comprised the most intelligent and talented, and Group 4 was regarded as the "dumb-dumb" group. I was put in the latter. Even at the young age of ten, I saw that the individuals in Group 1 were all white and that Group 4 contained the racial and ethnic students and those whites who were regarded as "trash." With respect to the assumption that Asians are good in math, I withdrew from college algebra three times before I flunked the course and had to change my major from psychology to English literature because there was no way I could pass the required statistics course. When I took the GRE I barely made it on the scale for mathematical ability. In the range of 200–800, I received something like 320.

The model-minority stereotype is a gross generalization of disparate Asian immigrant populations that vary in terms of ethnicity, immigration history, linguistic facility, education, and economic class.[21] Camouflaged by the notion of model minority are the unexpressed questions "Model of what?" and "Model for whom?"[22] On the one hand, the phrase "model minority" could imply that Asian Americans are exemplary, despite the fact that they happen to be "colored" and, as such, still inferior to the dominant white society. This understanding is hardly flattering to Asian Americans. On the other hand, the phrase could mean that Asian Americans are exemplary, and other racial ethnic groups should take after them. The model minority stereotype, then, becomes more of a critique and a denigration of other racial groups rather than a compliment to Asian Americans.

It is no accident that articles hailing Asian Americans as the "superminority" and the "whiz kids" emerged particularly during the Cold War of the 1950s and the racial conflicts of the 1960s:

> The narrative of Asian ethnic assimilation fit the requirements of Cold War containment perfectly. Three specters haunted Cold War America in the 1950s: the red menace of communism, the black menace of race mixing, and the white menace of homosexuality. On the international front, the narrative of ethnic assimilation sent a message to the Third World, especially to Asia, where the United States was engaged in increasingly fierce struggles with nationalist and communist insurgencies, that the United States was a liberal democratic state where people of color could enjoy equal rights and upward mobility. On the home front, it sent a message to "Negroes and other minorities" that accommodation would be rewarded while militancy would be contained or crushed.[23]

Asian Americans are held up as living proof that racial minorities can succeed in America, presumably by the sweat of their brow and not by civil rights demonstrations or protests. Using the model-minority stereotype as a weapon, whites tell blacks and Latinos/as that "Asian Americans do not 'whine' about racial discrimination; they only try harder."[24] The supposed accomplishments of Asian Americans divert attention away from the fact that racial discrimination is a structural feature of U.S. society, produced by centuries of systematic exclusion, exploitation, and disregard of racially defined minorities.[25] Blame for any social disparities falls on the other racial minorities, who "whine" about racial discrimination. White construction of the model-minority stereotype has as its antithesis the construction of other racial groups, such as blacks, as the "deficient" or "depraved" minority.

The model-minority stereotype buttresses the dominant ideology of the United States as a just and fair society, in which all its citizens compete on a level playing field. All foreign immigrants and racial minorities who have worked hard and played by the rules can be readily assimilated and succeed economically. White America judged and rewarded Asian Americans not "by the color of their skin but by the content of their character."[26] Significantly, some Asian American students have espoused the stereotype as a means of upward mobility and white approval. These students are primarily immigrants who have bought into the ideology of white America as the land of opportunity and dismissed any racial episodes as the isolated acts of single individuals. American-born Asians, however, are more likely to be wary of the model-minority stereotype and view any racial incidents as part of a larger social problem.

Following the model-minority stereotype can backfire on Asian Americans.[27] The perception of Asian American success in higher education often rebounds in anti-Asian attitudes. White students become threatened by and resent the growing number of Asian students in classrooms. They fear that so-called hordes of Asian students distort the grading curve, and many refuse to register for sections containing a large Asian critical mass. The zero-sum perception that Asian American gains denote white American losses often results in violence, as the Detroit death of Vincent Chin demonstrates. The Michigan congressman John Dingell angrily accused "little yellow men" for the economic hardships of Detroit automakers, rather than placing blame on the fact that domestic cars are not as skillfully made or as fuel efficient as Japanese imports.[28]

The perpetual-foreigner and the model-minority stereotypes work in tandem to construct contradictory images of Asian Americans in general and Chinese Americans in particular. As perpetual foreigners, they become a secondary caste that can be exploited and used. They are perceived as aliens in their own land, even though their citizenship often goes back several generations. When they ostensibly excel as model minorities through industry and entrepreneurial talents, they become a threat to be contained or destroyed. These two stereotypes make more complex the nature of U.S. race relations, which have usually operated under a black/white binary. Rather than functioning on the color axis, racial discrimination against Asian Americans operates on the axis of citizenship, casting Asian Americans as the perpetual foreigner. Colluding with this stereotype is the pigeonholing of Asian Americans as the model minority, which at times benefits them compared to other ethnic groups while simultaneously obscuring the countless ways in which they are marginalized and victimized by racism. It is through these two lenses that I view the book of Ruth.

The Book of Ruth

The social matrixes in the book of Ruth are rich. They include male/female, husband/wife, mother/son, mother-in-law/daughter-in-law, owner/overseer/laborers, mother's house/father's house, native resident/foreigner, and so forth. These relations are forged through marriage, friendship, widowhood, sexual attraction, economic and labor arrangements, immigration, and political amity or enmity. As the wealth of global interpretations of Ruth attests, the story is a "mine or mosaic of social relations, where readers can take their pick."[29] With the plurality of different readers comes a plurality of differing, often antithetical, interpretations. Juxtaposed to the more positive readings of the book, as an enchanting bucolic story about female empowerment and romantic heterosexual love, are others that see a more ambiguous and unsettling narrative.[30] I follow the lead of other people of color and allow the ambiguity of the text to favor a reading against the grain.[31] The usual optimistic and romantic readings of Ruth obscure issues of ethnicity, economic exploitation, and racist attitudes about the sexuality of foreigners that are evident in the text. Refracting the story of Ruth through the prism of the Asian American experience, I argue that, in its own way, the ideology of the text constructs Ruth the Moabite as a model minority and perpetual foreigner.

Ger *and* Nokriyah *in Ruth*

The book of Ruth utilizes two words to describe foreigners: *ger* and *nokriyah*.[32] A *ger* is a foreigner who has immigrated into and taken up residence in a society in which she or he has neither familial nor tribal associations. Although granted some protection under the Holiness Code (HC) and Deuteronomic Code (DC), the *ger* is not a full-fledged member of the Israelite community but someone of different and lower status. Ruth is not called a *ger*. The term is used to describe Elimelech's sojourn to Moab with his family (Ruth 1:1). However, because Ruth takes advantage of the laws about gleaning for the poor, the *ger*, and the widow (Lev. 19:9–10; 23:22; Deut. 24:19–22), the text implies that Ruth is a *ger*.

When Ruth encounters Boaz's kindness for the first time, she falls on her face and exclaims, "Why have I found favor in your sight, that you should take notice of me, when I am a foreigner [*nokriyah*]?" (Ruth 2:10). The text has Ruth acknowledge in direct speech her status as a foreigner in Judah. The connotation of *nokri* is generally negative, highlighting the person's otherness and separateness from the dominant culture.[33] We will see that the negativity of the *nokri* is particularly underscored by the fact that Ruth was a Moabite, one of Israel's traditional hated enemies. If Ruth was written during the time of Ezra and Nehemiah, the use of *nokriyah* in the mouth of Ruth is significant. Intermarriage between the exiles and foreign women (*nashim nokriyot*) (Ezra 10:2, 10; Neh. 13:26) was severely condemned. Note that the nemesis of Lady Wisdom is the Foreign

Woman[34] in the book of Proverbs, whose author shares Ezra's and Nehemiah's Persian-period ideologies.[35] Some interpret the marriage of Boaz to the *nokriyah* Ruth as a critique of Ezra's and Nehemiah's policies against foreign marriages.[36] Others argue for an earlier context for the composition of Ruth, perhaps as an apology for David, to remove the taint of Moabite descent.[37] I maintain, however, that, whatever the date, the negative connotations of Ruth's foreignness implied in *nokriyah* are not completely erased in the book.

Ruth as a Model Minority

In the construction of Ruth as the model minority, her Moabite ancestry is of prime importance. Ruth is not simply from any foreign nation but from Moab, whose entanglements with Israel have been antagonistic. According to Gen. 19:37 the Moabites were the spawn of a drunken incestuous encounter between Lot and his eldest daughter. Numbers 25:1–3 blames the idolatry of Israelite men, who "yoked" themselves to the Baal of Peor on the bewitching sexuality of Moabite women. The seer Balaam, hired by the king of Moab to curse the Israelites, ends up blessing them and cursing Moab instead (Num. 22–24). Moab, along with Ammon, refused to offer bread (*lehem*) and water on Israel's journey from Egypt and was thus denied admittance to the assembly of God, even down to the tenth generation (Deut. 23:3–4). The irony is that Elimelech and his family must immigrate from Bethlehem (House of Bread) to Moab because of a famine in Judah.[38] But this flight comes at a great cost: the patriarch and his two sons die in Moab, leaving three impoverished widows and a threatened patriline.

The deeper the enmity between Moab and Israel, the greater the valor in Ruth's resolve to embrace the latter and its God. Her rejection of Moab and its negative links with Israel transforms her into the Jewish convert par excellence. In rabbinic interpretation Ruth was the daughter of a Moabite king when she rejected her homeland and its false deities to become a God-fearing Jewess—loyal daughter-in-law, modest bridge, renowned ancestor of Israel's great king David.[39] Ruth's *hesed* (generosity, compassion, and love) toward her mother-in-law in accompanying Naomi to a strange land and in supporting her by gleaning is recognized by Ruth's future husband and provider. Boaz exclaims that the Israelite God, under whose wings she has sought refuge, will fully reward Ruth (2:11–12). If the book was written as an apology for the Moabite ancestry in David's line (cf. 1 Sam. 22:3–4), Ruth the faithful convert purges the line of any foreign stain.

Indeed, Ruth is not only the model convert but also an exemplar for the Jewish people. According to André C. LaCocque, "[Ruth's] 'heroism' is to become more of a Judean than those who are Judean by birth! Retrospectively, one can say that her fidelity toward the people and their God provides a lesson to those who should have been her teachers."[40] LaCocque further adds that the central theological message of the book is the meaning of *hesed*, which Ruth epitomizes for the people: "A non-Judean shows the way to the Judeans, precisely in an era where the respect for the latter had become the very condition of membership in the Second Temple community."[41]

In her article "Ruth, the Model Émigré," Bonnie Honig criticizes readings that turn the book into "a kind of nationalist narrative that Ruth's story does not only nor unambivalently support."[42] She outlines the two problems for the present discussion that inhere in the concept of the model émigré. According to Honig, dominant readings of Ruth fall into two categories that correspond to the two major responses to immigrants. On the one hand, immigrants are welcomed for what they can bring to a nation, whether it is diversity, talents, energy, novel cuisines, or a rekindled sense of national pride that had attracted the immigrants in the first place. On the other hand, immigrants are dreaded because of what they will do to the nation (burden the welfare system, weaken the common heritage, and so forth). Ruth's decision to leave her natal land for Israel reconfirms Israel's identity as the Chosen People, a people worthy of being chosen. Nevertheless, Ruth's relocation does not mean that Israel is now a borderless land, embracing all foreigners, even the hated Moabites. "Israel is open only to the Moabite who is exceptionally virtuous, to Ruth but not Orpah."[43]

The construction of Ruth as the model émigré is similar to the model-minority stereotype of Asian Americans. Ruth is held up for propagandistic purposes, either to expunge any contamination of Moabite descent for David or to critique Ezra's and Nehemiah's policies against intermarriage. She thus reveals what a virtuous foreigner can teach the nation. As model minorities, Asian Americans supposedly exemplify traditional values, such as respect for elders, industry and hard work, and family loyalty. Similarly, Ruth incarnates the quality of *hesed* in her overwhelming devotion to her mother-in-law; in her willingness to support her by diligently gleaning in a strange man's field, not resting "even for a moment" (2:7); and in her conversion to another God. As Ruth the Moabite teaches Judeans the meaning of *hesed*, Asian Americans educate others on how to be "good" minorities who know their place in a white society. Nevertheless, just as Asian Americans remain perpetual foreigners in the land of their birth, Ruth's disappearance in chapter 4 after the birth of her son leads one to question whether Ruth has been successfully assimilated as a foreigner into Judean society or ultimately abandoned once she preserves the male lineage.[44]

Ruth the Perpetual Foreigner

The flipside of the model-minority stereotype for Asian Americans is that of the perpetual foreigner. This Janus-like phenomenon is also apparent in the book of Ruth. Just as Asian Americans are consistently perceived as being more Asian than American by the dominant white society, so is Ruth continually called Ruth the Moabite, rather than Israelite, even after her immigration (1:22; 2:2, 6, 21; 4:5, 10). Ruth seems to lose this qualifier after she finally gives birth to a son (4:13), but it comes at the cost of not being recognized as his mother (4:17).[45] Naomi's ultimate incorporation back into the community is manifested by her displacement of Ruth as Obed's mother. This displacement implies that the revitalization of this community and the continuation of the patriline toward David's monarchy depend not only on Ruth's exemplary character but also on her marginalization as a foreigner.[46]

As Chinese Americans were economically exploited for cheap labor, particularly during the 1800s and early 1900s, so is Ruth's foreign labor exploited by both Naomi and Boaz. Jack M. Sasson and Athalya Brenner argue that 1:16–17, which is usually read as Ruth's tender pledge to Naomi, is actually a verbal contract in which Ruth submits her person to the wishes of her mother-in-law.[47] The "love" (*'hb*) that Ruth has for Naomi (4:15) can connote the relationship between an inferior to her or his superior, such as the one between a vassal and his lord.[48] This interpretation would explain, for example, why Ruth alone goes out to glean and why she easily acquiesces to Naomi's dangerous proposal to seduce Boaz on the threshing floor. She might have had little choice in the matter.

Issues of class, especially as they intersect with ethnicity and gender in Ruth, are also underscored in a perceptive analysis by Roland Boer.[49] In Marxist fashion Boer notices who owns the means of production, namely, the land, and who actually works it in the book of Ruth. The economic gulf between Boaz, as owner of the land, and Ruth, as foreign gleaner of the land's leftovers, is wide. Boaz does not work in the fields as do his reapers or his overseer, but rather, he commands them. "In other words, he lives off the surplus labour of those who do work."[50] His seeming munificence toward Ruth (2:8–9, 14–16) is that of one who has more than enough already. He can afford to dole out a little something for Ruth. In this regard Boaz's injunction to Ruth not to work in another man's field (2:8) may be motivated more by economic rather than personal interests. Boaz has already been told that Ruth "has been on her feet from early this morning until now, without resting even for a moment" (2:7). She continues the grueling work of gleaning until evening, and then she beats out an *ephah* of barley (2:17), which weighs somewhere between thirty and fifty pounds.[51] Boaz knows good foreign help when he sees it, and his so-called generosity can be read as offering inducements to keep Ruth's productiveness for his own benefit. Although Boaz does not acquire economic capital from Ruth's labor, he certainly reaps much social capital and prestige in the Israelite community as a benefactor of widows. We will see shortly that Boaz will eventually acquire land as economic capital through Ruth's person. Ruth continues to toil in his field "until the end of the barley and wheat harvests" (2:23). Boer quips, "This is hardly benevolence, but more like pure exploitation."[52]

Naomi does not work in the fields either. She too lives off the labor of Ruth the foreigner, whose actions she directs: urging Ruth to continue the nonstop work of gleaning, instructing her to make herself attractive to seduce a man in the middle of the night, and ultimately taking Ruth's child as her own. Some justify Naomi's absence in the field to her old age or the fact that she still grieves the loss of her husband and sons. Others think she is hard at work in the invisible domestic sphere while Ruth works outside the home. However, within the economics of the text, Naomi is more aligned with Boaz than with Ruth, especially when kinship intersects with ownership of the means of production. As related kin, Naomi and Boaz are complicit regarding "that piece of land" (4:3) that belonged to Naomi's husband, Elimelech. Another kinsman has a better claim to redeem this land, but Boaz is able to trump this claim by means of Ruth's body. "On the day you acquire the field from the hand of Naomi, you are also acquiring Ruth the Moabite, the widow of the dead man, to maintain the dead man's name on his inheritance" (4:5). By her kinship with Boaz and by strategically using Ruth to preserve the lineage of her husband, Naomi ultimately dislocates Ruth as Obed's mother.

Marxist feminists have often noted the deficiency in Marxist theory in not fully incorporating into its theorizing on class women's productive labor and their reproductive (or sexual) labor in the continuation of the species.[53] These labors interconnect most clearly in the person of Ruth. Exhausting herself by working the land for Boaz and Naomi, Ruth also becomes the reproductive means by which Boaz and Naomi profit economically. In Boaz's case, Ruth becomes the stumbling block that prevents the land from falling into the hands of Mr. So-and-So, who cannot marry Ruth and beget a son through her without jeopardizing his own inheritance (4:6). Through Ruth, Boaz is thus able to enlarge his holdings. And Ruth's birth labors in producing a son secure Boaz's patriline and Naomi's economic place in the community.

Other aspects of Ruth's sexual exploitation in the text work hand in hand with Ruth's foreignness. Foreign women in the Hebrew Bible have a long tradition of erotic allure and sexual insatiability. Witness Madame Potiphar, Delilah, the queen of Sheba, Solomon's foreign wives, Jezebel, the whore of Babylon, and the Foreign Woman in Proverbs. These women bring about the downfall of men through their sexuality. Asian American women also suffer under similar exoticization by white American males in the images of Suzie Wong, Madame Butterfly, the submissive lotus blossom, the seductive geisha, the Mongol slave girl, and the treacherous Dragon Lady.[54] Catering to the sexual fantasies of white men, the flourishing global trafficking of Asian women's bodies is built on such stereotypes.[55] Male domination and colonial supremacy coalesce here in the sexual depiction and exploitation of the foreign woman.

Lingering over Ruth is the notorious tradition of the Moabites as the perverse progeny of incest, whose women sexually seduced the Israelites away from YHWH (Num. 25:1–3). Ruth is particularly vulnerable to sexual harassment and violence in the fields by the male farmhands, who may regard her as "easy" because she is a Moabite, one of "those" women.[56] To protect his industrious worker and keep her working in his field, Boaz shields Ruth from these "attentions" by ordering his men to keep their hands to themselves (2:9).

The reputed carnality of foreign women injects greater ambivalence into the narrative of Ruth and Boaz on the threshing floor (Ruth 3). Biblical commentaries are rife with speculation on whether Ruth and Boaz "did it" that night. If intertextual parallels are drawn between Lot's daughters (Gen. 19) and Tamar (Gen. 38), Ruth did indeed "do it" with Boaz.[57] All three stories involve a threat to the patriline because of the death of a male. The fiancés of Lot's daughters are killed in the destruction of Sodom. God slays Er and Onan, leaving Judah's lineage in jeopardy. Elimelech and his sons die in Moab. In all three stories women take the initiative to restore and continue the lineage. Further, foreignness is attached to all three. Lot's daughters become the progenitors of the Moabites and Ammonites. Tamar is most likely a Canaanite, and Ruth is a Moabite. All three adopt sexually unorthodox means to achieve their purposes. Lot's daughters collude in an incestuous encounter with their father. Tamar pretends to be a hooker at the side of the road. Ruth marshals her charms to seduce Boaz on the threshing floor. All three take advantage of the men's inebriation from too much wine.[58] Certainly Lot's daughters and Tamar succeed in having sex with their targeted males, becoming pregnant with sons as a result. If the story of Ruth follows the same literary pattern, Ruth and Boaz consummated their union on the threshing floor, issuing in the birth of David's grandfather.

Whether Ruth and Boaz had sex that fateful night should not distract us from the economic urgency that compelled Ruth the foreigner to go to the threshing floor in the first place. Here I am in complete agreement with Katharine Doob Sakenfeld (who does not think the couple "did it") that

> no woman should have to do something so socially unacceptable in Israelite culture as to approach a man in the dark of night, at risk of discovery and public humiliation, and possibly severe legal penalties in order to put food on her family's table for the longer term. This is not a slightly adventurous tryst. It is a desperate act by a desperate person.[59]

While some white feminists may be appalled at the notion that the key to a woman's happiness is the Cinderella story of finding and seducing a rich man who will become her patron, for many destitute women in the third world such a hope is often one of the few options available.[60] Sakenfeld relates a story about a young impoverished Filipina who was recruited to go to a wealthy foreign country as a "dancer." In response to her pastor's suspicions that she was destined for the Asian sex trade, the girl pointed to the book of Ruth: "Ruth put herself forward attractively to a rich man in hopes that he would marry her and take care of her family. I am doing the same. Hopefully a rich man from that country will choose me to marry and will look after me and my family. God made things turn out right for Ruth and God will take care of me too."[61] The adverse consequences of global capitalism were brought home to me recently in Hong Kong, where it is not uncommon for Filipina domestic help (whose working conditions are often deplorable) to seduce the male head of household and sometimes engineer a divorce in order to better her situation. In these cases, as in the book of Ruth, economic survival often forces impoverished women to acts they would never do otherwise, literally spending their lives "in tears amid the alien corn."

Conclusion

Seen through the eyes of the dual Asian American experiences of being a model minority and perpetual foreigner, the book of Ruth holds in dialectical tension the positive and the more-ambivalent interpretations of the story. On the one hand, the book of Ruth is a (fairy) tale about a devoted widow who rejects her homeland and her idols to accompany her mother-in-law to a new country. In this scenario, Ruth becomes a model émigré (*ger*)—a model convert—who teaches the Chosen People the true meaning of God's covenantal *hesed*. She is an exemplar of female empowerment, initiative, hard work, family loyalty, and upward mobility. And to top things off, she does get the guy in the end.

On the other hand, Ruth is also the perpetual foreigner—a *nokriyah*—whose consistent label of Moabite implies that she, not unlike Asian Americans in the United States, is not fully assimilated in the text's consciousness of what it means to be Israelite. Ruth's foreignness is the linchpin in the economics of the text. It sets her apart from those characters who do not work in the book but who appropriate her labor and her body. Chinese American labor contributed to the building of a nation, but their efforts went unacknowledged.[62] So also does Ruth's labor in the field and especially in giving birth to Obed play a major role in strengthening the Davidic line and the formation of the state, but she too disappears at the end. The insidious economic picture that surfaces in the book of Ruth is that the Israelites—in the persons of Naomi and Boaz—are those who do not work, who exploit and live off the surplus labor of the foreign Other. Naomi assimilates into the world of Israelite men, the landowners who possess the means of production, while the foreign female worker, Ruth, vanishes when her body is exhausted. Ruth's story thus becomes an indictment against those of us who live in the first world and exploit the cheap labor of developing countries and poor immigrants from these countries who come to the first world looking for jobs.

Notes

1. Bearing the title of a male Gentile is the book of Job.
2. For complete bibliographical citations, see Gale A. Yee, "'She Stood in Tears amid the Alien Corn': Ruth, the Perpetual Foreigner and Model Minority," in *They Were All Together in One Place? Toward Minority Biblical Criticism*, ed. Randall C. Bailey, Tat-siong Benny Liew, and Fernando F. Segovia, Semeia Studies 57 (Atlanta: Society of Biblical Literature, forthcoming).

3. Mia Tuan, *Forever Foreigners or Honorary Whites: The Asian Ethnic Experience Today* (New Brunswick, NJ: Rutgers University Press, 1998), 1–35; Angelo N. Ancheta, *Race, Rights, and the Asian American Experience* (New Brunswick, NJ: Rutgers University Press, [1998] 2000), 44; Iris Chang, *The Chinese in America: A Narrative History* (New York: Viking, 2003), xi–xiii; Frank H. Wu, "The Perpetual Foreigner: Yellow Peril in the Pacific Century," in *Yellow: Race in America beyond Black and White* (New York: Basic Books, 2002), 79–129; Leslie Bow, "Making Sense of Screaming: A Monkey's Companion," in *Screaming Monkeys: Critiques of Asian American Images*, ed. M. Evelina Galang (Minneapolis: Coffee House Press, 2003), 489. Such encounters are not limited to Asian Americans. For the Chinese Dutch equivalent, see Ien Ang, "On Not Speaking Chinese: Postmodern Ethnicity and the Politics of Diaspora," *New Formations* 24 (1994): 1–18.

4. For example, Wu, "Perpetual Foreigner"; and Ancheta, "Introduction: Neither Black nor White," in *Race, Rights, and the Asian American Experience*, 1–18. See also Richard Delgado and Jean Stefancic, *Critical Race Theory: An Introduction* (New York: New York University Press, 2001), 67–86.

5. I am using as a springboard here the discussion of racial formation in Michael Omi and Howard Winant, *Racial Formation in the United States: From the 1960s to the 1990s*, 2nd ed. (New York: Routledge, 1994), 52–76. For Omi and Winant, racialization is the extension of racial meaning to a relationship, social practice, or group.

6. Ancheta, *Race, Rights, and the Asian American Experience*, 64; Tuan, *Forever Foreigners*, 8. See also Stuart Creighton Miller, *The Unwelcome Immigrant: The American Image of the Chinese, 1785–1882* (Berkeley: University of California Press, 1974).

7. See Paulla Ebron and Anna Lowenhaupt Tsing, "From Allegories of Identity to Sites of Dialogue," *Diaspora: A Journal of Transnational Studies* 4, no. 2 (1995): 131. This article consciously tries to construct tools for dialogue among racial and ethnic minorities; in this case, between African Americans and Chinese Americans. See also Edward M. Bruner, "Tourism in Ghana: The Representation of Slavery and the Return of the Black Diaspora," *American Anthropologist* 98, no. 2 (1996): 290–304.

8. This was brought home in a public way during two winter Olympics when the Asian American skater Michelle Kwan failed to win gold. The MSNBC headline in 1998 read, "American Beats Kwan" when Kwan finished second to teammate Tara Lipinski. In 2002 the *Seattle Times* described Kwan's loss to teammate Sarah Hughes as "American Outshines Kwan, Slutskaya in Skating Surprise."

9. For a readable account, see Chang, *Chinese in America*. Also see Ronald Takaki, *Strangers from a Different Shore: A History of Asian Americans* (New York: Penguin Books, 1989); and Ronald Takaki, *A Different Mirror: A History of Multicultural America* (Boston: Little, Brown & Co., 1993).

10. For a personal account, see "Detroit Blues: 'Because of You Motherfuckers,'" in Helen Zia, *Asian American Dreams: The Emergence of an American People* (New York: Farrar, Straus & Giroux, 2000), 55–81.

11. In particular, see Chang, *Chinese in America*, 236–60.

12. Andrea Louie, *Chineseness across Borders: Renegotiating Chinese Identities in China and the United States* (Durham, NC: Duke University Press, 2004), 97.

13. Except for reading *The Analects*, I have dabbled in all of the above.

14. Louie, *Chineseness*, 104.

15. I explored this more fully in Gale A. Yee, "Yin/Yang Is Not Me: An Exploration into an Asian American Biblical Hermeneutics," in *Ways of Being, Ways of Knowing: Asian American Biblical Interpretation*, ed. Mary F. Foskett and Jeffrey Kah-Jin Kuan (St. Louis: Chalice Press, 2006), 152–63.

16. See Gale A. Yee, "The Impact of National Histories on the Politics of Identity," *Journal of Asian and Asian American Theology* 2 (1997): 108–12.

17. See Kosuke Koyama, *Waterbuffalo Theology* (Maryknoll, NY: Orbis Books, 1974); and Kosuke Koyama, "Waterbuffalo Theology—After 25 Years," *PTCA Bulletin* 11, no. 2 (1998): 5–9.

18. See esp. Louie (*Chineseness*), who examines issues of Chinese identity through an in-depth ethnographic study of the In Search of Roots Program, sponsored by the PRC and certain Chinese American organizations. The intentions of the program are to bring young Chinese Americans to the villages of their ancestors to learn about the greatness of Chinese culture. The underlying motive of the PRC is to encourage Chinese American economic investment in China, their "true" homeland. Louie draws conclusions for Chinese identity from the PRC perspective, especially in its agenda for the In Search of Roots Program, and about how this agenda is negotiated and often subverted by the Chinese American students who participate in it. Also see Ang, "Not Speaking Chinese," 12–13.

19. See "The Model Minority: Asian American 'Success' as a Race Relations Failure," in Frank Wu, *Yellow: Race in America beyond Black and White* (New York: Basic Books, 2001), 39–77; Keith Hiroshi Osajima, "Asian Americans as the Model Minority: An Analysis of the Popular Press Image in the 1960s and 1980s," in *Contemporary Asian America: A Multidisciplinary Reader*, ed. Min Zhou and James V. Gatewood (New York: New York University Press, 2000), 449–58; and Sumi K. Cho, "Converging Stereotypes in Racialized Sexual Harassment: Where the Model Minority Meets Suzie Wong," in *Critical Race Feminism: A Reader*, ed. Adrien Katherine Wing (New York: New York University Press, 1997), 203–20.

20. In the popular media, see the fears about the "yellow peril," Fu Manchu, Dragon Lady, and Ming the Merciless from the planet Mongo, documented in Robert G. Lee, *Orientals: Asian Americans in Popular Culture* (Philadelphia: Temple University Press, 1999), 106–44.

21. Lucie Cheng and Philip Q. Yang, "The 'Model Minority' Deconstructed," in *Contemporary Asian America: A Multidisciplinary Reader*, ed. Min Zhou and James V. Gatewood (New York: New York University Press, 2000), 459–82.

22. Wu, *Yellow*, 59.

23. "The Cold War Origins of the Model Minority Myth," in Lee, *Orientals*, 145–79, quotation on 146.

24. Wu, *Yellow*, 44.

25. Omi and Winant, *Racial Formation*, 69.

26. Quoted from Dr. Martin Luther King Jr., "I Have a Dream" speech, August 28, 1963.

27. Wu, in *Yellow*, devotes a section called "Backlash from the Myth" (67–77).

28. Zia, *Asian American Dreams*, 58.

29. Musa W. Dube, "Divining Ruth for International Relations," in *Other Ways of Reading: African Women and the Bible*, ed. Musa W. Dube (Atlanta: Society of Biblical Literature, 2001), 180.

30. Alta C. van Dyk and Peet J. van Dyk, in "HIV/AIDS in Africa: Suffering Women and the Theology of the Book of Ruth," *Old Testament Essays* 15 (2002): 215–24, classify these

differing readings under four categories: (1) reading with the grain of the text (positive); (2) a romantic reading (even more positive); (3) a feminist perspective (against the grain); and (4) "a man, trapped by the slyness of two women." See also Madipoane J. Masenya, "*NGWETSI* (BRIDE): The Naomi-Ruth Story from an African–South African Woman's Perspective," *Journal of Feminist Studies in Religion* 14, no. 2 (1998): 82–85.

31. See Robert D. Maldonado, "Reading Malinche Reading Ruth: Toward a Hermeneutics of Betrayal," *Semeia* 72 (1995): 91–109; Laura E. Donaldson, "The Sign of Orpah: Reading Ruth through Native Eyes," in *Ruth and Esther: A Feminist Companion to the Bible*, ed. Athalya Brenner, Second Series ed. (Sheffield: Sheffield Academic Press, 1999), 131–44; Kwok Pui-lan, "Finding a Home for Ruth: Gender, Sexuality, and the Politics of Otherness," in *Postcolonial Imagination and Feminist Theology* (Louisville, KY: Westminster John Knox Press, 2005), 108–11; Francisco García-Treto, "Mixed Messages: Encountering *Mestizaje* in the Old Testament," *Princeton Seminary Bulletin* 22, no. 2 (2001): 159–71; and Wai-Ching Angela Wong, "History, Identity and a Community of *Hesed*: A Biblical Reflection on Ruth 1:1–17," *Asia Journal of Theology* 13 (1999): 3–13. For others who preserve the ambiguity and complexity of the text, see Amy-Jill Levine, "Ruth," in *The Women's Bible Commentary*, ed. Carol A. Newsom and Sharon H. Ringe, expanded ed. (Louisville, KY: Westminster John Knox Press, 1998), 84–85; Danna Nolan Fewell and David Miller Gunn, *Compromising Redemption: Relating Characters in the Book of Ruth* (Louisville, KY: Westminster John Knox Press, 1990); and Tod Linafelt and Timothy K. Beal, *Ruth and Esther*, Berit Olam (Collegeville, MN: Liturgical Press, 1999).

32. For what follows, see Christiana van Houten, *The Alien in Israelite Law* (Sheffield: JSOT Press, 1983); Rolf Rendtorff, "The *Ger* in the Priestly Laws of the Pentateuch," in *Ethnicity and the Bible*, ed. Mark G. Brett (New York: E. J. Brill, 1996), 77–88; L. A. Snijders, "The Meaning of *Zar* in the Old Testament," *Oudtestamentische Studiën* 10 (1954): 89–110; Harold V. Bennett, *Injustice Made Legal: Deuteronomic Law and the Plight of Widows, Strangers, and Orphans in Ancient Israel* (Grand Rapids: Wm. B. Eerdmans Publishing Co., 2002), 38–48; Christopher T. Begg, "Foreigner," *Anchor Bible Dictionary* 2 (1992): 829–30; and John R. Spencer, "Sojourner," *Anchor Bible Dictionary* 6 (1992): 103–4.

33. Rendtorff, "*Ger* in the Priestly Laws," 77; Begg, "Foreigner," 829.

34. In Hebrew: '*ishshah zarah*, which parallels *nokriyah* in Prov. 2:16; 5:20; and 7:5. *Nokriyah* parallels '*eshet ra'*, evil woman, in 6:24, and *zonah*, harlot, in 23:27.

35. For a full discussion, see Gale A. Yee, "The Other Woman in Proverbs: My Man's Not Home—He Took His Moneybag with Him," in my *Poor Banished Children of Eve: Woman as Evil in the Hebrew Bible* (Minneapolis: Fortress Press, 2003), 143–65.

36. See André C. LaCocque, *Ruth: A Continental Commentary*, trans. K. C. Hanson (Minneapolis: Fortress Press, 2004), 18–27; Victor H. Matthews, *Judges and Ruth*, New Cambridge Bible Commentary (Cambridge: Cambridge University Press, 2004), 208–10; and Frederic W. Bush, *Ruth, Esther*, Word Biblical Commentary (Waco, TX: Word Books, 1996), 30. For an overview of the issues of dating, see Katrina J. A. Larkin, *Ruth and Esther*, Old Testament Guides (Sheffield: Sheffield Academic Press, 1996), 18–25; and Katharine Doob Sakenfeld, *Ruth*, Interpretation: A Bible Commentary for Teaching and Preaching (Louisville, KY: John Knox Press, 1999), 1–5.

37. Murray D. Gow, *The Book of Ruth: Its Structure, Theme and Purpose* (Leicester: Apollos, 1992), 132–33, 199–205.

38. Moab had reasonably good agricultural land, which was productive even when other parts of Palestine were hit by famine. According to 2 Kgs. 3:4, King Mesha of Moab bred

sheep and used to deliver one hundred thousand lambs and the wool of one hundred thousand rams to the king of Israel. See Max Miller, "Ancient Moab Still Largely Unknown," *BA* 60, no. 4 (1997): 194–95.

39. Katheryn Pfisterer Darr, *Far More Precious Than Jewels: Perspectives on Biblical Women* (Louisville, KY: Westminster John Knox Press, 1991), 72. According to Zohar, *Balaq* 190a, Ruth was the daughter of Eglon, king of Moab, whom Ehud assassinated (Judg. 3:12–30) (cited in Mishael Maswari Caspi and Rachel S. Havrelock, *Women on the Biblical Road: Ruth, Naomi, and the Female Journey* [Lanham, MD: University Press of America, 1996], 85).

40. LaCocque, *Ruth*, 24–25.

41. Ibid., 28.

42. Bonnie Honig, "Ruth, the Model Émigré: Mourning and the Symbolic Politics of Immigration," in Brenner, ed. *Ruth and Esther: A Feminist Companion*, 51.

43. Ibid., 55–56.

44. See Levine, "Ruth," where she states, "It is the reader's task to determine whether this book affirms Ruth or ultimately erases her, whether she serves as a moral exemplar or as a warning against sexually forward Gentile women" (85).

45. Although space constraints limit my discussion, the issue of surrogate motherhood and its exploitation of poor and ethnic women looms here, as it does in the Sarah and Hagar story of Gen. 16. Also on the horizon is the practice of white Americans adopting female Chinese babies abandoned at birth. It remains to be seen whether these babies will be fully accepted as "Americans" or also tagged as perpetual minorities in spite of having white adoptive parents.

46. Honig, "Ruth, the Model Émigré," 73–74.

47. See Jack M. Sasson, *Ruth: A New Translation with a Philological Commentary and a Formalist Folklorist Interpretation*, The Biblical Seminar, vol. 10, 2nd ed. (Sheffield: Sheffield Academic Press, 1989), 124–25; and Athalya Brenner, "Ruth as a Foreign Worker and the Politics of Exogamy," in *Ruth and Esther: A Feminist Companion*, 158–62.

48. See William L. Moran, "The Ancient Near Eastern Background of the Love of God in Deuteronomy," *Catholic Biblical Quarterly* 23 (1963): 77–87; J. A. Thompson, "Israel's 'Lovers,'" *Vetus Testamentum* 27, no. 4 (1977): 475–81; and Susan Ackerman, "The Personal Is Political: Covenantal and Affectionate Love ('*Aheb*, '*Ahaba*) in the Hebrew Bible," *Vetus Testamentum* 52, no. 4 (2002): 347–58. Dube, in "Divining Ruth," also notes a slave-to-master relationship between Ruth and Naomi rather than an expression of mutual love (192).

49. Roland Boer, "Terry Eagleton: The Class Struggles of Ruth," in his *Marxist Criticism of the Bible* (London: T. & T. Clark International, 2003), 65–86.

50. Ibid., 79–80.

51. Bush, *Ruth, Esther*, 133.

52. Boer, "Terry Eagleton," 83.

53. See Heidi Hartmann, "The Unhappy Marriage of Marxism and Feminism: Towards a More Progressive Union," in *The Second Wave: A Reader in Feminist Theory*, ed. Linda Nicholson (New York: Routledge, 1997), 97–122; and Heidi Hartmann "Some Conceptual Problems in Marxist Feminist Analysis," in *Women's Oppression Today*, rev. ed., ed. Michèle Barrett (London: Verso, 1988), 8–41.

54. Aki Uchida, "The Orientalization of Asian Women in America," *Women's Studies International Forum* 21 (1998): 161–74. The Asian Woman fetish of white men has been

explored in the novel by Mako Yoshikawa, *One Hundred and One Ways* (New York: Bantam Books, 1999). "One hundred and one ways" refers to the number of ways a geisha was supposedly able to "unlock (men's) bodies with a groan" (9).

55. Rita Nakashima Brock and Susan Brooks Thistlethwaite, *Casting Stones: Prostitution and Liberation in Asia and the United States* (Minneapolis: Fortress Press, 1996).

56. See Michael Carasik, "Ruth 2,7: Why the Overseer Was Embarrassed," *Zeitschrift für die alttestamentliche Wissenschaft* 107 (1995): 493–94; and David Shepherd, "Violence in the Fields? Translating, Reading, and Revising in Ruth 2," *Catholic Biblical Quarterly* 63 (2001): 444–63.

57. For analyses of the similarities among these three narratives, see Harold Fisch, "Ruth and the Structure of Covenant History," *Vetus Testamentum* 32, no. 4 (1982): 425–37; Esther Fuchs, "Structure, Motifs and Ideological Functions of the Biblical Temptation Scene," *Biblicon*, no. 2 (1997): 51–60; and Ellen Van Wolde, "Intertextuality: Ruth in Dialogue with Tamar," in *A Feminist Companion to Reading the Bible: Approaches, Methods and Strategies*, ed. Athalya Brenner and Carole Fontaine (Sheffield: Sheffield Academic Press, 1997), 426–51.

58. Wine is implied in Gen. 28:12–13, since it is the festive time of sheep shearing.

59. Katharine Doob Sakenfeld, "At the Threshing Floor: Sex, Reader Response, and a Hermeneutic of Survival," *Old Testament Essays* 15 (2002): 174.

60. See, for example, Musimbi R. A. Kanyoro, "Biblical Hermeneutics: Ancient Palestine and the Contemporary World," *Review and Expositor* 94 (1997): 373.

61. Katharine Doob Sakenfeld, "The Story of Ruth: Economic Survival," in *Realia Dei: Essays in Archaeology and Biblical Interpretation in Honor of Edward F. Campbell, Jr., At His Retirement*, ed. Prescott H. Williams Jr. and Theodore Hiebert (Atlanta: Scholars Press, 1999), 221.

62. The famous picture of the white men posing at the completion of the transcontinental railroad has not a Chinese face in sight.

Part 2

Reinventing Spiritual Traditions

Chapter Four

Spiritual Buffet

The Changing Diet of America

Jung Ha Kim

I doubt that anyone driving along the interstate highways from the Bible Belt to Yankee New England expects to experience a dramatic moment of enlightenment. Myriad automobiles carry bumper stickers with a range of messages, a snapshot of public temperament and spiritual yearning: Jesus Is the Way; Karma, Karma, Karma; Minds Are Like Parachutes: They Only Function When Open; Black Is Beautiful; Seek and Ye Shall Find; Shop until You Drop; Think Globally, Act Locally, Pray Specifically; Om. . . . Tuning into one radio station after another on the road, one finds popular rock groups and rappers vocalizing lyrics that are reminiscent of Sunday school homilies and yet are sharply cynical or apocalyptic. All this seems to be quite American. While one station plays a song of the Irish rock quartet U2 ("I went out walking with a Bible and a gun; the word of God lay heavy on my heart"), another station plays rap by Snoop Dogg about the voice that offers the dying body "eternal life forever" after being gunned down in "Murder Was the Case." Neo-Christian lyrics—such as, "Would you hold my hand when you see me in heaven?"; "Faith lies in the way of sin"; and "When Jesus left Birmingham"—are, perhaps, so familiar to American ears that they are rarely listened to as important windows for

This chapter is a revision of "Sources outside of Europe," in *Spirituality and the Secular Quest*, ed. Peter H. Van Ness (New York: Crossroad, 1996), 53–71. As pointed out in an essay that originally appeared in a volume in *World Spirituality: An Encyclopedic History of the Religious Quest*, the term "non-Western" (and "Western," for that matter) was used heuristically. My intention is not to reiterate a binary mode of thinking but to differentiate the Western roots of contemporary spiritual experimentation from that of the non-Western influences. See also Nami Kim's chapter in this volume, which is an in-depth probing of the term "Asian" in "the 'indigestible' Asian."

viewing American unorthodoxies and for recognizing the parareligious yearnings embedded in these songs.

"Millions of Americans are searching for some clearer understanding of the core principles of religion and how they can be applied to the daily experience of living as well as to humanity's common destiny on this planet," said Bill Moyers, television producer and commentator, at a weeklong annual gathering of the Religion Newswriters Association.[1] Hiring a full-time religion correspondent for the first time in the history of network television, the late Peter Jennings of *ABC World News Tonight* justified his decision in this way: "Religion and spirituality are playing a much larger role in American life than what is generally portrayed [on television news]."[2] Whether one interprets the religious references of the new crop of rock icons and the new spiritual concerns of network television as expressing "religious doubt and the struggle to come to terms with the possibility that there may not be a God" or as "symbols of a thirst for values that transcend the fast-buck ethos of corrupt commercial cultures," it is long overdue to take note of the public's quest for spirituality, a quest worthy of recognition and analysis.[3] Cultural workers, such as rock stars, rappers, and anchorpersons, are prime candidates for playing the role of social critics and secular prophets in the contemporary cultural milieu. For spirituality is far from disappearing on American soil; rather, "it went underground and took expression outside of the religious establishment."[4] Navigating between the religious and the secular, people are creatively and eclectically pursuing their own quest for meaningful spirituality. What needs to be documented and critically analyzed is this subtle change that has been taking place in the United States, a nation in which 90 percent of the population claims a religious preference and more than two-thirds of the adult population believe in the existence of angels.[5] The subtle change is the widespread adaptation and appropriation of non-Western traditions into contemporary American spirituality.

This chapter, then, sheds light on the non-Western sources, and, more specifically, the Eastern sources, of the contemporary quest for spirituality; I demonstrate how this quest encompasses a syncretistic and eclectic interweaving of religious traditions of the West and the non-West. Consequently, deeply community-based Asian sources of spirituality are being transformed into highly privatized and individualistic experiences of spirituality in the United States.

Determining what is at stake in such attempts at appropriating non-Western traditions naturally leads to further questions. For example, what does it mean to be spiritual? How do different people experience and express spirituality? How have non-Western traditions and cultural practices been adopted so as to become more American? Are non-Western sources sufficiently homogeneous to be addressed collectively? How does the transplantation of religious and cultural values of the non-West influence the bifurcation of religious and secular identities in the United States? What can one say about the contemporary quest for spirituality in light of recognizing diversity within the United States?

To address the foregoing questions, this study brings three topical areas into dialogue with one another: the boundary between spirituality and religion, the privatization of abundant spiritual supplies from the non-West, and the politics of appropriating the East in the United States. I use these perspectives and constructs to focus and analyze the rich manifestation of sources that are appropriated and incorporated in contemporary spirituality in the United States and to stimulate further questions and discussions regarding the political economy of spirituality along the axes of history, colonialism, and religion.

Although it risks what is commonly thought of as coherence and objectivity, locating my autobiographical vantage point is in order. For I believe that the hermeneutical perspective of a study is deeply embedded in the author's life circumstances and is, thus, inevitably political. I defy the general academic perspective that true and pure knowledge is fundamentally nonpolitical. Moreover, by making my idiosyncrasies and biases explicit, I strive to make this study more accountable to the subject matter that I identify and analyze.

An Autobiographical Vantage Point

I am a hyphenated American of Asian descent, constantly straddling cultures that are disparate and at times contradictory. Born as the first daughter to North Korean parents in South Korea, I was raised in a Buddhist temple, spent much of my childhood in Japan, followed my parents to the United States as an involuntary immigrant at age twelve, and never stayed in one place longer than five years until age thirty. Thus I consider myself not only a multicultural but also a multireligious person. I have at various times been a Buddhist, a Confucian, a Taoist, a shamanist, a Zen Buddhist, a Shintoist, an Americanist, and a Christian.

I attend a local Protestant church and participate in its community life, and I also practice sitting meditation (that is, *zazen*) whenever possible. I venerate both living and dead ancestors, and I especially commemorate my late grandmother, who raised me, and my late father, who brought me into this land and became the root of my identity as a hyphenated American. At work I tend to conduct research projects that are community oriented rather than individually inclined. Although formal educational training in the fields of religion and sociology can explain this tendency to some extent, my conscious efforts not to bring shame to the communities and people with whom I deeply identify and to which I belong may be the primary reason for my choice of research methods and projects.[6]

My being a multicultural and multireligious person whose spiritual experiences are ever fluid and syncretic does not, however, guarantee greater sympathy for highly eclectic borrowing from other traditions by contemporary Americans questing for spirituality. For I believe that all representations and appropriations of other cultures serve purposes for particular groups of people, especially groups who have more privileges in the market economy of capitalist society. The main goal in such an economy is to commodify anything and everything that can be marketed, including spiritual sites and styles—from Native Americans' ancestor graveyards to the "exotic" lifestyles of Indian yogis.

Native Americans' religious usage of peyote is an instructive case in point. Peyote, or more specifically, the hallucinogenic drug extracted from this variety of cactus plant, has a long history of religious ceremonial usage among Native Americans in Mexico and the southwestern United States. Late nineteenth-century U.S. Indian policies condemned its usage along with other Native cultural practices, and peyote has generally been defined as an illegal drug by federal policy and statute. In the twentieth century special exemptions have been given to Native American religious usage of peyote—most recently the American Indian Religious Freedom Act of 1978. However, since the 1960s non-Native interest in peyote has disrupted the peyote cult in two ways. First, unauthorized harvesting (and merchandizing) of peyote buttons in Mexico and Texas has endangered supplies. And more recently, increasing claims of membership by non-Natives in the Native American church, often by persons interested only in the peyote, have created cultural and institutional tensions. As a result, the Native American Church of North America has ruled that non-Natives cannot be enrolled in the church, in order to prevent others from commodifying the community's religious usage of peyote as individual inducement of hallucination.[7]

However brief, the preceding autobiographical discussion provides the hermeneutical lens through which this chapter has been written. I now turn to three relevant issues highlighted earlier as important for delineating various contours of contemporary spirituality in the United States.

The Boundary between Spirituality and Religion

Just what does it mean to be religious? This question is intrinsically related to other questions, such as, What does it mean to be spiritual, and how do people experience and express spirituality?[8] Sociologists have generally assumed that every religion and its organizations are composed of largely two systems—belief and ritual—that are based on a conception of the sacred.[9] Thus scholars and practitioners (not mutually exclusive categories of people) have historically been inclined to draw boundaries between faith and practice and between religion and spirituality.

Noting that "spirituality" is "a notoriously vague term," Peter H. Van Ness claims, "Its scholarly meaning comes from reports of inner experiences offered as personal counterparts to religious doctrines and institutions."[10] Pointing out both different and overlapping aspects of what the words "spiritual" and "religious" mean, he also states that "some instances of spiritual discipline have long and intimate associations with organized religion; others do not."[11] Alternative conceptions are possible. For some people spirituality means one's "manner of being" religious and "of being a follower" of his or her religion.[12] Some define it more behaviorally as "a set of behavior repertoires that is formal and ceremonial."[13] Others accent disciplines, describing spirituality as "the disciplined rehearsal of right attitudes."[14] Still for others, it is "the fullest possible actualization of what [a person] is in his heart . . . wherein the totality of all the dimensions and capacities and contents of his life (soul) are brought to conscious unity in realization."[15] In short, being spiritual does not preclude one's allegiance to a particular institutionalized religion, yet neither does it require such an allegiance.

Calling for a humanistic value system—"the religion of the spirit"— Walter Lippmann contends that a dichotomous categorization of religion and spirituality needs to be reassessed in light of a highly individualized and rapidly changing society:

> In an age when custom is dissolved and authority is broken, the religion of the spirit is not merely a possible way of life. In principle it is the only way which transcends the difficulties. . . . The religion of the spirit does not depend upon creeds and cosmologies; it has no vested interest in any particular truth. It is concerned not with the organization of matter, but with the quality of human desire.[16]

Resonating with this call for a more humanistic religion of the spirit, Martin E. Marty states that critics of religion charge American religion with being "too political, too compromising, too institutionally self-seeking to provide room for spiritual development."[17]

What is more, discerning what spirituality means to different people can be met with some suspicion and even hatred from both the right and the left wing of the political spectrum. On the one hand, given the reality of deeply privatized spiritual experimentation in the United States, a resort to spirituality may mean a resort to a false consciousness that ignores and disguises the systemic causes for social and religious problems as matters of individual mentality and perception. On the other hand, the acknowledgement of parareligious and post-Christian spiritual experimentation as peculiarly American, and so as entirely legitimate ways of satisfying people's spiritual needs, may push persons who adhere to traditional religion to feel the need to defend their orthodoxies in the name of world religions and their historical establishments.

However one defines spirituality, what appears to be undeniably present in attempts to draw boundaries between religion and spirituality is the duality built into Western conceptualizations. As Pablo Richard demonstrates, Western civilization has been—from its origin in Hellenistic and Greco-Roman civilization—based on a distinction between matter (that is, the body) and spirit (that is, the soul). Reinterpreting Aristotle's dualism of body and soul, Richard contends that the "soul is regarded as the realm of the spiritual and of encounter with God, and the body is regarded as the material realm and the site of sin."[18] This conceptualization of the soul as dominant over the body was, in fact, the underlying framework for the domination of "master over slave, of man over woman, of adult over child, and of the human being over animal and nature."[19] In other words, spiritual life in the West necessitated that people experience alienation from their bodily experiences, exploitation in human relationships, androcentrism in gender relations, hierarchy in social relationships, and anthropomorphism in attempts to subdue and control the natural world. Thus to be spiritual in a Western religious sense entails, for example, observing the Christian Lenten season as a time of self-denial (that is, bodily denial) and sacrifice, and Easter Sunday as a day of remembering how the Spirit-God triumphantly overpowers the human bodily experience of death through resurrection.

Critical of the spirit/body dichotomy underpinning much Christian spirituality, the Cuban American theologian Ada María Isasi-Díaz advocates the term "praxis" to denote a more holistic understanding of spirituality. Warning against equating praxis with practice, she argues, "praxis is both intellectual enterprise as well as action."[20] Much-needed attempts to integrate the mutually exclusive dualism in the West, such as the spirit and the body, man and woman, knowledge and action, master and slave, and humanity and nature, are prevalently taking place in a variety of forms in different social groups. Efforts to take seriously the mundane and bodily experiences of the human life are also widespread in the secular quest for spirituality in contemporary America. For example, in order to advocate women's full and equal access to various levels of organized religious institutions and to foster liturgies and spiritualities that are more reflective of women's bodily experiences, some feminist circles are actively working to provide safe spaces for women both within and without the context of established religions. Reclaiming the preferential option for the poor and the oppressed as the core messages of the Christian good news, "people of colors"[21] and the dispossessed[22] are increasingly denouncing the tendency of the dominant culture to marginalize certain racial ethnic peoples, and they are challenging the assumptions of the universalized, one-size-fits-all God. James H. Cone's *A Black Theology of Liberation*, first published in 1970, is a prime example of a theologian radically rethinking the Christian message from such a vantage point, specifically from the experience of the oppressed African American community.[23] Rita Nakashima Brock and Rebecca Ann Parker's *Proverbs of Ashes* also exemplifies a critical reassessment of the violence-provoking Christian atonement theology from the feminist perspective.[24] And pointing to self-evident deterioration of natural resources and the environmental costs of the process of modernization and postmodernization, Native Americans and other environmentally conscious groups are urgently promoting nonanthropocentric and nondualistic perspectives toward the natural world. Native American religious thinkers such as the late Vine Deloria Jr. have contributed to shaping these new perspectives while at the same time offering distinctive but influential proposals about the nature of God and human spiritual life in order to sustain natural resources.[25]

These and other efforts searching for a more holistic and life-embracing spirituality are evident in various spiritual movements, such as creation spirituality, Goddess spirituality, 12-step spirituality, feminist spirituality, self-help spirituality, ecofeminist spirituality, men's spirituality, kenosis spirituality, and image design spirituality. They are also visible in classes and workshops devoted to tai chi, transcendental meditation, hatha yoga, therapeutic touch, extrasensory perception, and the reading of tarot cards. Many non-Western sources of spirituality—eclectically and syncretically mixed on American soil—can be found in these contemporary attempts to address and correct Western dichotomies, to affirm the human dimensions of life, and to accommodate rapidly changing everyday realities in a highly pluralistic society.

Thus these attempts at eclectically borrowing, mending, and quilting various traditions to fulfill contemporary quests for spirituality in the United States exemplify what others have called American characteristics. Numerous scholars and travelers have been fascinated by the diverse nature of American national characteristics; Alexis de Toqueville, Paul Tillich, and Reinhold and H. Richard Niebuhr are relevant examples. They noted that Americans are pragmatic, individualistic, optimistic, utilitarian, and yet deeply religious. For such a future-oriented people to turn away from the organized religions of the West and to turn to non-Western sources in their quests for more meaningful spiritual lives, something must have happened. What Lee H. Yearly calls "spiritual regret" is an intriguing explanation. Spiritual regret, according to Yearly, "arises from the sense, however implicit, that the traditional ways of dealing with distinctions among religions are deficient, that they fail to meet adequately the specific demands the modern situation produces."[26] Spiritual regret is, then, considered a virtue based on the recognition that "extremely varied, legitimate religious ideals exist and that no person can possibly manifest all of them."[27] Akin to the feeling of regret, perhaps, is another emotional construct, nostalgia. According to Renato Rosaldo, nostalgia is "a particularly appropriate emotion to invoke in attempting to establish one's innocence and at the same time talk about what one has destroyed," such as childhood memories.[28] What is peculiar about nostalgia is its "process of yearning for what one has destroyed as a form of mystification."[29] In short, nostalgia—especially in the context of "imperialist nostalgia"—revolves around "a paradox: a person kills somebody, and they mourn the victim."[30] Whether spiritual regret or imperialist nostalgia, people's longing for what they have lost or destroyed is certainly taking place in the spiritual realm. Needless to say, however, not all non-Western spiritual traditions are considered equally corrective or alternative sources for addressing spiritual quest in the United States.

The Privatization of Abundant Spiritual Supplies

Non-Western sources in general, and Asian traditions in particular, have influenced the spirituality of the United States in various ways. Peter W. Williams has articulated three areas in which Asian traditions have had an impact on the United States: "ethnic religions," "export religions," and "new religions."[31] This threefold designation is based on distinguishable categories of adherents: Asian immigrants and their descendants in ethnic religions; predominantly Euro-Americans in export religions; and an eclectic cadre of countercultural, cross-religious, and intellectual practitioners in new religions. Although Williams's categorizations are mostly designed for discerning religious groups, they apply also to the spiritual quests of many people in the United States. All three types of religious groups—and also their typical spiritual experiences—are demonstrative of what Marty calls the "merits of borrowing" from other traditions and cultures.[32] And I argue that implementing these merits of borrowing is a peculiarly and categorically American notion. The process of Americanizing Eastern sources entails more than merely transplanting cultural traditions in the United States; in the fuller sense, it means "becoming acculturated, adopting a distinctively American way of living and looking at the world as its own."[33]

For borrowing to be perceived as a merit, people need to assume at least one thing: an equal access to sufficient supplies. For if some can take out but others cannot, then borrowing becomes privilege or exploitation—something other than meritorious. How and why, then, did people resolve what Yearly calls spiritual regret by turning to other cultures and traditions as abundant supplies for borrowing? Although the transitions from rural to urban and from a preindustrial to a technologically advanced society seem to be the two most salient historical facts to which one can point as the broad causes of spiritual regret, I refer to more recent historical phenomena and argue that at least the following two demographic sources have been instrumental in making the cultural milieu of borrowing from other traditions more acceptable in the United States: (1) the emergence of the baby-boom generation, and (2) the changing demographic landscape.[34]

Baby boomers made up roughly one-third of the nation's population by 1990.[35] Consequently, their values, practices, beliefs, and opinions determine much of the social norms in the United States. Depicting America's religious landscape by focusing on the boomer generation from the 1940s to the 1990s, Wade Clark Roof claims that as Sunday school children of the 1950s arrived at their adolescence in the 1960s, they became unchurched in record numbers, thereby fundamentally altering the religious landscape in America. By the 1980s, however, some of these unchurched people had turned to evangelical and fundamentalist faiths; some had gravitated to New Age beliefs; and some had completely defected from organized religion. As this generation of un-, re-, and postchurched reached midlife in the 1990s, they placed more emphasis on creative and eclectic spiritual projects that are characteristic of the reemergence of spirituality and cultural pluralism in the United States.[36] Many turned to the East for spiritual and cultural insights.

While baby boomers have turned away from more traditional spirituality and organized religions and have freely moved in and out across religious and secular boundaries, people of colors also have actively promoted cultural and religious pluralism by providing cogent criticisms of the cultural hegemony of the dominant group(s) in the contexts of both the religious and secular realms. Mottoes such as God Is Black; Allah Is the One; Black Is Beautiful; God Is Rice, Rice Is God; God Is Red; and *En la lucha* are so widespread that their usage overlaps racial and ethnic boundaries. Illustrating the increasingly diverse landscapes of people living in the United States, in 1993 *Time* magazine featured a computerized face of Miss America in the year 2050 on its cover and entitled the multiracial face "Melting Pot." She is 15 percent Anglo Saxon, 17.5 percent Middle Eastern, 17.5 percent African, 7.5 percent Asian, 35 percent southern European, and 7.5 percent Latino. Although these percentages are somewhat skewed from the projected racial ethnic makeup of the nation's population in the second half of the twenty-first century, the éclat of portraying how presently dominant Euro-Americans will slip into numerical minority in the United States is an astute argument. Thus, contrary to traditional spirituality's dependence on homogeneity, the fact of demographic pluralism will continue to promote more heterodox and syncretic quests for spirituality. The history of Christianity, for example, also illustrates that the "orthodox rejection of syncretism has to do not with the purity of faith [and praxis], but with who has the right to determine what is to be considered normative and official."[37]

These two distinct demographic factors—baby boomers and people of colors—were instrumental in establishing the broader historical and political context of the United States wherein individualistic consumerism and borrowing of non-Western spiritual sources become possible (although the consequences of such processes have not been equally beneficial to these two categories of people). For substantiating the claim that individualistic consumerism is the underlying political and economic climate for eclectic borrowing of spirituality from non-Western sources, I rely on Ronald Delattre's dual usage of the word "supply," with the word having both economic and religious meanings in his term "supply-side spirituality." Delattre claims that among many consistent and important themes in the nation's history is "the assumption that abundance (variously interpreted) rather than scarcity, plenty rather than poverty, is the destiny of Americans (when religiously interpreted) as spiritual children of God."[38]

He also claims that this assumption is distinguishably American. After reiterating an Emersonian conviction that "man is born to be rich, or inevitably grows rich by the use of his faculties; by the union of thought and nature,"[39] Delattre proceeds to argue that supply-side spirituality is, then, based on the conviction that abundance rather than lack is natural and that anything less is "an unnatural condition that can be overcome through the right application of a spiritual power, and that such power is at human disposal."[40]

America's entitlement to abundance is evident in various articulations and pursuits of the American Dream as well as in the obsessive drive to acquire consumer goods even at the cost of accumulating personal and national debts and international trade deficits. Moreover, in searching for more exuberant lifestyles and spiritual experiments, people turn to the availability of abundant supplies from both within and without their communities. As a means to fulfill the promise of an ever-abundant supply-side spirituality, then, many Eastern sources of spirituality have been transplanted, appropriated, and represented as peculiarly American. Consequently, life journeys that afford to assume abundant supplies of such sources can take place in at least two ways. On the one hand, the journeys can lead to a way of life that seems "affirmative, optimistic, expectant, energetic, and confident."[41] On the other hand, by assuming an unlimited availability of sufficient supply, people can accumulate debts and eventually face bankruptcy.

The Politics of Appropriating the East

I now turn to discussing specifically the politics of appropriating Eastern sources of spirituality as American. Much of the spiritual experimentation that is based on the merits of borrowing in contemporary America can be seen as a ubiquitous effort to transform the Western mentality of, to use Benjamin Disraeli's phrasing, "The East is a career"[42] to "The East is a way of life." When Disraeli said that the East is a career, "he meant that to be interested in the East was something bright young Westerners would find to be all-consuming passion," especially in the first half of the twentieth century when the "Orient" was flourishing as an academic field for studying about the Other and "Orientalism" was flourishing as a "Western style for dominating, restructuring, and having authority over the Orient."[43] After World War II and in conjunction with the increasing liberation of so-called third-world countries from the colonial occupation of Western countries, explicit forms of domination by the superpower(s) in global politics became no longer acceptable or possible. As is suggested by the image and vocabulary of the global village, interdependence among the world's nations necessitated by mutual survival has induced the West to apply more subtle ways of representing and appropriating the non-West. Thus borrowing from Eastern sources for spirituality and adapting them as American can be seen as a new and subtle form of controlling and possessing the Other—that is, as a neocolonial attempt by the West to dominate its former colonies. For in consumption-driven societies, spirituality is, as with other consumer goods, easily commodified and marketed. As bell hooks says, fresh varieties of spirituality are "continually commodified and offered up as new dishes to enhance the white palate—that the Other will be eaten, consumed, and forgotten."[44]

Needless to say, not all forms of appropriation and representation of the Other are necessarily ill intended, nor do they always result in disservice to a particular source community of people. The process of borrowing from the Other is not predictably linear. In other words, some of the sources of Eastern spirituality have undergone unexpected transformations through the process of Americanization. For instance, deeply gendered and hierarchal practices of Confucian ritual and relational dynamic have been filtered and interpreted through the Western perception as the cosmic complementarity of the yin and yang. Gender-conscious people have turned to the teaching of Confucius as a source of a nondualistic principle of complementarity and as a possible corrective to sexist dualities in the United States. While non-Western sources of spirituality have been appropriated according to borrowers' specific needs and desires, this process has also brought unintended and yet profound changes in the ways in which people understand and experience their spirituality in general. For example, a Zen-style sitting meditation has been well adopted as a part of Christian practice. The stillness and sense of tranquility it provides have become highly sought after by Christians and non-Christians alike. And many Christian retreat centers offer Zen-style sitting meditation in their program. Stated otherwise, then, even in the process of representation and appropriation of the Other, a fundamentally two-way traffic of Americanizing the East and "Orientalizing" the West can be observed (even though this mutual impact may be unintentional).

Regardless of the subtle mutuality between Americanizing Asian sources of spirituality and Orientalizing Western spirituality, appreciating the Other must not be equated with appropriating the Other. This point cannot be overemphasized. From a global perspective, the political and economic realities that enable "white people to roam the world, making contact," are part of the world history.[45] Furthermore, the readiness of Americans to interpret their acts of exotic consumption as gestures of acknowledging the Other is revealing. Contrary to the commonsense belief that all forms of mutual exchange are mutually beneficial, the politics of representing and appropriating the Other in the West is based on the unequal configuration of power and varying degrees of economic and cultural privilege. In order to further document the multidimensional contours of the political economy and to muster both the potentially colonizing and the transforming process of Americanization of the sources of Asian spirituality, a few illustrations are in order.

The process of Americanizing ancient sources of Eastern spirituality is exemplified in Gertrude Stein's ability to recast traditional religious images by creating an alternative spirituality.[46] Her fictive spiritual identity—a "Chinese Christian"—is emblematic of how an assumption of abundant supply in one's searching for meaningful spirituality can explicitly and implicitly bring about transformations of both Western and Eastern spirituality in the name of Americanization. At the outset Stein's Chinese Christian is critical of the androcentric spiritual hegemony that is deeply embedded in institutional religions of the West. At the same time her Chinese Christian exhibits a self-conscious effort "to render Europe's perception of China, the colonizer's view of the colonized." Drawing from the images of the "Oriental" as mystical, female-referenced, and always being represented and appropriated by the non-Oriental, the Chinese Christian cultivates the quiet and stillness of contemplation as a spiritual act.[47] Knowledge of Chinese traditions is made to yield a set of activities that one can borrow and perform in order to experience rich spiritual experimentation in the West. This is also reminiscent of what Edward W. Said states about the Oriental experts: "What is required of the Oriental expert is no longer simply 'understanding'; now the Orient must be made to perform, its power must be enlisted on the side of 'our' values, civilizations, interest, goals." He also warns that this in turn will require "a new assertion of control, this time not as the author of a scholarly work in the Orient but as the maker of contemporary history, of the Orient as urgent activity."[48]

Chinese Christian spirituality does not merely blend Eastern and Western traditions into an alternative spirituality that is female identified and contemplation oriented. It also further privatizes spiritual quests by cultivating the desired state of consciousness through personal meditation, indeed, through individually catered lists of how to sit still, empty one's mind, maintain a sense of tranquility, and so forth. Chinese Christian spirituality is, then, made to be ultimately anti-institutional and highly individualistic. In the process of Americanization, therefore, deeply communal rites of conducting sitting meditation in the East have become the highly privatized spiritual discipline of individuals.

To account for some of the fundamentally different understandings of what constitutes spiritual and religious experiences in the West and the East, I refer to N. J. Demerath III's observation comparing Japanese and American religious beliefs and behaviors. Demerath points to a national Japanese survey taken in the early 1990s that indicates that some 70 percent of Japanese describe themselves as "religious indifferent," while their behavior suggests otherwise. There are credible statistics showing that "as many as 120 percent of Japanese are religious (if one relies on shrines and temple registration) or as few as 10 percent if one looks at regular participation within a given faith community." People do not experience conflict of being affiliated with more than one religious organization, since neither Buddhist temples nor Shinto shrines in Japan demand mutually exclusive membership. Based on these data he concludes, "If there is a tendency for Americans to maximize their religiosity, there is an opposite tendency among both the Japanese and Chinese to minimize it."[49] Although Demerath does not explain why these opposite tendencies exist, the notion of an interdependent self (that is, a communal self) in the East seems to be a salient factor. In monistic philosophical traditions of the East, a human being is thought to be by nature interdependent with others. Thus conducting rituals of ancestor veneration and making pilgrimages to shrines and temples, for example, are matters pertaining to the community and not to individuals. Because a premium is placed on collective welfare, people living in the East appear to be indifferent to highly individualistic experiences of spirituality and religiosity. It is, hence, ironic that some of the deeply community-oriented Asian sources of spirituality have been transplanted and appropriated as highly individualistic experiences in the spiritual lives of people in the United States. Along with Westernizing ancient Eastern traditions through the process of feminization and exotification, people in the United States have privatized the originally communal experiences of the Asian tradition.

A more-diffuse yet no-less-influential phenomenon of the impact of Asian spirituality in American art provides another case in point. Many forms of traditional Chinese art have been shaped by Taoist sensibilities. This has given a distinctively spiritual complexion to arts such as poetry and painting, both in the experience of a creative artist and in the experience of the aesthetic observer. In his study *Creativity and Taoism*, Chang Chung-yuan identifies several relevant principles of Taoism, including the yin and yang complementarity as the natural dynamic of the reconciliation of opposites and *ziran* as the disposition toward spontaneity and naturalness. Both figure in Hsieh Ho's celebrated canons of painting, informing especially the idea of *qiyun*, in which the painter seeks to become spontaneously a vehicle for a cosmic rhythm that achieves manifestation on the painted canvas. That is, the artist becomes one with nature and the human community.[50] Especially through the influence of Chan (Zen in Japanese) Buddhism, this Chinese spiritual sensibility and artistic practice influenced other Asian nations, particularly Japan. In *Zen and Japanese Culture* Daisetz T. Suzuki explains how Zen Buddhism informs Japanese practices such as Haiku poetry, landscape painting, and the tea ceremony. In the twentieth century this influence has also reached U.S. shores. Poets as diverse as Allen Ginsberg and W. S. Merwin show strong Buddhist influences. Asian visual art has influenced American painters in varying degrees, as is evident in the work of Georgia O'Keeffe, Ad Reinhardt, and Morris Graves. This Asian spiritual influence extends beyond well-known artists. For some years Julia Cameron and Mark Bryan have led popular workshops cultivating the spiritual dimension of art, and Cameron has published a widely read book entitled *The Artist's Way: A Spiritual Path to Higher Creativity*.[51] From the cover image of cranes flying near Mt. Fuji to quoted epigrams by Lao-tzu and the Buddha, the book gives ample evidence that the spiritual ethos of American artists is much informed by Asian traditions.

In conclusion, I have argued that many non-Western varieties of spirituality have become peculiarly American, in order to meet the needs of people's spiritual quests in the United States. This Americanizing of the Other has been shaped by a number of factors, such as the changing of the demographic landscape of America, the phenomena of spiritual regret and imperialist nostalgia, the assumption of abundant (spiritual) supply, and the political and historical climate of the merit of borrowing. All of these factors have been instrumental in directing the complex and rapid unfolding of the American saga of eclectic spirituality and will continue to do so. As Charles S. Prebish contends, "Among religious experiments in America, the one surviving and having long-lasting influence would be those that can, on the one hand, stimulate or elicit the power of spiritually transforming experience and faith and, on the other hand, channel that power into disciplined action."[52] Indeed, eclectic and syncretic adaptation and appropriation of Eastern sources of spirituality have survived thus far in the United States because they have elicited "the power of spiritually transforming experiences and faith."[53]

And since spirituality deals not only with ritualistic repertoire for the individual's well-being but also with people's deeply grounded historical quest for community survival, spiritual experimenters in America also need to be mindful of both explicit and implicit consequences of the assumed merits of borrowing and appropriation of Eastern sources of spirituality. Appreciating the Other, however, must not be equated with appropriating the Other, and acts of consuming "exotic" spiritual commodities must not be equated with acknowledging spiritual traditions of the Other. For even at the seemingly unlimited availability and abundant supply of the spiritual buffet, one must balance the desire to abandon with the need to keep to a healthy diet.

Notes

1. Quoted in Christopher Herkinger, "News Media Lack Soul, Moyers Says," *Atlanta Constitution*, May 7, 1994, B1, 3.
2. Michael J. Paquette, "Covering News of the Spirit: Religion Reporter Knows Her Calling," *Atlanta Constitution*, May 7, 1994, B1.
3. Guy Garcia, "Religion and Rock," *Atlanta Constitution*, January 8, 1994, E1.
4. Wade Clark Roof, *A Generation of Seekers: The Spiritual Journeys of the Baby Boom Generation* (New York: HarperCollins, 1993), 242.
5. For the statistics cited, see Nancy Gibbs, "Angels among Us," *Time*, December 27, 1994, 67–68.
6. Highlighting the difference between "shame" and "guilt," Herbert Fingarette makes the common but mistaken assumption that shame is concerned with "mere appearances rather than moral realities. . . . Guilt is an attack upon oneself, whereas shame is an attack upon some specific action or outer condition. Shame is a matter of 'face' or embarrassment, of social status. Shame says, 'change your ways; you have lost honor or dignity.' Guilt says 'change yourself: you are infected'" (*Confucius: The Secular as Sacred* [New York: Harper & Row, 1972], 30).
7. A 1990 U.S. Supreme Court ruling partially reversed the 1978 statute. For the history of U.S. law on peyote, see Omer C. Stewart, "Peyote and the Law," in *Handbook of American Indian Religious Freedom*, ed. Christopher Vecsey (New York: Crossroad, 1991), 44–62. For evidence regarding the disruption of the peyote cult, see Omer C. Stewart, *Peyote Religion: A History* (Norman: University of Oklahoma Press, 1987), esp. 332–36; and David E. Aberle, *The Peyote Religion among Navaho* (Chicago: University of Chicago Press, 1982).
8. N. J. Demerath III, "The Moth and the Flame: Religion and Power in Contemplative Blur," *Sociology of Religion* 55, no. 2 (1994): 108.
9. Émile Durkheim, *The Elementary Forms of Religious Life* (New York: Free Press, 1965).

10. Peter H. Van Ness, *Spirituality, Diversion, and Decadence: The Contemporary Predicament* (Albany: State University of New York Press, 1992), 12.

11. Ibid., 13.

12. Gustavo Gutierrez, *Las Casas: In Search of the Poor of Jesus Christ*, trans. Robert R. Barr (Maryknoll, NY: Orbis Books, 1993), 96.

13. John J. Macionis, *Sociology*, 5th ed. (Englewood Cliffs, NJ: Prentice-Hall, 1995), 488.

14. Susanne K. Langer, *Philosophy in a New Key*, 3rd ed. (Cambridge, MA: Harvard University Press, 1957), 153.

15. Arnold B. Come, *Human Spirit and Holy Spirit* (Philadelphia: Temple University Press, 1959), 17.

16. Walter Lippmann, *A Preface to Morals* (Boston: Beacon Press, 1960), 327–28.

17. Martin E. Marty, "The Spirit's Holy Errand: The Search for a Spiritual Style on Secular America," *Daedalus* 96, no.1 (1967): 109.

18. Pablo Richard, "Treatise on Politics," in *Spirituality of the Third World: A Cry for Life*, ed. K. C. Abraham and Bernadette Mbuy-Beya (Marykoll, NY: Orbis Books, 1994), 105.

19. Ibid.

20. Ada María Isasi-Díaz, *En la lucha/In the Struggle: A Hispanic Women's Liberation Theology* (Minneapolis: Fortress Press, 1993), 170.

21. While participating in a panel with four other women and me, Satako Yamaguchi used the term "women of colors" rather than "women of color" in order to "make [the] diversity visible." This occurred in a session titled "The Impact of National Histories on the Women in Religion" at the 1994 annual meeting of the American Academy of Religion in Chicago.

22. "The dispossessed" is a term borrowed from Jacqueline Jones, *The Dispossessed: America's Underclass from the Civil War to the Present* (New York: Basic Books, 1992).

23. James H. Cone, *A Black Theology of Liberation*, 3rd ed. (Maryknoll, NY: Orbis Books, 1995).

24. Rita Nakashima Brock and Rebecca Ann Parker, *Proverbs of Ashes: Violence, Redemptive Suffering, and the Search for What Saves Us* (Boston: Beacon Press, 2001).

25. Vine Deloria Jr., *God Is Red*, 2nd ed. (Golden, CO: Fulcrum, 1993).

26. Lee H. Yearly, *New Religious Virtues and the Study of Religion: The University Lecture in Religion, 1994* (Tucson: Department of Religious Studies, Arizona State University, 1994), 15.

27. Ibid., 12.

28. Renato Rosaldo, *Culture and Truth: The Remaking of Social Analysis* (Boston: Beacon Press, 1993), 70.

29. Ibid., 71.

30. Ibid., 69.

31. Peter W. Williams, *American Religion: Traditions and Cultures* (New York: Macmillan, 1990), 417.

32. Marty, "Spirit's Holy Errand," 111.

33. Robert Redfield, *The Little Community and Peasant Society* (Chicago: University of Chicago Press, 1960), 430.

34. Baby boomers are people born in America between 1945/1946 and 1964/1965. See Roof, *Generation of Seekers*; and Steven M. Tipton, *Getting Saved from the Sixties: Moral Meaning in Convention and Cultural Change* (Berkeley: University of California Press, 1982).

35. Roof, *Generation of Seekers*, 5, 269.
36. Ibid., 243.
37. Ada María Isasi-Díaz and Yolanda Tarango, *Hispanic Women: Prophetic Voice in the Church* (San Francisco: Harper & Row, 1988), 68.
38. Ronald Delattre, "Supply-Side Spirituality: A Case Study in the Cultural Interpretation of Religious Ethics in America," in *Religion and the Life of the Nation: American Recoveries*, ed. Rowland A. Sherrill (Champaign: University of Illinois Press, 1990), 87.
39. Ralph Waldo Emerson, "Wealth," in *Selected Writings*, ed. Brooks Atkinson (New York: Modern Library, 1990), 140, quoted in Delattre, "Supply-Side Spirituality," 93.
40. Delattre, "Supply-Side Spirituality," 93.
41. Ibid., 98.
42. Benjamin Disraeli, quoted in Edward W. Said, *Orientalism* (New York: Vintage Books, 1979), 5.
43. Said claims that "Orient" and "Orientalism" are "man-made" ideas that "have a history and a tradition of thought, imagery, and vocabulary that have given [them] reality and presence in and for the West" (*Orientalism*, 3).
44. bell hooks, *The Black Looks: Race and Representation* (Boston: South End Press, 1993), 39.
45. Ibid., 29.
46. Gertrude Stein, *Everybody's Autobiography* (New York: Cooper Square, 1971), 190.
47. For an excellent study addressing the issue of searching for a woman-centered spirituality and of blending the East and the West, see Linda Watt, "Can Women Have Wishes? Gender and Spiritual Narrative in Gertrude Stein's *Lend a Hand or Four Religions*," *Journal of Feminist Studies in Religion* 10, no. 2 (1994): 49–72.
48. Said, *Orientalism*, 238.
49. Demerath, "Moth and the Flame," 108, 109.
50. Chang Chung-yuan, *Creativity and Taoism: A Study of Chinese Philosophy, Art, and Poetry* (New York: Harper & Row, 1970), esp. 11–13, 210.
51. Daisetz T. Suzuki, *Zen and Japanese Culture* (Princeton, NJ: Princeton University Press, 1973); and Julia Cameron, *The Artist's Way: A Spiritual Path to Higher Creativity* (New York: Putnam, 1992).
52. Charles S. Prebish, "Asian-American and Euro-American Buddhism: An Increasingly Unfriendly Partnership" (paper presented at the 1994 annual meeting of the American Academy of Religion, Chicago). See also Robert S. Michaelson, *The American Search for Soul* (Baton Rouge: Louisiana State University Press, 1975).
53. Allen E. Richardson, *East Comes West: Asian Religions and Cultures in North America* (Cleveland: Pilgrim Press, 1985), 4, 65, 151.

Chapter Five

May You Storm Heaven with Your Prayers

Devotions to Mary and Jesus in Filipino American Catholic Life

Rachel A. R. Bundang

Summer vacation, 1998. *One hundred years of freedom—"freedom" in name only.*

Attending the Philippine Independence Day parade in Manhattan in June 1998 hardly seemed the best way to observe the politically and historically tarnished celebration of the 1898 centennial of the island nation's liberty "won" after three and a half centuries of Spanish colonial rule. The cruel irony of the anniversary, which has born witness to a stunted, hobbled, incomplete freedom, only raised for me the usual questions of ethnicity, identity, and authenticity to nag and gnaw. It made me want to flee New York for a while.

I escaped the thumping bass, hot concrete, and vertical, claustrophobic funk of the city for a slower pace and fled home to the humid flatness of Florida. While on familiar territory there, primarily in the Jacksonville

I wish to thank the following for their assistance and encouragement throughout the multiple incarnations of this work: Rudy V. Busto, for directing me to the work of Robert Orsi on hearing the original version, to help me connect social history and theology; Michael Campos and Orlando Espín, for thinking with me about popular religiosity; Jane Naomi Iwamura and Paul Spickard, for earlier comments; Charles Gallagher, SJ, then archivist of the Diocese of St. Augustine (Florida), and Diane Grey, archivist of the *Tampa Tribune* research library, for sources; Aida McKinney, coordinator of the main Santo Niño circuit in northeast Florida; and the Bundang family and the prayer communities they introduced to me in Jacksonville and Tampa, Florida. I also thank the Church of St. Paul the Apostle (New York); the Asian North American Religion, Culture, and Society Group (ANARCS) of the American Academy of Religion; and the Asian Pacific Americans and Religion Research Initiative (APARRI), for the opportunities to present those earlier versions.

area, I was invited to participate in and observe Filipino American Catholic prayer groups, both in the homes of the hosts and in these groups' pilgrimages on the road. In living rooms and bedrooms I saw lovingly tended home shrines to Jesus and Mary that to me, as a species of Asian Pacific American, Generation X, post–Vatican II Catholic, were eerie and disturbing, yet beautiful and imaginative in the devotion they showed. And at the altars in these niches of holiness sat large baskets, brimming with handwritten petitions. I heard stories, sometimes accompanied by photos, of purported miracles that were reminiscent of medieval hagiography: the sun and moon spinning, statues weeping, communion hosts bleeding, and rosaries turning to gold. I saw scores of Marian icons, as well as little statues of the child Jesus dressed up as everything from the Infant King to a Little League player. I walked through a weathered, hand-hewn Stations of the Cross, with each cross inscribed with a prayer and reflection fiercely dedicated to the unborn child. I rode up flat highways and down dirt roads for hours in a minivan with middle-aged immigrant Filipinas as we visited Marian apparition sites. For some reason—maybe because I was the youngest or a novice of sorts to these trips—my seat in that van was always next to a solid three-and-a-half-foot-high statue of the Virgin Mary, whom these women had seat-belted down for her protection. This was about as far from *Thelma and Louise* or any other buddy movie, for that matter, as one could imagine. At every pothole, Mary's tin, gold-painted crown would spin around on her head, and the rosaries strung around her hands would clatter against her blue-and-white ceramic folds. For *merienda*, the midday meal, we hauled out the cold, garlicky chicken *adobo*, plus rice, fruit, and soda from the trunk at the rest stops for a picnic lunch.

Every now and then I would step outside of myself and think, This is all so surreal. With an immigrant daughter's ambivalence and fierce questioning about what her parents do, I found it hard to believe that I was witnessing devotions seemingly from another place and time. It was difficult, too, to acknowledge that people I knew, some more intimately than others, engaged in such practices. In retrospect I am not sure I was successful in invoking or suspending the anthropological, cinematic, or even theological eye at the right times. But reflection on this trip yields proof of Asian Pacific American life east of California[1]—and religious life, at that. It is a life that on many levels blurs the line between alien and familiar, even for the insider/outsider.

In emigrating from the Philippines to the United States, Filipino American Catholics have brought with them the practice of forming and participating in home-based prayer circles as part and parcel of their culture. Wherever a minimum critical mass in the Filipino American population is reached, typically a first-generation immigrant will set up, promote, and coordinate the local circuit. These circles are often devoted to a localized Mary (such as *Ang Birhen ng Antipolo*, Our Lady of Peace and Good Voyage),[2] Jesus *(Ang Santo Niño*, the Infant Jesus of Prague),[3] both at once, or, less often, a wholly different saint altogether. Membership, they say, is open to all, and on a rare occasion non-Filipino faces turn up to observe, if not participate. Presently the overwhelming majority of participants in such groups are post-1965 first-generation women averaging forty years of age or more. Some circles are charismatic or mystical in nature and practice, while others are much more straightforward and matter-of-fact.

A set of prayer circles based in a Filipino American Catholic community in northeast Florida serves as a case study here, putting ethnography in the service of theology to offer a snapshot of an alternative moral community. Questions such as the following will be considered:

- How do these prayer circles function, and what purposes do they serve? Do participants understand their practices as escape, empowerment, or something else altogether? Are these practices merely markers of identity, heritage, continuity, or difference? How do they hold and shape memory, particularly of "home"? Is prayer only women's work? What do generational and gender differences in participation mean?
- How do different moral communities compete, collaborate, or intersect? For instance, how has the institutional Catholic Church responded to these prayer circles? How are the participants otherwise involved in institutional religious life—Catholic or not?
- What is the value and reach (or limitation) of this kind of exercise of moral and spiritual leadership? What resources and challenges do these communities provide their members and the community beyond?

These reflections come with a few disclaimers. First of all, in my discussion of these questions, my approach bears the dual sensibilities of the religion scholar and the Catholic lay minister. Especially in the latter capacity, it is my duty to cultivate a community: faithful and seekers alike, laity and clergy alike, educated in, empowered by, and engaged with their faith-seeking reason, not just being blindly obedient, whether to doctrine or tradition. Second, with concern for careful interpretation, it is critical to strive for accuracy and balance in presenting Catholicism, particularly to an audience who may not be Catholic. It is the lot of Catholic theologians these days to live, as the proverb goes, in "interesting times," when dual demands for intellectual freedom and doctrinal orthodoxy exist in such great tension, so that critical thinking and theological imagination, taken together, seem more a threat than a promise.[4]

Most important, I present to you the place and the people of this community that is my home. This is the place where I grew up, so the dual impulse to expose and yet protect is there. Embedded in this chapter is a critique of community as expressed through traditional Filipino religiosity and through the ways that many Catholic churches, at least in the countless places "east of California," have yet to take the challenge of social, cultural, and spiritual diversity within the Church seriously. For Filipino American Catholics of the 1.5 generation and onward, relating to the faith we have inherited from our parents in ways that are constructive, meaningful, and mature is often difficult. We observe rituals and devotions that may be visually rich and culturally significant but feel spiritually alien or, worse, crippling in our efforts to live culturally integrated and spiritually coherent lives in places and times beyond our parents' wildest dreams. How do we reimagine and engage Catholic tradition in ways that are liberating and transformative for ourselves and our communities?

While I do not always agree with or understand fully the faith and beliefs as expressed by this community, the believers and devotees undeniably find there a sustaining strength and power that feed the heart and mind, the spirit and imagination. My hope is that I can fairly honor both the scholarly demands of this project and my personal commitments to everyone involved. The point of this chapter is not to engage in Mariological analysis, historiography, or debate.[5] Rather, the goal is to explore theological method as well as provide empirical goods. In articulating a method, the question is how—in the best traditions of feminist, ethnic studies, and postcolonial approaches—we can compellingly craft a theology that is collaborative and rooted in a community's particular experience, self-understanding, and integrity. Although the language may be different, the people whose stories and questions provide the substance would ideally recognize themselves in the theology being put forth. And as for empirical goods, a look at this community and these practices will provide more raw material for study and reflection on the role of lived religion and popular religiosity—*iyong teolohiya at relihyon ng mga tao*, the theology and religion of the common person—in Catholic life and in the study of Asian Pacific American religiosity in general. As we shall see, these Filipino American Catholic devotions reveal a great deal about how this particular community understands the relationships between the human and the divine, especially as experienced in diaspora.

I was first introduced to the Santo Niño almost at the beginning of the circuit in this community of Jacksonville, Florida. In 1985 there was a death in my immediate family. And as a gesture of offering solace in the midst of the grief, another Filipino family had arranged for the weeklong devotion to visit our home soon afterward.

The coordinator of the novena[6] circuit, usually an older woman who is supposed to model piety, escorts the current host and the statue to the home of the next sponsoring family. The prayers are recited in various languages—English, Spanish, Tagalog, and other Philippine dialects—and last for at least an hour; they include the full rosary, some litanies (such as the Marian Litany of Loreto, endorsed by Sixtus V in 1587), prayers to Jesus (both as crucified savior and as infant king), St. Francis, St. Michael the Archangel, and various faces of Mary (as Fatima, Antipolo, Guadalupe, Peñafrancia, and others). Then come songs, again in the three main languages. At the close is fellowship over food. On each day of the novena devotees follow a basic menu of recommended prayers, perhaps along with some extra prayers as suggested for special intentions. The prayer booklet also includes a list of "very important things to do when asking favors." Women tend to lead the prayers in these meetings. Any children or husbands present usually come at the behest of their mothers and wives rather than of their own volition, and they tend not to be as vocal or fervent in their expressions of devotion; sometimes they even retreat to their own corners while the service goes on, but they are never really free to refuse to participate. At the end of the week the sponsoring family sends off the "guest," the Santo Niño, with a farewell prayer. Thus the statue and the devotion go house to house. One need not know the host or be invited; it is enough to call, find out the location, and show up to pray. As Cristina Reyes observes, "It is considered an honor to have the statue of the Santo Niño, evident by the long waiting list to host a novena."[7] The calendar fills up well over a year in advance, and many families are repeat hosts, usually as close as possible to a significant anniversary—usually that of the death of a loved one.

The Filipino American community in northeast Florida has since grown large enough to support at least five separate circuits, each run by at least two coordinators and serving several neighborhoods. In the twenty or so years that these groups have existed and flourished locally, the number of adherents has grown, but so has the length of the prayer services.

The current edition of prayer booklets, for example, exists as grainy third- or fourth-generation copies. Compared to the first edition, these have many more prayers venerating Mary in additional guises: not just as Fatima, for example, but also as Guadalupe, Patroness of the Americas.[8] The Santo Niño's presence in the home demands reverent, obedient, and consistent participation from beginning to end. In another variant, one group devoted to the Twin Hearts of Jesus and Mary meets weekly, year-round. Here the novena is followed by a charismatic prayer and healing service, where people speak in tongues and claim to be "slain by the Holy Spirit." The faithful interpret these gifts as markers of chosenness by God, of worth in God's eyes, of spiritual readiness to be consecrated.

In addition to these prayer circles, members of the groups regularly seek out opportunities to go on pilgrimages. In the late 1990s two vision-aries—Nancy Fowler of Conyers, Georgia, and Vimer Nagun of Pasco County, Florida (in the rural outskirts of Tampa)[9]—were popular among participants in these groups because of their proximity; they made for an easy day trip from the Jacksonville area, roughly a four- to five-hour drive each way. The members also make sure to perform what one could call other works of piety. In fact, to paraphrase Qoheleth, for this group, "piety, piety, all is piety." The more prayers one says, the better. These works do not include participation in activities of direct service to church or community—although most do serve in some visible, public liturgical function, most often within the context of the Mass as a lector, sacristan, or the like—but rather in rituals, in traditional acts of personal spiritual obligation and nourishment: going to Mass daily if possible, venerating the Blessed Sacrament, wearing scapulars, and fulfilling other similar per-sonal devotions. Some also join special confraternities such as the Legion of Mary as a further communal commitment in devotion. For better or worse—and often out of unknowing or a misplaced or highly traditional humility—there are domains and activities that are stigmatized, in a way, as belonging or relegated exclusively to a dedicated priest or religious per-son, and they highly respect these hierarchies and boundaries.

The deep and abiding devotion to Mary is arguably rooted in the fact that Spain's first steps in colonizing the Philippines were concurrent with the Council of Trent (1545–63).[10] In its effort to slow the march of the Protestant Reformation, the council clarified and codified doctrines, teachings, and practices they considered central to the faith, including the honoring of Mary and the saints. So it was likewise with the Santo Niño devotion, which originated in Spain in 1556 and eventually came under the special sponsorship of Discalced Carmelites in Prague a few decades later. Another consideration is the Tridentine insistence that Scripture cannot stand without tradition as an arbiter for what is true, good, and central in Christian life; "tradition" is understood to include both devotional literature and devotional or pietistic acts. In other words, the Filipino American Catholicism of the generations represented in these prayer circles bears the indelible stamp of the teachings from the Council of Trent as filtered first through colonial Spain and then further reinforced through subsequent dogmas promulgated during the First Vatican Council (1869–70 [officially closed in 1960]).

In addition to the legacy of Spanish Catholicism, one must also consider the world in which these practices and beliefs were received and ultimately transformed. Prior to the Spaniards' arrival, many indigenous tribes such as the Tagalogs in the region now known as Luzon had evolved a roughly egalitarian social order that was reflected in their mythology; men and women wielded power and held authority in equal measure. Moreover, there is a tradition of *babaylanes*, or priestesses: women (or feminized men) serving as gateways and intercessors to the divine in matters of sacred ritual.[11]

Clearly the fact that these devotions endure shows that these rituals, this faith, and this community are very much alive and present. Yet the differences seem so jarring—and make their devotions seem so anachronous—when juxtaposed with the broad (and, overall, arguably more progressive) texture of Catholicism in the United States after Vatican II (1962–65). This group tends toward a faith so "conservative" or "traditional"—for lack of more satisfactory terms—that they will often promote the disputed cause of Mary as co-redemptrix, equal to Jesus the Christ in the economy of salvation.[12] The struggle for liberation, as they understand it, is not so much for the eradication of evil and injustice on all fronts here and now, but rather, it turns explicitly toward the eschatological and cosmological, toward the distant but imaginable future when God will set all things right. The changes and reconsiderations set in motion by Vatican II are, more often than not, criticized as being too liberal. For example, participants decry the loss of a concrete sense of sin, as well as changes in the liturgy—things that reflect a rethinking of theological anthropology and of ecclesiology. One incensed woman, a coordinator of one of the Santo Niño circuits in Jacksonville, explains:

> Liberals are not *real* Catholics. . . . All a priest needs to do is say the
> Mass every day, even if there are no people there. It is their priestly
> obligation. If Jesus wanted a woman priest, he would have made one

of his mother. After 2000 years they want to change [the faith]! . . . It is better to stay on the side of Jesus.[13]

Perhaps no doctrine or belief in the Church has demanded more correction more often than that of Mary: who she is, what she does, what she means. For these believers she is a special, unique model of faith and holiness. Through these devotions and through the words of the visionaries, they heed and embrace Mary as "the eschatological icon of the church."[14] Her teachings are simple: come, pray, and repent. The unspoken but understood promise is that she will do her best to intercede and plead the supplicant's cause to God (as Jesus). In exchange the faithful are to strive for unflinching obedience to God's will.

In contrast to Mary's invitation, Jesus as the Infant King issues a command, coupled with a promise (often inscribed in prayer cards and booklets): "The more you honor me, the more I will bless you." He calls the faithful "to humility, simplicity, and sincerity—to become little in order to become great and pleasing before Christ the King."[15] Devotional texts idealize and bring home the call to a childlike faith:

> Being a follower of Christ demands courage, decisive action, maturity. But coupled with these must always be humility, candor, confidence—those virtues of childhood. It is these virtues that Jesus is recommending. A child accepts himself for what he is. Undismayed by falls and setbacks, he gets up again and begins over. A child is confident: he trusts his parents, believes what they tell him, and asks simply for what he needs. And a child is honest; his forthright candor and simplicity in dealing with others can help us to see what our relationship with God and our neighbor should be.[16]

Prayer circles such as those formed in this immigrant community constitute an island of stability in a place vastly different from the home left behind; in them, devotees exert control and assert their worth through their diligent participation. And therein lies the appeal of these devotions to the imagination. These are religious enclaves of communities that, on one hand, think of themselves as being in exile or diaspora, yet, on the other hand, are rerooting, especially in the succeeding generations.

For several decades now Filipinos have come to northeast Florida mostly through some affiliation with the military installations there[17]—as employees, family, and so forth. This city is a classic southern urban area that, despite some demographic shifts and the passage of time, is still very much a place that is black-and-white in its rhetoric and understanding of race, and it is overwhelmingly Protestant as well. The influx of Asians (mostly Filipino, with growing numbers of Vietnamese, Koreans, and Chinese) and Latinos (more Caribbean than South or Central American) started in earnest in the 1960s. But only in this past generation, from the 1980s onward, has the Filipino population shifted its weight, with an increasingly heavier count among second- and third-generation families. The 2000 U.S. Census estimates that Filipinos account for approximately 1.5 percent of the local population, or some ten thousand persons, while there is still a steady stream of new immigrants. Now the children and grandchildren of the generation represented by these prayer groups' participants are giving the community its newfound and ever-deepening stability.

Such is the climate in the wider community. But in terms of Catholic church life, there has not been much sustained or systematic thought on the diocesan level about outreach to and nurturing of the Asian Pacific American Catholic community. It has long taken them for granted—and also left them, as immigrants, to take care of their own. Filipino American Catholics, in this case, tend to fold into the population of their local parish and attend and participate there in individual works of piety. Despite annual celebrations of observances such as the *Santacruzan* (Search for the Holy Cross) each May[18] and the Feast of the Black Nazarene each January,[19] ethnic identity gets downplayed and submerged in the larger notion of Church, both local and global. These celebrations are organized by ethnic community groups that are social or cultural by intent rather than directly or explicitly affiliated with the diocese or any single parish, although they may be hosted by a parish. In larger areas where there is a critical mass of a given ethnic group, a diocese will establish and foster ethnic apostolates to serve these groups in more culturally specific ways than what normally takes place in the average parish church. For instance, in Boston, where the stable, nonstudent Filipino population is just reaching a critical mass, this has meant setting aside one Sunday a month to celebrate Mass as a community, usually in English with Tagalog songs, and then having a potluck supper afterward. And of course there are the special occasions, such as *Simbang Gabi*, the tradition of late night–early morning Mass during the octave before Christmas. Miami, Washington, D.C., New York City, Chicago, and other cities each have something a little different for their respective Filipino populations.

On the West Coast, with its more established and internally diverse communities, dioceses have a slightly longer history of having developed plans and campaigns for ethnic pastoral ministry in APA (Asian Pacific

American) communities. In northeast Florida, however, the Diocese of St. Augustine houses all its racial and ethnic outreach under the single heading of "multicultural ministry."[20] However, nothing formal exists to serve the specific needs and concerns of APAs, save the temporary help of an imported priest on occasion (to conduct liturgies in native languages, for example) or the existing and often overtaxed structures and personnel at the basic parish level. This is an incomprehensible oversight, given the significant proportion, long-standing presence, and devoted participation of Filipinos—with Vietnamese and others as more recent arrivals—in the local churches. And the visible, progressive "browning" of the pews in the parishes indicates that the numbers are still growing. To their credit, it is the first generation who bring the power of memory of culture, through faith life and otherwise—helping to sustain the traditions actively, problematic or outdated as these may sometimes be.

Do these people put Mary, the Santo Niño, and these other figures rather than God at the center of their spiritual lives? What do they represent for those who venerate them? What significance do they have to the Filipino American community?

Mary and the Santo Niño are vital indeed to the Filipino American religious imagination, and these devotions reinforce for participants who they are as Catholics and as immigrants, faithful to the Church (idealized as what was practiced "back home") and faithful to their root culture. However, the role and status accorded to these objects of devotion can seem disproportionate to and even at odds with official Church teaching—even under the most generous "big tent" Catholicism—which would make space for ecumenical rapprochement and affirm Christ as the heart and foundation of the faith. Jacques Bur reminds us what "officially" counts most, and why:

> We must emphasize the difference between the appearances of Mary and those of the risen Christ.
>
> The appearances of Christ are attested by the Gospel accounts. Their authenticity is guaranteed by revelation. As the foundation of the faith of the apostles and the resurrection of Jesus for us, they are also the foundation of our faith in the resurrection.
>
> By contrast, the appearances of Mary are not the foundation of our faith in the resurrection, and the Church does not oblige us to believe in them.

The private appearances reported in the course of the history of the Church, even those of Christ, are not guaranteed by the authority of revelation or the infallible *magisterium* of the church.[21]

One can see these devotions, then, as a divergence from official teaching, or, more generously, as an alternate tradition. The moral communities provided by these prayer circles compete, collaborate, and intersect with the institutional Catholic Church. The coordinators claim that their work has been approved by the local bishop. What groups like these best show is that Filipino American Catholics tend to emphasize highly personal connections with faces of the divine through devotions. In comparison, Vatican II's reforms recentered the faith in community as manifested in liturgical life, specifically in the Eucharist. To oversimplify a bit, familial intimacy with the divine—rather than the open table of Eucharist—is the dominant metaphor for these participants' religious lives. Mary is the embracing Mother, Jesus is the child to be cared for, and both model the everyday holiness that all should strive to emulate. Each one's power lies, in a way, in their need to be heeded, their vulnerability at the hands of another, their powerlessness—troubling things all for those reading with postcolonial, feminist, and liberationist eyes.

But what is the significance of all this veneration to the life of this community? Is it only veneration, or does it—as some argue—cross the line into idolatry?

For the [Santo Niño] devotees, it isn't enough to go to church. For them, Sunday Mass is about the entire community of Roman Catholics. Friday night [when this group convenes] is how the devotees have taken one aspect of Catholicism and made it something of their very own. But most of all they pray so that they do not forget who they are—Filipinos.[22]

For a community teetering between alienation and acculturation, these prayer circles serve as vessels of memory and as sites of refuge against the wider world, of resistance against the pull or demand to assimilate, and of spiritual resources to deal with their trials. The greatest trial is their strong sense of exile: from their geographic and cultural "home," which is "back there," that is, in the Philippines; sometimes from their families, especially in the difficulties they have with their children, who wrestle with the pulls of assimilation and acculturation differently from them; from their Church, which—in its more progressive impulses and moments and despite its best intentions—they feel is leaving them behind. This textured sense of exile turns the focus of their prayer on the eschatological.

By casual observation one notable thing about the laity of the Filipino diaspora in the United States—and not just this group—is their virtual lack of involvement in faith-rooted work, such as church-sponsored social justice or social change initiatives, per se, whether as volunteers or as paid staff, as opposed to public ritual or liturgical leadership as noted earlier.[23] Questions of political and economic justice are not always or explicitly tied to religious impulse or reasoning. The sacred and the secular world orders merged to a certain point in the Philippines, making possible, for example, the People Power revolutions of 1986 and 2001. Nonetheless, the social and moral climate, at least within Filipino American communities in diaspora in the United States, is individualistic, looking out primarily for the interests of self and, at most, family while compromising the cohesion and consciousness of the greater community. In other words, the communitarian ethic extends only so far and no further. At worst, Filipino Americans—Catholic or not—are no more than a "lumpen community" (in the sense of *Lumpenproletariat)*—an aggregate of people who may coexist but do not necessarily share experiences, goals, or agendas, let alone a common vision of what it means to be a people or a sense of accountability toward and care for one another, for whatever reason. The language of this people's faith and the rhetoric of their religious lives are not so much those of seeking political and social liberation from day-to-day disappointments and injustices but more those of seeking spiritual courage, freedom, and strength. For these Filipino Americans the driving force is the hungry search for intimacy and merit in the eyes of the divine—however embodied—and bestowing or withholding of favors, signs, graces, and miracles; and part of the trick is their persistence, their constancy in pursuing relationship with Jesus, Mary, or the saint of choice. They find victory in the small steps, in the tiniest movements.

At the risk of overgeneralization, one could readily conclude that since the Counter-Reformation, the Church has jealously guarded and conserved revelation, claiming that the authority of a presider's office—the presider being the public leader of liturgy and ritual, most often the ordained, by default—outweighs any evidence he can offer; the faithful or the seeker need only believe. But devotions such as these force the question of what counts more in the life of faith: revelation or intimate personal relationship with God? Is this sort of religion or faith thus lived out peripheral to or even divorced from the real world? For so many of these prayer group members, the rituals and mind-set do take over their lives: one need only note, for example, the great care given to tending the shrines, icons, and statues; or the sometimes staggering amount of time (and, in many cases, money as well) invested in prayer and pilgrimage. The power, efficacy, and value of prayer, especially as an expression of faith and as a way of honoring relationship with God, both individually and collectively here, are not under question. But the language and rhetoric of these practices, which emphasize (an almost) abject humility before God as well as mortification of both soul and flesh, may not ultimately be helpful as a strategy for coping with the reality of striving and struggle that most immigrants face. Rather, they may instead prove a liability for the health and survival of this community. No matter whom the object of veneration, there is a danger that these devotions reinforce the colonized notion of unworthiness as something to be expiated with our colonized love of—perhaps even obsession with?—martyrdom and victimhood. For example, how can a liberating interpretation of Mary—say, one that emphasizes her prophetic discernment and her humanness[24] as much as her obedient submission or sorrowful witness—be communicated and understood? Or if one is to emulate the Santo Niño and become childlike in relationships, is this not infantilizing? The believer is encouraged to drop everything into God's hands, underscoring a sense of helplessness that only deprives or diminishes the believer's capacity and taste for agency, especially moral agency. In other words, the agency is lost in the piety. And—speaking from a theologian-daughter's perspective—if survival in exile is the point, then at what point does the piety, as beautiful and rooted in the gnarled knots of faith, culture, and identity as it may be, become life denying rather than life giving?

The idea of "storming heaven with one's prayers"—a striking phrase that my mother voiced as her wish for me in my spiritual growth—is profoundly beautiful as a powerful statement of faith. However, it is just as troubling as a statement of utter humility that seems to surrender the faculties needed for discernment and the agency needed to survive the unknown; even if this humility is one before God, the colonial undertones are inescapable. Armed with the trademark tools that feminist method and postcolonial sensibility afford—the hermeneutic of suspicion, the dangerous memory, and the reconstructive impulse guided by wisdom and imagination—in the transformed circumstances in which we find ourselves, a renewed, engaged, more nourishing, and coherent vision of Filipino American faith community can be discerned and articulated.

As this prayer group and communities like it live into their faith and their experiences of immigration and acculturation, it would be worth revisiting them time and again as occasions of what could be called narratives of petition and grace that are scripted and lived out. It would be interesting to read this community's life of faith in dialogue with Elizabeth A. Johnson's work on the communion of saints, including Mary, and with Latino/a theologians' work on popular Catholicism. Johnson, for example, thinks that in Vatican II's christocentric turn, important and needed as it is, the American church in particular has forgotten the meaning and promise of sainthood. She discusses the shift from early Christian notions of saints as companions to the notion, under Rome's imperial consolidation, of saints as patrons and intercessors in what we now think of as the traditional cult of saints: here again the communitarian spirit gives way to the intimacy of unequals. Johnson considers the impact of loss and the promise of recovery of the sense of sainthood, of participation in the life of holiness among all women and men through time, even across the boundary between life and death. In other words, the path to holiness is necessarily relational.[25] One might also add "incarnational," for sainthood comes from the lived experience of the faithful, the friends and lovers of God. If, indeed, Filipino American Catholics relate to the saints and the divine as hierarchical[26] family rather than as a more textured and varied group of friends, each uniquely wise and devoted, one would hope for reinterpretation and reimagination of what such relationships could look like and how they could function—and perhaps how something more egalitarian and liberative might be mirrored and developed in our own persons and communities. As phrases such as "cloud of witnesses" attest, saints are a rich and vibrant part of our tradition and our faith, and sainthood as such deserves to be reconsidered in ways that are more edifying, more historically honest, and potentially more liberating as well.

On another front, in the study of popular religiosity, especially in Catholic communities, work in Latino/a religious studies has proved illuminating.[27] Read respectfully and critically, they can inform approaches to and understandings of Asian Pacific American—and especially Filipino American—religious experience and theology because the immigration narratives and decolonization and acculturation struggles are comparable, common experiences that are theologically formative. For instance, it is worth considering whether *mestizaje* and *nepantla*—or their equivalent counterparts in Filipino culture—are valid categories for discussing Filipino American Catholic experience.[28] Putting the two bodies of theological inquiry in conversation with each other can further inform how we do church and think about ecclesiology in a postcolonial community and, more fundamentally, how we discern what frameworks might best help us to understand and even heal this postcolonial sense of psychic, physical, and spiritual dislocation.

As Filipinos—Catholic and otherwise—immigrate, acculturate, and establish themselves here, the challenge lies in thinking critically about the intersections of faith and culture in order to undergo what the dissident, exiled filmmaker Marina Feleo Gonzalez, in a 1997 interview, called another project for "decolonization of the soul." For example, what messages about femininity and womanhood are being passed on, rebelled against, and contested? What do notions of home, exile, community, and memory mean now, in this new place? How do we critique the social order—of power and authority in a variety of spaces—that undermines our well-being as a people and the well-being of all people? Whether in or out of the Church, we have to cultivate our community ethic, our sense of purpose, and our understanding of why exactly we are here and what we are supposed to do.

And on a pastoral note, further study and engagement of the serious generational, cultural, and faith gaps in this Filipino American community are warranted. In order to exert more influence in the local Church and have it be more responsive, especially as the population grows, there must be critical and creative approaches to cultivating a sense of community and faith life between and of the immigrant (parent) contingent and the following generations (children). These gaps need careful attention if the community is to grow beyond mere cultural Catholicism and to mature in faith. In classrooms and parishes, homes and neighborhoods, countless young Asian Pacific American Catholics—and not just Filipino American—have confessed their alienation, hostility, and even indifference to the Church because they find their religious needs, experiences, and expectations to be vastly different from those of their parents; likewise, parents find their children's relative lack of care bewildering and frustrating. Sadly, they often do not share a common language or vision of being Church together. But this is something that can be crafted with time, attention, and discernment.

Notes

1. "East of California" refers to the West Coast–centric, and indeed, California-hegemonic scholarship typical in Asian Pacific American (APA) Studies until relatively recently. While California remains a powerhouse in terms of the field's institutional presence and strength, this past decade has seen remarkable growth in other geographic areas as APA

diasporas have migrated and settled more widely. A parallel claim may be made for APA social and cultural organizations.

2. Also known by her Spanish name as *Nuestra Señora de la Paz y Buenviaje* or formal Tagalog name as *Ang Mahal na Birhen ng Kapayapaan at Mabuting Paglalayag*. In 1626 Governor-General Juan Niño de Tabora took her image from Acapulco to the Philippines; the image got her name from the fact that she made a total of six round-trips between Manila and Mexico and was considered a protector in the perilous crossings of the galleon trade. She eventually came to rest in the Philippines, and her devotees make pilgrimages to the shrine in Antipolo, Rizal, each day to pay homage.

Given the particular fervor of Marian devotion in the community being studied here, it is important to note that a majority of the Filipinos who have settled in the Jacksonville area come from the Philippine province of Zambales, northwest of Manila—perhaps better known to U.S. readers as the site of the former Clark Air Base and Subic Bay Naval Base, as well as the Mount Pinatubo volcano. Zambales is the home of the devotion to the *Ina Poon Bato* (Our Lady of the Sacred Rocks), the oldest known image of Mary to appear in Asia; this manifestation of the Blessed Virgin is known as the protector of the Aetas (a local tribe), analogous to Guadalupe in her relationship to the indigenous of Mexico. See Antonio Pigafetta, *Magellan's Voyage: A Narrative of the First Circumnavigation*, ed. and trans. R. A. Skelton (New York: Dover, 1994). Pigafetta's 1521 account is recounted in brief in *The Philippines at the Spanish Contact: Some Major Accounts of Early Filipino Society and Culture*, ed. F. Landa Jocana (Manila: MCS Enterprises, 1975). See also "What is *Ina Poon Bato?*" http://www.udayton.edu/mary/questions/yq2/yq353.htm.

3. For samples of typical devotional literature, see author unknown, "Devotion to the Infant Jesus of Prague" (Rockford, IL: Tan Books, 1975); Ludvik Nemec, "The Infant Jesus of Prague" (New York: Catholic Book Publishing, [1979] 1986); and author unknown, "A Catholic Devotion to the Infant Jesus of Prague," http://www.infantjesus.com/index.html.

4. See Luke Timothy Johnson, "After the Big Chill: Intellectual Freedom and Catholic Theologians," *Commonweal* 133, no. 2 (January 27, 2006), http://www.commonweal magazine.org/article.php3?id_article=1499.

5. For a range of traditional sources on Mary, from documents to apparitions to art and icons, see the holdings of the Marian Library International Marian Research Institute at the University of Dayton, http://www.udayton.edu/mary/marypage21.html. See also George H. Tavard, *The Thousand Faces of the Virgin Mary* (Collegeville, MN: Liturgical Press, 1996); and Hilda C. Graef, *Mary: A History of Doctrine and Devotion* (Westminster, MD.: Sheed & Ward, 1999).

For a sample of more-contemporary takes on Mary, see Rosemary Radford Ruether, *Mary: The Feminine Face of the Church* (Philadelphia: Westminster, 1977); Ivone Gebara and Maria Clara Bingemer, *Mary: Mother of God, Mother of the Poor* (Maryknoll, NY: Orbis Books, 1989); Elizabeth A. Johnson, *Truly Our Sister: A Theology of Mary in the Communion of Saints* (New York: Continuum, 2003); and Jaroslav Pelikan, *Mary through the Centuries: Her Place in the History of Culture* (New Haven, CT: Yale University Press, 1998).

6. Although the Santo Niño devotion is observed a week at a time rather than for the nine days of a novena proper, adherents still consider and call it a novena in practice.

7. Cristina Reyes, "Cathollicism [*sic*]—Filipino Style," *Prism* (November 1995), http://www.journalism.sfsu.edu/www/pubs/prism/nov95/22.html.

8. Guadalupe has been honored as the Patroness of the Americas for over four centuries now; Pius XI extended her patronage to the Philippines in 1935.

9. Fowler's last public vision was supposed to have taken place October 13, 1998. As for Vimer Nagun, he was extremely popular in this Filipino American prayer group from northeast Florida because of the cultural consonance. At the time this research was first presented, in 1998, Nagun was seventeen years old. He claimed to have visions of Mary, and sometimes other saints as well. He first went public with these claims in January 1996. In the August 15, 1996, *Tampa Tribune* article titled "Religious Sightings Bring the Faithful to Teen's Doorstep," excerpted below, the journalist Steven Orlando first makes note of Nagun's apparitions; it is probably no coincidence that August 15 marks the Feast of the Assumption (of Mary, body and soul, into heaven), a Holy Day of Obligation in the Catholic Church. Many faithful, Filipino and otherwise, would drive for miles into the middle of nowhere to pray with him and learn from the messages Mary would send him.

> Vimer says he had at least 500 conversations with Mary, the mother of Jesus Christ, since July 8, 1995. The apparitions, he says, happen about 6:40 p.m. every day except Sunday. The faithful gather daily at his central Pasco County home.
>
> He says he also has seen Jesus and a host of angels and saints, including St. Patrick, St. Francis of Assisi, and Michael the Archangel.
>
> The youngest of six, Vimer says Mary delivers messages to him. He writes them in a spiral notebook while kneeling on his front porch before a crucifix and statues of Mary and Jesus.
>
> Many of the messages condemn abortion. Others mention the Second Coming, offer blessings, and call for prayers.
>
> As for why he sees the apparitions, the Zephyrhills High School junior says little.
>
> "I don't know," he said. "I really don't know." . . .
>
> Vimer said he first told others of his experiences in January [1996]. They began gathering one Saturday a month at the grotto at Saint Leo Abbey [where the visions first took place].

The Diocese of St. Petersburg was extremely hesitant to authenticate his visions, warned the faithful to keep their distance, and prohibited its priests from saying Mass or leading prayers at the site.

Some other late twentieth-century sightings around the world that have had staying power and a continued following include those in Medjugorje, Bosnia-Herzegovina (since 1981), with the six visionaries; Veronica Leuken with Our Lady of the Roses in Bayside, Queens (from 1970 until her death in 1995); and, of course, Nancy Fowler in Conyers, Georgia. But the Church has not officially recognized anything as legitimate since Fatima, nearly eighty years ago, in Portugal.

10. Ferdinand Magellan landed in the archipelago in 1521, and governorship was established by 1563. The Council of Trent ran not continuously but in three sessions: 1545–49 under Pope Paul III; 1551–52 under Pope Julius III; and 1562–63 under Pope Pius IV.

11. See Mary John Mananzan, *Woman and Religion*, 3rd ed. (Manila: Institute of Women's Studies, St. Scholastica's College, 1998); Herminia Menez, *Explorations in Philippine Folklore* (Manila: Ateneo de Manila University Press, 1998); William Henry Scott, *Barangay: Sixteenth-Century Philippine Culture and Society* (Manila: Ateneo de Manila University Press, 1994); Vicente L. Rafael, *Contracting Colonialism: Translation and Christian*

Conversion in Tagalog Society under Early Spanish Rule (Durham, NC: Duke University Press, 1993); and Melba Padilla Maggay, *Filipino Religious Consciousness: Some Implications to Missions* (Manila: ISACC, 2002).

12. Vatican II documents such as Pope Paul VI's 1964 *Lumen Gentium* (8.60–65) teach that Mary is not equal to Jesus. His 1974 *Marialis Cultus* further provides guidelines for "the Right Ordering and Development of Devotion to the Blessed Virgin Mary." See also Jacques Bur, *Pour comprendre la Vierge Marie dans le mystère du Christ et de l'Église* (Paris: Cerf, 1992).

13. Aida McKinney, interview by author, tape recording, Jacksonville, Florida, July 1998.

14. Louis Bouyer, *The Seat of Wisdom: An Essay on the Place of the Virgin Mary in Christian Theology* (New York: Pantheon Books, 1962), quoted in Jacques Bur, *How to Understand the Virgin Mary* (New York: Continuum, 1996), 57.

15. Nemec, "Infant Jesus of Prague," 9.

16. Author unknown, "Catholic Devotion to the Infant Jesus of Prague," 15.

17. Remember that the Philippines was a U.S. colony (1898–1946); Philippine nationals were enlisted in the U.S. Navy—initially to serve as stewards, in most cases—since the beginning. After the Philippines was "granted" its independence in 1946, the 1947 Military Bases Agreement between the two nations allowed the United States to recruit Filipino citizens. In exchange for a term of service in the U.S. Navy, Filipino nationals were granted citizenship. Later this extended to gaining permanent residency and eventual citizenship for dependent relatives. The agreement expired in 1992, when the leases for U.S. bases in the Philippines were not renewed, so the land and facilities reverted to Philippine control. See Marina Claudio-Perez, "Filipino Americans," http://www.library.ca.gov/assets/acrobat/filipino.pdf.

18. The *Santacruzan* is a festival, complete with religious-historical beauty pageant in full costume, celebrated each May. It reenacts and commemorates Queen Helena and her son Constantine the Great's search for the Holy Cross, which they find in Jerusalem and take back to Rome, to much rejoicing (See *"Flores de Mayo at Santacruzan"* (Flowers of May and the Holy Cross), http://www.seasite.niu.edu/Tagalog/Cynthia/festivals/flores_de_mayo_at_santacruzan.htm. See also Felina Lazaro et al., *"Santacruzan:* The Queen of Filipino Festivals," http://www.hagonoy.com/lbcorpus/halbc007.html.

19. Each January 9 a life-size statue of Jesus—taken by galleon from Mexico to the Philippines in 1606 and housed at St. John the Baptist Church in Quiapo, Manila—is paraded on a gilded carriage through the streets near the church. The faithful and those seeking healing or other miracles aim to touch the statue, hoping for some kind of blessing or transformation. See "Feast of the Black Nazarene," http://www.seasite.niu.edu/TAGALOG/Cynthia/festivals/philippine_festivals_fs.htm.

    As practiced by Filipino American Catholic communities in northeast Florida, this ritual means processing around the church property and saying the rosary plus prayers specific to the feast day while carrying a likeness of the Quiapo statue. And, as with the Santo Niño novenas, the ritual ends with a community meal.

20. In 1998 the diocese had two separate ethnic apostolates: one for Hispanic ministries and the other shared jointly by blacks and Native Americans (all terminology theirs). It is unclear when the shift to a single office and point-person took place.

21. Bur, *How to Understand the Virgin Mary,* 123.

22. Reyes, "Cathollicism."

23. There are, of course, isolated cases of laity involved in faith-rooted work and religiously motivated social action movements. At most, they may consider the work they already do—in nursing and medicine, teaching, social work, or even military service, for example—as a brand of ministry. But this is rare.

24. It is with relatively recent documents such as Paul VI's *Marialis Cultus* (1974) that we see a shift to efforts to promote Mary as a champion of the marginalized, dispossessed, and oppressed and as a "power woman" that modern women could perhaps look to or identify with. The point is to honor her role in salvation history and encourage proper celebration in liturgy and prayer life.

25. See Elizabeth A. Johnson, *Friends of God and Prophets* (New York: Continuum, 1998), esp. 305–25.

26. Or imperial, or feudal, or patriarchal family, for that matter.

27. See, for example, Orlando O. Espín, *The Faith of the People: Theological Reflections on Popular Catholicism* (Maryknoll, NY: Orbis Books, 1997); Orlando O. Espín and Gary Macy, eds., *Futuring Our Past: Explorations in the Theology of Tradition* (Maryknoll, NY: Orbis Books, 2006); and María Pilar Aquino, Daisy L. Machado, and Jeanette Rodríguez, eds., *A Reader in Latina Feminist Theology: Religion and Justice* (Austin: University of Texas Press, 2002).

28. Here *mestizaje*, or mixing, refers to both miscegenation and cultural fusion. *Nepantla* is originally a Nahuatl word, now often used by Chicana/o theorists and artists to refer to *tierra entre medio*, an in-between, ever-shifting, liminal space. See, for example, Gloria E. Anzaldúa and AnaLouise Keating, eds., *This Bridge We Call Home: Radical Visions for Transformation* (New York: Routledge, 2002); and Pat Mora, *Nepantla: Essays from the Land in the Middle* (Albuquerque: University of New Mexico Press, 1993).

Chapter Six

Ancestral Returns

Reexamining the Horizons of Asian American Religious Practice

Jane Naomi Iwamura

To Return Once Again

"Who will light incense to the dead when I am gone?" asks the mother of Asian American journalist Andrew Lam. Her sister, Lam's aunt, replies, "Honestly, I don't know. None of my children will do it, and we can forget the grandchildren. They don't even understand what we are doing when we pray to the dead. I guess when we're gone, the ritual ends." Lam continues to speak of his mother's pain and a "certain twinge of regret and guilt" he feels regarding an obligation that he can never totally fulfill because of his American upbringing.[1]

Ancestor veneration—rituals that honor the dead and ensure their continued existence—is an integral part of East Asian religious systems. Its expression takes on many forms: from *jingzu* in China to *chesa* for Koreans to Vietnamese *ngay gio* and Japanese *senzo kuyo*. The specificities of these various rituals in different Asian and Asian American contexts range from offering various sacrifices to deities on behalf of the ancestors and to the ancestors themselves in order to sustain their existence to performing ritual acts that remind us of their lives and deeds and the web of interdependence that links us to one another. We would not be here if not for our

Portions of this chapter first appeared in *Amerasia Journal* 22, no. 1 (1996): 162–67. I would like to thank Kwok Pui-lan, Rita Nakashima Brock, and the PANAAWTM collective for their feedback on the chapter and especially for their unflagging support throughout the years. Their commitment to Asian and Asian American women's voices in theology and ministry is a continual inspiration. I would also like to thank Rudy V. Busto, David Kyuman Kim, Leng Lim, Young Mi, Angela Pak, Haeyoung Yoon, David Yoo, and Joan May Cordova for making the initial piece possible, and Rachel Bundang and Anne Joh for sharing the journey.

ancestors, and they would easily pass away if it were not for us. Such acts of veneration also instill in the practitioner a sense of the dialogic relationship between the past and the present—one that is intimate and binding.[2]

While the majority of Asians now living in the United States are Christian,[3] practical and psychic remnants of these traditions linger. It is not uncommon for Asian Americans to observe ancestral rites alongside their Christian faith and honor the dead in transformed ways (memorial services and filial piety "preached from the pulpit").[4] The significance of family and ancestors still greatly informs the ethos of Asian American religious life and underwrites structures of feeling that uniquely shape Asian American religious identity.

Christian or non-Christian, however, Asian Americans—especially second and subsequent generations—often hold ambivalent views toward ancestor veneration and Asian religious folk practices. There is a multitude of reasons for this (some of which I explore in this chapter). It is true that religious practices and identities are bound to change given the impact of migration, acculturation, and other social forces, as well as the decisions we make in our everyday lives. However, it is important to think about what we have given up in the process and consider ways that we can retain the spiritual legacy of our Asian ancestors and maintain our commitments to them, while remaining true to ourselves and our contemporary environment.

My Japanese American immigrant grandparents and great-grandparents traveled to the United States with ancestors in tow. While only one of my grandmothers ever made it back to Japan, their families were never too far away. Through their stories and spiritual practices, they nurtured bonds that stretched across time and space to link samurai and rice farmers (in Japan) with engineers and peach farmers (in the United States). With my grandparents' passing (as well as that of my mother), I, too, hear their query: "Who will light incense for us now that we have gone?"

In 1993 I had just finished my master's degree in theological studies at Harvard Divinity School. While I had become familiar with the works of such philosophers of religion as Hegel, Feuerbach, Kierkegaard, and Kant, and also with the contemporary theological efforts of Gordon D. Kaufman, Sallie McFague, James H. Cone, and Virgil Elizondo, my connection to these Christian-based thinkers was always somewhat remote. Only when I was asked to organize a panel on religion for the Association for Asian American Studies (AAAS) did I begin to explore sources closer to home. For my presentation on the panel, I harnessed my training in theological method and invoked the spirit of my grandmothers—both devout Buddhists—to speak on a phenomenon that was close to my heart: the notion of ancestors.

My aim in bringing these two seemingly disparate traditions together —Christian constructive theology and Japanese American folk religion— was threefold: (1) to call attention to the spiritual and psychic loss we suffer in a white Christian society, (2) to address the need for a theological vision that takes Asian religious frameworks seriously, and (3) to offer a practical method for (re)creating this vision. Ideally, such a method would challenge essentialized notions of Asian religions as well as ward off the temptation to appropriate these notions uncritically with little consideration of their history and use.

In the presentation I gave at the AAAS (which subsequently appeared in *Amerasia Journal*), "Homage to Ancestors: Exploring the Horizon(s) of Asian American Religious Identity," I made an attempt at such a methodology. What follows here is a reworking of this early effort. At the time, I drew from that with which I was most familiar: Japanese American religious experience. I then discussed the factors that "distance" Asian Americans from the spiritual practices of our forebears and explored a threefold approach to reconfiguring ancestor veneration in an American context— retrieval, reexamination, and reconstruction.

More than a decade has passed since I penned "Homage to Ancestors." The piece still remains close to my heart—a true expression of my view of where we need to go in terms of Asian American religious belief and practice. I appreciate the opportunity to return to my earlier work. While I have attempted to clarify my points and provide additional examples, the integrity of the original essay remains and will hopefully still be of use to theologians, students, pastoral care workers, and engaged practitioners.

The View from Here

As a Japanese American, family was always important, and not simply my immediate family, but also all those Iwamuras, Tanakas, and Shiraishis who had come before, creating bonds that stretched across the Pacific and back again. Even those of whom we had little record or no account were still remembered in their absence (for example, my grandmother Ruki's family). I grew up with a sense that even if one died and "came to be white ashes,"[5] that one's spirit would live on through family remembrance. This sensibility was cultivated through everyday acts and rituals—the stories my grandmothers would tell, regular visits to the cemetery, irregular correspondence and gifts between us and relatives back in Japan, and a continual chain of memorial services.[6] It was also reinforced by the poignant memory of the empty place setting that would appear at my grandmother's dinner table long after my grandfather's death. Yes, I knew that family was important, but I did not always appreciate the ways in which my heritage encouraged my view.

The closest I came to articulating this phenomenon seemed to reside in the Japanese notion of ancestor and the ritual of ancestor veneration. In Japan, ancestor veneration centers on *ie*:

> *Ie* is a social system based upon one idea of a family. The word *ie* has three meanings: (1) a house or dwelling place, (2) family or home, and (3) lineal kinship or lineage originating from an ancestor and maintained generation after generation by a succession of patriarchs. These three meanings are in fact closely related as shown by the fact that a family—or any family—is supposed to have a genealogy of its own and also by the fact that a family lives in a house.[7]

The conception of family invoked here is not determined by bloodline but rather by social consideration. Indeed, a male individual biologically unrelated to a family can be adopted or brought in as an heir, look after the family property and shrine, and continue the household line.

The Issei, or first generation of Japanese Americans to migrate to the United States (my grandparents), brought with them this sense of family. For many of these immigrants the practice of ancestor veneration existed alongside their Buddhist faith and was incorporated into their daily religious practice. However, the Issei's strong identity as Jodo Shin Buddhists—a more centralized and missionizing sect of Japanese Buddhism —unwittingly paved the way for the eventual demise of ancestor rituals. The Buddhist "churches" that these Japanese Americans established began to appear more and more like their Christian counterparts in terms of devotional practices and mood. Faith in Amida Buddha (a central tenet of Jodo Shin) shared a striking affinity with faith in God and became increasingly the focus of Japanese American Buddhist life; ancestor veneration had no similar parallel in American culture.

Living in the United States set Japanese Americans further adrift from traditional ancestral rites. For the Nisei (second-generation) Japanese Americans, ancestor veneration made even less sense. It did not fit well with a society that espoused independence and individuality, understood itself spiritually as "one nation under God," and became increasingly organized according to nuclear family units. As Nisei attempted to distinguish themselves from their Issei parents and make their way in the United

States—a society acutely hostile to their existence—old-world practices were readily abandoned and new-world sensibilities adopted.[8] Second-generation Japanese Americans transformed the Jodo Shin church into an American institution that focused squarely on Buddhism's relevance in the modern world. The ancestral dimensions of Buddhist practice were viewed as cultural vestiges that prohibited Buddhism from being truly considered on par with Christianity and other so-called world religions.

In addition to these changes, there was the distance—the physical distance—between Japan and America. There was little opportunity to really know one's relatives "back home" except through occasional letters and photographs. To many of us Sansei (third generation), these photographs hold the faces of strangers; the pictures of the ancestral property we look on as someone else's home. The memory and significance of these connections seems to have "passed away" with our Issei grandparents and great-grandparents.

What we do remember are the rituals—simple ceremonies to which we were often witness. In a poem Susan Mukai writes,

> Everyday at dinnertime
> Obachan goes to the obutsudan.
> Bows deeply once, then
> then places the rice offering
> inside the paper doors.
> She strikes the bell I am
> forbidden to touch.
>   Clear, clean tone lingers in mid-air
>   commingling with the sweet incense
> Grandma and the Nembutsu.
> Jichan, she is so faithful.
> do you know?
> She bows again, turns
> smiles, "Oboenasai, kore omaeno desu."
> I don't understand, but I nod.
> And we walk to the kitchen.[9]

"*Oboenasai, kore omaeno desu.*" "Please learn, remember: this is yours." And we often do, as my memories have shown. We look back and discover that, despite all the factors that distance us, ancestors preside; they "speak through dream."[10] Although elusive, these spirits maintain a power over us; they predict our values, our actions; they guide us intuitively through life.

To pay homage we must return to the ancestral site; this site is not a geographic location or a particular moment in time, but rather, it is found deep within each one of us. To return it is first necessary to understand the path by which we have traveled so far, the forces that have set us adrift and have distanced us from our ancestors.

Distancing

Ancestor veneration rituals are modeled after the patriarchal and patrilineal structure specific to East Asian societies. As East Asians settle in America, these traditional Asian systems are contested by new ways of understanding "family," alternative values (for example, independence, autonomy), and different socioeconomic conditions. East Asians who migrate to the United States, along with their descendants, live and work within a configuration of social relations that does not encourage or support traditional ancestor veneration.

In addition, East Asian sacred rituals are forced to adapt to a particular institutional structure in order to be fully recognized. For one, the central site of religious practice in the United States is usually understood as separate from the home (for example, church, temple), and for another, affiliation is established on a voluntary, individual basis. Since Japanese ancestor veneration does not readily fit either one of these models, transmission becomes difficult in an American setting. This is further compounded by the limited engagement with, and appreciation of, Asian and Asian American cultures as a whole. Within the U.S. context, second, third, and subsequent generations of Asian Americans have little reason to engage in ancestor veneration and other Asian religious practices beyond their cultural commitments and sense of family obligation.

The academy is one venue that offers the opportunity of return: East Asian Americans are able to study ancestor veneration and more fully understand its function and practice. However, understanding the ritual in this setting can also distance Asian Americans from their spiritual heritage in an unusual manner. First of all, since initial scholarship of Asian spiritual practices and "religious" rituals was done by European and Euro-American scholars, the language and terms by which we rediscover them can be tainted by Orientalist perspectives and racist overtones (for example, "syncretism," "ancestor cult," "myth"). Second, the scientific approach that the academy espouses in relation to all phenomena is based on instrumental rationality. This particular lens views ritual and spirituality in terms of functionality (for example, psychological, social, political), instead of grappling with the practice in more holistic ways and considering its meaning in historical context.[11]

A complex set of factors distances East Asian Americans from practices such as ancestor veneration. This distancing is both positive and negative, which perhaps can explain feelings of ambivalence that Asian Americans may have toward their spiritual heritages. On the one hand, new ways of looking at one's inherited tradition can have a "liberating" effect, freeing Asian Americans from the oppressive structures that operate in their respective Asian cultures. On the other, we have lost touch with valuable human resources that can lend meaning, inspiration, and strength to our lives.

Re-site-ing

The question we must ask ourselves is, Where do we go from here? As an Asian American scholar committed to approaching religious and spiritual phenomena from a perspective that is community based and interdisciplinary, the questions become the following: How can I capture the religious experience of Asian Americans in a way that is respectful of their practice and recognizable to them? How can I best bring to light the religious subjectivities of Asian Americans and the worldview that frames them? What intellectual and spiritual resources can I potentially give back to the community?

The method I would like to propose turns on a metaphorical understanding of one's relation to the past: "The relation between past and present . . . requires . . . a willingness to intervene destructively as well as constructively, to shatter received wisdom as well as reconfigure that debris in new and arresting ways."[12] It is in this manner that I approach the notion of ancestor veneration and my Asian spiritual heritage as a whole. I envision three dimensions to this process: retrieval, reexamination, and (re)construction.[13]

The first dimension is retrieval. We must foster scholarship and understanding of Asian spiritual and philosophical traditions from an Asian American point of view. This includes study of texts and historical and contemporary practices and rituals in Asia and Asian America. "Retrieval," in the sense I am proposing, challenges and extends the boundaries of current scholarship on Asian "religions" and on American religious history. New hermeneutical lenses and philosophical concepts need to be developed in order to uncover and understand fully Asian American spirituality. For instance, examination of institutionalized expressions of religion (e.g., temples) is necessary, but taken as a comprehensive measure of Asian

American spirituality is highly misleading; a practice such as ancestor veneration that is often done privately in one's home is easily overlooked. Asian American spirituality and self-understanding often permeate all areas of life, making inadequate the study of even formalized rituals. This is eloquently stated by a Japanese American minister speaking about the members of his rural congregation in central California:

> A sense of silence envelops you and you relate it to Buddhism: a silent, individual spiritual understanding of the world. No words, no doctrines, no scriptures. Just fog around you and the sound of your pruning shear slicing through canes and the mist of your breath floating before you like incense: farming and Buddhism as a way of life.[14]

We must pay special attention to features such as these and to other contemporary expressions and practices in the Asian American community and discern their spiritual function and significance. In relation to traditional forms of ancestor veneration, we can perhaps examine how this ritual has been transformed in a U.S. setting. We must also look at rituals that have not traditionally been considered in a spiritual and philosophical light but involve a similar sensibility: for example, the annual pilgrimages of Japanese Americans to Manzanar and other World War II internment camps;[15] cultural celebrations and festivals;[16] and artistic expressions such as dance, visual expressions, and literature.[17] Such work is already underway, but still more needs to be done.

A second dimension entails reexamination. Critical perspectives reveal the oppressive dimensions of the practice and how it has been used to justify and reinforce a social order that denies full personhood to women and other "outcasts." We need to scrutinize a practice closely, although some would interpret this scrutiny as an "act of rebellion"—one that upsets the cosmos of our ancestral practice, therefore upsetting our ancestors. The narrator in Maxine Hong Kingston's *The Woman Warrior* speaks of the displeasure of her "No name" aunt whose story she reveals: "I do not think she always means me well. I am telling on her, and she was a spite suicide, drowning herself in the drinking water."[18] Within the traditional social configuration, No Name Woman's transgressions are a disgrace, and it is best that she is forgotten. But to most contemporary readers, her story is a tragic one, demonstrating the destructive dimensions of this configuration. How does one reconcile oneself to a practice that has such a history? Can it be remodeled so that the unjust aspects are not perpetuated? Yes. Indeed, I believe it is our duty and obligation to do as best we can to bring about such a transformation. Reexamination, critical analysis, constitutes the first step in this process of setting things right.

While we need to critically interrogate the structures that underwrite ancestor veneration and other Asian religious practices, we also must examine our motivations and role in claiming these practices. We must recognize that these rituals also lay claim on us. Rooted in long-standing traditions that are culturally defined, ancestral practices draw on particular epistemologies that can challenge our commitments and concerns. Here we must be careful not simply to pick and choose what we find most attractive, but rather, we need to deal with the intricacies of the practice. For example, a feminist-inspired approach of ancestor veneration may call on us to transform the practice in liberating ways. However, the ritual also continually pushes us to wrestle with ancestors "closer to home"—family connections and lineages—no matter how painful these connections may be. In this manner, Asian spiritual heritages can become avenues through which we seek new types of resolutions and insights and expand our own worldview.

The third dimension comes from conscious and imaginative (re)construction.[19] It is the dimension that, I believe, is the least widely acknowledged and least creatively explored. The shattering of received wisdom is the prevalent road for academics, who analyze, differentiate, and deconstruct. However, as scholars and as individuals committed to a larger community, can we say that we are acting responsibly when all we do is simply tear up, break down, and then hand over the shattered pieces? We, too, as community-based intellectuals have an obligation to creatively reconfigure the debris. We must strive to generate or at the very least support those who venture new spiritual and philosophical understandings: to make an offering . . . to give back . . . to replace.

Reconstructing involves focusing on what one hopes will be retained. In relation to the concept of ancestor, I would like to emphasize the sensibility it helps to cultivate, which views social relationships and solidarity as primary, which recognizes interdependence as characteristic, and which fosters responsibility and obligation to others. This "right relation" is not only something to be pursued in regard to our contemporaries but also in respect to those who have come before and those who are to come after.

But we might also think of ways in which the concept and ritual need to be revised in order to maintain their relevance. One way to transform the practice is to acknowledge all human beings that have gone before as our ancestors, that is, "democratize" the concept and ritual. Another alternative would be to (re)claim a lineage, that is, (re)construct historically overlooked, unrecognized genealogies (for example, those of women).[20]

Illustrations of this can take the form of historical reconstructions, reworking of myths and rituals, and imaginative journeys.

With a renewed sense of ancestor, we can begin to make the ritual more inspiring, insightful, and meaningful. This is already taking place: many Japanese Americans who still maintain an *obutsudan* (Buddhist home altar)[21] in their homes choose to include the *ihai*[22] of all deceased family members and not just those of male progenitors. There are also altar variations that radically depart form the traditional *obutsudan*. The most memorable one that I have seen consists of a simple arrangement that includes a candle, dried petals as incense, and uniquely framed pictures of the deceased family members. It is placed unconventionally in the busy dining area, where the family is readily reminded of the ancestors' presence and the ancestors in turn can enjoy the everyday goings-on of the household. Still another Japanese practitioner—a college student—keeps a small Buddhist altar in his dorm room. Photos of family members do not adorn his shrine (since most of them are still living), but, rather, an image of Malcolm X is placed before his altar. By maintaining the altar, this student not only pays homage to his Japanese religious heritage but also to the slain black leader, who serves as his inspiration.

An example of a transformed ritual on a much grander scale was realized at the Annual Conference of the World Council of Churches Assembly in 1991 in which Chung Hyun Kyung, a Christian feminist liberation theologian from Korea, brought together oral text, visual images, and Korean and Australian aboriginal dance ("Come, Holy Spirit—Renew the Whole Creation").[23] A large part of Chung's presentation was given over to naming, hence remembering the lives of those who were abused, displaced, forgotten, and violated throughout history—paying altar tribute to hungry ghosts, a transformed ancestor veneration.

While more traditional variants of ancestor veneration may appear elusive among Asian Americans, the sensibility that informs the ritual persists. The metaphor of ancestor remains an important organizing principle that inspires the work of Asian American scholars, artists, and filmmakers. Andrew Lam's work, which began this essay, is a case in point. Another example is Loni Ding, who reconstructs the history of Asians in the United States in her three-part series *Ancestors in the Americas*. Ding is known for her distinctive "documemoir" approach to ethnic filmmaking. Through the retrieval and reexamination of disparate source materials— "archeological sites; graves; rocks; pots, pans and dishes; Asian folklore; customs and sayings; as well as more conventional primary documents such as census records, legislative reports, and period newspaper clippings"—she reaches back in time and re-creates an intimate sense of the past.[24] She then reanimates this vision for her audience through the use of "first-person archetypes" that narrate the story and give voice to "the experiences of a different group of pioneers traditionally left out of the public record."[25] Similar to ancestral rites that blend history, memory, and imagination, Ding conjures ghosts who refuse to be forgotten, and her filmmaking becomes an act of ritual remembrance.

Indeed, a return to ancestral veneration can lead not only to personal transformation (through everyday practice) but also encourage social and political change. Loni Ding's filmmaking is an example of the way in which a consideration of ancestors leads to a renewed consciousness of the Asian American historical struggle. The annual pilgrimage to Manzanar functions in a similar manner, blending spiritual recovery with political awareness.[26] The two-day event includes cultural performances, political speeches, an interfaith ceremony, and obon dancing. While a new interpretive center has been built on the grounds (now a National Historic Site), the cemetery remains the focal point of the pilgrimage. The interfaith service, led by ministers, Buddhist reverends, and Shinto priests, takes place at the stone monument, or Soul Consoling Tower, in the heart of the cemetery. Here pilgrimage visitors gather to remember the eighty-six people buried there, and also more broadly to honor the ten thousand Japanese who suffered the tragic injustice of those interned on the premises during World War II. Through offerings of flowers and other objects, and by participating in the obon dance, visitors pay homage to Japanese American ancestors. They do so not only to remember the Issei and Nisei who suffered racial oppression at the hands of the U.S. government but also to insure that other Americans do not befall a similar fate. These rituals direct the visitor's attention to the past, but they do so for the sake of the present and future. The poet Janice Mirikitani's words capture this spiritual dynamic well:

> Footsteps lead to destiny.
> We dance honoring ancestors
> who claim our home,
> and freedom to pursue our dreams.
> Our voices carve a path for justice:
> Equal rights for all.
>
> We prevail.
> Our future harvested from generations.

From my life
opens countless lives.

The journey continues . . .[27]

Such an ambitious undertaking of retrieval, reexamination, and reconstruction of ancestor veneration and other Asian and Asian American spiritual traditions is necessary. First, it gives back to the community by offering life resources that have the potential to provide orientation and meaning. Second, it pays tribute to our intellectual ancestors; it expands existing scholarship by offering substantive material and challenges current notions of Asian and Asian American religions. For example, it encourages the religious studies scholar to look beyond institutionalized forms of religion; it reconsiders what is viewed as religious and as spiritual; and it contributes to the discussion of religion and social structures.

Seeing ourselves and our work in continuity with our ancestors' spiritual understanding in this way preserves the integrity of their experience. "Re-site-ing" becomes "reciting" the spiritual texts that our ancestors' lives represent; it is perhaps the greatest homage we can pay to them.

Notes

1. Andrew Lam, "Who Will Pick Up the Ritual When I Am Gone?" *Audrey* (June 2003): 57.
2. See, for example, Wan-Li Ho, "Respecting Our Ancestors: Christianity and the Confucian Tradition," *Commonweal* 134 (January 14, 2005): 10–11; Jonathan H. X. Lee, "Pilgrimage of the Spirit: Connecting with My Ancestors," *Review of Vietnamese Studies* 2, no. 1 (2002), http://hmongstudies.com/Lee2002.pdf; idem, "Ancestral Veneration in Vietnamese Spiritualities," *Review of Vietnamese Studies* 3, no. 1 (2003), http://hmongstudies.com/Lee2003.pdf; and Fei Xiaotong, "The Shallowness of Cultural Tradition," in *Land without Ghosts: Chinese Impressions of America from the Mid-nineteenth Century to the Present*, ed. R. David Arkush and Leo O. Lee (Berkeley: University of California Press, 1989). In Fei's essay he reflects on the differences between American and Chinese cultures, especially their conceptions of the past.
3. From the Pilot National Asian American Political Survey, 2000–2001. Responses are drawn from the survey question "What is your religious *preference*?" (emphasis added) and may not reflect the hybrid nature of Asian American religious identity. According to the study, 46 percent of Asia Americans identify themselves as "Christian." The category "Christian" here includes those who self-identified as "Protestants," "Catholics," and "Christians." It is interesting to note that the next highest category of religious preference is "None" (19 percent), which may reflect the fact that Asian religious practices (such as ancestor veneration) do not fit neatly into American definitions of religious affiliation based on a world-religions model. See Pei-te Lien and Tony Carnes, "The Reli-

gious Demography of Asian American Boundary Crossing," in *Asian American Religions: The Making and Remaking of Borders and Boundaries*, ed. Tony Carnes and Fenggang Yang (New York: New York University Press, 2004), 40.

4. For an extended discussion of the ways in which Korean American Protestant Christians have blended the ancestor veneration ritual (*chesa*) into their Christian practice, see Su Yon Pak et al., "Resourcing the Life Circle: The Practice of Re-membering the Generations Before," in *Singing the Lord's Song in a New Land: Korean American Practices of Faith* (Louisville, KY: Westminster John Knox Press, 2005), 45–55.

5. "On White Ashes" (*Hakkotsu no Gobunshō*) is a letter written by the fifteenth-century Buddhist priest Rennyo Shonin that is regularly read at Japanese American Buddhist funerals.

6. In Japanese Buddhist culture, memorial services (*senzo kuyo*) are held on the forty-ninth day (after the person has expired) and the one hundredth day. These services then take place to mark the first-year anniversary of the death, third-year, seventh-year, thirteenth-year, etc. Because of this cycle, Japanese American Buddhists frequently attend these services.

7. C. Takeda, "Family Religion in Japanese: *Ie* and Its Religious Faith," in *Ancestors*, ed. William H. Newell (The Hague: Mouton Publishers, 1976), 119. Ancestor veneration is also organized according to incorporate *dozoku* groups in which extended family is included and founding ancestors of a particular household (*honke*) are venerated. A particularly good discussion of *ie* is found in Dorinne K. Kondo, *Crafting Selves: Power, Gender, and Discourses of Identity in a Japanese Workplace* (Chicago: University of Chicago Press, 1990), 121–31.

8. The Second World War had a harrowing effect on Japanese Americans, not to mention their religious practice. Buddhist ministers (and Buddhism by extension) were the first to be interned. Families felt compelled to eradicate any trace of their connections to Japan and to Japanese culture, including their *obutsudans* (home altars). Many of these *obutsudans*—often the centers of religious practice—were burned or abandoned. When Issei and Nisei entered the camps, they were subjected to government-sanctioned "Americanization" programs that further reinforced a sense of alienation from their Japanese heritage. While Japanese Americans still found ways to maintain and foster their religious commitments during this period, they (and their progeny) still suffer the long-term effects of this oppression.

9. Susan Mukai, in *Rising Waters* 2 (Santa Cruz: Asian American Studies Planning Group, University of California at Santa Cruz, 1977), n.p.

10. Joy Kogawa, *Obasan* (Boston: David R. Godine, Publisher, 1981), 22.

11. There are exceptional cases here, mainly carried out in the classroom. Scholars have become increasingly sensitive to the ways in which Asian ritual traditions are carried out in "communities of practice." As Tracy Sayuki Tiemeier notes, "I do invite the students to think more critically about these traditions *as* traditions within particular religious communities that have their own inner logics (even if they are changing and porous) of spiritual diagnosis, path and goal, and have vibrant lives within matrices of beliefs, practices and communities" ("Retrieving 'Asian Spirituality' in North American Contexts: An Interfaith Proposal," *Spiritus* 6 [2006]: 228–33, quotation on 231–32, original emphasis). The number of courses on Asian American religions (versus Asian religions) also provides opportunities for critical engagement.

12. Martin Jay, *Force Fields: Between Intellectual History and Cultural Critique* (New York: Routledge, 1993), 1. In *Force Fields* Jay attempts to bring together and discuss different

historical strands of cultural criticism. Jay's insights that the given quotation represents I find especially apt since I interpret his project as one in which he struggles to make sense of his lineage or ancestors, albeit intellectual ones.

13. These dimensions do not follow one after the other, but, rather, they occur simultaneously. It is useful to compare the framework I propose with others, such as those offered by Elisabeth Schüssler Fiorenza, in which she unfolds a hermeneutics of suspicion, proclamation, remembrance, and creative actualization (*Bread Not Stone: The Challenge of Feminist Biblical Interpretation* [Boston: Beacon Press, 1984]). Another interesting delineation is found in Mitsuye Yamada, *Desert Run: Poems and Stories* (Latham, NY: Kitchen Table, Women of Color Press, 1988), in which she suggests returning, resisting, and connecting.

14. David Mas Masumoto, *Country Voices* (Del Rey, CA: Inaka Countryside Publications, 1987), 145.

15. See, for example, Joanne Doi, "Tule Lake Pilgrimage: Dissonant Memories, Sacred Journey," in *Revealing the Sacred in Asian and Pacific America*, ed. Jane Naomi Iwamura and Paul Spickard (New York: Routledge, 2003), 273–89; and Jane Naomi Iwamura, "Critical Faith: Japanese Americans and the Birth of a New Civil Religion" (in progress).

16. See, for example, "Belief and Practice: Buddhist Obon Festival," *Religion and Ethics Newsweekly*, July 18, 2003, http://www.pbs.org/wnet/religionandethics/week646/belief.html.

17. An especially good example of literary analysis that pays attention to Asian (American) religious practice is Teruyo Ueki, "Obasan: Revelations in a Paradoxical Scheme," *MELUS* 18 (1993): 5–20.

18. Maxine Hong Kingston, *The Woman Warrior: Memoirs of a Girlhood among Ghosts* (New York: Knopf, 1976), 16.

19. I am extending the understanding of religious concepts as products of "imaginative construction" as Gordon D. Kaufman offers in his *The Theological Imagination: Constructing the Concept of God* (Philadelphia: Westminster Press, 1981); and idem, *In Face of Mystery* (Cambridge, MA: Harvard University Press, 1993).

20. There are certain "disabilities" of which one has to be aware when constructing one's ancestral lineage in such a way. See Toni Morrison, "Rootedness: The Ancestor as Foundation," in *Black Women Writers (1950–1980): A Critical Evaluation*, ed. Mari Evans (Garden City, NY: Anchor Press / Doubleday, 1984), 339–45, where Morrison offers the example of Hagar and Reba in her *Song of Solomon* (New York: Knopf, 1977), as an instance of "the female who reproduces the female who reproduces the female," which diminishes relationships to and with men, and as a result, their "abilities" (344). Morrison is correct to point out that "if we don't keep in touch with the ancestor then we are, in fact, lost" (344). The overall project I have proposed brings with it the ominous and cautionary warning to those who undertake it (or not): "When you kill the ancestor you kill yourself" (344). I thank Young Mi Angela Pak for bringing Morrison's insightful piece to my attention.

21. I explore Japanese American *obutsudans* in greater depth in "Altared States: Exploring the Legacy of Japanese American Butsudan Practice," *Pacific World: Journal of the Institute of Buddhist Studies* 3, no. 5 (2003): 275–91.

22. An *ihai* is a certificate on which the Buddhist and given names of a deceased person are written.

23. For the written text, see Chung Hyun Kyung, "Come, Holy Spirit—Renew the Whole Creation," in *Signs of the Spirit: Official Report, Seventh Assembly*, ed. Michael Kinnamon (Geneva: World Council of Churches, 1991), 37–47.

24. Loni Ding, "Some Conceptual Concerns in Producing *Ancestors in the Americas*," Ancestors in the Americas, http://www.cetel.org/docu.html.

25. "An Interview with Loni Ding, director of *Ancestors in the Americas*," AsiaSource, http://www.asiasource.org/asianamerica/ding.cfm.

26. See Doi, "Tule Lake Pilgrimage"; and Iwamura, "Critical Faith."

27. Mirikitani's poem appears on memorial sculptures erected in the Japantowns in San Francisco, San Jose, and Los Angeles. The landmarks, funded by the California Civil Liberties Pubic Education Program (CCLPEP), were commissioned to represent the "moving history" of Japanese Americans. I transcribed the poem during my visit to the Los Angeles landmark on November 4, 2006.

Part 3

Reorienting We-Self

Chapter Seven

Cooking without Recipes

Interstitial Integrity

Rita Nakashima Brock

I burst through the door of a low, light-green stucco cottage and scream, "They have taken my mother! The Communists have kidnapped her and are brainwashing her!" This nightmare began to interrupt my childhood sleep after my family moved from Okinawa to Kansas. I was six at the time. In the dream I had struggled up a thick, jungle-covered hillside to the cottage. My mother was captive behind the locked doors of the hut, hidden in a pine forest. To find her I had stolen quietly between neighborhood houses into the woods, weakly lit by the late afternoon sun. I could see my mother through a dirty window, tied to a chair. I shouted through the murky glass, "Mother, do you know me? Ayako, it's Rita!" Her blank stare left me feeling as if the ground had dissolved under me and a whirlpool of despair sucked me under.

I was bereft of my mother in Kansas. We had been relocated there by my white American stepfather, and she had ceased to speak to me in Japanese, forcing me to switch from our common mother tongue into a language alien to us both. We spoke without mutual fluency; and although I understood her silences, I did not know I understood them. Our primary connections were sustained by food.

Every December a large cardboard box arrived from Fukuoka, Japan. On Christmas morning our family opened it, knowing that my mother would be delighted with the *nori*, *aji-no-moto*, dried tuna, and *somen* and *udon* noodles that would sustain us for the year. Until I stayed at school all

---

This is a revised version of "Interstitial Integrity: Reflections toward an Asian American Women's Theology," in *Introduction to Christian Theology: Contemporary North American Perspectives*, ed. Roger A. Badham (Louisville, KY: Westminster John Knox Press, 1997), 183–96.

day, my mother based my lunches around treasures from that box. When our family sat down to dinner, she had often cooked two meals. She put greens or black-eyed peas, pork chops, and cornbread before my father. My mother, younger sister, and I ate rice, sliced vegetables she pickled herself, and meat fried until it was crispy.

Sometimes I watched her prepare dinner. She mixed the bread batter and poured it into a hot, cast-iron frying pan before putting it in the oven. We all loved the crunchy dark brown crust that formed from the hot pan. She rinsed the rice, measured the final water with her fingers, put a piece of *kombu* in it, and let it steam on the stove. Sometimes she experimented, frying rice with leftover roast beef or peas, or she tempura-fried asparagus and broccoli. My father avoided the Japanese dishes, while we three women sometimes shared his southern food. We all had salad and pie. Unbeknownst to my father, who loved my mother's cooking, she spiced his food with soy sauce and *aji-no-moto*. Although she owned several American cookbooks, she rarely used them, and her Japanese and fusion dishes were always improvised. This experimentation and indifference to recipes characterize not only my own cooking style but also the way I have lived my life.

My identity resembles my mother's eclectic meals, a fusion of ingredients annealed by the fires of growing up on three continents as a Japanese, mixed-race woman and a liberal Protestant educated in the second half of the twentieth century in U.S. schools. This cross-cultural process has resulted in a consciousness I call "interstitial integrity." Integration brings many diverse parts together, the way a collection of ingredients finally makes a dish. Integrity is how we know ourselves and make choices that sustain our values in relationship with others. It is a complex, evolving process over time, captured in moments of self-awareness and self-acceptance—brief interludes of consciousness that appear within the tossing turbulence of many people and places.

"Interstitial" comes from *interstitium*, and it is used in biology to describe tissue situated in vital organs. The tissue is not organ tissue, but, rather, it connects the organs to one another. Interstitial tissue lives inside things, distinct but inseparable from what would otherwise be disconnected. It is a channel of life in and out of things separated and different. It makes a living, pulsating unity, both many and one. Without interstitiality, parts of my life would wither and die, unnourished by the connective tissues of memory that constantly flow in and out of my consciousness. Interstitial integrity is how I improvise a self, recognizing the diverse cultures and experiences that have made me who I am. It is how I mix a life together from myriads of ingredients.

Myths of Purity

I have found that constructing a life as a mixed-race, Asian North American woman has been a countercultural process. The United States prefers its citizens to be pure racial types and monolingual people who can be categorized easily as friend or foe, elect or damned, patriot or terrorist. This emphasis on purity is deeply embedded in the founding myths of the society. It continues to structure relationships in the larger culture racially, religiously, and sexually. In understanding that I have an American identity and citizenship, I have sought to take responsibility for the ambiguities of this identity, especially in relation to the liberal Protestant religious tradition that is mine and that is embedded in many of the worst aspects of American history.

Calvinist Puritans in North America believed they were the elect of God who had arrived at a Promised Land. Disillusioned with their attempts to reform England and feeling like persecuted victims of empire, they believed they could overcome their history and start over. They would create a new covenant with God based on the biblical church. Their covenant would redeem humanity through the destruction of the sinful world and the restoration of its primordial innocence in Eden. They lived by an arc of mythic time, which pushed forward by looking backward. The arc ran from its pristine beginnings in the New Testament, through the present time of corruption, to a new and millennial future that would re-create or restore the innocent and pure past. The arc created their relationship to the present as a problem to be endured and overcome. They could not see what was directly in front of them or relate to the land and its people except as dimensions of their myths. The conquest of native land, genocide, and slavery were required to bring the end times to pass, part of the struggle against evil.[1]

The Puritans viewed Native Americans in three ways: as agents of the devil, especially the French papists; as instruments of divine judgment against Puritan sins; and as the original inhabitants of Eden, which they would replace with a New Eden. Puritans who respected Native Americans were regarded as apostates and traitors. When the Puritans were devastated in the King Philip War with the Indians, their Reforming Synod of 1679 did not determine that the cause of their defeat was their treatment of Native Americans. Instead, they concluded that their losses were divine punishment for their lack of sufficient piety.

This piety was grounded in a Protestant suspicion of the senses. The sufficiently pious lived in the world based on an imaginary vision of what they were living toward. The elect should avoid acute, sensory attunements to what was immediately in front of them. Sensory appreciation of the world was suspect because it was corrupted by sin, and attention to the senses interfered with the ability of believers to read and hear the Word of God. This antisensual Puritan piety led to a religious sensibility that was intensely subjective and extremely self-centered. It was ethically blind to relationships in present time and space. At the same time, it lived in a constant state of insecurity. As the Cherokee scholar Laura E. Donaldson notes, "Colonizers were frequently haunted by a sense of insecurity, terrified by the obscurity of the 'native mentality,' and overwhelmed by indigenous societies' apparent intractability in the face of government."[2]

As inheritors of this Puritan legacy, Americans live by myths of pristine beginnings, noble founding fathers, and the belief that Americans are always on the side of what is right. American myths of humanity are based on an arc of time that begins with "natural man," who is victimized by evil and who will be restored in the future by continuing to believe in what is good and pure. This myth of primordial restoration requires an illusion of innocence and belief in a mission that God protects and blesses, and it views American ideas and values as signs of progress toward a better world.[3]

This Christian narcissism of purity and piety informs what Renato Rosaldo has called imperialist nostalgia. Human beings whom imperial colonizers have fought, subdued, and disempowered are recast in the imagination of the colonizers. Faced with guilt about their destructive past, imperialists seek to reclaim their lost innocence. They think of their victims as noble savages, residing in their subjective imagination in the pristine past. Native Americans come to embody "natural" man, just as they were once thought of as inhabitants of Eden. As this mythic icon and stereotype, Native Americans symbolize the colonizers' redemption, as the colonizers imagine them to have been uncontaminated, preconquest ideal types.[4]

Calvinist thinking about Genesis and the myth of primordial restoration, especially, led to one later strand of imperialist nostalgia that connected Native Americans and Asians through ideas of nature. The Puritans believed that God had created the world as good and that studying nature provided some access to divine intelligence, which reflected the importance of Christian humanist thinking on John Calvin. Jonathan Edwards (1703–58) asserted that the human mind and the world were, ultimately, an emanation of God's mind. He believed, however, that sin corrupted human capacities to access this truth.[5]

Ralph Waldo Emerson (1803–82) drew on Edwards's intellectual legacy about nature and God, but he rejected the emphasis on sin. Emerson believed the human mind, through nature, had direct access to God. He condemned conventional forms of Christianity and valorized self-reliant men who trusted this access and refused social conformity. Emerson, as the model of self-reliance, had a conventional household maintained by his wife, his mother, three female servants, and a gardener. For Emerson the true position of nature in regard to man is akin to woman's position in regard to man. Nature is subordinate to mind. It has little value in itself, but rather, it attains value as it reflects and supports man in his ever-changing internalizing of nature as a guide to spiritual life. "All the facts in natural history taken by themselves have no value, but are barren, like a single sex. But marry it to human history, and it is full of life." Woman's relation to man was the relationship of Asia to the West. This use of Asia reflected Emerson's interest in Hinduism and Confucianism at a time when European humanists were fascinated with India and China as cradles of human origins and civilizations. "I call her Asia," Emerson said of his wife. Asia meant a grand, "natural" faith; mystery; flow; and passive contemplation—all of which could be consumed by the active, masculine West. A mystical relationship to nature—that is, Asia—could unite the self with the cosmos. Emerson reported a dream in which the world shriveled to the point he was able to swallow it whole. His Self was All and all consuming. The Western Man embodied the Soul, which was given natural spirituality by Asia. Each man was the god of his own Olympus going it alone.[6]

Emerson's use of Asia is part of a long historical legacy grounded in mythic understandings of the earth as divine creation. From as early as the fourth century CE, the Ganges in India was sometimes identified as the fourth river of Genesis 2. Many medieval navigation maps of the fifteenth century followed this identification of the Ganges with paradise, marking Eden as a forbidden island off the coast of Cipangu, today's China. Columbus likely used such maps when he set off to India in the "Orient," literally east, which was the direction of Eden and the direction Europe's churches faced. He sailed west to reach the east, believing paradise to be at the nipple of a round globe. There he believed he would find the gold and jewels flowing out of paradise, that is, the Edenic milk flowing from the nipple, the milk of the Ganges.[7]

Primordial myths of restoration run into the future while gazing backward. In Columbus's time, apocalyptic fevers ran high, and the end of the world was predicted to arrive in 1650. Columbus thought he would be the messiah of a new age to come by finding paradise in Asia. Instead, he became the harbinger of colonialism and genocide, like King Midas, turning life into cold cash. Asia, too, had its myth of colonization based on a unifying idea of Asian identity. In 1641 Japan closed its doors to the West to avoid being colonized, only to reopen them in the mid-nineteenth century to colonize its neighbors. Nami Kim's chapter in this volume addresses the Japanese colonialist use of Asia, at nearly the same time as Emerson used it in the United States.[8]

During Emerson's time, feminists such as Elizabeth Cady Stanton sought to oppose the Christian subordination of white women based on Genesis 2 by dismantling the primordial myths of Christianity. *The Women's Bible*, published in 1898, drew on Christian humanism, the founding myth of American democracy, and the strand of Calvinist Christianity that also influenced Emerson.[9] At this same time, Protestant Christian white women, who could not obtain equal rights to preach and teach in their churches, sailed to Asia to convert "Oriental" women. The women missionaries ignored indigenous traditions, imposing their Victorian, Christian values on women they believed were even more oppressed than themselves. As Kwok Pui-lan has noted, this white colonialist religious pattern was repeated during the 1970s by some white American feminists who argued that their feminism would save women of color.[10]

In the late nineteenth century, after they confined Indians to reservations, white imperialists, afflicted by guilt, turned to Native Americans to restore their own imaginary, mythic relationship to what they thought of as natural. In addition, the white West required the mysterious foreignness of Asia for its own salvation. To discover "true" Asian religions, they ignored Asian America, reaching across the Pacific for their salvation in a reversal of the missionaries who took Christian salvation to Asia. In 1979 a white male scholar of Buddhism published a book on American Buddhism that ignored the largest number of Buddhists in North America, Asian Americans, who have been practicing it for many generations and brought it from Asia. He perpetuated the perception that white male imperialists are the experts on "true" Buddhism, which they import pristine, directly from Asia, in the elite versions taken from male-dominated practices in Asia, a transmission of male dominance that interpreted Buddhism in mythic Protestant terms as individual salvation.[11] In most forms of Buddhism in Asia only an elite, highly trained few, mostly men, undertake the study of texts or the rigorous practices of meditation to benefit others, who support them by giving alms to begging monks. These exchange relationships of generosity spread merit through the entire community but are not part of the way white Americans practice Buddhism. In 1975 Gary Snyder, a poet who studied Zen in Japan, won a Pulitzer Prize for *Turtle Island*, which intertwines Asian and Native American religions as the nature-oriented traditions that will restore Euro-Americans to the environment.[12]

Notions of the Native American noble savage and true Buddhist of Asia have been imported into the American primordial myth, now operating in what has been called America's Third Great Awakening. One major aspect of this religious revival is the movement away from organized religion to spirituality. Many who claim to be spiritual but not religious borrow Asian religious practices, romanticize nature, and fetishize Native Americans. White, New Age feminists relate to women of color, just as white men relate to men of color, as nostalgic imperialists. The cultural practices of real human beings are sanitized and idealized, uprooted from their long history in highly organized, community-based cultural systems, and transplanted into American primordial myths, where they are individualized as echoes of Emerson's salvation in nature.[13]

The past half century of cultural conflicts, U.S. imperial aspirations, and the rise of the Religious Right have sought to reassert Protestant versions of the American restoration myth in the face of an increasingly globalized world. Those who cling most fiercely to restoration myths fail to note the complexities of ethical decisions or the often-tragic consequences of even the best moral choices. The American restoration myth struggles under the cumulative weight of what it cannot remember and what it increasingly cannot understand in a world resistant to American hegemony.

Restoration myths starve the society. In seeking to move into a better future, people live always partly in an imaginary world, dissociated and unable to integrate the fullness of being that eludes them. They are, therefore, the least equipped to understand themselves or their relationships. They use theoretical or imaginary ideals to drive the world forward. They live outside the present, which the loss of primordial creation has made dangerous. They are easily emotionally manipulated, which drives the powerful engine of consumerism. Those who live inside myths of restoration leave behind too much destruction and too little love, settling for hope in an imaginary future, while remaining perpetually unrequited and lonely.

White Male Integrity and the Other

I did not grow up in an Asian American community, and I had little inoculation against white American hegemony. I received my picture of America and Americans from my stepfather and the military bases of my childhood, which had a distinctive class structure of enlisted men, officers, and their related dependents. I learned that a person of integrity sustains a system of ethical principles, which measure good and evil, true and false, and insider and outsider. A person should hold these values independent of influence. The masculine self, head of all dependents, is supposed to be autonomous, stoic, and self-possessed. Women are, unfortunately, permeable, acquiescent, dependent, and too emotionally bonded to others. Women, if we are good, maintain one form of impermeability: sexual chastity. Good women, therefore, function as gateways to male access to females.

I also imbibed the racial stereotypes of American culture, which set men and women of color against the integrity of the white imperialist. Asian men were stereotyped as obsequious, servile, and feminine, like the character Hop Sing in the old Western series *Bonanza*. As mysteriously exotic and dangerous, Asian men became sinister evil geniuses or exotic Kung Fu gurus who rescued white people. A *Yellow Book* television advertisement in August 2006 satirizes this last stereotype by depicting a clueless young white man who seeks knowledge from a spiritual teacher. The teacher is played by David Carradine, who was also Kwai Chang Caine in the 1970s successful classic television Western series *Kung Fu*.

Westerns epitomize the powerful male loner who avenges victims and fights for justice. In the *Kung Fu* series Buddhism empowers the solitary male avenger, Caine. He was born of a Chinese mother and white American father and was raised as a Shaolin monk before traveling to the West. Chinese Buddhism is pictured as an apparition of white nostalgia, and Carradine, a white actor, is an apparition of a mixed-race person. Caine's Chinese life appears in mystical, soft-focus fogs—the studio used for filming the scenes of China was once the set of *Camelot*. Whenever Caine faces an evil villain, he flashes back to his pure, foreign spiritual roots. Then he defeats his evil opponent and saves the innocent.

The 2006 advertisement ridicules the original show's mystifications of Buddhism, exposing it as a commercial product for Western consumption. Carradine pokes fun at his guru role by exaggerating its religious mystifications while referring the seeker's every question to the *Yellow Book* for all necessary knowledge of life. Carradine sells pizza, reinforces his original association with Caine, and inscribes his role as guru in American capitalist terms by saying it is a material world. He draws out the phrase "dot com" into a resonant chant, "dot commmm." The advertisement's coy, self-referential, ironic, entertaining, deconstructionist tone was popular in the white religion academy during the Clinton years.[14]

Subjected to stereotypes about Asian women, I grew up feeling both invisible and too visible in relation to white men. I was the target of sexual advances based on stereotypes. At the same time I felt I had to enact some of these stereotypes or become totally invisible. To escape orientalization in adolescence, I studied makeup techniques to make my round face look more oval and tried perms to keep curled my straight, lank hair. I attempted to colonize my flesh, to remove its stigma of race and foreignness, to become American. Asian women were Dragon Ladies who connived with evil Asian men, or we were submissive, sweet, and accommodating Lotus Blossoms who loved their white male subjugators. Sexually sophisticated Suzie Wongs or Miss Saigons were updated Madame Butterflies. These fantasies about Asian women are lived out in the contemporary mail-order bride phenomenon, sex tourism to Asia, and the trafficking of poor Asian women and girls to American brothels.[15]

David H. Hwang ridicules these stereotypes in his award-winning play *M. Butterfly*. The play uses the true story of a hapless white diplomat, named Gallimard, who is in love with what he thinks is a gorgeous Chinese opera singer named Song Liling. However, Liling is a man highly skilled at playing women, a fact that eludes the culturally ignorant Gallimard, who does not notice that men can perform feminine roles in Chinese opera. Gallimard mentions his love of the story of Madame Butterfly to a Chinese official, played by the same actor who is the beautiful Song. Gallimard's romantic vision is met with scorn.

Imagine the reverse, the Chinese man asks. A blonde cheerleader in Texas falls deeply in love with a rich Japanese businessman who promises to return to marry her. Pregnant, she spurns a marriage offer from a Kennedy and waits for her love while raising their son. Then, when she discovers he has married a beautiful, kind Japanese woman, she kills herself so he can take their son and raise him in Japan with his wife. In his complex, postcolonial allegory of East Asia and the West, Hwang exposes the cultural ignorance, political stupidity, rape mentality, and narcissism of the Western colonial mind. He concludes his play with the onstage transformation of the Western man into the fantasy of his obsessive, narcissistic love, Madame Butterfly, who kills herself as the final lights are extinguished.[16]

Imaginary Homelands

Madame Butterfly was my mother's favorite story, but she did not read the story through the lens of a white male imperialist. For her the story was about a woman betrayed by love who fought to survive. My mother, too, waited for a man, my Puerto Rican father, who left her with their child and never came back. She found another, better man to marry, whom she followed to the United States with both the child of her first love and the child of her husband, my younger sister. She did not see herself as a suicidal heroine, but she identified with what Butterfly felt in the face of love betrayed and lost. It touched her deeply and, perhaps, helped her feel better about her choice to survive rather than die.

When I arrived with her in Kansas in 1956, Japan was a hated country. Many days as a child, after I spent my waking hours seeing few Asian faces, I would catch a sudden glimpse of myself in a mirror and be startled by the face peering back. It looked strange, even to me. My mother began to seem foreign and opaque. I took refuge in remembering Japan as a place where I was loved and protected, a lush world, in stark contrast to the dry, brown prairies of Kansas and the hostile white schoolmates who called me "dirty Jap." Japan eventually receded into an "imaginary homeland," a term Salmon Rushdie used to describe his childhood memories of India, uninformed by visits. Japan also became my version of a primordial myth of innocence.[17]

Reality, however, was much more complex. In my nightmare it might seem that the feared Communists were Americans and that safety was Okinawa. Perhaps, however, the dream was my attempt to disrupt my nostalgia for Japan. The house of Communist captivity was deep in the pine forest of my childhood Japan, not the brown prairies of Kansas. Even as I clung to an imaginary homeland, I sought to find acceptance in the only place I spoke the language. I had no choice but to become an American, and I wanted to belong. Maybe I sought to free my mother from being Japanese so I could have the American mother I wanted in Kansas, a sign of how bewildered I felt in my struggle to disorient and reorient my life in the United States.

In 1964, about a year after my nightmare ceased to haunt me, my father was sent to Landstuhl, Germany, on a three-year tour of duty. Although we lived with him on a U.S. military base, my art and history teachers encouraged me to explore German history and culture. In cities such as Frankfurt, Mannheim, and Cologne I was transported from Kansas to Oz through beautiful churches; sumptuous palaces; exotic foods; art museums; and operas, symphonies, and ballets. I immersed myself in the language and culture of a people whom my stepfather, a prisoner of war in World War II, despised.

At the same time that I absorbed German culture, my friends and I created a hermetically sealed oasis of American life within the walls of our military base. We watched old versions of American television shows on the base broadcast system, danced to Motown music at our local teen club, studied in schools with imported American teachers, attended church led by American ministers, and bought American snacks at the military post exchange. As we constantly compared our memories of the United States with life "on the economy," Germany fell far short. In our America everything was better. But what my friends described as home in Chicago, San Antonio, and San Francisco were places I had never been. They sounded as strange to me as Germans and Germany had seemed when I first arrived. I learned homesickness for places I had to imagine, since I lacked real memories, while pretending not to like a land I found wonderful.

When I finally returned to Japan during my senior year in college, I looked forward, finally, to the one place I was not a stranger. I discovered I was no longer Japanese. I could barely understand the language and could not speak it. My hand gestures were too big, and I walked too boldly. While neither the United States nor Germany was home, Japan was irretrievably lost. I would have to learn to live in the interstices of several worlds, to live with several worlds inside me, not simply one or even two, while struggling to make a life neither totally within nor totally outside these worlds.

The Creation of Asian America

Asian America is a palimpsest. The traces of Asia's many races, cultures, and religions are written myriad times over its single surface. The first and oldest layers of immigrant texts are from China and Japan, with smaller groups from India, the Philippines, and Korea. None used the term "Asian American." After the 1965 Immigration Act the numbers of Koreans, Filipinos, Vietnamese, Cambodians, Hmong, Pakistanis, Indians, Thais, and Pacific Islanders grew significantly. The use of "Asian American" emerged to identify a political movement. It also became a racial designation, however inadequate. At the beginning of the twenty-first century and in the wake of 9/11, the movement began to pay better attention to Muslims and those from West or South Asia.[18]

The politics of Asia and the United States are continually rewritten on the Asian American palimpsest, obliterating parts of old faded script on the parchment with fresh ink. On the one hand, tensions among Asian countries arrive with new immigrants to North America. For example, the Japanese colonization of Korea and China is sometimes relived in the suspicions of Korean and Chinese immigrants against Japanese Americans. These antagonisms erupted in the 1990s with new evidence of Japan's forced sexual slavery of Asian women before and during World War II.[19] On the other hand, in the Asian American movement, whatever transpired in Asia is often overwritten by the racial politics of the United States. Our histories and cultural traditions, layered into an ad hoc, pan-Asian story, are inscribed in English, our one common language. We engage a common struggle against racism, create friendships across old national boundaries, and enact forms of hospitality organized around eclectic potlucks.

This system of layers—of identities claimed and denied, of old conflicts sublimated and transplanted, and of hybrid forms integrated interstitially—characterizes the development of an American identity from Asians and their descendants. It is the story of race and immigration on North American soil. Whiteness is itself also a construct of racialized identity related to the history of Europeans in Europe and transplanted into an identity constructed by colonization and contact with Native Americans, enslaved Africans, Latinos, and Asian Americans. In the nineteenth century non-British immigrants, such as the poor from Ireland, had to prove their whiteness in court to gain naturalized citizenship.[20]

Interstitial integrity more accurately describes how human beings construct a self in any culture. We draw life from every relationship in our lives. We are imprinted with the voices that give us language, the emotional inflections and words by which we identify feelings, the body rhythms we enact, the ways we examine the world and interact with it, and the knowledge that we come to make our own. We do not choose the others who live in us, but nonetheless, they are how we become who we are. We are constituted by these complex relationships to the world as we internalize them. Korean Americans refer to *nun chi* (literally, eye measure). *Nun chi* is the ability to observe, assess, and make judgments based on a self-possessed awareness of living in multiple worlds while maintaining an attitude of concern and compassion. It is exercised by the practice of memory and reflection on values in context. It is being present while being aware of being present and examining what we hold together as we weave it.[21]

My self is a constant conversation, sometimes even a conflicted, cacophonous argument. I am as much the traces of Japanese grammar, which shaped my first fluency in language, and the cultural sensibilities of my first caregivers as I am my education in U.S. military schools and liberal higher education. My Japanese family practiced Shinto rituals for weddings and Buddhist funerals, finding value in both traditions. My mother handed me an idealized version of my early life in Japan, so I can only infer what courage and skill it took for her to survive in the aftermath of war with a mixed-race child in a xenophobic culture. She worked as a nurse at a U.S. military hospital, married one of the American medics, and erased my birth father by never speaking of him.

From my stepfather I learned an enlisted man's suspicion of authority and from my mother a respect for teachers and doctors. My father, a white southerner who grew up on a farm, was direct and blunt, while my mother was indirect and emotionally reserved. My mother felt superior to Koreans and Chinese, as my father did to African Americans; but I grew up on integrated U.S. military bases, where my best friends were as likely to be Latino or black as white. The only racial group I tended to avoid was Asian Americans, who made me uncomfortable because they reminded me of what I was trying to overcome in becoming American.

Growing up in Asia, North America, and Europe, I struggled to understand the experiences and relationships of my life, to harmonize their dissonances so that I would be less of a mystery to myself. I studied Japanese in college and graduate school, which helped me understand my thinking patterns and values. I did not, however, regain fluency. I fought conflicting impulses to know and not to know a language my mother had worked so hard to help me forget. In my study I learned that nouns and verbs are fluid and changeable, but verbs are of greater importance. The more artful and less direct a communication, the more it shows appreciation for the intelligence of the listener and the more it gives breathing space for negotiation between people. In addition, the choice of words differs according to the relationship of speaker to listener, which requires social knowledge and sophistication. Men and women speak different forms of Japanese. Women speak in longer, more diplomatic ways than men, even to each other. Children also use a distinctive discourse, and when speaking in front of or to children, adults adopt their language. Everyone avoids, whenever possible, the use of the singular, first-person personal pronoun "I," although men use it more often. The avoidance of "I" orients the listener to the action taking place in a nexus of relationships because this nexus is more important than a single actor. The actor is only one part of the whole meaning of what happens. Frequent use of "I" and direct and blunt speech are regarded as egotistical and socially stupid.

This sense of fluidity of forms, of larger wholes, indirect speech, and the limits of "I" thinking inform my commitment to interstitial integrity and the improvisational mix by which I have made a life. In understanding the complexities of American myths of restoration and purity, I seek to undermine their colonial structures of race and gender and their obsessions with purity and victims. I do so as one who chooses not to avoid the ambiguities of being a woman of color in the United States. At the same time, I believe that the history of U.S. politics and its current imperialist actions compel me, as a liberal Christian and feminist committed to justice, to refuse to limit my sensibilities to national politics or an Asian American framework. I have a responsibility to claim forms of power and agency handed to me by citizenship and education and to deepen my attunement to historical and material realities in order to understand how to use power wisely, for life.[22]

Living with Interstitial Integrity

The struggle to be an Asian American woman, its complexities, disappointments, and struggles, was captured in Maxine Hong Kingston's landmark work *The Woman Warrior: Memoirs of a Girlhood among Ghosts*, first published in 1976. This book defies pure categories such as fiction or nonfiction, history or myth, autobiography or story. In it Kingston describes her mother's "talk-story" of her life as a healer and conqueror of ghosts in China. Kingston imagines her mother's strength and capacity to survive in China as her being a strong eater. A strong eater is undeterred by strangeness, by what others regard with anxiety or suspicion. A strong eater can handle what has no recipes, life off the menu.

Kingston describes the struggle of her strong-eater mother to survive within the structures of gender and culture in the Chinese American community in Stockton, California, and within a racist and sexist society. Kingston's observations about family and community capture the ambiguity of being a Chinese American woman. In that community, Wendy Ho observes,

> The daughter, as her mother before, and each in her own challenge and degree, attempts to disrupt and subvert the discourses which confine their potential. Both their stories and voices generate an interactive and multiple sense of their similarities and differences as mothers/daughters, of their possible complicity in traditional/ dominant power configurations and strategies of appeasement, and of their subversive signifying strategies for survival. . . . There is no unified, centered tradition in her communities in America that allows [Kingston] as a Chinese American woman to speak easily and forthrightly about her own person. The self is often fragmented, split and invisible to the self and is defined directly by a conflicting web of interpersonal relations and roles.[23]

Women, gays, lesbians, bisexual and transgender people, and those of mixed race are often pressured not to challenge sexism, homophobia, and racism in Asian American communities. To preserve their dignity and resist racism, women sometimes work to hide domestic violence, sexual abuse, forced marriage, and poverty. But the dominant white society carries the dangers of its myths of restoration and its othering of Asian Americans, an alienation Kingston vividly describes when she beats up a Chinese classmate who reminds her too much of herself.

Since our arrival to North American shores in large numbers in the late nineteenth century, Asian and Pacific Islander women have worked for justice, not only for ourselves and our compatriots but also for people in other countries. Refusing to split ourselves into Asian or American, many of us have worked on both frontiers at once. As the Asian American feminist theorist and filmmaker Trinh T. Minh-Ha notes, "The struggle is always multiple and transversal—specific but not confined to one side of any border war."[24] The twenty-year existence of Pacific, Asian, North American Asian Women in Theology and Ministry (PANAAWTM) is a current example of such multiple and transversal work among women. It has provided many of us a place to explore interstitial integrity. It is a community of strong eaters.

Interstitial integrity helps us be attuned to the fullness of life, to appreciate its many pleasures, and to participate in its ever-changing rhythms and patterns, rather than to be starved by unrealized hopes or a thin nostalgic past. While we remember the poisons of racism, sexism, and colonialism, we do not choose to harm the only lens by which we relate to the present or to let past traumas determine our choices now. Instead we seek to understand the complex relationships of our lives, sifting through the toxins and retrieving the rich morsels of life, nourishment that can sustain a lifetime of work for justice and for peace.

Mitsuye Yamada, a Nisei feminist poet, was a child when she was imprisoned in World War II. Her family was sent to the Manzanar Internment Camp in the arid Owens Valley in California. For years she did not speak of her anguish and anger about this injustice. In "Thirty Years Under" Yamada describes the three decades that held her humiliation and wounds "in a cast iron box / sealed it / labeled it / do not open . . . forever." She chose silence partly as a strategy to protect her daughter, to shield her from the poisons of racism and the horrors and humiliations of internment. Her silence created an unspoken gap between them that was only bridged when she and her daughter visited Manzanar, and her daughter listened to her describe life in the camp. Yamada's experience illuminates a love that is deepened by being grounded in space and time and a process of achieving insight by evoking historical memory and being attuned to what is right in front of us.[25]

The silence of prisons must be shattered; the silence of beauty and love must be received with gratitude. In 1988 Yamada's *Desert Run* was published, with poems and stories about her experience of internment. She says she spent years hating the desert as a reminder of her humiliation until a friend who loved it took her camping. She began to see the desert as her friend did, with the kind of healing and grace that love gives us. Yamada notes, "I spent 547 sulking days. I watched the most beautiful sunsets in the world and saw nothing." Reflecting on the desert's silences, she says she was too young to hear them during internment. But as an adult, she can feel the silences of wilderness and wildness, the tacit unspoken presence of love, and the hidden legacies of life passed on to her.[26]

With her new eyes Yamada remembers the Chinese men who built the Western railroad, buried in shallow, sandy graves, "the genetic code of Asian ancestral ties." She writes of resistance and of her family's legacy of resilient, resourceful women, which she has inherited and passed on. Her desert poems conclude with her "aging woman body spread-eagled on the ground," reaching to the four points of a future in which "my hometown this earth" will be a place of life, like the desert she now can see in all its living beauty, as it was, as it is. Yamada describes the future in terms of space, grounding it in what is, rather than placing it illusively out of reach. Her woman body is the interstitial tissue, the integrity that holds healing and life. She attunes herself to the connections of her poignant, compassionate, complex life. Yamada is reborn, created anew, by a fullness of life. She holds many-layered multiworlds together with memory, silence, and speaking and by a deep commitment to justice, to beauty, and to love.[27]

This is the meaning of spirit in flesh, to find what is sacred by taking into our lives all that has touched us. Interstitial integrity is this spirit in us, our struggle to hold the many in the one. We endeavor to make sense and meaning out of the multiple social locations, the hybrid cultures, and the many powers of death and life that are placed before us. Interstitial integrity is our ability to lie down, spread-eagled, reaching to all the many worlds we have known, all the memories we have been given, tempered in the cauldrons of history and geography in our one body. We find our value in taking our small place in long legacies of life incarnating spirit in bodies. Through such legacies, we participate in shaping our many worlds, and we grow in wisdom and beauty and live on in the traces we leave in others, so they, too, might cook without recipes.

Notes

1. Unlike Martin Luther, John Calvin maintained that paradise could be found on the earth. In 1650, long after medieval navigation maps had stopped indicating a possible earthly location for paradise and had begun showing the Americas and the conquest of the native inhabitants, Calvin published a commentary on Genesis, which contained a map with paradise located in Iraq. See Christoph Auffarth, "Paradise Now—But for the Wall Between, Some Remarks on Paradise in the Middle Ages," in *Paradise Interpreted: Representations of Biblical Paradise in Judaism and Christianity*, ed. Gerard P. Luttikhuizen (Leiden: E. J. Brill, 1999), 168–79. Richard T. Hughes and C. Leonard Allen, in *Illusions of Innocence: Protestant Primitivism in America, 1630–1875* (Chicago: University of Chicago Press, 1988), describe liberal and conservative versions of Calvinist myths and the way they structure time mythically.

2. Laura E. Donaldson, "The Breasts of Columbus: A Political Anatomy of Postcolonialism and Feminist Religious Discourse," in *Postcolonialism, Feminism, and Religious Discourse*, ed. Laura E. Donaldson and Kwok Pui-lan (New York: Routledge, 2002), 52; Joy Gilsdorf, *The Puritan Apocalypse: New England Eschatology in the Seventeenth Century* (New York: Garland, 1989); and Alden T. Vaughan and Edward W. Clark, *Puritans among the Indians: Accounts of Captivity and Redemption, 1676–1724* (Cambridge, MA: Belknap Press of Harvard University Press, 1981).

3. Hughes and Allen, *Illusions of Innocence*.

4. Renato Rosaldo, *Culture and Truth: The Remaking of Social Analysis* (Boston: Beacon Press, 1989); see also Ronald Niezen, *Spirit Wars: Native North American Religions in the Age of Nation Building* (Berkeley: University of California Press, 2000).

5. Conrad Cherry, in *Nature and Religious Imagination: From Edwards to Bushnell* (Philadelphia: Fortress Press, 1980), summarizes Edwards's idealism: "Only ideas of things give them their status in being. Qualities such as color or shape, which we may out of habit attribute to things in themselves, are no more *in* the things than pain is in a needle; they are 'strictly nowhere else but in the mind'" (46, original emphasis). See Hughes and Allen, *Illusions of Innocence*, for a discussion of Erasmus's influence on Calvin, especially in the former's appeal to ancient philosophers and Christian antiquity, a form of humanist primordialism (7–8). Ronald Niezen, in "Apostles of the New Age," in his *Spirit Wars*, connects New Age "nativist" assumptions surrounding indigenous North American traditions and Asian Buddhism (194–216).

6. Ralph Waldo Emerson, *Selections from Ralph Waldo Emerson*, ed. Stephen E. Whicher (Boston: Houghton Mifflin Co., 1960), 33, 124, 478. An overview of Emerson can be found at http://plato.stanford.edu/entries/emerson/.

7. The medieval mapping of Asia as paradise is discussed in Valerie I. J. Flint, *The Imaginative Landscape of Christopher Columbus* (Princeton, NJ: Princeton University Press, 1992). See also Donaldson, "Breasts of Columbus," 41–61.

8. Caroline Walker Bynum and Paul Freedman, eds., in *Last Things: Death and the Apocalypse in the Middle Ages* (Philadelphia: University of Pennsylvania Press, 2000), describe the various apocalyptic fervors and their causes. Columbus's particular messianic expectations are examined in Kirkpatrick Sale, *The Conquest of Paradise: Christopher Columbus and the Columbian Legacy* (New York: Knopf, 1990); and it is analyzed in feminist postcolonial terms in Catherine Keller, *Apocalypse Now and Then: A Feminist Guide to the End of the World* (Boston: Beacon Press, 1996).

9. Stanton edited *The Women's Bible*, which included a number of noted feminist authors who wrote commentaries on key texts on women in the Bible. The text is available at http://www.sacred-texts.com/wmn/wb/index.htm.

10. Kwok Pui-lan, *Postcolonial Imagination and Feminist Theology* (Louisville, KY: Westminster John Knox Press, 2005); and Kwok Pui-lan, "Unbinding Our Feet: Saving Brown Women and Feminist Religious Discourse," in *Postcolonialism, Feminism, and Religious Discourse*, ed. Laura E. Donaldson and Kwok Pui-lan (New York: Routledge, 2002), 62–81.

11. Charles S. Prebish, *American Buddhism* (North Scituate, MA: Duxbury Press, 1979).

12. Gary Snyder, *Turtle Island* (New York: New Directions, 1974).

13. Evan Eisenberg, in "Managers and Fetishers," in his *The Ecology of Eden* (New York: Knopf, 1998), deconstructs romantic views of nature, religion, and deep ecology. He argues that they are too subjective to have significant impacts on policy and social change. He also criticizes those who view scientific progress as salvation, in effect dismantling the dissociated thinking at both ends of the primordial restoration myth: pristine nature and the millenarian future.

    Criticisms of the colonization of Native American rituals were championed by the American Indian Movement and are found throughout much of Native American scholarship. Among the earliest was Vine Deloria Jr., *God Is Red: A Native View of Religion* (New York: Putnam, 1973), whose work is also collected in *Spirit and Reason: The Vine Deloria Jr. Reader*, ed. Barbara Deloria, Kristen Foehner, and Sam Scinta (Golden, CO: Fulcrum, 1999). See also Andrea Smith, *Conquest: Sexual Violence and American Indian Genocide* (Cambridge, MA: South End Press, 2005), chap. 6.

14. Jane Naomi Iwamura deconstructs such Western fantasies of Asian religious traditions in "The Oriental Monk in American Popular Culture," in *Religion and Popular Culture in America*, ed. Bruce Forbes and Jeffrey Mahan (Berkeley: University of California Press, 1999), 23–43. Her 2001 dissertation at the University of California at Berkeley is titled "The Oriental Monk in American Popular Culture: Race, Religion, and Representation in the Age of Virtual Orientalism." Creators of the original television series announced a prequel in production about Caine's Chinese training. More information can be found at http://www.en.wikipedia.org/wiki/Kung_Fu_(television).

15. Asian Women United of California, eds., *Making Waves: An Anthology of Writings by and about Asian American Women* (Boston: Beacon Press, 1989); Judy Chiu, "Social and Economic Profile of Asian Pacific American Women: Los Angeles County," in *Reflections on Shattered Windows: Promises and Prospects for Asian American Studies*, ed. Gary Y. Okihiro, Shirley Hune, Arthur A. Hansen, and John M. Liu (Pullman: Washington State University Press, 1988); Deborah Gee, filmmaker, *Slaying the Dragon*, National Asian American Telecommunications Association, San Francisco; and Trinh T. Minh-Ha, *When the Moon Waxes Red: Representation, Gender, and Cultural Politics* (New York: Routledge, 1991).

16. The author viewed this play during its first year on Broadway at the Eugene O'Neill Theater March 20, 1988–January 27, 1990. The production received Tony Awards for best play and best featured actor for B. D. Wong as Song Liling, as well as a best actor nomination for John Lithgow as Gallimard. Hwang also won a Pulitzer Prize for Drama. For more, see http://www.ibdb.com/production.asp?ID=4497.

17. Salmon Rushdie, *Imaginary Homelands: Essays and Criticism, 1981–1991* (New York: Viking, 1991). For Asian American analyses of orientalism, see Michael Omi and Dana

Takagi, eds., "Thinking Theory in Asian American Studies," *Amerasia Journal* 21, nos. 1–2 (1995). Edward W. Said, a Palestinian American, analyzes British hegemony in the Middle East and does not address the nuances of life in Asian America. However, his analysis of the European colonialist mind-set in *Orientalism* (New York: Penguin, 1995) has been important in Asian American Studies. Kwok Pui-lan develops a groundbreaking feminist theological analysis in her *Postcolonial Imagination.*

18. William Wei, *The Asian American Movement* (Philadelphia: Temple University Press, 1993). See also Tomoji Ishi, "Contemporary Anti-Asian Activities: A Global Perspective," in *Asian Americans: Comparative and Global Perspectives*, ed. Shirley Hune et al. (Pullman: Washington State University Press, 1991); Gary Y. Okihiro, "Is Yellow Black or White?" in his *Margins and Mainstreams: Asian Americans in History and Culture* (Seattle: University of Washington Press, 1994); and Okihiro et al., *Reflections on Shattered Windows.*

19. For the story of forced sexual slavery, see Nami Kim, "'My/Our' Comfort *Not* at the Expense of 'Somebody Else's': Toward a Critical Global Feminist Theology," *Journal of Feminist Studies in Religion* 21, no. 2 (2005): 75–94; and the book I coauthored with Susan Brooks Thistlethwaite, *Casting Stones: Prostitution and Liberation in Asia and the United States* (Minneapolis: Fortress Press, 1996).

20. Catherine M. Eagan, "'White,' If 'Not Quite': Irish Whiteness in the Nineteenth-Century Irish American Novel," *Eire–Ireland: Journal of Irish Studies* (Spring–Summer 2001), http://findarticles.com/p/articles/mi_mOFKX/is_2001_Spring-Summer/ai_80532344; and Noel Ignatiev, *How the Irish Became White* (New York: Routledge, 1996).

21. Information provided by Mary Paik, McCormick Theological Seminary, April 29, 1995, in a conversation about an earlier draft of this chapter.

22. For a description of recent work I have undertaken for social change in relation to U.S. imperialism and its uses of conservative religion, see Rita Nakashima Brock, "Fantastic Coherence," *Journal of Feminist Studies in Religion* 21, no. 1 (2005): 155–73.

23. Wendy Ho, "Mother/Daughter Writing and the Politics of Race and Sex in Maxine Hong Kingston's *The Woman Warrior*," in *Asian Americans: Comparative and Global Perspectives*, ed. Shirley Hune et al. (Pullman: Washington State University Press, 1991), 225–38, quotation on 237. Kingston's novel was reprinted by Random House in 1989. For examples of Asian American women's activism, see Asian Women United, *Making Waves;* and Rita Nakashima Brock, "Private, Public, and Somewhere in Between: Lessons from the History of Asian-Pacific American Women," *Journal of Feminist Studies in Religion* 12, no. 1 (1996): 127–32.

24. Trinh, *When the Moon Waxes Red,* 16.

25. Their story is part of a documentary film, *Mitsuye and Nellie: Asian American Poets*, about two feminist poets and friends, Mitsuye Yamada and Nellie Wong (San Francisco: Light-Saraf Films, 1981). Yamada's poetry about internment is in her *Desert Run: Poems and Stories* (Latham, NY: Kitchen Table: Women of Color Press, 1988), 2.

26. Yamada, *Desert Run,* 11.

27. Ibid., 84.

Chapter Eight

Violence and Asian American Experience

From Abjection to *Jeong*

Wonhee Anne Joh

> Violence is, always, an exploitation of that primary tie, that primary
> way in which we are as bodies, outside ourselves and for one another.
> Judith Butler, *Precarious Life*

My children and I were suddenly attacked on the streets of a quiet New Jersey suburb. It was the first Saturday after September 11, and we had gone out for our usual Saturday morning breakfast on Main Street. I remember noting the American flags that were draped over railings and store awnings and off building rooftops. Smaller cars had at least one tiny flag flying from a window or antenna, while larger SUVs displayed large flags waving off their hoods. I felt very uneasy, but I told myself not to worry since we had gone out for Saturday breakfast at this place for years and the town was a familiar place to us.

While leaving the restaurant, we were stopped at an intersection when the crossing guard began to wave his arms and shout obscene words at us. Rather than drive off, we got out of the car to counter his comments. This was a lethal move. As soon as we left the safety of our car, we were targeted by a mob that appeared suddenly and expectedly out of nowhere. The crowd pushed us around and yelled, "Go back to where you came from!"

Other motorists and pedestrians just passed by without even pretending to look, avoiding all eye contact and any obligation to intervene. I called the police out of sheer terror. When they finally arrived, they merely dispersed the crowd but did nothing else. They did not even bother to write up the incident. I was told that if I wished I could go over to the station and write up my own report to be on file. I proceeded to do so out of rage, humiliation, a sense of injustice, and a will that this incident should be recorded and not forgotten. It was my way of claiming some power and agency in a situation where we felt powerless. On our way back home my son asked me a question that continues to haunt me. Bewildered at a not-yet-named injury and aching with an innocence on the brink of vanishing, he asked, "Why didn't the police help us?" For my son this event marked the loss of his confidence in the American practice of democracy and was the moment when he began to reflect on his place and relationship to the U.S. nation-state. It was remarkable for me to witness his growing attachment to a Korea that he knew so little about. He was shifting his nationalism from the United States to Korea.

As for my response to this incident, I continue to struggle with the deep and constant need for justice. It is often the case that such deep desire for justice draws me into the dynamics of a too-simplistic "us" versus "them." Because the dynamics of oppression are never simple, holding justice and love together is often not an easy task. Often, it is easier to point the finger at the "evil" in "them" than acknowledging our ways of participating in oppression. My personal struggle is always to work toward radical and lasting justice while simultaneously recognizing and holding fast the humanity in the other. Then how is it possible for me to work toward justice without a violent turn toward the other? For me, this has been made possible by a Korean concept called *jeong*.[1]

Introducing *Jeong*

In Korean contexts *jeong* saturates daily living and all forms of relationships. As a cultural concept and practice, *jeong* encompasses but is not limited to notions of compassion, affection, solidarity, vulnerability, and forgiveness. Many Koreans often feel that *jeong* is more powerful, lasting, and transformative than love. *Jeong* makes relationships "sticky" but also recognizes the complex and dynamic nature of all relationalism. While *jeong* works to resist oppression and suffering, it does not have elements of retaliatory vengefulness. When *jeong* is present among sufferers and the oppressed who do not forget justice, these same oppressed people preserve an element of forgiveness for those who participate in structures of oppression. Presence of *jeong* in the Korean cultural context does not mean that there is no oppression and violence among Koreans. Korea, like most other contexts, has covert and overt forms of sexism, racism, and classism along with other forms of individual and systemic structures of violence.

Let me share an example. As in many other patriarchal cultures, sexism and violence against women are rampant. The presence and practice of *jeong* does not mean that violence against women is completely eradicated. However, *jeong*, as practiced by and between women who are victims of patriarchy, helps them to form networks that not only help them survive such brutal victimization but also enable them to form solidarities that allow for the creation of movements to confront and resist various manifestations of violence. Participants of these movements and networks are both men and women. Although all Koreans may not always practice my understanding of *jeong* precisely in these ways, I am stretching this concept and inviting us to examine what I understand to be liberative about *jeong*.

Jeong may seem to be a form of love. Yet *jeong* is difficult to categorize in relation to the notions of love that have often been fragmented as eros, philia, and agape. Like eros, *jeong* is an intense and vital mode of bonding, but unlike eros, it is less susceptible to the romanticization of love as erotic or sexual attraction. One of the common metaphors for *jeong* that I have often heard is that *jeong* is "sticky." This stickiness is not fusion without distinctions but the kind of stickiness that understands that we are, whether we want to admit it or not, always connected to one another. Because we are constituted in and through relationality with all others, *jeong* recognizes that we are indebted to others as well. Like philia, or friendship, *jeong* has a strong sense of relationality, but unlike philia, it does not depend on equal regard and mutuality in order to flourish. Finally, like agape, *jeong* often involves dramatic sacrifices in relation to others, even vis-à-vis an oppressing other; but unlike many renderings of agape, *jeong* is not a self-emptying self-sacrifice. It is certainly not self-abnegation. In contrast to self-sacrifice, *jeong* is an intentional, wise, and knowing decision to relinquish that recognizes not only the dignity and worth of oneself but also that of others. In this context, though, agency is not relinquished. It is inaccurate to say that *jeong* perpetuates passivity and powerlessness. Rather, choosing to live by and through *jeong* is to claim one's agency and power in a situation of powerlessness. At times sacrifice in *jeong* works to restore life in the face of forces that destroy life.[2]

I believe that *jeong*, while mindful of justice, highlights the necessity of *jeong* for the other in the work of justice. *Jeong* thus suggests a distinctive way of relating love and justice. In this regard Reinhold Niebuhr's observation of equality and rights offers an insight. He argues that justice cannot be achieved through some kind of precise formula or equation of rights. My understanding of *jeong* as an intentional relinquishment that aims at and creates restorative dignity resonates with Niebuhr's thinking when he observes, "Love must strive for something purer than justice if it would attain justice. Egoistic impulses are so much more powerful than altruistic ones that if the latter are not given stronger than ordinary support, the justice which even good men [*sic*] design is partial to those who design it."[3] *Jeong* manifests itself in unique combinations of these different dimensions of love, justice, and restorative dignity, transgressing boundaries between oppressor and the oppressed, finding ways to mix resistance and embrace amid oppressive relations, and giving birth to new forms of love and justice. *Jeong* does not compromise with those who perpetuate violence and oppression. Rather, the power of *jeong* allows us to recognize the seriousness of the suffering of the oppressors even as we resist their oppressing practices. *Jeong*, in other words, emerges in the interstitial space between the self and the other, between the oppressors and the oppressed.[4]

There are dimensions to love prevalent in many communities that, I think, resemble *jeong*. There are those communities that recognize the interdependence, rather than the independence, that allows life to flourish. These peoples—whether Africans deploying notions of Umbuntu (idea of humanity toward others best conveyed through the maxim "I am because we are") or Indians expressing concepts such as Ahimsa (largest love or love force)—well recognize that a communal and relational way of being in the world benefits not only humanity but also all of creation, and it is the key to our social and planetary recovery and survival. Many of the peoples and cultures who daily practice that which is similar to *jeong* also have been exploited historically and know suffering and violence in their bones. For example, many people who have experienced the violence of poverty, emigration, war, genocide, racism, sexism, homophobia, forced labor, and state-sanctioned torture often seem to hold on to what resembles *jeong* because it is what ultimately gives them dignity in the face of such inhumanity. A woman who experiences domestic violence may or may not love her abuser, but she might hold on to *jeong* for the other because it is not only about holding on to the kernel of the abuser's humanity but, more important, *jeong* prevents her from the abyss of inhumanity and also restores to her her dignity and agency. *Jeong* does not discourage separation and autonomy, but rather, *jeong* works to help us be mindful that we are always in relation to the other.

Something like the Korean notion of *jeong* seems to be emerging in a number of academic discourses, especially among intellectuals who reflect on historical oppression, such as postcolonial theorists, who have recently made a surprising turn by calling for love. Gayatri Chakravorty Spivak, for example, dares to hope in a "postcolonial love" as a supplement that will allow for different peoples and movements to develop and maintain strength and duration, to stick, we might say, as "the strongest mobilizing discourse in the world, . . . the supplementation of collective effort by *love*." Michael Hardt and Antonio Negri also call for political love as the motivating factor of the multitude. For "without this love, we are nothing."[5]

While I agree with these ideas, I still find that "love" often does not convey the breadth, depth, and complexity of all our ways of being with one another. When we speak of love, it often seems conditional and restrictive. For example, either I love the other or I do not. Either you are with me or you are not. Friend or Foe. Good or Evil. Abused or Abuser. People also have argued that one should love where the condition of reciprocity and mutuality is present. This is an ideal state, which one would wish for all relationships. However, we know that frequently this is not the case. *Jeong*, though, is neither conditional nor restrictive, because one cannot will or determine when, where, or with whom one can experience *jeong*. Sometimes, even in relationships of animosity, *jeong* emerges despite our best efforts to block it out, because we cannot prevent glimpsing the image of ourselves mirrored in the other. When one sees one's self mirrored in the face of the other, one knows in the deepest recesses of one's heart that complete severing is not the solution. In this way *jeong* is even more expansive and generous than love, even in the context of relational complexity. We will return to the notion of *jeong* in the final section, after making a necessary turn in the next section to examine a specific way by which violence occurs.

Violence and Racial Abjection

> Abject peoples are those whom industrial imperialism rejects but cannot do without: slaves, prostitutes, the colonized, domestic workers, the insane, the unemployed. . . . Inhabiting the cusp of domesticity as its constitutive, inner repudiation: the rejected from which one does not part. . . . Abjection is that liminal state that hovers on the threshold of body and body politic—and thus the boundary between psychoanalysis and material history.
>
> Anne McClintock, *Imperial Leather*

The expression of *jeong* is especially difficult for the "abject peoples" to whom McClintock refers here. However, it is within cultures of abjection that *jeong* often emerges, and so the notion of abjection needs to be examined closely. In the incident I narrated at the beginning of this chapter, outright and blatant racial violence erupted in the aftermath of 9/11. My experience of that instance reminded me once again that still I was considered foreign. I have lived in this country for most of my life, and most of my identity has been shaped by my location in the United States. After many physical, psychic, and emotional returns to Korea, my search for so-called roots had led me back to my rootedness in the United States. My self-proclaimed identity as a Korean American is now a political act of defiance. It is a political decision in that I claim my right to belong fully in this context. Although my experience of being Korean American is deeply complex, I would insist that it is unique. Being Korean American in the United States is different, for example, from being part of a diaspora of peoples in the United States. "Diaspora" means that a person feels not at home in one context precisely because this person is aware that there is an elsewhere where she or he feels she or he once belonged. By contrast, my claiming a Korean American identity is a specific political act of resistance designed to create home against the persistent violence of racism. This act of claiming the United States as the site of belonging involves confronting the hegemony of whiteness that determines who and what is meant by "American."[6]

Who is an American? As far as mainstream assumptions go, does skin color matter in those split-second processes of identification of whether one is an American? As far as the Department of Immigration and Naturalization Service is concerned, one can become a U.S. citizen through "naturalization." No one mentions, however, whether one is then an American also in the minds of one's fellow citizens or in the functioning of the society. Is there or should there be a connection between being American and being a citizen? How does an ethnic person become white and American? Is it still necessary to become white to become American? Is being American raced? Gendered?

To answer these questions, we need to think more deeply on the experience of abjection, a helpful notion described by the psychoanalyst Julia Kristeva.[7] "Abjection" can be defined as an operation of the psyche that requires the expulsion and exclusion of that which threatens the formation of one's identity. The myth of white superiority is one of the ways that a particular white identity expels others as abjects. Here I am only highlighting how racism works in the process of abjection. What this process assumes is that one's identity is shaped and formed in opposition and as antagonistic to the other. The abject is understood as that which the self sees as the unclean, foreign, and improper. Abjection does not take place based on race alone. Racism is one among many modes of abjection, but it is surely one of the most prevalent ways by which abjection takes place. However, other abjects are also constructed within racialized and ethnic groups. Violent abjection can be experienced by a variety of groups: white women, the poor, those restrictively defined to geographical regions, sexual minorities, and those with disabilities, for example. Moreover, if we continue to understand abjection as part of the process of individual identification, then we come dangerously close to normalizing the violence that is part of this process of rejection.

One can argue that if our collective identities are formed in antagonistic relationships to others and if our collective or individual identity relies on rejecting what is different, then it seems unavoidable that violence will always be present. The alternative I suggest is for us to find ways of becoming subjects that are not opposed to one another by abjecting the other. What we need are ways of becoming subjects in relation to subjects.[8] It is toward this end that the notion of *jeong* is helpful.

Expulsion and abjection of racial and/or gender differences rely on violence against whatever is perceived to be the other to some dominant/ normative self. Thus it is important to interpret the narrative of the U.S. nation's white collective psyche precisely because the inner psychic formation, when moving from the individual to the collective dimension, has had political repercussions. Within the U.S. body politic we must be prepared to ask whether democratic politics and policies depend on recurring acts of disavowal and violence against the abjected other.[9]

In *America Right or Wrong*, Anatol Lieven notes that in times of national crisis, especially when borders and boundaries are threatened, a concerted and deliberate effort is mounted to form an illusion of a united nation. Lieven observes that nationalism (and patriotism) surface only by violence that stamps down the other, both within and without its body politic. When white power is threatened and its dominance seems precarious, it attempts to stabilize the nation, the body politic, through defense of its traditional culture and ethnicity. In order to shore up defense of the vital collective interest, ferocious measures are used to sanction internal social violence within the nation. However, such attempts to police the porous boundaries of the nation fail to recognize that such attempts amputate that which is inextricably inseparable.[10]

There is a direct historical reciprocity of national identity and racism, or what Charles Mills refers to as a racial contract. A racial contract of inclusion and exclusion, revulsion and pseudo-attraction all work to form a "consensual hallucination." This contract is an exploitative one where all whites, according to Mills, are beneficiaries. Such an agreement functions as a "meta-agreement" that is inclusive of the epistemological, political, and moral dimensions of life. Mills goes on to argue that the phenomenon of racism and the logic of white supremacy are crucial in many ways for maintaining domination. Especially important is that such logic of domination is something that is psychically required in order to justify systems and structures of white supremacy. Such a racial contract is built on the threat of violence at work in the processes of abjection—a threat whereby the violated recipient is just as implicated in violence as the agent of violence. Dominant Euro-American subjectivity is often formed in a binary structure of subjectivity that must become antagonistic to the other as it must simultaneously reject and negate the other.[11]

In arguing against the U.S. racialization of Asian Americans as "Orientals," Robert Chang notes just how important it is when we claim ourselves as Asian Americans. "Asian American, in contradistinction with Oriental," he notes, "is in some sense a national identity, a claim to a proper place in America."[12] The relationship between Asian Americans and white Americans is fraught with the violence of racism that Asians in Asia often do not understand. While Asian Americans do well to understand the violence of imperialism as experienced by Asians, Asians also would do well to discern how the engine of this imperialism works within the United States against Asian Americans through the violence of white racism. Mutual understanding of differing oppressions might lead us to formulate new ways of participating in liberation movements that are inter- and intranational and that might possibly propel us toward a vision of cosmopolitanism, if not planetary consciousness of shared struggles without erasing the particularity of these experiences.[13]

Kristeva writes extensively of how the psyche has to have the other as object in order to become a speaking subject. The abject is everything that the subject feels necessary to expel in order to create a state of its own subjectivity. The abject, once expelled, then marks the boundaries and the borders of the self as both deeply repressed inside and expelled outward by the psyche. Hence the abject is that part of us we desperately attempt to repress and expel, as we become a speaking subject. The subject understands the abject as threatening the fabric of her or his social order. The abject continues, however, to defy the subject's comfort in clear and absolute lines of demarcation and must constantly be jettisoned from the self. Inasmuch as the abject is jettisoned, it is experienced as garbage; in short, the abject is the refused refuse. Abject peoples often internalize their status as abjected. For those of us who internalize in this way, seeing ourselves as garbage is horrific. Not only are we severed and expelled by the oppressing other (the dominant/normative self) but we sever and expel ourselves in order to become a subject. This implies at best an ambivalent relationship with the self and at worst a form of self-hatred. This self-hatred, in turn, comes at the cost of our continuously projecting onto others those parts of ourselves we find to be garbage.

The abject haunts the subject as its outwardly projected boundary. Yet it is a boundary that unwillingly is transgressed: the subject cannot divorce herself or himself from that which she or he abjects. The abject is, as Kristeva tells us, "something rejected from which one does not part." Having fabricated an anxious border between subject and other, abjection reveals a society's precarious hold over the fluid and disorderly interplay of individual and collective psyches. Abjection is thus not something to be overcome but that which must be acknowledged and embodied as irreparably part of ourselves.[14]

Dominant psychoanalytic theories presuppose that the relationship between the subject and the other is antagonistic. I argue that the process of becoming a separated self is at its core violent and that such a violent process produces an ongoing cycle of violence stemming from the individual and moving to the collective psyche. Antagonism and exclusion are part of identity in a white racist society; otherwise, it would be impossible to have autonomous identities. I propose an alternative way to understand self as distinct from others without antagonism—a way in which the subject recognizes its intimate connection with other differentiated subjects as subjects. In order to dismantle our impulse to kill or erase the other in order to feel we exist, we must first learn to become subjects without the oppositional other. Since the cycle of abjection occurs in most all of us, all of us are in need of learning new ways of becoming subjects. Individual psychic formation is crucial in shaping the dominant collective psyches that often reflect the national and social psyche, and the psyche of the nation-state cannot help but be political. For violence is indeed a violation of our most primary ties in the connections between individuals to others and to the collective.[15]

As one racialized group in the United States, Asian Americans are abjected to maintain dominant white subjectivity.[16] In contrast, when Asian Americans assert that they are Americans, rooted and invested in this land, they question the construction of dominant white U.S identity—the kind that sustains white supremacy. Indeed the presence of racialized Asian American bodies at once reaffirms and threatens white identity.[17]

Many peoples have been racialized in the history of the United States, and different communities experience abjection differently. Karen Shimakawa notes the disparate ways that racialization and the experience of abjection take place. She uses the category "assimilable versus inassimilable abjection" to speak of how abjection plays out in the minds of the white dominant subject.[18]

In the face of such public exercises of abjection as occurred to my family just after 9/11, we must ask how we can resist the violent brutality that simmers underneath our identities when we encounter the violence of the dominant identity. In the face of this violent abjection, is it possible to respond constructively for emancipatory praxis without retaliation or retribution? In my own case, when faced with the violence of abjection, I also experienced the incredible impulse to respond with a violence of my own. One wonders if Frantz Fanon might have been right when he insisted that violence could serve as psychotherapy for the oppressed. Fanon pressed his belief that one can only recover one's self through violence, while at the same time he was also repulsed by violence no matter where it was generated.[19] One is compelled to ask, then, Has violence become endemic?

In the story with which I began this chapter, one of the reasons that the people who witnessed the violence of the mob could not and would not make eye contact with us was perhaps that they were exposed as participants and beneficiaries of this racial contract. By not helping us they revealed that they were unwilling to break the racial contract. In so doing they unconsciously relied on the violence of white racism to maintain their privileged position by accepting the abjecting of racialized others. They affirmed a contract that requires a person either to be the instigator of violence against the other or to be subjected to violence as the abject.

Overall, then, in this situation of racial contract, someone like me is pushed to excise, in my case, my Asianness in order to function as an American in the United States. If I do not do so, I become invisible or subject to violence. Often the situation comes down either to "Go back to where you came from" or "Shut up and play dead." Thus it has been crucial for me to examine both the dominant white narrative of belongingness and exclusion, in the light of abjection.[20]

How might we overcome violence? How can we practice an ethics of respect for irreconcilable differences? Is it possible to seek justice and mutuality without erasing all our particularities into a form of universalization?[21] Such questions emerge when we witness the cycles of violence attending the process of abjection. Only when we recognize the abject as a profound part of our psyche is it possible to overcome violence and make the mandate "Love your neighbor as yourself" even a remote possibility.[22] The need for this recognition returns us to the notion of *jeong*.

Face of An(O)ther: Engaging *Jeong*

Jeong, therefore, emerges within the interstitial realm of relationalism. *Jeong* is rooted in and thrives in relational matrices. As it emerges through connectedness, it works as a relentless faith that abjection does not have the final word.[23]

Unfolding the Korean character of *jeong* reveals its multidimensional characteristics. Its multiple shades of meaning derive mainly from the notion of heart. *Jeong* emerges within connectedness to unravel abjection and enhance the process of becoming a self in relation to the other. If we shift to theological discourse, my claims for *jeong* resonate with the metaphor of the unleavened bread that rises with yeast, as used in an analogy for the kingdom of God. For the arising of *jeong* (like the small yeast) within relationality is what generates the power for emancipatory praxis. Possibility for *jeong* resides in the contact zone, the interstitial space between the self and the other. This interstitial space where *jeong* comes forth is made possible when we see the other through our hearts.

Rita Nakashima Brock has noted, "We know best by heart." She posits that when we live within the fullness of our hearts, our brokenness becomes whole and healed. Such "fullness of the heart" creates and sustains our sense of relational interconnectedness. According to Brock relational existence is the "heart of our being, our life source, our original grace."[24] *Jeong* is a form of relationality that is more than interdependence. It is a mode of interdependence that is fostered when agents of love embrace even a form of sacrifice, but this is not the self-sacrifice that feminists so rightly critique. By challenging absolute lines of demarcation between the self and the other, *jeong* does require, in certain instances, the decision to put the other before ourselves. This kind of relationality, however, is deeply based on an ethics of mutual recognition and resonance that counters violence, defined as the oppositional and individually oriented process of subject formation and abjection examined above.

In *jeong* one knows that asserting one's subjectivity by rejecting the other is brutal. This does not mean that *jeong* is not confrontational or that it reifies relations of domination and powerlessness. In Korean culture I have experienced relationships between people who do not give up on the other in their relationship of *jeong*; these are individuals who have a sense of obligation to pose even the most confrontational of challenges, starting their challenge with, "Because I have *jeong* for you, I need to be honest and say this to you." *Jeong* allows us to have hope even in the capacity of the oppressor to be transformed. However, it does not mean that we languish in a kind of hope that waits for change to take place. Rather, it is because of *jeong* that we are compelled to move continuously to demand change and justice. *Jeong* recognizes not only our connectedness but also the dignity and worth of both the self and the other.

Jeong is able to wedge itself into the smallest gaps between the oppressed and the oppressor. *Jeong* is powerful precisely because it is an emancipatory and healing power, even in relationships that have been reduced to simple binarism, as is often the case between the oppressor and the oppressed. *Jeong* contests the existence of and pronouncement of binarism. In this regard, the notion or experience of *jeong* has gradations and levels of thinness and thickness, that is, it exhibits weaker and stronger forms of relationality.

Overall *jeong* replaces dichotomies with more inclusive frameworks for understanding the self and the other. While clear systemic oppressions must be critically analyzed and resisted, *jeong* also recognizes the brokenness and pain of the oppressors because of the fear that drives them to commit violence and mete out death toward the other. Ultimately it is this intimate existential recognition of the self, mirrored in the other, that leads to transformation of the heart.[25] This recognition can happen to each one at different times or to both simultaneously.

Jeong emerges in the in-between space created by the juxtaposition of suffering and justice, between death and life. Because *jeong* is so difficult to define yet so concretely known in everyday practice, Koreans have analyzed many forms of *jeong*. One of the more common is the distinction between *mi-eun jeong* and *go-eun jeong*. Many Koreans share the notion that the former is a form of *jeong* that emerges even when one is in an antagonistic relationship with the other, while the latter emerges in relationships of mutuality and reciprocity. A popular saying in Korea precisely embodies this collective solidarity that might be uncomfortable for the Western individualistic sensibility: "You die, I die; You live, I live," or, in another context, "I am because we are." These sayings actualize the form of *jeong* that emerges within relationality and community. Boyung Lee's chapter in this volume gives an example of the strength of communalism and relationality when she writes about *uri*. The "we" in Korean is often used interchangeably with the singular subject. This epistemology of "we" is what is necessary in our resistance against violence that lies at the root of abjection.[26]

As I indicated in the first section, *jeong* is not unique to Koreans alone. Whenever the communal is emphasized and honored, I have found the presence of *jeong*. Although it might have a different name in that context and is stressed in different ways, *jeong's* notion of relinquishment creates dignified restoration. Lack of *jeong* is most noticeable in cultures that have adopted capitalist, individualist notions of the self and the violent projections necessary to sustain this sense of self in opposition to the other. *Jeong* threatens a culture that values individualism and separation while devaluing communal interdependence and the interconnectedness of all.

Jeong addresses and redresses that whole process of abjection at the heart of violence that is the basis of American racism. *Jeong* requires two, the self and the other, that allow the subject to cross the boundaries of the self and be the other. This form of *jeong* provides identification through difference without abolishing or assimilating differences. Because the power of *jeong* is not confined within particular borders, boundaries, divisions, and dichotomies, justice can come through the restorative work of *jeong*.[27]

In speaking of racism and abjection I have focused on the situation of Asian Americans in the United States. This focal point does not signify a prioritization or privileging of Asian American experiences of violence. Asian Americans must attend not only to violence experienced within the United States but also to violence experienced elsewhere, often because of U.S. involvements. The woman identified as Nicole in Kwok Pui-lan's chapter in this volume is an example of how rampant and pernicious violence has become in our world and indicates the urgency of ending cycles of individual and social violence. The dangers that threaten the existence of life do not come only from sources outside of the human heart. They are reflections of our vulnerability, mirrored in others, which has turned into hostility toward others.

As I acknowledged above, my initial response to the antagonism I experienced after 9/11 was an impulse to be violent in return. However, I remembered grieving the tragedy of September 11 along with others. I too grieved for those who were and continue to be victims of U.S. violence both outside and inside of the United States. I recognized the pain of those lashing out to me. It did not justify what they did, but I understood the pain. My sense of *jeong* allowed me to discern the fear and hatred that the events of 9/11 generated. I could see the pain and also knew that we will grieve for a long time. Our vulnerability was manipulated by the powerful to benefit those who only understand capital and violence.[28]

Jeong lives in saying both a yes and a no in relation to the suffering it bears: no to violence and abjection and a simultaneous yes to the power of *jeong* to seek ways beyond this violence and abjection. One is able to recognize the vulnerability of the other by looking beyond the hardened heart of the other. *Jeong* exists even within, especially within, relationships not based on mutuality. At the heart of the transgressive power of *jeong* is its presence, its emergence even within the terrain of confrontational and oppositional relationships and often in the absence of mutuality and equality.

We dream, hope, and live with, by, and through the heart. In a culture that poses heart against mind, we must note the importance of the heart metaphor in Christianity. When we live with heart we cannot stay immune to the other. The suffering of the other becomes my suffering; her and his joy, my joy, in a relationship that is frequently but not necessarily that of reciprocity. If we do not have heart we do not have life. *Jeong* emerges within relationships; it emerges with contact. It is important to keep in mind that ordinary relations, the matrix for practicing *jeong*, are crucial for both personal and corporate life. Such praxis of *jeong*, entailing both fidelity and courage, cannot help but be prophetic witness and resistance to powers of death as it manifests itself in domestic and international spheres. The logic of love and the logic of justice, often pitted against each other, must be held together; for the bifurcation between subject and abject are false, just as the binary of oppressor and oppressed fails to offer the possibility that we are covictims in the long run. *Jeong* and justice must work together in overcoming violence. Let us remember that there are people, we, us, *uri*, who are already on the road toward justice and wholeness.[29]

The agency of oppressed peoples, I argue, springs from their awareness of how vital *jeong* is for their survival. Some may wonder if here I privilege *jeong* over love. More accurately, I present *jeong* as a dimension of love, one that often has been erased or repressed, especially in dominant Western culture's discussion of love.[30]

In future work I hope to recover a robust, prophetic love in the work of emancipatory movements by seeing them infused with *jeong*. Because *jeong* is complex, not everyone does or will experience *jeong* the same way. I invite us, though, to stretch a little more. As Michael Franti sings, "Is your love enough or can you love some more?"[31] That "some more," I suggest, can be ushered into our lives by the practice of *jeong*. Through this practice, through reclaiming this imperfect *jeong*, one might possibly give continuous rebirth to our subjectivities in relation to others as subjects and thereby learn to live, not annihilate—always already being taught by one another to live with and through *jeong* rather than violent abjection.

Notes

1. For a theopolitical articulation of this concept, see Wonhee Anne Joh, *Heart of the Cross: A Postcolonial Christology* (Louisville, KY: Westminster John Knox Press, 2006).

2. See JoAnne Marie Terrell, "Our Mothers' Gardens: Rethinking Sacrifice," in *Cross Examinations: Readings of the Cross Today*, ed. Marit Trelstad (Minneapolis: Fortress Press, 2006), 33–49.

3. Reinhold Niebuhr, *Moral Man and Immoral Society: A Study in Ethics and Politics* (New York: Charles Scribner's Sons, 1947), 266. See also M. K. Gandhi, *Non-violent Resistance (Satyagraha)* (Mineola, NY: Dover Publication, 2001); and James M. Washington, ed., *A Testament of Hope: The Essential Writings and Speeches of Martin Luther King Jr.* (New York: HarperCollins Publishers, 1991), 5–74.

4. This transgressive power of *jeong* comes close to what Nelson Mandela wrote: "No one is born hating another person because of the color of his skin, or his background, or his religion. People must learn to hate, and if they can learn to hate, they can be taught to love, for love comes more naturally to the human heart than its opposite. Even in the grimmest times in prison, . . . I would see a glimmer of humanity in one of the guards, perhaps just for a second, but it was enough to reassure me and keep me going" (*The Long Walk to Freedom: The Autobiography of Nelson Mandela* [Boston: Little, Brown & Co., 1994], 622). Mandela's brutally long prison term might remind us that real transformation takes time.

5. Gayatri Chakravorty Spivak, *The Critique of Postcolonial Reason: Toward a History of the Vanishing Present* (Cambridge, MA: Harvard University Press, 1999), 332–34, quotation on 383, emphasis added; and Michael Hardt and Antonio Negri, *Multitude: War and Democracy in the Age of Empire* (New York: Penguin Press, 2004), 350–58, quotation on 352. Also see Catherine Keller, *God and Power: Counter-Apocalyptic Journeys* (Minneapolis: Fortress Press, 2005), 113–34.

6. Much has been written about the significance and the impact of 9/11 on U.S. foreign policy. Such attention was and continues to be necessary as our policies on war, invasion, terrorism, torture, and corrosion of democracy continue to inflict suffering on many peoples and nations despite persistent calls for change. As much as attention on U.S. foreign policy is necessary and important, it is also necessary that we not fail to examine critically our domestic policies, especially as they pertain to the ongoing construction of a particular kind of national identity that is done at the cost of constructing and expelling its own other, foreigner, alien, stranger, abject.

7. Julia Kristeva, *Powers of Horror: An Essay on Abjection* (New York: Columbia University Press, 1982).

8. Kelly Oliver, *Subjectivity without Subjects: From Abject Fathers to Desiring Mothers* (New York: Roman & Littlefield Publishers, 1998), 81; and see Drucilla Cornell, *The Imaginary Domain: Abortions, Pornography and Sexual Harassment* (New York: Routledge, 1995).

9. For an excellent discussion of how the figure of the immigrant functions as abject in the formation of national identity, see Bonnie Honig, *Democracy and the Foreigner* (Princeton, NJ: Princeton University Press, 2001).

10. Anatol Lieven, *America Right or Wrong: An Anatomy of American Nationalism* (Oxford: Oxford University Press, 2004), 58; and see Karen Shimakawa, *National Abjection: The Asian American Body Onstage* (Durham, NC: Duke University Press, 2002), 131.

160	*Wonhee Anne Joh*

11. Charles Mills, *The Racial Contract* (Ithaca, NY: Cornell University Press, 1997), 14–19. For an incisive indictment against white racism, see the poet Amiri Baruka's controversial poem "Somebody Blew Up America," http://www.counterpunch.org/poem1003.html. What is most often not acknowledged in psychoanalysis is the privileged position of the dominant identity. Kelly Oliver argues that often these unexamined and privileged positions influence the many ways in which identity is shaped and even deformed. As Oliver notes, theories that do not start from the subjectivities of those othered, but rather from the dominant subjectivity, presuppose a need to exclude some other to fortify and shore up itself in order to reassure that all subjects are alike: "We level differences, we develop a normative notion of the subject formation based on one particular group, gender or class of people" (*The Colonization of Psychic Space: A Psychoanalytic Social Theory of Oppression* [Minneapolis: University of Minnesota Press, 2004], 2). Most of psychoanalytic theory, poststructuralism, and even deconstructionism presupposes an antagonistic relationship between the self and the other, the subject and the object, and the individual and the society.

12. Robert Chang, *Disoriented: Asian Americans, Law, and the Nation-State* (New York: New York University Press, 1999), 5. For an excellent discussion on the construction of political identities of peoples, see the most recent work of Ernesto Laclau, *On Populist Reason* (New York: Verso, 2005); see also Judith Butler, "Competing Universalities," in *Contingency, Hegemony, Universality: Contemporary Dialogues on the Left*, ed. Judith Butler, Ernesto Laclau, and Slavoj Žižek (New York: Verso, 2000), 136–81.

13. Another political reason for the claim to Asian American citizenship comes from the desire to participate in the democratic process. Chantal Mouffe notes, "If the task of radical democracy is indeed to deepen the democratic revolution and to link diverse democratic struggles, such a task requires the creation of new subject positions that would allow the common articulation . . . of antiracism, antisexism and anticapitalism" (*The Return of the Political* [New York: Verso, 1993], 18); see also Chantal Mouffe, *Democratic Paradox* (New York: Verso, 2000). Also refer to Robert Young's discussion of "Tricontinentalism," in his *Postcolonialism: An Introduction* (Oxford: Blackwell, 2001), 211–16.

14. Kristeva, *Powers of Horror*, 9. The Oedipus complex attempts to account for the emergence of the speaking subject. This psychic process has been traditionally understood as divided into two stages: presubjectivity and the period following, which allows entrance to the symbolic at the cost of abjecting or repressing the semiotic. See Martha Reineke, *Sacrificed Lives: Kristeva on Women and Violence* (Bloomington: Indiana University Press, 1997), 22.

15. See Ernesto Laclau, *Emancipation(s)* (New York: Verso, 1996), 52–53.

16. For further excellent analysis of how racism has functioned and continues to operate in maintaining white hegemony in the United States, see Ronald Takaki, *Iron Cages: Race and Culture in Nineteenth-Century America* (New York: Oxford University Press, 2000).

17. In the United States different social acts and policies of anti-Asian racialization have been ways by which Asian Americans have been marked as abjects. This violent process of abjection, so insidiously carried out and brutally exercised, has been experienced by many other racialized groups who make up the body politic of this nation. Asian Americans are not the exception. However, let me offer an example that points to the different ways that white racism functions toward Asian Americans. I have often found that a white person (who assumes her or his American identity by virtue of skin color) will hardly ever ask an African American where she or he comes from. However, even if one is a third-

generation Japanese or Chinese American, we can be sure that the same white person will assume that the Asian American is not American. It is rare when a white person does not ask, "So, where are you from?"

18. Karen Shimakawa, *National Abjection: The Asian American Body Onstage* (Durham, NC: Duke University Press, 2002), 39. For further discussion on how racism works in the process of dominant national-identity formation within the United States, see Anne Anlin Chen, *Melancholy of Race: Psychoanalysis, Assimilation, and Hidden Grief* (Oxford: Oxford University Press, 2001); and Sara Ahmed, "The Skin of the Community: Affect and Boundary Formation," in *Revolt, Affect, Collectivity: The Unstable Boundaries of Kristeva's Polis*, ed. Tina Chanter and Ewa Plonowska Ziarek (Albany: State University of New York Press, 2005), 95–112.

19. Frantz Fanon, *The Wretched of the Earth* (New York: Grove Press, 1963), 35–106.

20. Due to space constraints I cannot delve deeper into the complexity of this assertion. I am aware, though, of how our identities are often constructed along and through different, dense, and often conflicting positions. Such intersectional identities, cutting through multiple sites that make up who we are, also position us in these sites at different times. As such, one might be the instigator of violence against the racialized abject, even as in a different situation, this same racialized abject male can mete out violence to another gendered and sexed female. This female might also find another way of abjecting another female.

21. Julia Kristeva, *Strangers to Ourselves* (New York: Columbia University Press, 1991), 2; see also Cecilia Sjoholm, *Kristeva and the Political* (New York: Routledge, 2005), esp. 59–86.

22. For an interesting interpretation of the mandate "Love your neighbor as yourself," see Slavoj Žižek, Eric L. Santner, and Kenneth Reinhard, *The Neighbor: Three Inquiries in Political Theology* (Chicago: University of Chicago Press, 2005).

23. Ashis Nandy explains the importance of recognizing that there are no "pure" positions that can even be said to be a constant, for he goes on to note that

> what looks like an obfuscation and compromise with evil may be seen also as a truer understanding of the oppressors whose suffering and decadence is, for once, taken seriously by their victims, who bear the responsibility of being both the subject and object of "history." What looks like a failure to make cognitive distinctions may in fact be a recognition that the popular modern antonyms are not always the true opposites. This century has shown that in every situation of organized oppression the true antonyms are always exclusive part versus the inclusive whole . . . not the past versus the present but either of them versus the timelessness in which the past is the present and the present is the past, not the oppressor versus oppressed but both of them versus the rationality which turns them into co-victims. (*The Intimate Enemy: Loss and Recovery of Self under Colonialism* [Delhi: Oxford University Press, 1983], 99)

24. Rita Nakashima Brock, *Journeys by Heart: A Christology of Erotic Power* (New York: Crossroad, 1988), xiv, 7.

25. Walter D. Mignolo, *Local Histories/Global Designs: Coloniality, Subaltern Knowledges, and Border Thinking* (Princeton, NJ: Princeton University Press, 2000), 338.

26. I am well aware that this notion of the "we" can be rightly critiqued, especially from the feminist perspective, as one that includes dynamics of coercion. Is it possible to have difference, to have autonomy, while at the same time affirming the importance of the communal? Many who so well know violence of abjection have relied and depended on the

collective, the sense of "we" to mobilize collective resistance against violence. Judith Butler also examines the necessity of the "we" as she observes that "we are something other than 'autonomous' in such a condition, but that does not mean that we are merged or without boundaries. It does mean . . . that when we think about who we 'are' and seek to represent ourselves, we cannot represent ourselves as merely bounded beings, for the primary others who are past for me not only live on in the fiber of the boundary that contains me, but they also haunt the way I am, as it were, periodically undone and open to becoming unbounded" (*Precarious Life: The Powers of Mourning and Violence* [New York: Verso, 2004], 27, 28).

27. Julia Kristeva, *Tales of Love* (New York: Columbia University Press, 1988), 368, 15. See also G. W. F. Hegel, "Love," in *The Hegel Reader*, trans. and ed. Stephen Houlgate (Oxford: Blackwell, 1998), 31–33.

28. For an excellent anthology on feminists responding to violence, refer to Elizabeth A. Castelli and Janet R. Jakobsen, eds., *Interventions: Activists and Academics Respond to Violence* (New York: Palgrave Macmillan, 2004).

29. Nelson Mandela, a person who knew both the depths of violence and the power of love as liberating force, writes, "For to be free is not merely to cast off one's chains, but to live in a way that respects and enhances the freedom of others. The true test of our devotion to freedom is just beginning" (*Long Walk to Freedom*, 624).

30. The African American, feminist poet Nikki Giovanni's poems powerfully argue how this form of love, which I refer to here as *jeong*, is what sustains the African American family and community in the face of the continuing violence of racism in its many dimensions. Moreover, her poetry signifies how this particular form of bond is often brutally undermined, dismissed, and, especially, erased by white racism. In her poem "Nikki Rosa," Giovanni writes, "And if you become famous or something they never talk about how happy you were to have your mother all to your self"; she ends with "and I really hope no white person ever has cause to write about me" because "even though you remember your biographers never understand." See http://project1.caryacademy.org/echos/poet_Nikki_Giovanni/samplepoemsnikkigiovanni.htm (accessed May 9, 2007).

31. Michael Franti and Spearhead, " Is Love Enough?" in *Yell Fire!* CD (New York: Anti, 2006).

Chapter Nine

Bitter Melon, Bitter Delight

Reading Jeremiah Reading Me

Lai Ling Elizabeth Ngan

Bitter Melon

Once upon a time there was a melon patch with a variety of melons growing next to each other—winter melon, honeydew melon, shrimp-colored honey melon or cantaloupe, and bitter melon. The children watched eagerly for the cantaloupe and honeydew to ripen, but when they passed by the bitter melon, they made disparaging and disgusted noises to indicate their displeasure. The bitter melon cried out to its Maker, "Why have you made me so distasteful to these little ones? Why couldn't I be more welcomed like the cantaloupe or honeydew, or at least accepted like the winter melon?" All the Maker would say was, "You are who you are supposed to be, and you, no less than the others, have a place under the sun."

Bitter melon—genus: *Momordica*, species: *M. charantia*. Also known as balsam pear or balsam apple, bitter melon is called *kugua* in Chinese, *karela* in Hindi, *pavakka* in Tamil, and *pare* or *parai* in Malay and Indonesian.[1] This tropical melon produces green, oblong fruits with a shiny, waxy, and wrinkly skin. It is among the most bitter of vegetables, and the smaller and more wrinkled it is, the more bitter its taste. Enjoying bitter melon is an acquired taste. When first exposed to it, most children and even adults find the taste disagreeable; however, many people gradually find themselves enjoying the bitter taste and dishes cooked with bitter melon. I am one such convert—now, bitter melon is one of my favorite vegetables in the world. Bitter melon is widely grown in Asia, and Asian immigrants in North America continue to enjoy its bitter taste in their native cuisines. In Asian restaurants in North America, however, it is not commonly found on the menu. Asian restaurant owners may prepare and

163

serve it to their staff and even tell their loyal customers that bitter melon is available, but except in ethnic restaurants that cater primarily to Asian customers, bitter melon is off the menu.

The bitter melon is a useful metaphor for the Asian immigrant experience in North America. Waves of Asian immigrants who came to North America have experienced and shared in a bitter history.[2] Many immigrants came to the New World to escape poverty and war, and for the promise of a better life for their families, job opportunities, and the possibility of greater freedom and security. Many of our Asian forebears, however, endured racially based persecutions, cruelty, and ostracism. Early immigrants were often restricted to ethnic ghettoes. Chinese immigrants in San Francisco, California, were forbidden to venture beyond Broadway Street, the "Big Street," after dark, at the threat of violence and death. Sometimes entire communities of immigrants were driven out of the towns in which they resided, put on boats, and sent back to their countries of origin.[3] For the first half of the twentieth century in the United States, most Chinese males were not allowed to bring their wives into the country, essentially creating bachelor societies in Chinatowns. Some of the immigrant gold miners were beaten, robbed, and even killed. The first anti-immigration law enacted in Congress targeting a specific ethnic group was the Chinese Exclusion Act of May 6, 1882.[4] The suffering that these Chinese immigrants endured was truly "eating bitterness."[5]

European immigrants likewise experienced ethnic discrimination in their early days in the United States, but subsequent generations have been able to assimilate relatively seamlessly into a white American society if they were also white. The same, however, cannot be said of immigrants from Africa, Asia, and South America whose skin color, facial features, and physical statue are sufficiently different from the white majority. Asian Americans, even those whose families have been here for several generations, continue to stand out as a distinct group. The stereotypical image of Asian Americans is that we are model minorities, a label that pits Asian Americans against other minority groups. Because of our external features we are also marked as perpetual foreigners.[6] No matter how many generations Asian Americans have been in America, we are often considered as outsiders, and our loyalty is easily placed under suspicion.[7] Sadly, Asians, and more recently Middle Easterners, often have to prove themselves twice as capable and twice as loyal in comparison to other ethnic groups who can blend more easily into the dominant society.

I moved from California to Texas ten years ago, and my early experience in Waco was indeed culture shock. I was accustomed to being around lots of Asians at the seminary where I taught, and I was ministering at a Chinese church, where my Asianness was not an issue. When I arrived in Waco, however, there were hardly any Asians around. A local Chinese pastor said that there were less than one hundred Chinese in a city of one hundred thousand, including students and restaurant workers.[8] All of a sudden having Chinese food became very important. I was excited to see a sign on the window of a Vietnamese restaurant advertising that it carried Asian groceries. On entering, however, the Asian grocery consisted of two shelves of sparsely placed canned goods that were long past their expiration dates. The owner approached and advised me that his store was not where I should shop and that I should go to Dallas or Houston to get my groceries.

I went to a Sam's Club after church one day in my Sunday best. When I walked into an aisle, a girl of twelve or thirteen stared at me with horror on her face and began to back away from me. Perhaps I was the first Asian she had seen, but it was disconcerting that my appearance would cause such fear in her. The initial experiences of being different from the dominant society awakened my sense of being Chinese; I was an outsider. The early years in Waco were indeed difficult. I was not sure if I could adjust and make this my home; I was lonely for the faces of other Asians, and I wondered if I would ever be accepted. I struggled and argued with God about this call to come to Texas. I was sure of the call, but did it have to be so difficult and disorienting? I think the bitter melon is a fitting metaphor for my early years in Waco.

The life of Jeremiah as depicted in the Bible can also be characterized as a bitter melon, as someone who ate bitterness. He was a prophet who could not change who he was or deny his call. He had the difficult mission of pronouncing indictments and YHWH's judgments against his people. This made him a threat and an object of derision to his fellow citizens. Since God brought me to Texas, did I have a mission also? Jeremiah's bold complaint to God did not change the bitterness of his experiences, but at some point in his life, he made peace with being who he was meant to be. He proclaimed,

> Your words were found, and I ate them
>   and your words became to me a joy
>   and the delight of my heart;
> for I am called by your name,
>   O LORD, God of hosts.
>   (Jer. 15:16)[9]

As Jeremiah found delight in God's word, can I find delight in Jeremiah, a book that is in the word of God? What can I learn from Jeremiah's courage and life? How might his story give me strength for my journey?

I am interested in the book of Jeremiah because I can identify with his experience. Jeremiah struggled long and hard with his call to be a prophet of YHWH. He was the son of Hilkiah, of the priests in Anathoth, in the land of Benjamin. He was probably a descendant of Abiathar, who was banished from Jerusalem after Solomon ascended the throne (1 Kgs. 2:26–27). Although Jeremiah was born into a priestly family, he did not serve as a priest. He was not a native of Jerusalem; he was an outsider with an unwelcome message.

Jeremiah was faithful in proclaiming YHWH's message, trying to point the people of Judah back to a covenantal relationship. His life as a prophet was so difficult that he wrestled with God about his bitter experiences. The questions that intrigue me about Jeremiah are these: As someone who was pushed to the margins in his society, who was distrusted and despised by his fellow citizens, how did Jeremiah act and react in these circumstances? How does the text portray his relationship with YHWH? How is he a model that I might follow? How does the book of Jeremiah speak to life and hope? These are some of the questions that will form the backdrop of my inquiry into the formation of Jeremiah as a prophet.

Asian American Biblical Hermeneutics

Before proceeding with a look at the prophet Jeremiah, a word about Asian American biblical hermeneutics seems appropriate. Like its Asian counterpart, it is highly contextual.[10] Asian American biblical scholars are usually trained in historical-critical methods in graduate institutions in North America or Europe and often use these methods in their interpretation of the Bible. We are, however, also aware that our social locations— our social, political, historical, and economic realities—play a major role in how we read and interpret the Bible. Our social location as a marginalized group heightens our awareness of the injustice perpetrated not only on Asian Americans but also on all minority groups. This location also sensitizes us to our complacency and participation in oppressive structures. A contextual reading of the biblical text would recognize this matrix from which our readings occur.

As a woman, I am also aware of the disenfranchisement of women in the Asian and Asian American community, especially in religious communities. Some churches refuse to ordain women and allow them a large role in the business of the church; others refuse to allow women on the platform, reserving it as a male-only space; still others allow women to work only with children or in the kitchen but do not permit women to preach or teach or serve communion. All of these practices claim support from biblical verses; but the Bible also proclaims the good news of equality among gender, race, and social class (Gal. 3:28). Churches are set up with a male-dominated hierarchical structure that harms both males and females. The interpretation of Scripture that supports such structures needs to be reexamined to bring a more-balanced, *shalom* (wholeness) perspective on how to live as God's people in the world.

As with many Asian American Christians, the Bible has a significant place in my life. I am a convert from Buddhism. My experience of God is of God revealed through Jesus Christ. In the Baptist tradition the Bible as the Christians' sacred Scripture is sufficient for faith and practice, for determining what I believe and how I live.[11] My interest in the Bible is not only to understand the text in its ancient context but also to sort out what it may mean for me and for all of God's people in the present.

As I am constructing the meaning in the biblical text, however, the text is constructing me. The reading and searching for meaning inevitably alter one's inner self. One does not come away unchanged. A dialogue occurs between the reader and the read, a light shines on the landscape of the heart, and sometimes something shifts in the reader. I find reading the Jeremiah of the text has this effect on me. The text is re-forming my assessment of the meaning of my life and vocation. It redefines life's circumstances and puts them into a greater context. It enlarges my valuation of life in this world. Something shifts in my understanding and in the way I see. As I am reading Jeremiah, Jeremiah is reading me.

Jeremiah the Prophet

The prophet Jeremiah is recognized as an important figure in the Bible not only by the length and placement of the book that is named for him but also by his inclusion in the list of prophets cited at Caesarea Philippi. When Jesus asked his disciples who did people identify as the Son of Man, the disciples answered, "Some say John the Baptist, but others Elijah, and still others Jeremiah or one of the prophets" (Matt. 16:14).

Who is Jeremiah? What can we know about him? The book of Jeremiah has more historical and personal information about the prophet than any other prophetic book in the Bible. Jeremiah studies, however, have long made a distinction between the "Jeremiah of history" and the "Jeremiah of the text."[12] While traditional interpretive approaches seek to reconstruct an authentic life of the historical prophet from the text, what seems more feasible and preferable from an exegetical standpoint is to recover the Jeremiah who is characterized and presented in the text. This is the Jeremiah with whom this study is engaged.

Struggle with Identity, Call, and Mission

Jeremiah's Story

The book of Jeremiah begins with a description of his call by YHWH: "'Before I formed you in the womb I knew you, / and before you were born I consecrated you; / I appointed you a prophet to the nations'" (Jer. 1:5). In spite of his protest, YHWH commissioned him to be a prophet and promised him protection from his adversaries.

He was a "lad" when YHWH called him (Jer. 1:6). The commissioning of Jeremiah is reminiscent of the call of Isaiah (Isa. 6:6–7). Whereas a seraph touched Isaiah's lips with a live coal from the altar, it was YHWH who put out the hand and touched Jeremiah's mouth:

> And the LORD said to me,
>   "Now I have put my words in your mouth.
>   See, today I appoint you over nations and over kingdoms,
>   to pluck up and to pull down,
>   to destroy and to overthrow,
>   to build and to plan."
>
> (Jer. 1:9–10)

The unpopular proclamations Jeremiah was instructed to cry out made him persona non grata. Where are the flattering words and supportive oracles for the king and his court? Where are the pronouncements of blessings for the king and his sons? Where are the affirmations of unwavering loyalty to the monarchy? Jeremiah's earlier pronouncements against Judah may be brushed off as the delirium of a mad man, but his insistent cries of "Violence! Destruction!" made him an irritant and a threat to state security. His judgment oracles and prophetic acts could be read as acts of sedition. His insistence on submission to the Babylonian yoke made him an outright traitor. To make Jeremiah stop speaking, he was beaten and put in stocks (Jer. 20:1–2), arrested and threatened with death (Jer. 26:7–11), forced to become a fugitive (Jer. 36:19–26), and thrown into a cistern and left to die of hunger (Jer. 38:4–13). Even his kinfolk from Anathoth plotted against his life (Jer. 11:21–23). Such was the life of the prophet.

In his forty years as a prophet of YHWH, Jeremiah experienced much hardship and bitterness; he was rejected and persecuted by his own people, and he saw the fall of his nation and the exile to Babylon. After the assassination of Gedaliah the governor in 583 BCE, Jeremiah and Baruch, his friend and scribe, were forcibly taken to Egypt by a group of Judeans who wanted to escape the Babylonian wrath. This is the last of what we know about Jeremiah.

My Story

I am a Chinese who was born and raised in Hong Kong in a devout Buddhist family. Even though I attended a Catholic school and began to believe at an early age that Jesus is God, my parents made it clear that conversion to Christianity was not permitted. At my maternal grandmother's persistent urging, however, we children were eventually allowed to attend her church. I started attending this Baptist church when I was fifteen and had a conversion and call experience at the age of seventeen, just prior to leaving Hong Kong for school in the United States.

As a people who were long dominated by foreign powers and colonized by the British, my family was one of those that had bought into the myth of European superiority and had internalized racism to the extent of desiring the physical stature and facial features of Westerners. To give me double eyelids like the Europeans, my mother repeatedly drew lines on my eyelids with toothpicks until permanent lines were formed. Similar to some of my Chinese friends from Hong Kong, I was instructed to pinch my nose bridge continually in an attempt to raise the height of my nose. Such childhood experiences reinforced the message that because I was not like the Europeans, I was not desirable.

I had lived most of my life by values my mother had tried to instill in me, abiding by the virtues of a traditional Chinese female who is genteel, quiet, and deferential. Like the legendary beauty Yang Guifei of the ninth century BCE, a royal concubine of the emperor of the Tang dynasty, I was not allowed to leave the house except for unavoidable outings such as going to school and to ballet and piano lessons. We were not permitted to talk back to elders, and any decision of significance was dictated by my parents.

After coming to the United States at the age of seventeen, I continued to play this role. I felt that unrealistic expectations were sometimes placed on me, as if I represented all Chinese and all Asian women. Some people expected me to be a stereotypical Asian woman like those represented in movies, or an imagined China doll: genteel, quiet, deferential, and perhaps secretly a kung fu expert. Except for being a kung fu expert, I was living up to other people's stereotypes and expectations.

During the first year in a boarding school in California, I began to observe that American girls and women were permitted more say in their lives. How I wished to be like them. The day I first became aware of this desire to be an American—that is, a white American—was also a day of great disappointment. For most of my life I was ashamed to look at myself in the mirror since only fair skin and Euro-American facial features were considered beautiful. One morning while I was absentmindedly washing my face at the sink, I looked up into the mirror and found to my great horror that I was not white. "But I am white," I declared. At least that was how I had felt for several years, long enough to have forgotten that I am Chinese. I was distraught at the thought that no matter how white I may feel inside, I could never be white enough. My outside will always be yellow. I will always be different from my white friends. I was a "foreign" student from Hong Kong who had become Americanized. I was not American, but I was also not Chinese anymore. I grew to accept the fact that I could not be white, but I did try to emulate white American culture and values because I genuinely respected my professors who taught me through college, graduate school, and seminary. Except for a female music professor, all my professors were white males. They taught and mentored me, and I felt privileged to have had them as my teachers, but they could not teach me to be who I am, a Chinese American woman.

After studying biology in graduate school, I again felt God's call to ministry and attended seminary in the San Francisco area. My vocation took a different direction. Through struggle and discernment and what I believe to be God's leading, I now teach Hebrew Bible at a Baptist seminary in Texas.

I found that it was relatively easy to be a Chinese American in California. The Bay Area has a large population of Asian Americans with significant political clout. Many agencies and legal advocacy groups exist that look out for immigrant and minority groups' rights. To live in the middle of Texas, however, is a different story. Shortly after arriving in Texas, I became even more aware that I am not white, not male—and not Texan. I spoke with the wrong accent, so well-meaning friends tried to teach me to speak "proper" Texan English. Some friends advised me jokingly that in order to become a Texan I would have to run over an armadillo with my car. What a horrifying suggestion.

The newfound interest in my Chinese heritage was forged after I came to Texas. Thrust into this situation, I needed to find my roots. My awareness of being on the margins due to my race and gender initially deepened my sense of inferiority and voicelessness, but good friends encouraged me to become my true self and to speak from my place as a Chinese American woman. It took a series of illnesses, however, before I began to reassess my life. Who am I? Who am I meant to be? The process of finding my true self was a grace-filled journey, albeit a long and painful one. It took me even longer to be able to embrace God's call as a prophet. I am glad for everything that I have experienced because all of it shaped me into who I am and prepared me for the transformation into the real me. My consciousness has been raised as to the suffering that minorities and women endure every day. I have been given new sight and must speak according to what I see. How can I not? I find this place on the margins to be exciting because it is at the margins that life and creativity occur.[13] I am becoming the person who I am meant to be, and I travel this journey with others who also seek life, healing, and wholeness for all beings.

Relationship with God: The Prayers of Jeremiah

The prophet Jeremiah is known as the weeping prophet in some Christian circles because of the many laments he intoned for his people and himself. He was torn between the wrath that God was going to inflict on the Israelites and the pain that God and his fellow citizens were inflicting on him. He was assailed from every side. His prayers are often called confessions in Jeremiah studies, but they are more in the nature of complaints and arguments with God.[14] These prayers paint the depth of Jeremiah's spirituality and his relationship with God.

Ann and Barry Ulanov, scholars who teach and write in the area of psychiatry and religion, conceptualize prayer as "primary speech": "It is that primordial discourse in which we assert, however clumsily or eloquently, our own being. If we are ever honest with ourselves, it is here that we must be, though we are often not sure about who it is that we are talking to or how well we are talking or that we are even talking."[15] Prayers are not speeches about God but speeches to God. As conversations between the pray-er and God, they involve speaking and listening. Whether one perceives an answer from God, prayers state who we really are and where we are in our beings; they reveal one's interiority.[16] Jeremiah's prayers, therefore, can serve as windows to the interiority of the prophet. The interest here is not to reconstruct a psychological profile of Jeremiah but to explore the relational features that may illumine the source of his strength.

The prayers of Jeremiah are found in five blocks of material. The first prayer, Jeremiah 11:18–12:6, was occasioned by a plot from Jeremiah's kinfolk in Anathoth to kill him. Taking the form of a lament, Jeremiah asserted his innocence and trust in YHWH and pleaded his cause with YHWH. God promised vengeance on those who sought his life. Apparently the judgment was delayed, and the wicked continued to prosper. Using lawsuit language, Jeremiah questioned YHWH's resolve to punish the treacherous, and YHWH countered that the worse was yet to come.

The second prayer, Jeremiah 15:10–21, came out of persecutions and insults from the people to whom he had been prophesying. Because of his vocation, he was cursed and ostracized. This prayer shows the complex emotional struggle that went on in his inner being. One moment Jeremiah bemoaned his birth and existence (Jer. 15:10); at another moment he was in inexplicable joy. However, he put the responsibility for his suffering on God:

> Know that on your account I suffer insult.
> . . . .
> under the weight of your hand I sat alone,
>   for you had filled me with indignation.
> Why is my pain unceasing,
>   my wound incurable,
>   refusing to be healed?
>   (Jer. 15:15b, 17b-18a)

In spite of his suffering, he found the word of God to be pleasurable:

> Your words were found, and I ate them,
>   and your words became to me a joy
>   and the delight of my heart;
> for I am called by your name,
>   O Lord, God of hosts.
>   (Jer. 15:16)

Jeremiah recognized the pain and the joy of being God's prophet. Nevertheless, he accused God of being like a deceitful brook that is unreliable. Perhaps Jeremiah had contemplated quitting his vocation, for YHWH's reply presented an ultimatum:

> If you turn back, I will take you back,
>   and you shall stand before me.
> If you utter what is precious, and not what is worthless,
>   you shall serve as my mouth.
>
> (Jer. 15:19)

There was no word of comfort, only a call for Jeremiah to return to his task and the promise of triumph over his enemies.

The next three prayers did not receive a direct reply from God. The third prayer, Jeremiah 17:14–18, is a cry to God to save him but punish his persecutors. The people taunted him because of the delay of God's judgment. Jeremiah must have felt like a fool. He cried, "Violence! Destruction!" yet imminent destruction was nowhere in sight. Jeremiah's reputation as a prophet was at stake, and so was the truthfulness of YHWH's word. The fourth prayer, Jeremiah 18:18–23, is a prayer for revenge. He had been interceding for the people to whom he brought YHWH's words; now he prayed for their total destruction without mercy. His enemies continued to plot to kill him, and he wanted YHWH to pour his full wrath on them. In the fifth prayer, Jeremiah 20:7–13, Jeremiah accused God of overpowering him.

> O Lord, you have enticed me,
>   and I was enticed;
> you have overpowered me,
>   and you have prevailed.
> I have become a laughingstock all day long;
>   everyone mocks me.
>
> (Jer. 20:7)

When he tried to reject his mission, however, he found that he could not:

> Then within me there is something like a burning fire
>   shut up in my bones;
> I am weary with holding it in,
>   and I cannot.
>
> (Jer. 20:9b)

YHWH and Jeremiah's enemies had become indistinguishable (Jer. 20:7, 9). His only consolation was that YHWH of hosts was with him "like a dreaded warrior," and the downfall of his enemies was sure (Jer. 20:11).

The way Jeremiah spoke with God suggests that he was also a friend of God. Not only did he understand the pathos of God and share God's pain and anguish concerning the wayward Judahites, but also his relationship with YHWH was close enough to allow complaints and fights. Politeness aside, he argued with God, and God sometimes answered back, and sometimes the prophet's accusations and God's answer were both harsh toward each other. The gloves were off, so to speak. The prayers were honest to God; and God and Jeremiah wrestled like Jacob's wrestling at Peniel (Gen. 32). Jeremiah did not want the job, but God promised strength and triumph. He wanted to give up his call, but God offered him a chance to return. He trusted God, yet at times he found it difficult to trust. Jeremiah needed God's support and protection. Dare we say that God needed Jeremiah as a partner?

Friendship with God

Jeremiah, a friend of God who dares to argue and wrestle with God, is a role model to whom all Christians can aspire, not just Chinese American Christians. Many Asian American Christians, however, would not dare to think of God as a foe or argue with God even when experiencing Joban trials. The piety of most Asian American Christians would forbid the voicing aloud of such blasphemous thoughts even in the most desperate circumstances. We have been socialized by family in traditional values of revering elders and obeying persons in positions of authority. If we are not permitted to question parents, teachers, or pastors, how much less would we be allowed to question God? In religious systems that insist on accepting everything, whether good or bad, as God's will and judgment, and every suffering or mishap as punishment for sin, there is no room for contesting one's experience as unjust and undeserved.

Women suffer a double restriction because hierarchical structure is compounded with patriarchal devaluation of women's place in society. How could women dare to argue and wrestle with God when the Deity is consistently portrayed as a male superior who is far above all superiors? My first experience of arguing with God came by accident. I had graduated from college with lofty plans for my future, plans of which any Asian parent would be proud. My grades and test scores should have guaranteed smooth sailing, but the plans I had envisioned were not materializing. It was a silly but intense fight, in retrospect, out of my distrust that God truly loved me. I fought, argued, cried, and complained for a month until I realized that God was holding me and waiting patiently for me to realize that

God had a plan for my good and not for my demise. There was no radical departure from my beliefs but a deeper understanding and growth in faith. I was learning to approach God boldly, trusting that God loves me even when I am angry and want to fight.

Our cautiousness in approaching God keeps us from conceiving of God as a friend, for such a notion brings God too near to the human realm. The Bible, nevertheless, teaches both the transcendence and immanence of God. God is the Holy One in our midst (Isa. 12:6). God is the totally Other, yet God became like us and came to us through the incarnate Christ. A Christian hymn encourages us with the thought of "what a friend we have in Jesus," and the Bible calls Abraham a "friend of God." But we humans? As God's friends? This is a theological concept to which we may be able to assent in the abstract but have difficulty accepting as a spiritual reality. For God and Abraham to come as friends, they would have to come as equals. As Frederick Buechner states in his book *Whistling in the Dark*, "It is something Abraham and God . . . do together. . . . He is not being Creature for the moment, and God is not being Creator."[17]

Asian American Christians need to remember that we not only are creatures of God, saved by grace, but we also can be friends of God. Sadly, we often keep God at a safe and polite distance. To be God's friend, however, we have to come close enough to wrestle with God, as did Jacob and Jeremiah. To wrestle with the Holy One is risky, of course—Jacob left the encounter with a permanent limp, and Jeremiah left with no relief from his bitter life—but to be close and be touched is better than being at arm's length from the Source of all being.

"To Pluck Up and to Pull Down"— Jeremiah as Prophet–Social Critic

Abraham Heschel's classic work on the prophets proposes that "the fundamental experience of the prophet is a fellowship with the feelings of God, a *sympathy with the divine pathos*, a communion with the divine consciousness which comes about through the prophet's reflection of, or participation in, the divine pathos."[18] In speaking of Jeremiah in particular, Heschel states that what happened to Jeremiah was "the overwhelming impact of the divine pathos upon his mind and heart, completely involving and gripping his personality in its depths, and the unrelieved distress which sprang from his intimate involvement."[19] Thus Jeremiah was a passionate participant in the anguish and pathos of God.

The constant drumbeat of Jeremiah's message was the apostasy of Judah. The people of Judah had committed the unimaginable.

> Has a nation changed its gods,
>> even though they are no gods?
> . . . .
>> they have forsaken me,
> the fountain of living water,
>> and dug out cisterns for themselves,
> cracked cisterns that can hold no water.
>> (Jer. 2:11a, 13)

Using images from Hosea, Jeremiah indicted the Israelites for whoring on every high hill and under every green tree (Jer. 2:20; Hos. 4:10–13). Like Isaiah's Song of the Vineyard, Jeremiah accused them of degenerating from a choice vine from the purest stock to become a wild vine (Jer. 2:21–22; Isa. 5:1–4). They will be punished with war and destruction, and they will be shamed like a thief who was caught (Jer. 2:14–19, 26–28).

Jeremiah's use of female metaphors for faithless Israel presents a problem that interpreters need to address. Jeremiah equated Israel with an adulterous wife who was justifiably divorced by her husband; she was a whore who prostituted herself to many lovers; she even waited by the waysides for them so that as the object of sexual violence by these lovers, she was the one to be blamed.[20] The prophet used metaphors of a "restive young [female] camel" and a "wild ass" in heat with uncontrollable sexual appetite for "strangers" to mock the people's unfaithfulness to YHWH (Jer. 2:23–25). Jeremiah's link of female metaphors with sexuality and the absence of such connection when using male metaphors are striking. Angela Bauer points out that "the sexuality of the female is identified as the problem. . . . The portrayal of the female as out of control sexually resonates with patriarchal descriptions of women despite reverse social-sexual realities."[21] Careful interpretation needs to dislocate the pairing of blameless male with sinful female, the notion that sexual desire is evil, and the right of men to use physical and sexual violence against women.

Jeremiah's message was also conveyed in prophetic acts. The story of the loincloth in Jeremiah 13 is an analogy that shows the need for Israel and Judah to be attached to YHWH; otherwise, like a loincloth that was buried on the banks of a river and left to deteriorate, they will become useless (Jer. 13:1–11). In Jeremiah 18 the prophet observed a potter making a vessel. The clay that was misshaped could be reshaped into another vessel as the potter willed. The lesson to Judah was a call to repent and return to YHWH so that God could devise a plan for their good, but the people refused (Jer. 18:1–12).

Another message was drawn from the faithfulness and obedience of the Rechabites (Jer. 35). These descendants of Jonadab (2 Kgs. 10:15), son of Rechab, obeyed the instruction of their ancestor to live an austere lifestyle. They lived as nomads in tents, did not sow or own houses or vineyards, and abstained from drinking wine. The Israelites, however, had persistently refused to obey God. In addition they had filled the land with the blood of the innocent, and even offered their children as burnt offerings to Baal (Jer. 19:4–5). Jeremiah demonstrated YHWH's judgment by breaking an earthen jug, signifying that God would break the people and the city with a breaking that could never be mended, a fate of death and destruction (Jer. 19:10–11; 35:13–15).

The people of Judah had also mistakenly put their trust in the temple in Jerusalem, assuming that it was a guarantee of special protection from enemies or harm (Jer. 7:4). But the Israelite covenantal religion demanded more than the pure worship of YHWH; it had moral obligations. In Genesis 18:19 YHWH states that the descendants of Abraham are to do righteousness and justice; but there was no justice or righteousness in Jeremiah's day (Jer. 5:1–5; 21:12; 22:3): "Will you steal, murder, commit adultery, swear falsely, make offerings to Baal, and go after other gods that you have not known, and then come and stand before me in this house, which is called by my name, and say, 'We are safe!'—only to go on doing all these abominations?" (Jer. 7:9–10). The Judahites suffered for want of good leaders who were true to YHWH. Whether rulers, priests, or prophets, they were all leading the people astray (Jer. 2:8; 5:30–31).

With New Eyes to See

Asian Americans who are aware of the harm of prejudice and injustice should take a lead in bringing about a more just society. No one should have to suffer the indignities of being considered as a lesser citizen—not white, black, brown, or yellow. We must speak up and be the voice of the voiceless and work to raise the heads of the downtrodden. The task of making things right is a labor not only for the sake of Asians and Asian Americans, but also one that must be extended to include all ethnic groups and persons of lower socioeconomic class, especially racial and ethnic women, who suffer double discrimination. Then every person can truly have equal rights and opportunities, and every person can truly have a place under the sun.

Educated and financially secure Asian Americans, however, are not always cognizant of the gulf between them and other Asian Americans who are struggling to get by and survive.[22] We are unaware of our privileges relative to those who are disenfranchised and may even turn a blind eye to our complacency and contribution to others' suffering. We are guilty of the injustices that we perpetrate against others in a lower socio-economic class, regardless of race and gender. As a matter of fact, not all Asian Americans have made it. Many Asian Americans, especially new immigrants, live below the poverty line, working in labor-intensive jobs such as in garment sweatshops, markets, and ethnic restaurants sixteen to eighteen hours a day, seven days a week. They are paid far below the minimum wage. Some live in squalid conditions and are confined to ethnic ghettos because of lack of English-language capacity and access to broader opportunities. They are looked down on by some Asian Americans who may consider them as ignorant, backward immigrants. We may be glad to have cheap Chinese food in restaurants and cheap T-shirts and other souvenirs from Chinatown, but the persons who labor to provide the services and goods that we enjoy are invisible. We do not recognize the struggles they face daily to survive in a strange land. We may even find them embarrassing because they lack the culture and sophistication of Western society and do not fit nicely into the "respectable" dominant culture. For those of us who are privileged Asian Americans, we have become, knowingly or not, the oppressors of our less fortunate brothers and sisters.

Asian Americans can be as guilty as anyone of racial prejudices against other nonwhite ethnic groups. Many of us have bought into the myth of white superiority. The internalized racism is insidious and damaging to all who harbor it. We may have appropriated the schematic of white superiority that gives a false sense of our inferiority in comparison to whites, but we may also have appropriated a false sense of superiority of our Asian-ness over African Americans, Latinos, Pacific Islanders, Africans, and so forth. We may even have a sense of our own ethnic superiority over other Asian groups. Perhaps it is ethnic pride or maybe it is the need to bolster self-confidence, but the tendency is to compare and put down other ethnic groups in favor of ourselves. As is often the case, one disenfranchised group is pitted against another, competing for limited resources and opportunities when we should be working together for the good of the whole community.

"To Build and to Plant": An Asian American
Christian Reflection on Jeremiah

Asian Americans are persons created by God, in God's image—a commonality that we share with all humanity. We cannot change who we are, nor should we desire to do so. We can be proud of our Asian ancestry and traditions—of our ancestors who came to North America, endured much hardship, and ate bitterness as often as they ate rice. They persevered. Their courage and tenacity were incredible. They were strong people. Their efforts to pave the way for subsequent generations have brought us to where we are today.

The work of full acceptance and appreciation of Asian Americans, however, is far from complete. In a world where racism, classism, and sexism are real, we must confront and eradicate the evil perpetrated by various kinds of prejudice. We must do our best to bring about a more just society, where everyone has a place under the sun. We cannot simply accept the status quo and enjoy the privileges that come from coalescing with the dominant culture while others are disenfranchised; we must seek to dismantle overt racism and other systemic discriminations such as classism and sexism. We have benefited much from the civil rights movement, but the dream of Dr. Martin Luther King Jr. is far from realized. How should we use our power and privileges for the betterment of society, to be the hands and feet of the powerless? I believe it is our role to be prophets who call our communities to accountability, to right what is wrong, and to let justice prevail.

We also need to pave the way for future generations. To teach and mentor the next generation is our obligation, not a luxury that can be ignored. Our ancestors have paved the way for us, and now it is our turn. To nurture the next generation of Asian and Asian American women is a task in which Pacific, Asian, and North American Asian Women in Theology and Ministry is actively engaged. We hope to instill in the next generations of Asian and Asian North American women an understanding of their rightful place in society and empower them to be change agents and prophets for the good of the world.

Asian Americans are like the bitter melon that cannot become a cantaloupe or honeydew, and not everyone will welcome us or our message for a just world. But bitter melons have their purposes and their place under the sun. A recent Google search for "bitter melon" turned up 546,000 sites. It turns out that bitter melon is not an obscure vegetable at all. Almost all of the Internet sites are companies marketing bitter melon powder and pills as treatment for various ailments. Chinese medicine has long recognized the usefulness of bitter melon in treating diabetes by lowering blood glucose, but now alternative medicine points to its potential use as a treatment for heart disease, certain types of cancer, and possibly HIV/AIDS.

Asian Americans have an important role to play in this society. Like the bitter melon and its medicinal uses, we can make a difference in forging a better world. If we accept and embrace who we are as Asian Americans in spite of the realities of an imperfect world, perhaps we too can rejoice in the impact that we can hope to make. We have an undeniable place under the sun. Perhaps, like Jeremiah, we will find joy and delight in our hearts for what God has done in us, for we are called by God's name.

Notes

1. See "Bitter Melon," http://www.en.wikipedia.org/wiki/Bitter_melon.
2. Ronald Takaki, *Strangers from a Different Shore: A History of Asian Americans*, rev. ed. (Boston: Little, Brown & Co., 1998); and Ronald Takaki, *A Different Mirror: A History of Multicultural America* (Boston: Little, Brown & Co., 1993).
3. During my college years in Riverside, California, one of my teachers took me to a section of town that had buildings with typical Chinese tile roofs. He told me that a long time ago, Riverside had a Chinatown, but one day, the whites in town took all the Chinese to Los Angeles, put them on boats, and shipped them back to China.
4. Iris Chang, *The Chinese in America: A Narrative History* (New York: Viking, 2003), 132.
5. "Eating bitterness" is a Chinese expression that refers to someone who has to endure severe hardship.
6. For a discussion of the use of "model minority" and the effects of being considered "perpetual foreigners," see Gale A. Yee's chapter in this volume.
7. Consider the Japanese internment camps during World War II, when Americans of Japanese ancestry from the West Coast were removed from their homes and confined to makeshift camps in desolated places in the United States; there were many instances that raised suspicion that Chinese Americans were unreliable and might be spies for China.
8. This figure was quoted in 1996. Since then Waco has seen a significant increase in many ethnic groups, especially Latinos, and some of the larger grocery chains carry a small selection of ingredients for cooking Chinese food. I still have to go to Dallas for periodic shopping ventures.
9. All scriptural quotations are from the New Revised Standard Version.
10. Jeffrey K. Kuan, "Asian Biblical Interpretation," in *Dictionary of Biblical Interpretation*, ed. John H. Hayes (Nashville: Abingdon Press, 1999), 70–77; Archie C. C. Lee, "Biblical Interpretation in Asian Perspective," *Asia Journal of Theology* 7 (1993): 35–39; Chan-Hie Kim, "Reading the Bible as Asian Americans," in *The New Interpreter's Bible*, ed. Leander Keck et al., vol. 1 (Nashville: Abingdon, 1994), 161–66; Tat-siong Benny Liew, ed., "The Bible in Asian America," special issue, *Semeia* 90/91 (2002); Mary F. Foskett and Jeffrey Kah-Jin Kuan, eds., *Ways of Being, Ways of Knowing: Asian American Biblical Interpretation* (St. Louis: Chalice Press, 2006).

11. Herschel Hobbs, *The Baptist Faith and Message* (Nashville: Convention Press, 1971), 25–27.

12. Timothy Polk, *The Prophetic Persona: Jeremiah and the Language of Self* (Sheffield: JSOT Press, 1984), 7–24.

13. Michael Walzer, *Interpretation and Social Criticism* (Cambridge, MA: Harvard University Press, 1987), 38.

14. Anson Laytner, *Arguing with God: A Jewish Tradition* (Northvale, NJ: Jason Aronson, 1990).

15. Ann Ulanov and Barry Ulanov, *Primary Speech: A Psychology of Prayer* (Louisville, KY: Westminster John Knox Press, 1982), vii–viii.

16. Ibid., 1.

17. Frederick Buechner, *Whistling in the Dark: An ABC Theologized* (San Francisco: Harper & Row, 1988), 50.

18. Abraham Heschel, *The Prophets* (New York: Harper & Row, 1969), 26, original emphasis.

19. Ibid.

20. See Angela Bauer, *Gender in the Book of Jeremiah: A Feminist-Literary Reading* (New York: Peter Lang, 1999), where she points out that the verb *shgl* translated as "been lain with" (Jer. 3:2) "carries the connotation of forced sexual intercourse" (50–51).

21. Ibid., 33–34.

22. Chang, *Chinese in America*, 348–88; Takaki, *Strangers from a Different Shore*, 424–32; Dušanka Miščevic and Peter Kwong, *Chinese Americans: The Immigrant Experience* (Westport, CT: Hugh Lauter Levin Associates, 2000), 174–94; Joel L. Swerdlow and Chien-Chi Chang, "New York's Chinatown," *National Geographic* 194, August 1998, 58–77.

Chapter Ten

No Garlic, Please, We Are Indian

Reconstructing the De-eroticized Indian Woman

Anne Dondapati Allen

From a culture that gave the world the Kamasutra, the erotic architecture of the Ajanta and Ellora caves, and the seductive undulations of the Bharatnatyam and Kuchipudi dances, the term "de-eroticized Indian woman" seems a contradiction. It is incomprehensible, at the very least, that two such contrasting realities would exist within the same cultural context and with such seemingly relative ease. The pen of the poet, the brush of a painter, the chisel of the sculptor, and the undulations of a dancer encapsulate in art and make accessible to the world the eroticism of the human body. This eroticism is only permitted, however, through flights of fantasy. That art offers creative freedom even in a traditional society such as India is neither new nor shocking. Male and female forms in the throes of graphic sexual encounters, however, stand in stark contrast to demure, sari-clad Indian women, who cast furtive, guilty glances at a world to which they are uninitiated. Some Indian communities claim that garlic can cause a woman to feel sexually aroused. Instead of the obvious "No sex, please, I'm Indian," we might say, "No garlic, please, I am Indian."

The chasm between the appreciation of the human body captured in stone and the everyday experience of women becomes evident in the epidemic of HIV/AIDS cases and their devastating impact on the women and children of India. The question that begs to be answered is why the consequences for women diagnosed with HIV/AIDS are so harsh and dehumanizing. The answer is found not in the disease itself but in how it is contracted. Unlike cancer or malaria, the HIV/AIDS virus is transmitted through sexual activity. This fact shrouds the diagnosis in shame, suspicion, scorn, and secrecy, and it places responsibility firmly on the individual. If HIV/AIDS were acquired through a mosquito bite, the diagnosis would not carry the taboo that it often does.[1] Women, who are seldom given the right to make decisions about their bodies, are penalized nonetheless, not only for contracting the disease but also for bringing shame on their families.

Some insights are easy to come by: in cultures that measure the productivity of women by motherhood, HIV/AIDS hinders their production of healthy sons, who guarantee the continuity of the ancestral line. Unable to fulfill her procreative functions, a woman is ostracized from the marital home and from her social and religious communities. Social ostracization sets in motion a series of penalties that are physically, psychologically, socially, and spiritually debilitating and render the woman incapable of providing for herself or her children. During a visit to a hospital in South India, Donald E. Messer, a practical theologian and advocate for victims of HIV/AIDS, captures the plight of Indian women infected by the AIDS virus:

> Outside the men's wards, women (mothers and wives of the sick) looked through the bar-like windows at what we were doing. Once we stepped outside, they greeted us with smiles and gestures of appreciation for the gifts. But outside the women's wards, no one looked through the windows. Those inside were terribly alone. . . . I learned that men spread the disease to their spouses and girlfriends, but women are blamed and often tossed out of the home. They not only die, they die alone.[2]

To address the HIV/AIDS crisis in India and its impact on women and children, we must examine the social and political processes that contributed to this situation. How did sexual activity come to be established as such a taboo for Indian women? I locate the genesis during colonial India in the 1800s and 1900s.

The Missionizing of Colonial India

Colonial rule in India was justified on the grounds of British "moral superiority" measured by three factors: the abject condition of Indian women, a supposedly degenerate culture, and the effeminacy of Indian men that rendered them presumably incapable of governing themselves.[3] Before the arrival of evangelical missionaries, the British presence in India was primarily a business venture, with strict entry restrictions. Increasing pressure from the missionaries forced the British Parliament to modify the charter in 1813, lifting entry restrictions and opening the way for

Protestant missionaries to enter the country.[4] With the arrival of the missionaries, the religious justification for the British presence in India, and their interference in the public and private realms, began in earnest.

The missionary goal was to bring light to a nation steeped in superstition and depravity. The will of God was for India to benefit from their missionizing and colonizing project. Initially the intended target of missionary efforts was upper-caste Hindus, but these efforts were largely unsuccessful. Missionizing efforts were then diverted to the more accessible lower castes, with greater success. Indian converts to Christianity consisted mostly of economically and socially disenfranchised groups. The observation, analyses, literature, and scholarly studies compiled by British administrators, missionaries, and scholars were intended to garner ideological and financial support; instead, these denigrated the social, cultural, religious, and economic conditions in India. While the missionaries' concern for social issues may have been genuine, they also significantly furthered the material and ideological basis of colonialism.

British missionaries in the second quarter of the nineteenth century radically transformed the relationship between the rulers and the missionaries and set in motion a process that inextricably linked the gospel with the imperial presence in the country. Although most known through its British presence, Christianity in India predates the arrival of European missionaries. This historical fact challenges the notion that prior to the arrival of British Christianity, the culture was depraved and in dire need of saving. Hence the collusion of the British administrators and British missionaries is even more significant given that cordial relationships did not exist with other European missionaries, including German, Dutch, and Portuguese Christians. The British collusion thus furthered the missionizing and colonizing enterprise, firmly establishing the British Empire in India.

Nationalism and the Construction of the Ideal Hindu Woman

Indian reformers and revivalists responded to the increasingly denigrating rhetoric about Indian culture and beliefs. As the nationalists attempted to argue with their colonizers, their responses took place within the constructs that the colonizers established. The nationalists accepted the analysis of moral and cultural degeneration, but they argued that reform lay in returning to India's past. They embraced what they deemed to be superior values within Hinduism, and their corrective lay in the rejuvenation of a weakened culture and religion and the restoration of the motherland to her prior glory. Colonizer and missionary rhetoric was thus countered by a revaluation of traditional Hindu culture, radically changing the course of the nationalist struggle.

The political, social, and religious decline of the culture was located in departure from traditional values and beliefs and the inadequacy of the Hindu male. Indian nationalists did not deny the abject condition of women. They argued that in India's glorious ancient past, women were afforded a superior status. Since the Indian male was inadequate, the liberation of the nation would have to come through the Indian woman. The nationalists constructed an ideal of womanhood from models in the past.[5] They therefore located the redemption of the nation within an unconquered, pure space—the body of the Hindu woman, who was uniquely qualified for the task, argues Tanika Sarkar, for several reasons:

> This body was disciplined by the Shastras alone and proved its capacity for pain and suffering, and therein lay the redemptive hopes of the whole community. The Hindu woman's body was molded from infancy by a shastric regimen of non-consensual, indissoluble, infant marriage, and by iron laws of absolute chastity, austere widowhood, and a supposedly proven capacity for self-immolation.[6]

The unconquered body of the chaste Hindu woman was the ground on which the redemptive story would be constructed. Out of the ashes of a people who were conquered and a culture that was violated would rise a nation that was wounded but not obliterated, sullied and yet impenetrable to the onslaught of an alien civilization, bruised but resilient—endowed with the image of Mother India. By acknowledging the fallenness of the nation, the nationalists achieved two significant goals: (1) they glorified the insurmountable, indomitable spirit of the nation, Mother India, in spite of the degeneration of the culture, and, thereby, they solidified the perception of a cohesive, continuous, and glorious past; and (2) they issued a challenge to men and women to restore Mother India to its past glory.

A more notable outcome was the unquestioning acceptance of this version of history for the sole purpose of creating a unified voice and a common vision for the country. If the Indian Hindu woman was constructed as the salvific figure for burgeoning nationalism, and her chaste body was the source for bringing forth a new India, the task of protecting, preserving, and prescribing approved codes of conduct would be legitimated and warranted. The argument that child marriage and sati would preserve the virginity and chastity of women seemed to be perfectly logical and rational. Women, in other words, would become the sacred sacrificial object to compensate for the inadequacy of the Indian male. Such a mind-set continues to prevail within large segments of Indian society even today.

Prevailing Constructs of Female Sexuality in India

Indian cultural contexts acknowledge female sexuality and desire, but they are described and valued to fit the agenda of patriarchal structures. On the one hand, female sexuality is considered synonymous with production of children. Female sexual desire, on the other hand, challenges the familial and communal control of procreation due to its purely personal, pleasurable experience. Constraints on women's sexuality are directly linked to the amount of property attached to the women, guaranteeing the purity and economic prosperity of the caste.[7] The higher the status, the greater the number of restrictions imposed on the women, irrespective of faith traditions. Any expression of women's sexuality outside the parameters of the patriarchal marital relationship invites judgment and condemnation from the community. Even within the marital relationship women's expression of sexual desire is regarded negatively. In contrast, male sexuality is not limited to procreation and does not require monitoring, thereby allowing for the expression of male sexual desire without its being condemned. Sexual desire in women, although found in religious beliefs, proverbs, folklore, and the subversive ways women claim their desire, is, nonetheless, viewed as an abject condition. It is characterized as inferior, irreversible, and destructive. Such views allow the society to regulate, discipline, and normalize all life stages of women to curb the condition. The hierarchical and negative construction of female sexual desire thus validates families, society, and religion as systems of control.

Discussions on sexuality have two places. Within the context of fertility and birth control, sexual intercourse is a sexless, necessary act for motherhood. Within the marital bond, sexual intimacy is a shameful act, to which a woman submits as part of her daily chore. Outside motherhood, it is an amoral, shameful, obscene act. Sex in singleness is sinful, and rape and sexual violence are the natural by-product of being unattached to a male.[8] In the first instance, desire and self-expression are divorced from the sexual experience, and in the second instance, the mere implication of desire and fulfillment is deemed immoral. This bifurcation is so commonplace in people's psyches that motherhood within marriage is the prescribed code, and singleness and infertility are unacceptable.

Women bear the social consequences for both dimensions of sexuality. With motherhood as the focal point of marriage, infertility is looked on as a bad omen and is almost always blamed on the woman. Sex becomes simply a means to an end, which itself is socially constructed. Virginity in singleness places the burden on women of disciplining their own bodies, making escape into a sexless marriage seem natural. Gabriele Dietrich notes that most conversations about sexuality take place at the point of a crisis and unfold as a discussion about "suffering." In this framework of suffering, "sexual desire and fulfillment of desire remain peripheral."[9] Furthermore, the physical pain of the birthing process is romanticized and normalized, whereas the pleasure of the sexual act and desire are demeaned and devalued. Suffering, pain, and shame become the rhetoric associated with being female, and they become the normalizing discourse generated and passed down through the generations. Strikingly absent is conversation about the experience of sexual desire. Conversation about one aspect of the body and silence about other aspects communicate explicitly what is judged to be normal and abnormal and produce shame about what cannot be discussed.

Subversion of Traditional Constructs of Womanhood

Subversion is a process by which disenfranchised groups surmount systemic oppression through subtlety by appropriating resources from within their cultures and faith traditions. Women subvert the constrictions of nationalist gender norms both by creating counternarratives and by using gender norms to appear conformist while becoming agents of power outside women's traditional confinement to home and motherhood. A. K. Ramanujan suggests that tales centered around and told by women provide a venue for expressing beliefs and customs contrary to those found in Hindu classics, allowing women to rid themselves of the societal shackles, if only in imagination.[10] This countersystem is crucial to the survival of women within an otherwise physically restrictive, emotionally stifling, and spiritually repressive world.

Oral traditions, particularly folk songs, provide another example of subversion. In a highly segregated North Indian society where intergender interaction is limited, songs provide an acceptable mode of engagement and communication. Ann Grodzins Gold explores the use of women's songs to subvert traditional notions of female propriety and conduct: "Rajasthani folk culture, transmitted in women's songs and stories, supplies many images of females that are simultaneously seductive and fertile, erotic and domestic, and positive. . . . This lore gives an impression of women as sexually playful and exuberant, taking pleasure in their own bodies and celebrating their bodies' capacities both for erotic engagement and for painful but fruitful birth giving."[11] These lighthearted songs seem to undermine the existing values systems; however, the humor does not devalue reproduction, and in fact, both pleasure and propriety seem to exist comfortably alongside each other.[12]

Women's songs are remarkable in their ability to move between the realities of their social circumstances and their created fantasy worlds without much tension. The songs explicitly describe female sexual desire, with graphic descriptions of women's bodies and even their demands on legitimate relationships with their husbands and illegitimate relationships with lovers that take place in clearly demarcated fantasies. The abjection of sexual desire within social gender hierarchies is subverted as the women's fantasies take flight within artistic expression.

Countersystems exist as a powerful media for communicating the unresolved conflicts giving voice to emotions, desires, and fantasies that subvert the social order without posing a tangible threat. The conflicts that are so easily resolved in mythology, such as Sita proving her chastity by surviving the ordeal of fire, find a less sensitive audience in real life. The conflicts become more pronounced, and the outcome is more harsh and unrelenting, forcing women to stay within the rules for appropriate social conduct. In fact, the clear demarcations between the good and the bad and the chaste and the unchaste are essential for the survival of women, particularly those who aim for a role beyond that of a daughter, wife, and mother.

Since religion is used as a tool to sanction and maintain the subjugation of women, some resourceful women have subverted the teachings of their religious communities and have used their traditions to give voice to their agency. Rajeswari Sunder Rajan suggests that, historically, women who have gained prominence in public leadership often owe their success to privileges of birth, such as caste, religion, family, or merit, with gender taking a backseat, as in the cases of Indira Gandhi, Benazir Butto, Khaleda Zia, and Sirimavo Bandaranaike. Their ascension to power during political crises took place at the expense of significant personal losses, since women leaders are expected to be de-sexed, unfeminine, or even masculine in their dress, mannerisms, interests, and engagement with people.[13]

This separation of the private/feminine and public/masculine/asexual is especially clear in the examples of Sadhvi Rithambara, Uma Bharati (Bharti), and Vijayraje Scindia. All three women draw on images, metaphors, and beliefs popular within the culture, and each is distinctive in her use of gender strategies. Scindia, born into a royal family, left the Congress party and severed ties with her son, unthinkable for an Indian mother. To mask her defiance of her female role, she presents a demeanor of piety with the white clothes customary for widows. Bharati, however, is described as a spirited, extroverted woman who seems to revel in the role the press affords her as the "sexy *sanyasin*" (something like a sexy nun), and as an unmarried woman she defies conventions of Indian womanhood. The unmarried Rithambara, with her oratory skills and explicit calls to violence, is known to have instigated riots in many regions. All three women share one crucial thing: celibacy; Rithambara and Bharati, both single women, flaunt their life as *sanyasins*, and Scindia maintains her widowhood in demeanor and dress, an outward sign of her celibacy. The resurgence of Hindu communalism in the late 1980s and 1990s afforded these Hindu women the opportunity to come to the forefront of the national political scene by relying on an alternate model of female leadership.

Through renunciation, both sexual and material, all three women gain access to people in all walks of life, offering an alternate model of leadership. Their celibacy is one of the most powerful tools in gaining the trust and reverence of the masses, and it also frees them from social conventions. Scindia, Rithambara, and Bharati have challenged normative gender roles, established their independence from male figures, and gained political clout through a clever use of religious knowledge and imagery; the furtherance of their personae by the dominant political parties is a testimony to the success of their strategies. In espousing a militant lifestyle and displaying political ambition and powerful oratory, all three women clearly demonstrate their power, all within the realm of religion.[14] Ironically, while all three women gain tremendous social power by virtue of being celibate; the tightly reined-in eroticism is romanticized by the audience, establishing them as the unattainable, desired object. Uma Bharati, the sexy *sanyasin*, for example, is a major draw for men.

Indian Christian Culture and Theology

In their attempts to establish the sovereignty of the British Empire, colonialists and missionaries justified their presence by citing the abject condition of Indian women. Nationalists countered this rhetoric by constructing an idealized past when women enjoyed high status in society. In their efforts to reclaim the sovereignty of the motherland, nationalists glorified the de-eroticized female body and its procreative capabilities. Two streams of discourse, colonialism and nationalism, worked in conjunction with each other to use the abject condition of women as the platform to further their respective agendas.

Indian Christian theology evolved in response to and in dialogue with the major political and national movements of the nineteenth and twentieth centuries. Christian converts were primarily socially and economically disenfranchised segments of Indian society who found Christianity to be a useful instrument for separating themselves from a life of degradation.[15] They did not intend to sever their caste affiliations and identities but to reconstitute them in such a way that it would further their agenda. This reconstitution of caste lines subverted an oppressive system, to the benefit of a previously powerless group. Their conversion to Christianity offered an acceptable strategy for maneuvering an unshakable social system, without complete renunciation of the Hindu social order. The old social structure with all the rights and privileges is thus replicated within a new faith, providing a communal identity and thus reinforcing codes of propriety.

The impact of conversion on converts varied depending on caste and class affiliations, but women bore the brunt of the maintenance of old social orders. In the intersection between colonialism and the Christianization of Indian society, the reconfiguration of gender roles evolved into a measure of one's status and upward mobility. The more upwardly mobile a particular family, clan, or tribe became, the more restrictive it became toward its womenfolk. Propriety, constraint, and chastity were established as a measure of respectability for women.

Indian Christian theology that arose in the nineteenth century in response to neo-Hinduism was mainly the work of high-caste converts to Christianity. In the hands of the Christian elite, theology advanced the interests of their caste communities. Hence it was guilty of maintaining oppressive gender norms as well as perpetuating caste structures. By excluding the voices of the oppressed and marginalized majority, Indian Christian theology became an instrument of "co-option" rather than "human liberation."[16]

As a minority religion that exists within a predominantly Hindu culture, Christianity in India has the difficult task of constantly defining itself. Minority religions, by necessity, live in tension with the secular and religious culture of the dominant group. In a culture and society in transition, articulating a minority religious identity involves a critical engagement with both the dominant culture and its particular religious traditions. An important part of this engagement is for Indian Christians to recognize the influences of the dominant culture on a minority religion's culture, tradition, worldview, and religious beliefs. The key is to find liberative resources within one's traditions that understand the full humanity of all people.

In spite of the fact that some attention has been given to the oppression of women, Christian theology in India has mimicked the larger culture in choosing to be silent around issues of female sexuality. Scholarship that does not include or acknowledge female sexuality is incomplete because it ignores this aspect of womanhood and uses it to validate and justify gender hierarchy and the subjugation of women. This silence especially reinforces negative images and attitudes about female sexuality and further perpetuates the system of women's oppression that Christians seek to challenge.

Nationalist rhetoric about female virtue as synonymous with a politically independent, culturally rich, and religiously superior India continues to be reproduced through various Christian systems. Negative attitudes toward women's sexuality impact every aspect of an Indian woman's life, including levels of education, social mobility, choice of partners, and even motherhood. Clearly defined codes of behavior are accompanied by blatant messages regarding the consequences of violating the code, with the burden of maintaining the family honor resting primarily on the Indian woman. The iconic status of the de-eroticized Indian woman is seriously threatened by sexual activity, and this in turn is directly related to the dehumanizing treatment of women with AIDS.

This is particularly true for Christian women in India, who are in dire need of a message that is transformative and liberative. Hindu religion has its share of goddesses who challenge normative gender constructs and provide Hindu women with resources within their tradition to reinterpret their faith. Most Indians are aware of the heroism of Hindu women in mythology and are not shocked when ordinary women draw on these narratives to argue their case. Christian women, unlike Hindu women, cannot appropriate subversive elements in Hindu mythology to rise above their circumstances. Unfortunately, Christian women are not given the resources within their tradition to resist injustice, and they are, in fact, penalized for questioning or challenging the teachings of their church. Scholars, religious leaders, and laity alike in Indian Christianity must bring all aspects of women's lives into conversation with our religious tradition. It is indeed time for the liberative message of Christianity to become a gift to all peoples, instead of the right of few.

One of the most transformative insights for the Indian Christian community is that God affirms sexuality. We worship a God who created man and woman in God's image and declared them both good. Not only is the creation of women a conscious, decisive act by God but it is one that affirms that no human being is complete in isolation. To be human embodiments of the Christ, we must all love others as gifts of joy and pleasure. Although many interpret the creation of humanity as a model of traditional heterosexual marriage, the text itself says the subordination of wives to husbands is the penalty of sin. In a redeemed state, adult love is lived out in mutuality and in the company of equals. When we live in the image of God, we celebrate the female body, as well as the male, including their pleasurable aspects, both as expressions of intimacy and relationality with each other and, sometimes, also to procreate. For Indian Christians our struggle must be to understand how this liberating truth may be both a counternarrative drawn from India's cultural traditions and a new, liberating truth drawn from our faith.

Notes

1. Donald E. Messer, *Breaking the Conspiracy of Silence: Christian Churches and the Global AIDS Crisis* (Minneapolis: Fortress Press, 2004), 2.
2. Ibid., xv.
3. Uma Chakravarti, "What Ever Happened to the Vedic Dasi? Orientalism, Nationalism and a Script for the Past," in *Recasting Women: Essays in Indian Colonial History*, ed. Kumkum Sangari and Sudesh Vaid (New Brunswick, NJ: Rutgers University Press, 1989), 35.
4. Eliza F. Kent, *Converting Women: Gender and Protestant Christianity in Colonial South India* (New York: Oxford University Press, 2004), 42.
5. V. Geetha, "Gender and the Logic of Brahmanism: Periyar and the Politics of the Female Body," in *From Myths to Markets: Essays on Gender*, ed. Kumkum Sangari and Uma Chakravarti (New Delhi: Manohar Publishers and Distributors, 2001), 50.
6. Tanika Sarkar, *Hindu Wife, Hindu Nation: Community, Religion, and Cultural Nationalism* (Bloomington: Indiana University Press, 2001), 143.
7. Joanna Liddle and Rama Joshi, eds., *Daughters of Independence: Gender, Caste and Class in India* (New Brunswick, NJ: Rutgers University Press, 1986), 64–65.
8. Gabriele Dietrich, *Women's Movement in India: Conceptual and Religious Reflections* (Bangalore: Breakthrough Publications, 1988), 87–88.
9. Ibid., 88.
10. A. K. Ramanujan, "Toward a Counter-System: Women's Tales," in *Gender, Genre, and Power in South Asian Expressive Traditions*, ed. Arujun Appadurai, Frank J. Korom, and Margaret Mills (Philadelphia: University of Pennsylvania Press, 1991), 33–53.
11. Gloria Goodwin Raheja and Ann Grodzins Gold, *Listen to the Heron's Words: Reimagining Gender and Kinship in North India* (Berkeley: University of California Press, 1994), 38.
12. Ibid., 44.
13. Rajeswari Sunder Rajan, *Real and Imagined Women: Gender, Culture and Postcolonialism* (London: Routledge, 1993), 105–15.

14. Amrita Basu, "Feminism Inverted: The Gendered Imagery and Real Women of Hindu Nationalism," in *Women and Right-Wing Movements: Indian Experiences*, ed. Tanika Sarkar and Urvashi Bhutalia (London: Zed Books, 1995), 158–67.

15. Kent, *Converting Women*, 239–40.

16. Sathianathan Clarke, *Dalits and Christianity: Subaltern Religion and Liberation Theology in India* (New Delhi: Oxford University Press, 1998), 37–41.

Part 4

Embodied Agency

Chapter Eleven

Salmon and Carp, Bannock and Rice

Solidarity between Asian Canadian Women and Aboriginal Women

Greer Anne Wenh-In Ng

June 21, 2006. National Aboriginal Day in Canada. Native songs, stories, and music filled the airwaves; in Toronto's Skydome, programs celebrating Aboriginal culture and spiritual traditions lasted all day. In churches, an Aboriginal Day of Prayer was observed either on this day or on the Sundays before or after it.

June 22, 2006. At long last, after decades of protest and lobbying by Chinese community organizations both national and provincial, the government of Canada, through Prime Minister Stephen Harper, made its official apology to the Chinese community for imposing a discriminatory head tax on Chinese immigrants from 1885 to 1923.[1] It was not until 1947 that the Chinese Immigration Act of 1923 (in popular parlance the Exclusion Act), which effectively barred all Chinese laborers from entering Canada, was repealed, and wives and children separated for decades could finally join their spouses and fathers.

It would be interesting to ask, How many Chinese Canadians listened in to some of those broadcasts of Aboriginal songs and stories on June 21, or attended any of the programs at the Skydome? How many Chinese churches in Vancouver or Calgary or Toronto incorporated some of the prayers for the June 21 Aboriginal Day of Prayer in their Sunday services the last two Sundays in June? The question would be especially applicable to congregations of The United Church of Canada, this being the twentieth anniversary of the denomination's Apology to First Nations communities that its highest church court, the General Council, made in 1986.

Conversely, we might wonder, on the day after their celebrations on June 21, how many Native persons and communities noticed the federal government's apology about the Chinese head tax?

This chapter by a first-generation immigrant Chinese woman of the post-1967, second-wave immigration is a tentative first step into relatively uncharted territory in search of a praxis of solidarity between Asian Canadian women and Native or Aboriginal women and communities. It is an attempt to make a road by walking, testing out the possibility of such praxis while being acutely aware of having usurped Native land on which to establish her home in the Asian North American diaspora in this first decade of the twenty-first century. What are some issues we can share, some issues in which we need each other's support, and some with which we can only be in solidarity? In other words, what potential is there for bannock[2] and rice and salmon and carp to appear on the same menu? And if they do, will their flavors clash or enhance one another? My reasons for embarking on such a venture are fourfold: personal, political, praxiological, and ecclesial. This venture is personal because of my desire to continue learning from, and not to lose the connections with, various Aboriginal individuals and communities since the mid-1980s;[3] it is political because I sense a timely need for these two nondominant communities to accompany and be in solidarity with each other within Canada in the neocolonial globalization context of today; and this journey is praxiological because Aboriginal people and Asian Canadians may come at questions of action and reflection with some perspectives that confirm each other's hunches and some that differ and challenge each other. Finally, this journey is ecclesial because of the challenge to move beyond the historical involvement of my denomination (The United Church of Canada) in "Christianizing" and "Canadianizing" attempts vis-à-vis Native communities to seek alternative possibilities of "becoming church" together.

Salmon and Carp, Bannock and Rice: A Historical Sketch

The relationship between Canada's non-European and nonwhite peoples, including its people of Asian ancestry, and its original First Nations peoples, is delicate. Not being part of the two colonizing nations, French and English—whose languages and cultural identities shaped the official bilingual and bicultural, primarily white nationhood of Canada—Chinese, Japanese, Sikh, and Hindu individuals and communities—who have contributed toward the building of the nation since the mid-1880s (the Japanese by their fishing as well as garden and vegetable farming on the west coast; the Chinese by being recruited to build the Canadian Pacific Railroad, which eventually linked the country from west to east)—have not had their constructive roles acknowledged. On the contrary, they have been systematically discriminated against with explicitly racist legislation and action. For the Chinese this included the imposition of a head tax followed by an immigration act that barred their entry until 1947. For the Japanese, even for its Canadian-born population, there was their enforced internment as enemy aliens during World War II and the prohibition of their returning to their properties and businesses after the war, resulting in their being dispersed east of the Rockies in Alberta, Saskatchewan, Manitoba, Ontario, and Quebec. It was not until the changes in immigration regulations in the 1960s (the elimination of country-of-origin quotas in 1962 and the institution of a points system for independent applicants in 1967) that Caribbean blacks, Koreans, and Filipinos began to add more "color" to the face of what up until then had been a predominantly "white" Canada.

The catch lies in this popular perception of a presumably white Canada. For of course there were many nonwhite faces in the population of the country before 1962—notably descendents of African slaves who had come to the Canadian colonies with their United Empire Loyalist masters at the time of the American Revolution and of the freedom seekers who made their way to various spots in Ontario via the Underground Railroad in the mid-nineteenth century. Most obvious of all, there were descendents of the original inhabitants of the land, now either confined to reservations set up under the Indian Act (1876) or living often in survivalist situations in Canada's urban centers, where they are usually "invisible" to these cities' other inhabitants.

Asian immigrants and Asian Canadians did not participate in the unequal land treaties with various First Nations, the establishment of Native reservations in almost every province, and the administration of residential schools that from the early 1900s to the mid-1970s arbitrarily took children from Native villages to "educate" and "civilize" (thus perpetrating cultural genocide as well as laying these children open to both physical and sexual abuse by teachers and administrators). Nevertheless they ended up benefiting from the system of land grab and now private ownership of at least the plots of land on which their residential homes stand. In this way Asian Canadians are unwillingly implicated in the injustice and continuing colonization meted out toward Native communities. The challenge is therefore twofold: for Asian Canadian Christians, on the one hand, to work together in solidarity with Aboriginals against structural and institutional racism and, on the other hand, to recognize their complicity in the colonization and oppression still being perpetuated by all non-Aboriginals and to live out their faith by beginning to work toward a just and right relationship with Aboriginal individuals and communities in the contemporary context. To explore such a challenge it is necessary to arrive at some understanding of the place of Canadians of Asian heritage, especially the women among them, in the larger scheme of Canada as a much-touted multicultural nation. I will do this in the following two sections: the first describes and analyzes the location of Asians and Asian Canadians in Canada's discourse of multiculturalism; the second deals with the location of Asian and Asian Canadian women within the segment of Canada's multicultural female population designated as women of color or visible minority women.

Asians in Canada's Discourse of Multiculturalism

Among those who benefited from the elimination of preference for European countries of origin for would-be immigrants (1962), and even more from the introduction of the points system for independent applicants (1967),[4] were middle-class, more educated, working-age Asians from Hong Kong and Taiwan and immigrants from South Asia, Korea, and the Philippines (some of these last came under the temporary-domestic-worker category). By the end of the 1960s their presence, together with earlier non-English, non-French immigrants, could no longer be ignored by the government of the day (the Liberal government under then prime minister Pierre Elliot Trudeau), resulting in a report in 1969 titled "The Cultural Contribution of the Other Ethnic Groups in the Report of the Royal Commission on Bilingualism and Biculturalism." While entrenching the English-French foundation of the nation, the government in October 1971 declared multiculturalism an official policy, with an emphasis on funding for programs aimed at cultural retention and cultural sharing by Canada's ethnocultural communities, including support for the teaching of heritage languages. The period of celebrating our differences had begun.[5] These getting-to-know-you cultural activities, alas, did not include any process for interaction between performer and visitor, nor was there a chance for reflection on common experiences of ethnocultural minorities, such as discrimination in school and workplace, obstacles to integration into the Canadian workforce for newcomers, or the persistence of being regarded as foreigner that second- and subsequent (often unto the fourth- or fifth-) generation members of nonwhite ethnic minorities experienced.[6] It is important to point out here that First Nations "are not mentioned in this discussion. They have always been seen as external to all the various ethnic and racial groups in Canada and indeed external to the Canadian nation itself. . . . The concerns of the First Nations have never been given any priority in discussions of Canadian nationhood, multiculturalism, or anti-racism."[7]

As the 1970s moved into the 1980s and incidents of racial tension in schools and other public places continued, it became clear that the song-and-dance tone of such a policy was flawed. There came increasing demands for equity in access to services and in employment, especially as the Charter of Rights and Freedoms (as integrated into the constitution that was repatriated from Britain in 1982) guaranteed equality rights. In the words found in section 15 (1) of the Charter,

> Every individual is equal before and under the law and has the right to the equal protection and equal benefit of the law without discrimination and, in particular, without discrimination based on race, national or ethnic origin, colour, religion, sex, age or mental or physical disability.[8]

The Multiculturalism Act of 1988 reiterated the commitment, stating that it "recognizes the diversity of Canadians as regards to race, national or ethnic origin, colour and religion as a fundamental characteristic of Canadian society." The act went on to claim that it was designed to "preserve and enhance the multicultural heritage of Canadians while working to achieve the equality of all Canadians in the economic, social, cultural and political life of Canada," and it was directed at all Canadians, not only racial minority communities. The act recognized Aboriginal communities as a distinct component of Canadian society, but it did not place the Aboriginal individual under the ethnic minority umbrella.[9]

In spite of such claims, however, the earlier Employment Equity Commission of 1984 had attested to the existence of systemic racism in education, the media, health services, employment, and the justice system for racial minority groups and individuals.[10] Four designated groups—women, Aboriginals, visible minorities, and persons with disability—were recognized in the 1980s as being especially disadvantaged where employment was concerned. A federally appointed task force in 2000—Equality Now!—made a series of strong recommendations for recruiting, appointing, and promoting visible minority applicants to the executive level in the public service sector, but it did not address the larger question of racism in Canadian society. Racism appears to be an issue usually denied by white managers responsible for hiring, leading to one scholar's discouraging conclusion that "as long as visible minorities remain objects of discrimination at a general social level, their achievements in Canadian work places will be limited."[11] Included among these visible minorities is a high number of Asians who were trained and qualified in Canada, not abroad. Nonetheless, by 2003, statistics show that although the number of women, Aboriginals, and persons with disabilities had reached their officially defined workforce availability, these groups were concentrated on the lower levels of employment, with extremely low figures at the management level. In Canada's public service sectors, "members of visible minorities have consistently lagged behind the other [three] groups."[12]

Asians among Women of Color and Visible Minority Women

Despite some original reservations about the designation "woman of color" (with its connotation of "colored woman" and of a color hierarchy coding shades of difference) for herself and other South Asian women, the Canadian feminist writer Himani Bannerji has reluctantly come to employ this term in solidarity with other antiracist feminists "as a term of alterity, or even of opposition to the status quo in spite of the statist nature of this concept in Canada."[13] The term "visible minority women," however, was more of a state designation, especially in the context of a conference that the Province of Ontario sponsored in 1983 to deal with issues of sexism, racism, and the work of women of different racial minority backgrounds. In 1986 a state-initiated National Conference on Immigrant and Visible Minority Women took place, with a resulting network, the National Organization of Immigrant and Visible Minority Women (NOIVMW). As "a creation of the Canadian state," the term "visible minority women" has been critiqued as "void of any race or class recognition" when applied to "such diverse groups as Native, South Asian, Black, Chinese and other non-white groups of women as 'qualitatively homogeneous,' since the racial histories of those groups could not be unified." In fact, one of the ironies of the national conference was that weightier issues of "Black women fighting around issues of employment or education, or South Asian women fighting for better wages in the garment industry," were subordinated to the internal question of who qualified as visible minority and who did not, putting them into conflict with one another. Another divide-and-conquer consequence, intended or not, was the fact that the National Action Committee (NAC) on the Status of Women, made up mostly of white (and middle-class) women and cast in the role of being more interested in issues of gender than race, claimed as their areas of concern issues such as abortion, daycare, and pay equity. These were issues the visible minority women's organizations believed they could not then address, although the specific issue of equal pay for Native, black, South Asian, and South East Asian women was one of the NAC's priorities.[14]

Another way in which immigrant women, the Asian women among them, were both racialized and gendered was the differential treatment meted to sponsored immigrants as opposed to independent immigrants under the points system as well as the discriminatory treatment given to non-European domestic workers—as opposed to British and European nursemaids and nannies. The former, often spouses, fiancées, or parents of independent immigrants, were not eligible for government-sponsored language training (accompanied by a living allowance) and had to abide by a ten-year dependency period on their (usually male) sponsors. The disproportionate number of women among the sponsored class meant that they found it much harder to integrate into the host society, could not more equitably contribute to the workforce (they had to take much lower-paid work due to lack of language and skills training opportunities), and often became vulnerable if the domestic situation became violent.

As for nonwhite domestic workers, many of whom were Caribbean black or Filipina, their contribution to the Canadian labor market was devalued to the point where, in spite of increasing demand for their services, they were not able to qualify as independent applicants under the points system. They could come into Canada only under temporary work permits, and they had to live with the same employer's family for at least two years before they were permitted to apply for landed immigrant status on their own. This circumstance did change, though, when regulations under the Foreign Domestic Movement of 1981–92 finally allowed non-white domestic workers to apply for this status without the two-year wait. Thus, as Sedef Arat-Koc, a Canadian university teacher and scholar who specializes in Canadian immigration policy and transnational feminism, has pointed out, an active antiracist and antisexist agenda must be developed to challenge status quo assumptions of "who 'builds' a nation (and who doesn't), who is a 'contributing' (as opposed to 'dependent') member of society and nation, and what are the values of housework, care-giving work, and different types of labour market work."[15]

The Complexity of Relationship between Asian Canadian and Aboriginal Women

Asian and Asian Canadian women's relationship with Native/Aboriginal/ First Nations communities is complex. On the one hand, because of the sharing of visible minority status within Canada, there is potential for solidarity. On the other hand, as part of the non-Aboriginal population who have benefited from privileges on a par to those of white Europeans, Asian and Asian Canadian women are seen to be oppressors. In the remainder of this chapter I will address the issues of how to discern a path by which to develop a greater understanding of each other's situation, to arrive at a more just relationship, and, ultimately, to be able to act together on issues of common concern and to stand in solidarity in matters of concerns specific to each.

As nonwhite women, both groups have to contend with white privilege and the assumptions of a Eurocentric Canada built on skin color as well as the violence they as women experience in their communities. Both communities have been marginalized and seen as Other in this land. Both need to claim their voices in telling the stories of their individual and community experiences, whether historically or in their contemporary lives.

In reflecting theologically on their history and experience, both groups can resort to a theology of the sinned against, building on the Korean concept of *han* (bitter suffering accumulated and repressed, sometimes over generations) to articulate their cry for justice.[16] For nonwhite women in Canada to effectively release their *han*, the Korean Canadian theologian Grace Ji-Sun Kim has suggested a Wisdom/Sophia Christology, which is established on a multifaith integration with the traditional Chinese and Korean devotion to Guan-Yin/Kuan-Yin (Kannon to Japanese women).[17] Where Scripture is concerned, Asian and Asian Canadian women will find it helpful to employ feminist interpretations when they are seeking liberation from patriarchal Confucian social oppression in church (and in their transplanted Korean or Chinese community ethos in North America), combined with a postcolonial lens when seeking justice from colonialist, racist oppression in their visible minority women's realities. A postcolonial lens in reading Scripture will also be helpful for Native and Aboriginal women.[18]

The search for potential commonalities can also turn to a comparison between elements of a Native and Aboriginal worldview with elements of an Asian (and to a lesser extent, Asian Canadian as represented by my ethnocultural tradition, the Chinese) worldview:

Native	*Asian*
A creation that covers all created things, living (plant, animal, human) and nonliving (rocks, trees, rivers)	The ten thousand/myriad things (*wan wu*) that cover all created things

The creator as Grandfather/ Grandmother	The Dao (ground of being), *Tien* (heaven) or *Shangdi* (Lord on High)
A variety of creation stories with stories of the flood	A variety of traditions (*Pang Gu, Nu Wa*) with stories of the flood
A link with ancestors that tends to be matrilineal	A link with ancestors that tends to be patrilineal
Name giving as transference of power within clan	Name giving by grandparents or parents that lodges hope in posterity
Oral history and tradition	Literary history and tradition
Land central: anchored in place	Linkage to ancestral land (not necessarily material but for purposes of preserving identity)

Depending on how much of one's traditional worldview is retained by either a Native or Aboriginal woman or by an Asian or Asian Canadian woman, the extent to which commonalities are shared will differ. When, however, both groups are faced with Christianity as usually interpreted by the contemporary West, with the latter's cultural emphasis on individualism as opposed to family/community, its linear/temporal/history emphasis against the centrality of spatiality/place in Native worldviews, or its dualistic tendencies versus the holistic tendencies of both Asian and Native ways, it is not difficult to infer that these two communities stand closer to each other on one end of the spectrum in categories such as creation,[19] humanity/anthropology, and community than with the white majority. The way these two different communities (or rather, the variety of communities within them) have been taught by Christian missionaries to forsake or abandon their traditional cultures' spiritual practices on conversion to Christianity is similar, although for one it may have happened in Asia and for the other it has happened within Canada. Thus a common issue is that of belonging to more than one religious and spiritual tradition, an issue about which Christians in both groups can share experience and insights. The shared struggle of both groups to remain whole by not giving up the legacy of their spiritual traditions as they strive to be faithful Christians is a theme that other essays in this volume explore more thoroughly.

How could groups of Asian Canadian women and Aboriginal and Native women share some of these commonalities? I recall an instance of this happening at a national church Sounding the Bamboo conference for racial ethnic minority women of The United Church of Canada held in Vancouver, British Columbia, in June 1997. This conference was the third Sounding the Bamboo conference, with the theme We Are Many, We Are One. As part of the conference's attempt to encourage participants to reclaim their spiritual roots via getting to know the creation stories in their cultures, Aboriginal women of that province were invited to give leadership in sharing Aboriginal creation stories and spiritual practices. In one segment of the program, participants moved progressively in a round of stations where Caribbean, Chinese, Korean, Japanese, and Native and Aboriginal creation stories were told or enacted. The Aboriginal leaders led worship one morning by conducting a smudging ceremony and by offering prayers to the four directions, while a Chinese leader led the group in tai chi exercises. Most participants found these activities to be both educational and empowering. It is encouraging to discover that, within a decade, Aboriginal women are becoming an integral part of the conference, serving with Asian and black Canadian women on the planning team. It is significant, too, that the 2007 conference theme is Sharing Wisdom and Growing Connections and that the four-day conference in 2007 will begin on June 21, National Aboriginal Day in Canada.

Individuals can also engage in acts of solidarity. Janet Yee is a fifth-generation Chinese Canadian activist. She tells the story of how, as a counselor for women suffering from violence, she once accompanied to the local police station three generations of First Nations women in one family to report on abuse the grandmother suffered in a residential school, domestic violence the mother endured, and sexual and physical abuse the teenage daughter survived. As they were going up in an elevator together, three white male police officers entered, their presence and sense of entitlement taking up all the space both physically and psychologically, almost obliterating the three Native women and Yee. It took her several moments of soul-searching to decide whether to do nothing and to be seen as "siding" with the officers, thus being on the "winning" side, or to risk taking some action without knowing what the consequences would be. Finally, she took a deep breath, holding it "as a shield, stretching as far left and right as the elevator wall. . . . I asked God about . . . learning to exist in our own bodies, about taking up space and not fear. Then I puffed myself up to move the police officers' bodies: to give us more room. We will share the space." The result was that the officers sensed a change and stopped their chatting. As they exited the elevator they turned around to acknowledge those whom they had ignored. "And the people I was with gazed back at them, too. We were full-bodied now."[20]

A more challenging contemporary test for solidarity arises when Asian and Asian Canadian women are asked to stand with Aboriginal sisters in their sisters' call to participate in their struggle to end violence against them at this midpoint of the World Council of Churches' Decade to Overcome Violence.[21] A word of caution, however, is in order here. In spite of commonalities that can be identified between these two communities, each group (with diverse communities within each, different First Nations within Native communities, and a range of Asian countries of origin among the Asian and Asian Canadians) is in many other aspects disparate from another. These differences need to be acknowledged and honored, not glossed over.[22]

In spite of commonalities, Asian and Asian Canadian women can also be seen as oppressors by Aboriginal women. As non-Aboriginals and as Christians, Christian women of Asian heritage in Canada are part of the church that has perpetrated spiritual and cultural genocide on Native and Aboriginal peoples, who continue to suffer from the effects of past oppression and current marginalization. In this sense, Asian and Asian Canadian Christian women need to stand, however painfully, with their (predominantly) white denominations and to recognize the need for *metanoia* and transformation.[23] While secular Canadian academic research seldom discussed these issues,[24] such reflections are found in church publications, both denominational and ecumenical.[25] For example, "seeking right relationships," a theme that runs through The United Church of Canada's most recent publications in this area, is premised on the possibility of eventual forgiveness and reconciliation from Native and Aboriginal communities.

The long-term goal is for the Christian community to move toward becoming a body of Christ that affirms each part for being what it is, in all its diversity, rather than presupposing a forced uniformity that pretends that differences do not matter. This goal of affirming all members of the body of Christ in their diversity is one in which Asian and Asian Canadian women, by their double identity vis-à-vis the white church and the Native and Aboriginal church, have an important role to play. It is a role that Asian Canadian Christian women will have to grow into because they also need to overcome the hierarchy of color oppression that they experience, an inevitable part of the systemic racism they have internalized.[26] Failure to acknowledge and deal with such internalized oppression will prove to be an obstacle to lasting alliance or solidarity with their Aboriginal sisters in this land.

Nurturing Justice-Oriented, Culturally Diverse Faith Communities

What are some pastoral and educational resources that can assist in attaining goals of becoming more egalitarian via culturally diverse churches and institutions? I suggest three areas with which to begin. First, we need to move beyond the basic knowledge of Canada required of immigrants applying for Canadian citizenship. We need to include the communal histories of exclusion and oppression of Aboriginal and Asian communities and of immigration history as well as antiracism education as part of theological and church education.[27] Second, we must continue past the nod to ethnocultural inclusivity of the annual observance of World Communion Sunday by developing relevant liturgies—liturgies of lament to mark Canada's histories of exclusion and oppression and liturgies of celebration for observing special days and Sundays in relation to these occasions as well as prayers and hymns that include personal stories and life stages of Asians and Asian Canadians and other minority members of a particular faith community. And finally, we need to move beyond polite greetings of "Good Morning" and "Hello" by participating in encounters with culturally and religiously diverse neighbors, including Aboriginal individuals and communities, and in projects, events, and movements for racial and gender justice within and outside the church. It must also be emphasized that these activities do not occur in a linear fashion, but rather, they overlap in the life of an institution or a congregation.

Beyond Citizenship Quizzes

One of the hurdles that would-be citizens in Canada have to face is the citizenship quiz, usually a general test of one's knowledge of Canada's geography (the names of the provinces and their capitals), political structure (the fact that the prime minister is the chief executive officer of the country, whereas the governor general is the representative of the British crown), and some milestones in Canadian history (Canada's so-called birthday as a confederation was July 1, 1867; the constitution was repatriated in 1982). In these questions, as in the usual history lessons taught at school, one seldom learns about the following: the colonization and conquest of Native and Aboriginal inhabitants via unfair treaties, the Indian Act, the cultural genocide and physical and sexual abuse perpetrated on Aboriginal children and youth in the residential schools up until the 1970s, the marginalization of black United Empire Loyalists after their arrival in Nova Scotia in the 1770s, the crucial contribution of Chinese railroad workers recruited in the 1880s to take up the most dangerous aspects of building a national railroad, or the way immigration regulations were skewed to the disadvantage of certain classes or races and ethnicities.

For members of Christian churches to be able to respect one another, it is paramount that all members, young and old, newcomer and old-timer alike, become acquainted with their country's (and their church's) whole history. Only with such truth telling can their faith in justice for all be grounded. This will entail convincing denominational units responsible for church membership and education to devote human and material resources to this enterprise, to conduct the necessary leadership training, and to include these components in their faith formation and Christian Education endeavors. At the same time, the churches also need to advocate the inclusion of these neglected histories in the school curriculum. "We have to get into the classrooms of the nation and have history taught in ways that are more truthful," is how the United Church's former moderator the Very Reverend Stan McKay, a member of the Cree nation, puts it.[28] Moreover, we must do this integration not only during Black History Month every February or Asian Heritage Month in May. As the African Canadian educator Carl E. James asserts, "The history of all peoples who have contributed to the building of Canada should be incorporated into Canadian history courses, [otherwise] . . . the message then being sent to students is that Canadian identity does not include the beliefs and experiences of all who have resided in and contributed to the development of Canada, in spite of official claims to the contrary."[29] We must also remind denominational educators and producers of resources that the interpretative lens employed in these attempts at recovery must be one of decolonization, rather than supposedly neutral.[30] This should also apply to any account of the denomination's home mission efforts, whereby they have brought the gospel to new immigrants, often devaluing these newcomers' cultures, languages, and spiritualities in the process. The repudiation of these dangerous memories will no doubt pose a challenge, even a threat, to the well-intentioned, benevolent, white hegemonic powers of state and church, but they must be uncovered and critically considered and examined if the church is to be truly a faithful and just church as it tries to become more culturally diverse.[31]

Beyond World Communion Sunday

In Canada it is likely that even the most monocultural white or ethnic congregation will, on the first Sunday in October, observe World Communion Sunday by singing an international hymn or two, by inviting someone (if available) in the congregation to read one of the day's Scripture lessons in one's native tongue, or by having the congregation say the Lord's prayer together in each person's language or dialect if the congregation is sufficiently diverse linguistically. The challenge is, then, What do churches do on the other Sundays of the year in order for the global and multicultural nature of the gospel and the church to become the norm rather than just a token gesture? One strategy is to incorporate these practices intentionally into worship as a matter of course, rather than as a once-a-year exception, and thus a token. Prayers of intercession during regular Sunday worship can refer to local, national, or global happenings (Canada's apology to the Chinese community for having levied the head tax is a good example), and life and work announcements can include community events sponsored by a variety of ethnocultural groups. The encouragement to attend National Aboriginal Day celebrations is another example. If the congregation has recently welcomed new immigrant members, their special occasions, such as the reunion of a parent or relative by recent arrival or the successful attainment of citizenship, could become a matter of thanksgiving and celebration.

Appropriate prayers will need to be written and newly composed lyrics to hymns could be attempted—a project in which younger members of the congregation can be invited to participate. Another strategy is to pay attention to special days that the world community observes, such as International Women's Day (March 8) and the International Day for the Elimination of Racial Discrimination (March 21) as well as cultural feast days that a specific Asian group celebrates, such as Lunar New Year's Day (first day of the first month in the lunar calendar) or the Mid-autumn Festival (fifteenth day-night of the eighth month in the lunar calendar). Which cultural festivals get celebrated will, of course, depend on which cultural groups make up the congregation.[32] The caution here is not to fall into a repeat of the song-and-dance type of multiculturalism activity, with its danger of exoticizing and orientalizing nonmajority cultures, but rather, congregations need to ensure that there is mutuality and an equal distribution of power as much as possible.

Beyond "Good Morning" and "Hello": Planned Dialogues and Encounters

One of the effective pedagogies for the nonpoor[33] is the employment of immersion experiences accompanied by relevant reflection. These could be church-sponsored group visits to historically significant sites with accompanying study and reflection—for instance, site visits to centers in southern Ontario marking the history of the Underground Railroad and World War II internment camp sites in New Denver and Kaslo in British Columbia.[34] Or they could be planned dialogues and encounters between a Christian church group and a non-Christian faith group, such as a local mosque or Buddhist temple, or between a non-Native congregation and a Native congregation, as The United Church of Canada's interchurch-interfaith project Circle and Cross[35] has suggested; this is a process whereby Aboriginal and non-Aboriginal church members have the opportunity to converse on the relationship between Christianity and Native and Aboriginal spirituality. Encounter experiences require preparation and heavy time and energy investment: much care and sensitivity must be exercised on both sides, especially on the part of the dominant or more powerful conversation partner.[36] Non-Native participants in the talking circles of Circle and Cross, for instance, had to learn from hard experience how to listen without interrupting and to respect oral cultures by refraining from overtly taking notes with pen and paper every minute. Gender dynamics in more traditional churches (both Asian and Native) could also suggest the appropriateness of dividing into gender-specific subgroups to facilitate greater ease in speaking and sharing.

Conclusion

For many first-generation immigrant Asians in Canada (not so much for Asian Canadians, who are Canadian born), the first line of Canada's national anthem, "O Canada, our home and native land," can scarcely apply. Yet we are now living in homes on what was originally Native land. In search of a praxis of solidarity, this chapter is a beginning exploration in how Asian Canadian women, both first-generation immigrant and subsequent-generation Asian Canadians alike, can learn to relate more faithfully and justly to the original inhabitants. These inhabitants and their descendents have too often been excluded from the nation-building schemes of the ruling state, including its "bravest" experiment of multiculturalism. But reflection and study as human activities can only propose and explore; to what extent these activities will bear fruit is ultimately dependent on the work of the Spirit, which is best expressed in the prayer-ful, invocative words of the theme of the World Council of Churches' Ninth Assembly in Port Alegre, Brazil, in February 2006: "God in your Grace, Transform the World." In this transforming grace, my trust is that both "The Grace of Difference"[37] and "The Grace of Sophia"[38] will play a significant role.

Notes

1. Beginning in 1885 with $50, the head tax reached $500, the equivalent to two years' wages in 1923.
2. Bannock is a bread made by deep-frying a dough of flour and water, and it is a favorite in Native communities.
3. I have been given the gift of these relationships. As a member of the faculty of the Van-couver School of Theology from 1986 to 1995, I was involved in the development of the Native Ministries Master of Divinity by Extension degree program, the first such post-baccalaureate degree program in the Western world.
4. See Valerie Knowles, *Strangers at Our Gates: Canadian Immigration and Immigration Pol-icy, 1540–1997* (Toronto: Dundurn Press, 1997), 145–78.
5. One prime expression of such programming was the annual Caravan multicultural fes-tival held in June for over twenty years in Toronto, whereby distinct ethnocultural groups, from Ukrainians and Hungarians to Chinese and Filipinos, offered food, folk dance, and music in community centers and church halls for the enjoyment and educa-tion of holders of "Caravan passports."
6. By the 1996 census approximately three in ten of the 3.2 million, or 11.2 percent, of the total population who self-identified as "visible minorities" were persons born in Canada (statistics cited by Tania Das Gupta, "The Politics of Multiculturalism: 'Immigrant Women' and the Canadian State," in *Scratching the Surface*, ed. Enashi Dua and Angela Robertson [Toronto: Women's Press, 1999], 190).
7. Ibid., 191, 192.
8. Carl E. James, ed., *Possibilities and Limitations: Multicultural Policies and Programs in Canada* (Halifax, Nova Scotia: Fernwood, 2005), 155.
9. For more on the Multiculturalism Act of 1988, see http://www.pch.gc.ca/progs/multi/policy/act_e.cfm.
10. Karen Mock, "Redefining Multiculturalism," *Canadian Diversity/diversité canadienne* 4, no. 3 (Fall 2005): 89.
11. Audrey Kobayashi, "Employment Equity in Canada: The Paradox of Tolerance and Denial," in *Possibilities and Limitations*, ed. Carl E. James (Halifax, Nova Scotia: Fern-wood, 2005), 162.
12. Ibid., 158–59.
13. Himani Bannerji, "The Paradox of Diversity," in *The Dark Side of The Nation: Essays on Multiculturalism, Nationalism, and Gender* (Toronto: Canadian Scholars' Press, 2000), 28–29.
14. Linda Carty and Dionne Brand, "'Visible Minority' Women: A Creation of the Cana-dian State," in *Returning the Gaze: Essays on Racism, Feminism and Politics*, ed. Himani Ban-nerji (Toronto: Sister Vision Press, 1993), 169, 178–79.

15. Sedef Arat-Koc, "Gender and Race in 'Non-discriminatory' Immigration Policies in Canada, 1960s to the Present," in Dua and Robertson, *Scratching the Surface*, 230.

16. For more on the concept of the sinned against, see Andrew Sung Park, *The Wounded Heart of God: The Asian Concept of Han and the Christian Doctrine of Sin* (Nashville: Abingdon Press, 1993); and Andrew Sung Park and Susan L. Nelson, eds., *The Other Side of Sin: Woundedness from the Perspective of the Sinned Against* (Albany: State University of New York Press, 2001).

17. See Grace Ji-Sun Kim, *The Grace of Sophia: A Korean North American Women's Christology* (Cleveland: Pilgrim Press, 2002).

18. Out of the plethora of works now available for reading the Bible from a postcolonial perspective, the following are a good place to start: R. S. Sugirtharajah, ed., *The Postcolonial Bible* (Sheffield: Sheffield Academic Press, 1998); R. S. Sugirtharajah, *Postcolonial Criticism and Biblical Interpretation* (Oxford: Oxford University Press, 2002); and Musa W. Dube, *Postcolonial Feminist Interpretation of the Bible* (St. Louis: Chalice Press, 2000).

19. An interesting alternative to the Genesis creation story has been suggested by the Cherokee writer Thomas King in his 2003 Massey Lectures, *The Truth about Stories: A Native Narrative* (Toronto: House of Anansi Press, 2003). "What if Adam and Eve had simply been admonished for their foolishness? I love you, God could have said, but I'm not happy with your behaviour. Let's talk this over. Try to do better next time. What kind of a world might we have created with that kind of story?" (27–28). For a discussion of the need to teach visible minority children and young people in North America their ethnoculture's creation stories in addition to Bible stories, see Greer Anne Wenh-In Ng, "Beyond Bible Stories: The Role of Culture-Specific Myths/Stories in the Identity Formation of Non-dominant Immigrant Children," *Religious Education* 99, no. 2 (2004): 125–36.

20. Janet Yee, "Racism: Moving beyond Denial: My Body, My Soul, and My Story" (The United Church of Canada's mission magazine), *Mandate*, May 2005, 21.

21. For more on this call from Canada's Native sisters, see Women's Interchurch Council of Canada, "Still Walking: Aboriginal Women Lead the Struggle against Violence," special issue, *Making Waves* 6, no. 1 (2006).

22. An earlier reflection on the challenging yet needful task for minority communities to learn to relate "horizontally" with one another may be found in the section titled "Intersecting Journeys within and with Other Nondominant Communities: Toward a Theology of Solidarity," in Greer Anne Wenh-In Ng, "Land of Maple and Lands of Bamboo," in *Realizing the America of Our Hearts: Theological Voices of Asian Americans*, ed. Fumitaka Matsuoka and Eleazar S. Fernandez (St. Louis: Chalice Press, 2003), 108–12.

23. Rebecca Todd Peters ("Decolonizing Our Minds: Postcolonial Perspectives on the Church," in *Women's Voices and Visions of the Church: Reflections from North America*, ed. Letty M. Russell, Aruna Gnanadason, and J. Shannon Clarkson [Geneva: World Council of Churches, 2005], 91–107) provides a sobering and challenging analysis of why the North American white church needs repentance so that it can be transformed.

24. For instance, Winona Stevenson's excellent historical account "Colonialism and First Nations Women in Canada," in Dua and Robertson, *Scratching the Surface*, 49–80, deals mainly with First Nations–white relations.

25. For this chapter these resources include The United Church of Canada, *Justice and Reconciliation: The Legacy of Indian Residential Schools and the Journey toward Reconciliation*

(2001), and the special issue of its mission magazine, *Mandate*, "One More Step: Living in Right Relationship: Twenty Years after the United Church's Apology to First Nations Peoples" (May 2005), together with three special issues of the Women's Interchurch Council of Canada's quarterly journal *Making Waves*: "Exploring Racial Diversity and Difference: Indigenous and Immigrant Voices Speak out on Racism in Church and Society" 1, no. 1 (2000); "Naming Racism, Speaking Truth to Power" 4, no. 2 (2004); and "Still Walking: Aboriginal Women Lead the Struggle against Violence" 6, no. 1 (2006).

26. For an understanding of how internalized racism by oppressed or nondominant groups has often led to cross-racial hostility and what can be done about it, see the section "Raising Awareness for Aboriginals and People of Colour," in *That All May Be One: A Resource for Educating toward Racial Justice*, ed. Greer Anne Wenh-In Ng (Toronto: The United Church of Canada, 2004), 48–52.

27. One denomination that has made a step toward such efforts is The United Church of Canada. At its Thirty-ninth Triennial General Council held in August 2006, the church made a commitment to make antiracism training mandatory for all its ministry personnel (that is, all persons in paid employment in the church).

28. The United Church of Canada, *Mandate*, May 2005, 4.

29. James, *Possibilities and Limitations*, 178.

30. As expressed on page 7 in The United Church of Canada, *Mandate*, May 2005, these six principles are (1) antiracism and decolonization, (2) holistic approach, (3) full participation of Aboriginal people, (4) whole community involvement, (5) healing and education, and (6) building right relations.

31. This is a challenge being taken up by The United Church of Canada, which in its Thirty-ninth Triennial General Council in August 2006 made a commitment to move toward being transformed into an "intercultural church" that will strive for "mutually respectful diversity and full and equitable participation of all Aboriginal, francophone, ethnic minority, and ethnic majority constituencies in the total life, mission, and practices of the whole church" (August 18, 2006, update by Jeff Cook, http://www.united-church.ca/gc39/news/1813.shtm).

32. In Toronto's Davenport-Perth Community Church, recent immigrants from Nigeria and other parts of Africa cooperated with Caribbean blacks to observe Black History Month, and an Ojibwa member of the official board introduced drumming as part of worship.

33. Alice Fraser Evans, Robert A. Evans, and William Bean Kennedy, eds., *Pedagogies for the Non-poor* (Maryknoll, NY: Orbis Books, 1987).

34. These site visits are among the learning experiences suggested in *God So Loved the People of the World*, the Canadian Council of Churches' resource for Racial Justice Week, March 19–25, 2006.

35. The most recent (2002–5) of The United Church of Canada's Interchurch-Interfaith projects, Circle and Cross, provides a process whereby non-Native and Native congregations engage in conversation about the relationship between Christianity and Native and Aboriginal spirituality. Its recommendations for adoption by and implementation of a series of follow-up strategies of education and celebration came before the denomination's Thirty-ninth Triennial General Council in August 2006, and they were affirmed by this national church body.

36. Anne Bishop, in her *Becoming an Ally: Breaking the Cycle of Oppression in People* (Halifax, Nova Scotia: Fernwood, 1993), discusses at length these types of encounters. See especially her suggestions in chapter 8 for people with power, 109–19.

37. Marilyn L. Legge in *The Grace of Difference: A Canadian Feminist Theological Ethic* (Atlanta: Scholars Press, 1992) devotes significant space to wrestling with elided minority voices in Canadian literature, in particular, the Japanese Canadian female experience in Joy Kogawa, *Obasan* (Toronto: Lester & Orpen Dennys, 1981); and Meti women's experience in Beatrice Cullerton, *In Search of April Raintree* (Winnipeg: Pemmican Publications, 1983), 144–65.

38. Kim, *Grace of Sophia*.

Chapter Twelve

When Justice Collapses

A Religious Response to Sexual Violence and Trafficking in Women in Asia

Nantawan Boonprasat Lewis

The Tragic Story That Challenges Our Ethical Response

On the return trip from Myanmar (Burma) to Phuket, Thailand, in February 2006, I picked up a *Bangkok Post* while boarding the plane and encountered a story that caught my attention. My traveling group, not realizing that I already had a copy of the *Post*, all passed their copies to me saying, "You've got to read this!" The story was titled "Righting Wrongs."[1] Readers of this chapter need to be warned that the parts of the story told here are vivid and painful.

Urairat Soimee, or Buo, a name given to her by her family, is dying from ovarian cancer that has metastasized into her liver, breasts, and other parts of her body, but she is determined not to die yet. "Not until justice is done," she vows. "I must use my own suffering to warn other women against falling into those devils' traps." She could, however, die any day. Looking at her picture in the newspaper, one could hardly imagine what she has already been through.

Buo has no hair—a result of the chemotherapy treatment. She wears a loose shirt to conceal a medical bag needed to relieve herself due to intestinal surgery a year ago. She was also recently in a hospital for a breast cancer operation. Nonetheless, she was up and around, telling everyone her story.

This story began when her husband was disabled after a car accident, leaving her to carry on the responsibility to care for him and her children. Buo cried most nights from feeling so much despair. She is an uneducated, poor, peasant mother of three from a northeastern town in Thailand. Her peasant life ended six years ago, though, when a rich neighbor told Buo that she was married to a Japanese restaurateur and was recruiting help

217

for their business in Japan. Buo, understandably, believed her. Buo's family could not afford a television or a radio. She had never heard of women being deceived to go into sex work in foreign lands.

Buo borrowed a large sum of money to pay for her trip to Japan. Once she arrived at Narita International Airport, she was met by another Thai woman, Dao, whose husband drove Buo to an apartment in Nagoya. She was immediately told that she was to work as a call girl. Buo was in disbelief. "My knees gave way," she said. "I was on the floor, crying and protesting." Her panic was to no avail, however, as Dao, the *mamasan*, laughed while pointing out that no one would have traveled to the apartment in Nagoya if she were told the truth. Buo was told that she had to pay back the cost of the trip, which was doubled to include the cost that Dao and her husband incurred in order to bring her to Japan. It would take five months to pay back this cost.

Gangsters were sent to inspect Buo's body. Dao's husband threatened to kill Buo, so she had no choice but to do as they instructed her. Buo counted each day until the end of the five-month period, while she was locked in a small apartment with other Thai girls who were also enslaved for sexual services. Soon enough Buo contracted a sexually transmitted disease, and yet she was forced to work. She had to service at least three men on each weekday and six men on weekend days. There was no day off, not even during her menstrual periods. Some men brutalized her body. When she said "No," she was beaten or raped. Even so, when the five months of contractual agreement ended, she was told that she still could not leave. She needed to earn more money in order to free herself. Furthermore, she was told that she had already been sold to another gang in town.

Out of desperation Buo contacted her friend and collaborated on a plan to escape. She and her friend were also able to secure help from another Thai, a man named Boon. When Boon arrived at the apartment, Dao, the *mamasan*, threatened to send the *yakuza* (hoodlum) to kill them if they tried to escape. Boon instructed Buo to run away while he tried to prevent Dao from carrying out her threat. When they were able to meet later in another town, Buo learned that Boon had killed the *mamasan*. Buo's friend reported the incident to the police in hope that they would be sent back to Thailand. After all, both of them had been forced into prostitution.

As the incident unfolded, the police transported Buo and her friend back to the town where the murder took place. Buo's friend was deported back to Thailand. Boon was sentenced to ten years in prison. As the trial went on, several human rights groups in Japan rallied for Buo's release.

Yet although Buo maintained her innocence, she was sentenced to solitary confinement for five years.

Three months into her imprisonment, Buo developed a sharp pain in her abdomen and learned that she had ovarian cancer. Her uterus and ovaries were removed, and she was given only two months to live.

Under pressure from various human rights groups, the Japanese authorities deported Buo back to Thailand. Buo left Japan with one regret: she was concerned with the fate of Boon, who had rescued her from the *mamasan*. Buo's friend who had helped plan the escape and had been deported earlier had since sued the woman recruiter in the village and her parents. They were convicted and are now serving a thirteen-year sentence. The National Human Rights Commission and the FACE (Fight against Child Exploitation) Foundation assisted Buo in filing a civil lawsuit against the woman recruiter and her parents. She won a 4.5 million baht (approximately USD 112,500) judgment against them. This lawsuit judgment is the first of its kind in Thailand.

Most women who are forced into the sex trade would live in silence for fear of social stigma and social condemnation. Buo chose the opposite. With death staring her in the face, she vows to fight on with one certainty: "I don't want anyone to suffer like me—ever again."

Those who are informed of Buo's heroic action and its transformative power are invited to tell her story to others. Unlike Maxine Hong Kingston's mother in *The Woman Warrior,* who for worthy reasons cautioned her daughter not to tell anyone about the suffering of women in her family, Buo's story challenges us to be public about the situations of women in the sex trade in Thailand and Asia. Buo's story is not an exception but, sadly, an example of tragic situations that millions of women are experiencing in Asia and around the world. More than anything else, their struggles should compel us to act together in identifying ways and means to prevent and end sex trafficking in women and sexual violence against them.

Owning the Struggle: A Personal Journey

The suffering of women in Southeast Asia is both a political and personal struggle for me, partly because I was born in that part of the world and partly because I am deeply committed to women's struggles for justice, equality, and the right to name their world. I first began my research on this topic in the early 1980s, when sex tourism in Asia was rapidly growing into a global industry and when AIDS was yet to be identified and named as a deadly disease directly linked to the sex trade. Sex tourism, sex trafficking in women, and AIDS—a disease that presents a serious threat to women's lives, their families, and the community—need our global attention. As I proceed to work on this issue, I have come to the realization that I am indeed chasing a moving target. I have come to terms with the ever-changing context of Thai society, the Asian region, and the global economy; how this affects the way we understand and respond to the situation; and how daunting this task continues to be. In this journey I am discovering new aspects, more information, and sometimes unexplored dimensions of discourse on this subject. Regrettably, it is not possible to discuss all of these in this chapter. There are times when this engagement creates frustration, as I see no end to the crisis. Nonetheless, my frustration means little in comparison to tragedies that women in the sex trade in Asia and around the world experience. Sex trafficking is a horrific form of violence against women and a grave violation of human rights. The plight of these women and their daring actions and strength, such as Buo's story, motivate me to persist in addressing the situation and renew my commitment to fight along until the day women are not forced to live such horrific lives.

I suggest that readers consider the following questions as a broader framework for my discussion: How do we, women and men of faith, together address this ongoing crisis of sex trafficking in women? What are some of the new perspectives or strategies—theologically, ethically, socially, and politically—that need further development to prevent or stop sex trafficking? What resources are there in our faith traditions that can inspire us to be a responsive community to the exploited and suffering poor? What do we do when, to use Nicholas D. Kristof's words, "justice [has] collapsed."[2]

It is crucial that a search for solutions begins with a critical understanding of the context of sexual violence and sex trafficking in women in Thailand and Asia. Due to space constraints, however, the discussion here is geared toward the current situation and the contributing factors from which the situation emerges. In addition, I pay special attention to the religious aspect of the situation, which does not generally receive adequate consideration from scholars, activists, and the public.

Defining the Term "Trafficking in Women"

It might be useful to begin with specific understanding of the term "trafficking in women" and its relation to the sex trade. In *The Traffic in Women*,[3] Siriporn Skrobanek, Nataya Boonpakdee, and Chutima Jantateero submit that trafficking is a form of migration that is done through coercion, violence, and deception. Trafficking can also be done voluntarily when one is faced with no choice but migrating in order to survive. Specifically, these authors view human trafficking as an aspect of migration in which women are currently the majority of those being trafficked for the purpose of prostitution. The United Nations Expert Group on Measures to Eradicate Violence against Women also suggests that traffic in women occurs in many forms: forced prostitution; forced domestic labor; false marriages, including mail-order brides; clandestine employment; and false adoption. The UN recently estimated that approximately one million children are being subjugated in slavery conditions in Asia.[4]

However, a concern here is with a particular form of trafficking: the sex trade that is an economic exploitation of women's labor and sexuality on a grand scale with accommodation from religious, cultural, political, and economic systems. Sex trafficking in women in Thailand today, regardless of whether it occurs at national or international levels, is a structural and global process. As the authors Pa Yaw and BARS[5] have pointed out, the Mekong subregion—that is, Myanmar, Laos, China's Yunnan Province, Cambodia, Vietnam, and Thailand—has become a major regional center for trafficking. It receives trafficking victims from all neighboring countries, including central Asia and Russia. Thailand is also a sending country of young females for trafficking to the United States; European countries, including the United Kingdom; Australia; Hong Kong; Taiwan; and Japan.

Current statistics provide a parameter of the situation in Thailand. The UN International Labor Organization suggests that between one hundred thousand and two hundred thousand Thai women and young girls work in the sex industry overseas. Other sources estimate that Thai women represent approximately 40 percent of Asian women working in the sex industry in Japan.[6] The Protection Project, a human rights research institute based in Washington, D.C., has calculated the figure to be between fifty thousand and seventy thousand.[7] The Foundation of Women in Thailand has suggested a higher number, estimating that at least eighty thousand to one hundred thousand Thai women were working in Japan by the end of the twentieth century, where numerous cases of sexual abuse, physical imprisonment, and other ill treatments were reported. In addition, beginning from the late 1980s when the sources of the supply of young women from northern Thailand shifted to ethnic women, mostly from the hill tribal communities, women from neighboring countries—that is, Myanmar, China, Hong Kong, Cambodia, as well as from Eastern Europe—were also recruited and taken to work in the sex industry in major cities such as Chiang Mai (a major tourist destination in northern Thailand); the Thai capital, Bangkok; Had Yai and Phuket in the south; and Pattaya on the eastern seaboard of Thailand.[8]

Sex Trafficking and the Feminization of HIV/AIDS

The spread of HIV/AIDS in the late 1980s was rampant in the sex industry. Sex work, where unprotected sexual practices are common, has become a major source of transmission of the HIV virus, AIDS, and other sexually transmitted diseases. By the late 1980s, the connection between the sex trade and HIV/AIDS could no longer be ignored. HIV/AIDS is a deadly disease that gravely threatens the well-being of the whole nation, its neighboring countries, and the continent. At the world AIDS conference in Bangkok in July 2004, many health officials signaled that "Asia faces an HIV epidemic that could rival Africa's."[9] This is partly because of the rapid expansion of AIDS into China, Indonesia, and Vietnam, whose populations comprise over 50 percent of the entire population of Asia. If India, which also struggles with the situation, is included on the list, the figure certainly will go much higher.

UN Secretary-General Kofi Annan announced in 2004 that "AIDS today has a 'woman's face.'" The secretary-general should know. Women represent almost 50 percent of AIDS cases worldwide. Eighteen and a half million of these women live in developing countries, fifteen million of whom are in sub-Saharan Africa.[10] Annan's statement also applies to Asia. A *Star Tribune* (Minneapolis, Minn.) editorial writer, Kate Stanley, who participated in the National Conference of Editorial Writers at the Fifteenth International Conference on AIDS in Bangkok in July 2004, filed the following report of her trip experience: "It's a woman's face, a stricken face—all eyes and cheekbones. It has a stark and hopeless beauty, but has forgotten the art of smiling. You sit on the bed and smooth black hair from the face; take the too-thin hand in yours—and the tears well up. . . . How could this married mother of a toddler, newly pregnant with her second child, be lying here fighting for her life?" Stanley asked.[11] Certainly there are explanations, some of which will be explored here.

Beyond the Sex Trade: HIV/AIDS in the Twenty-first Century

Since the late 1980s, when Asia was known as the next epicenter of HIV/AIDS in the world, sex tourism and various forms of commercial sex had been implicated as major contributing factors. Extensive research and writings by Thai, Asian, and other international scholars have aided the public and government officials' understanding of the ongoing epidemic.[12] In Southeast Asia both female and male sex workers are viewed as victims of the global economy; of the tourism industries; of internal warfare, such as the Burmese and Cambodian situations; of neocolonialism, militarism, and imperialism; and of racism, patriarchy, and the institutionalized, traditional values and moral system that privilege the haves and the powerful over the Other. All of these factors are interconnected and negatively affect the lives of most of the poor, including women, children, and their families. Several who study this issue also point out that globalization and a capitalist and patriarchal mode of development in Thailand have not only brought about a drastic change in society and social relations but have also decreased women's status in family and society and increased gender inequality. In addition, as Yot Santasombat suggests, there is a lack of understanding of gender and sexuality in Thai society during the time when sexuality is, again, rapidly transforming into a highly profitable commodity.[13] During the 1990s impoverished communities have also succumbed to the deadly HIV virus, which takes its toll on their lives and wreaks havoc in their families, communities, the region, and the nation.

Toward the end of the twentieth century, the conventional assumption about the AIDS epidemic and its direct cause—that is, sex tourism and same-sex sexual contact—has been challenged by socioeconomic reality and the nature of the disease. Attempts by the Thais, both by private and government sectors, as well as international humanitarian organizations and countries that provide funds, human resources, education, and so forth, have helped to address this epidemic. AIDS is no longer perceived as a problem solely facing intravenous drug abusers, those who receive transfusions of contaminated blood, gay men, or sex workers who service Western and Asian tourists. It has become a disease that derives from social and economic problems in countries where poverty abounds; where development is geared toward urbanization; and where there is a breakdown of family and community social relations as either husbands and wives, or both, migrate into urban sectors and engage in a new territory of social relations, and as family expectations of daughters and wives as the breadwinners increase. The problems are also exacerbated by cultural ideologies, attitudes toward sexuality, gender inequality, and violence against women. Many countries in Asia, such as Cambodia, Thailand, Myanmar, Indonesia, and the Philippines, despite their particularities, find themselves in a similar situation. Asia has been warned to learn from

Africa's hard lessons. A closer look at the situation in Thailand may shed some light on its evolving issues and the complex situation that we need to consider in order to develop adequate strategies to prevent and end sex trafficking.

Religious Responses to Violence against Women in Sex Trafficking

The Thai community as a whole has demonstrated concern and commitment to responding to the sex industry and HIV/AIDS. Various forms of action have been developed and implemented by all sectors of the society, including governmental and private sectors, community members, social activists, professionals, and academics. International organizations, both governmental and private, have also joined these efforts. It is beyond the task of this chapter to assess the effectiveness of these responses, but it is at least as imperative to critically examine religious and cultural factors, including certain complexities within the tradition that inform the Thai attitude toward the sex trade and its tolerance (at best) of the situation. It is also important to provide analytical understanding that can assist the current and future direction of the community's response. Additionally, the current situation of the sex trade and HIV/AIDS clearly indicates that factors contributing to the situation extend beyond the Thai border.[14] Therefore, to be effective, strategies to combat the situation must be developed with great attention to the cross-cultural, international, and interreligious context. More important, a reflection on Thai religious and cultural responses to this situation needs to take place within a consideration of the global context. To this end, at least three major areas need to be further examined: the concept of prostitution in Theravada Buddhist history, cultural tolerance of the sex industry in modern Thai Buddhism, and the common interpretation of sexual sin and karma in the case of prostitution in Thailand.

Prostitution in Early Buddhist Texts and the Development
of the Thais' Understanding of Prostitution: Some Ambiguities

Thai and Western feminist scholars have pointed out differences in the construction of the concept of prostitution in the Thai and Western contexts. In the West there is often the assumption that prostitution is primarily based on individual decision rather than cultural and structural circumstances. In *Thai Women in Buddhism*, Chatsumarn Kabilsingh, whose recent ordination as a monk bestowed on her the new title of Venerable

Dhammananda, discusses the concept of prostitution as it appears in early Buddhist texts. According to Kabilsingh, this traditional interpretation influences the history of the concept and attitude toward prostitution in Thailand.[15] The term "prostitute" in the early Buddhist text is *sobhini*, which is a short version of *nagar sobhini*, which means beautiful women who belong to the city. The King of Vajji assigned the name to women whose profession was state prostitute. During this time, women who were in the profession were trained in the entertaining arts and social skills, such as dancing, singing, poetry, and the art of creating sexual pleasure for men. These women were viewed as having high status and worked only for statesmen and royalty. At times they became a source of conflict among powerful men who desired them. To prevent this conflict the King of Vajji bestowed the *sobhini* with a special status; they were to belong to the city and could not be owned by particular men.

There was also a group of prostitutes with lower status called *ganika*, meaning a community of women who served the general public in the society. But the early Buddhist text mostly mentioned *sobhini*, some of whom encountered the Buddha. Several early texts, that is, the *Ambapali Theriyapadana* and the *Maha Parinibbana Sutta*, indicated that the Buddha did not condemn prostitutes. He expressed compassion toward them, and despite protests from his monks, he declared that, like others, prostitutes could attain enlightenment. As Kabilsingh points out, the Buddha viewed prostitution in terms of a state of human existence that was characterized by suffering.[16] There were several stories in the texts of prostitutes who turned away from the profession, became strong supporters of the religion and the *sangha* (community of monks), and won praise. One of them became a *bhikkhuni* (a female monk), took refuge in the Dharma (the teaching of the Buddha), and later became enlightened.

Undoubtedly such stories and attitudes, as well as the religious status of prostitutes in the early Buddhist texts, inform the historical development of prostitution and the public attitudes toward prostitutes in Thai society. The word *sobhini*, not *ganika*, was adopted to call women employed in prostitution. In the nineteenth century the words *Ying Nyarm Muang* (beautiful women of the city), which implied a similar status to *ganika* in early Buddhism, were also used interchangeably with the word *sobhini* to refer to a prostitute, suggesting the traditional Buddhist concept that she belongs to all. With this religious history of prostitution, as well as the practices of current and former prostitutes who followed examples of prostitutes in the early Buddhist texts in providing material support to temples in their towns and villages, it is understandable that there is a degree of tolerance and acceptance of the profession in the community. Kabilsingh also stresses that the Buddhist teaching encourages women to leave prostitution and seek refuge in the teaching of the Buddha.[17]

In addition, the concept of prostitutes as women who belong to all has led Thai men to view their sexual experience with prostitutes as not being in conflict with Buddhist moral conduct. To some men it is an exchange of cash and service. However, Kabilsingh has been quick to point out that this assumption does not imply that the sex trade is acceptable and the suffering of women is justified. For Kabilsingh, sexual relations are not for sale, and women are not sexual commodities. The sex industry as manifested in Thai society is partly a consequence of misinterpretation and misunderstanding of the fifth Buddhist moral precept on sexual violation of others.[18] However, there is a drastic difference between the social and historical context of early Buddhism and today's Thai Buddhist society, which raises a critical question of the moral attitude of men who sexually exploit women in the profession.

Cultural Tolerance and the Sex Industry in Modern Thai Buddhist Society

A commentary often heard in a discussion on the relationship between Buddhism and the sex trade is the degree of tolerance in Thai society and, in particular, the role of Buddhism in influencing Thai social values. If sex trafficking in women is viewed as morally wrong and unethical, why does the Thai dominant religious institution tolerate this situation? The late Waranee Pokapanitwong argued that in Thai Theravada Buddhism there is a clear division of church (religion) and state (government), where authority to administer society is given to the state, and religion, or the *sangha* (viewed as presenting the religious institution), is primarily concerned with spirituality.[19] There is also a long history of royal patronization of the religious institution, which formalizes the reciprocal relationship between religion and state.[20] The continuation of centralization of the religious institution under the central government, which was instituted in the early nineteenth century, is critical in defining and monitoring the role of the *sangha* in Thai society. Public opinion seems to reveal a preference that monks should not be involved in solving social problems. Although the AIDS crisis has affected the way Thai monks apparently view their role, their involvement in responding to the crisis is still on a voluntary and individual basis; they are thus unlikely to confront government policies or directly intervene in government agencies. According to Pokapanitwong, all of these factors must be taken into consideration in forming an opinion that Buddhism (as represented by the body of the *sangha*) provides cultural tolerance for commercial sex activities. Pokapanitwong submits that it is important to examine closely the role of the state (government) in influencing social tolerance toward diverse behaviors and its intervention (or not) in social relations in order to better understand the social tolerance of the sex industry. In addition, one must recognize various forces in the dynamic relationship among the nation, the state, and the global society. For Pokapanitwong, it is not possible to draw a conclusive opinion that Buddhism is an unchanging religious institution in the formation of Thai popular culture, since it is only one of many cultural factors interacting with traditional Thai beliefs and practices.[21] The globalized culture of capitalistic consumerism and accumulation also affects Thai practices, and it is this international culture that constantly negotiates with the power of the state.

When Justice Collapses: Bad Karma Revisited

A religious concept that is also influential in the thinking of the general Thai public regarding the sex trade is a popular belief that the plight of women in the trade is due to their bad karma, or *bap* in Thai. An early Buddhist text referenced a case of a woman who was born and became a prostitute because she insulted a *bhikkhuni* in her previous life. Thus this story inspired a popular belief that the life of suffering that a prostitute endures is self-inflicted. Current and former prostitutes who support their needy families and temples with income from sex work could be seen as acquiring merit that will benefit them in the next life. Prostitutes may also be viewed sympathetically by the community, which eases the prostitutes' regret and shame over their profession.

These religiously informed issues are just a few critical examples of the complexities in attitude and cultural treatment of women in prostitution that need further examination. There is certainly a need to develop an alternative interpretation of how the profession and the plight of women in it could be viewed from a religious and moral viewpoint that can restore and affirm the principle of life and gender equality of women in society. (This includes the principles of nonviolence and compassion, which the Buddha taught as keys to a sustainable and peaceful community.) Although this task remains formidable, we must challenge one approach without hesitation. To continue to view the plight and suffering of women in the sex trade merely as bad karma (an understanding that the women's bad actions in past lives are catching up with them) without examining other social, political, ideological, and economic factors doubly assaults the victims and further perpetuates their suffering while leaving the unjust socioeconomic system unchallenged. Such an ethical and theological analysis completely ignores the violence committed against these women in the names of religious and cultural patriarchal ideologies, national development, national security, global militarism, global capitalism, neocolonialism, sexism, and racism. As evident in the case of Asian women in the sex trade, when there is no gender equality, there is no justice. When justice collapses, there is no hope for a sustainable and peaceful society, much less for the women who suffer within that society. It is thus vital for religious communities, if we are to act together, to develop an approach that takes seriously the context from which the situation emerges, its contributing factors, and its connection with the larger international and interreligious contexts.

Religions, Resistance, and Activism: Toward a Long-Lasting Political Engagement

The situation and contributing factors of the sex trade and HIV/AIDS in Thailand and Asia as discussed in this chapter, including Buo's tragic story, call for an urgent ethical imperative. This life-threatening and death-dealing reality clearly indicates that much more needs be done, and all strategies and actions must be carried out in a consistent and coherent manner. The following actions are recommended as immediate and long-term strategies to address the situation.

- Responses to the sex trafficking of women need to include attempts to uncover counterinterpretations of patriarchal values and ideology embedded in the sacred texts and culture.
- Sex trafficking is contextually specific. As far as the Thai case is concerned, there needs to be more in-depth dialogue on the Buddhist concepts of sexuality and sexual morality for laity, especially young men and women, as well as for monks and religious scholars who transmit the knowledge and interpretations to the public.
- There is also a need for more scholarly work from other faith traditions. Sex trafficking is a global phenomenon. Religious responses must also come from world faith traditions to challenge the exploitative and brutal treatment of women, young and old.
- Efforts must be made to articulate a religiously inspired understanding of political engagement for social justice and social change. More interreligious dialogue on religious concepts and values that

motivate such political and social engagement needs to take place among religions of Asia: Buddhism, Confucianism, Islam, and Christianity.

- Rigorous civic engagement in monitoring laws on trafficking policy, on migration, and on the labor exchanges with the neighboring countries of Thailand, between Japan and Thailand, and other receiving countries in Europe and in North America must be ongoing.
- The community of women and men who are committed to working for justice must hold one another accountable and truthful in the journey. We must become, as Kwok Pui-lan suggests, a "transnational network,"[22] creating an imagined community in resisting all deadly forces and standing with those who are victimized by the culture of violence; employing political, social, and economic resources available to us to create space where their voices can be heard and their stories can be told and placed in an appropriate context so that remedies can be secured.

For the life of Buo and many other women who suffer greatly because of sex trafficking and HIV/AIDS, there is no waiting time. Their tragic situation is caused by personal, structural, and global factors. Strategies for change must be developed in such a conceptual framework. As death stares her in the face, Buo refuses to give in. She has fought with great resistance and determination the injustices that life has shown her. She is living her last days in a religious-activist manner and is determined to prevent others from succumbing to a situation like hers. Buo has defied her dying condition to ensure life for others. This kind of political engagement will likely save not only women in her community but also women in the world.

Notes

1. Sanitsuda Akachai, "Righting Wrongs," *Bangkok Post*, February 13, 2006, 1.
2. Nicholas D. Kristof, "A Woman without Importance," *New York Times*, March 28, 2006, 13.
3. Siriporn Skrobanek, Nataya Boonpakdee, and Chutima Jantateero, *The Traffic in Women: Human Realities of the International Sex Trade* (London: Zed Books, 1997).
4. Kristof, "Woman without Importance."
5. Pa Yaw and BARS, "Trafficking of Women in Asia," *Judson Research Center Bulletin* 5 (December 2005): 54–55.
6. Ibid., 55.
7. Bruce Bower, "Children's End," *Science News* 24 (September 2005): 200.
8. For a critical analysis of trafficking in Thailand and neighboring Myanmar, see Christa Foster Crawford, "Cultural, Economic and Legal Factors Underlying Trafficking in

Thailand and Their Impact on Women and Girls from Burma," *Cardozo Journal of Law and Gender* 12, no. 3 (2006): 821–53.

9. Juliana Omale, "Asia Learns from Africa's Hard Lessons," *Gender Links*, July 16, 2004, 3.

10. Jennifer Wisnewski Kaczor, *Global AIDSlink* (April–May 2004): 14.

11. Kate Stanley, "AIDS with an Asian Face," *Star Tribune* (Minneapolis), August 15, 2004, A5.

12. See Thanh-Dam Truong, *Sex, Money and Morality: Prostitution and Tourism in Southeast Asia* (Atlantic Highlands, NJ: Zed Books, 1990); Ryan Bishop and Lillian S. Robinson, *Night Market: Sexual Cultures and the Thai Economic Miracle* (New York: Routledge, 1998); Lisa Law, *Sex Work in Southeast Asia: The Place of Desire in a Time of AIDS* (London: Routledge, 2000); Jeremy Seabrook, *Travels in the Skin Trade: Tourism and the Sex Industry* (London: Pluto Press, 1996); Chris Lyttleton, *Endangered Relations: Negotiating Sex and AIDS in Thailand* (Bangkok: White Lotus, 2000); Yot Santasombat and Mae Ying Si Kai Tua, *Community and Prostitution in Thai Society* (Bangkok: Institute of Local Community Development, 1992); Niwat Suwanphattana, *The Community of Prostitution* (Chiang Mai: Women Studies Center of Chiang Mai University, 1998); and Cynthia Enloe, *The Morning After: Sexual Politics at the End of the Cold War* (Berkeley: University of California Press, 1993). For a critical examination of Thai Buddhist tolerance of the Thai sex industry, see, in particular, Waranee Pokapanitwong, "Buddhism and Sexuality in Thai Society," in *Gender and Sexuality in Thai Society*, ed. Ammara Pongsapit and Marjorie Muecke (Bangkok: Chulalongkorn University Press, 2005).

13. For further detail, see Yot Santasombat, "Understanding Gender and Sexuality in Thai Society," in Pongsapit and Muecke, *Gender and Sexuality in Thai Society*.

14. For a case in point, see Crawford, "Cultural, Economic and Legal Factors." See also Satoko Watenabe, "From Thailand to Japan: Migrant Sex Workers as Autonomous Subjects," in *Global Sex Workers: Rights, Resistance and Redefinition*, ed. Kamala Kempadoo and Jo Doezema (New York: Routledge, 1998), 114–23.

15. See Chatsumarn Kabilsingh, *Thai Women in Buddhism* (Berkeley: Parallax Press, 1991), 67–70.

16. Ibid.

17. Ibid.

18. For more detail, see Chatsumarn Kabilsingh, "Kao Kham Pantakit Tang Pet," in Pongsapit and Muecke, *Gender and Sexuality in Thai Society*, 41–60.

19. Waranee Pokapanitwong, "Reevaluation of the Site of Blame: Demystifying Buddhism and Thai Sexuality," in "Negotiating Rural Subsistence: Cultural Politics and the Commodification of Thai Female Sexuality" (Ph.D. diss., Rutgers University, 2003).

20. See, in particular, Somboon Suksamran, *Buddhism and Politics in Thailand* (Singapore: Institute of Southeast Asian Studies, 1982).

21. Pokapanitwong, "Reevaluation of the Site of Blame."

22. See Kwok Pui-lan's chapter in this volume.

Chapter Thirteen

Rice, Medicine, and Nature

Women's Environmental Activism and Interreligious Cooperation in Taiwan

Wan-Li Ho

Like many other Chinese families, my parents were genuinely influenced by the Confucian tradition, so it was natural for my family to celebrate festivals with our ancestors. In every important festival, my parents led us to the ancestral shrine that displayed the names of all our foremost ancestors to pay our respects to them. Simply gazing on this ancient roster made me feel like I was standing at the intersection of my family's past, present, and future; suddenly all my family history was vibrant and immediate, evoking in me a sense of community and belonging.

After the rituals we often gathered at a big, round table and, while standing, bowed our heads in prayer. As is typical in a Christian household, my father usually led the prayer. It began, "O Lord, thank you for bringing peace and safety to our family so far, and we hope that you will continue to bless us." As a Christian family, we nonetheless retained a strong Confucian and Taoist heritage, and it was important for us to both talk to our ancestors and pray to God, even as part of the same ritual. It was as though we worshiped in a church without walls, and we reached out to our ancestors.

After praying, everyone sat down around the dining table, where two chairs were left empty for our male and female ancestors. The meal included two bowls of rice, two pairs of chopsticks, and two cups of fine wine dedicated to the ancestors. My father, using a respectful tone, looked at the two empty chairs that were set up for ancestors and said, "*Tai Gong* (male ancestor) and *Tai Po* (female ancestor), please enjoy a meal with us." Because we sat together at the round table, everyone felt close to *Tai Gong* and *Tai Po*. At this point the family reunion banquet had really begun.

This entire ritual is an unforgettable part of my life. My father maintained these Confucian practices even while many Protestant churches were encouraging their members to shun such rituals. As he put it, "Without our ancestors, we would not be here, and therefore we should not stop paying our respects to them." He was convinced of the long-term significance of these rituals and unperturbed by combining seemingly disparate religious traditions.

My father drew on his Confucian ideas to respect our family's communion with our past, but it was his Taoist beliefs from which our family developed a deep love for Nature. My father wanted all of us children to enjoy the beauty of nature and carefully observe our world. He taught us to notice that the color of every leaf is different, the shape of each tree is unique, and the height of all mountains is not the same. He guided me to enjoy every bit of the beauty in day-to-day life. As I grew up, I was often reminded that if I sought to become a practitioner of the skillful employment of language, I must, in a deeper sense, be an artist of everyday living, harmonizing with nature both inside and outside. In this way a love of nature took root in my life.

My father thus raised me to be a Christian while also following the rules of Confucian moral conduct as well as the appreciation of nature inherent in Taoism. It all seemed natural to him, but as I grew older, I started wondering how a first-generation Chinese Christian like my father could live peacefully in simultaneous contact with different traditions and religions and how he could so easily mingle distinct religions. Whereas in Western thought about religious practice, religion has defined rituals and claims to ultimate and exclusive truth, my personal experience as a Christian in Taiwan suggested an entirely different form of religious fluidity.

Such ties among religious practices and philosophies are surely becoming more essential as our world grows smaller, and the potential for mutual enrichment instead of conflict must be developed as societies are pushed closer together. My academic work in religion has, for the past few years, focused on case studies of religious women in Taiwan engaged in environmental protection. Environmental protection (*huanbao*) is not a religious concept and does not relate to any specific theology per se. But in recent years many religious groups have begun to realize the need to address the global environmental crisis. They hold that religion provides an impetus for believers to become aware of their environmental responsibilities. Some of these groups are more involved at a theoretical and theological level, while others focus on praxis or pragmatic programs to improve environmental conditions. In Taiwan, religious women are pushing the meaning of religious practices into the social realm, and many are reexamining premises of their faiths in the process.

This chapter focuses on the work of three Taiwanese religious women's groups. Two are Buddhist: the Buddhist Compassion Relief *Ciji* Foundation (hereafter referred to as the *Ciji* Foundation) and the Life Conservationist Association (hereafter referred to as LCA); and the third is Christian: the Taiwanese Christian Ecological Center (referred to as the Ecological Center in discussion of its activities prior to 1998, when the name was changed. See below). The Ecological Center has been the only Christian group focused on environmental work in Taiwan for over a decade, and its founder is a woman. There are other Buddhist groups in Taiwan that have been involved in environmental work, but I have chosen to focus on *Ciji* and LCA because their founders and leaders are women and Buddhist nuns. In addition, these two Buddhist groups adopt distinct strategies in their environmental activism. The work of these three groups is representative of larger Taiwanese patterns of interdependence and strategies of activism in approaches to environmental protection.

While the groups have different religious orientations, they are working toward similar goals, and interreligious cooperation and dialogue have emerged as telling aspects of their work. While there is ample evidence of the great practical potential of interreligious cooperation, I found myself asking the same questions about these groups as I did about my father's religious practice: How do these religious women, affiliated with variant traditions, manage to cooperate so easily on practical and theoretical levels while working for environmental protection?

I found the answer in Taiwanese culture and its religious traditions. Its history of religious cooperation introduces new forms of interreligious dialogue that do not typically surface in Western discussions of dialogue. Before embarking on this discussion, though, I will first examine each of these three groups' religious and spiritual sources of influence with an emphasis on how dialogue and cooperation have taken shape in Taiwan among groups of religious women.

Buddhist and Christian Women's Ecological Movements in Taiwan

Some Buddhist perspectives have already made impressive strides toward linking ecological concerns with Buddhism.[1] New schools of thought are emerging on Buddhist environmental perspectives, and many organizations all over the globe are promoting action toward environmental protection. This is particularly true of Taiwan.

Buddhist Compassion Relief Ciji *Foundation* (Ciji)

The Buddhist Compassion Relief *Ciji* Foundation belongs to one of the major denominations in Taiwanese Buddhism. (The character *ci* means compassion and *ji* means relief.) As one of Taiwan's largest and most prominent social organizations, the foundation plays a significant role in Taiwanese religion and grassroots activism within the larger ecological movement. Its leader, Dharma Master Zhengyan, is a Buddhist nun.

In Taiwan, the story of the founder and the organization's humble beginnings are well known. Master Zhengyan started the *Ciji* Foundation in 1966 following two events. The first took place in a hospital when she saw a pool of blood on the floor from an aboriginal woman's miscarriage. The hospital had refused to admit her without a deposit, which the aboriginal woman did not have. This shocked and distressed Master Zhengyan. The second event was her encounter with three Catholic nuns, who tried to convert her to Christianity. Master Zhengyan had a long discussion with them. During their meeting the nuns commented that although Buddhists have the most compassionate doctrine, compared to Catholics, they devote little attention to the needs of the poor and the underprivileged in Taiwan. Master Zhengyan was deeply affected by this criticism and decided to do something about it.[2]

Master Zhengyan founded the *Ciji* Foundation in 1966 with thirty followers. They were mostly housewives who contributed as little as fifty cents (equivalent to USD 0.02) a day from their grocery money.[3] Thirty years later Master Zhengyan not only runs one of the finest hospitals in the nation, *Ciji* General Hospital, but also a training school for nurses, *Ciji* Nursing College, both dedicated to serving the poor.[4] By 1994 the foundation had over four million members (this is nearly 20 percent of Taiwan's population), of which 80 percent are women, mostly homemakers.[5] Today *Ciji* is the largest civic organization in Taiwan.

The foundation was selected as the foremost social movement in Taiwan in 1991, and the foundation has been awarded the Peace Wind Award (*He Feng*) for its environmental activism and influence in society. The majority of its leaders are women, and women play a leading role in environmental activities, such as recycling programs and teaching and practicing self-discipline and thrift. Master Zhengyan emphasizes "spiritual" environmental protection. "Our hearts," she believes, "like the environment, must be protected from pollutants, like garbage." She refers to these pollutants as the "Five Poisons—greed, anger, delusion, arrogance, and suspicion" and insists that to maintain spiritual balance and health we must avoid pollutants as best we can.[6]

One of the *Ciji* Foundation's most successful initiatives has been its recycling program, which in 2002 collected nearly 350,000,000 kilograms of paper, or the equivalent of 7.2 million trees.[7] Most of the money earned is then used for charitable works, such as funding hospital and school buildings and helping victims of natural disasters, such as the September 1999 earthquake in Taiwan. Thus they believe they are living their mission: "Turning Garbage into Gold; Turning Gold into a Loving Heart."[8]

Although *Ciji* adherents are not radical, the movement is a powerful, albeit "silent," social reform movement.[9] According to the *Ciji* Foundation, revolution must be preceded by internal transformation, so rather than seeking a political movement to enforce environmental protections, they seek an individual-based transformation with spiritual, personal roots. In 2002, for example, *Ciji* enlisted and organized over thirty thousand environmental volunteers throughout the island.[10] In addition, *Ciji* has established Environmental Protection Stations (*huanbao zhan*, EPS) to enable community activities to protect the environment.

All of the new activities and projects, like the old ones, flow directly from the messages and words of Master Zhengyan. Recently she has integrated and clarified her motivations for encouraging *huanbao* in a religious sense. Her three wishes are to purify minds, harmonize society, and free the world from disaster. These wishes have taken on environmental meaning: "Integrate your mind and body to care for the earth, and your spirit will be purified. If the community unites to protect life, society will be in harmony. When the earth is protected by the people, there will be no disaster under the sky."[11] Thus the message emphasizes that protection of the earth can help realize uniquely religious and spiritual goals of purity and harmony.

Life Conservationist Association

The Life Conservationist Association shares much with *Ciji*, yet it also demonstrates striking differences. While it is founded on Buddhist ideals, LCA is less concerned with personal development than it is with promoting and enforcing legislation for the protection of animals. Moreover,

LCA is unafraid to maintain a high, and often controversial, public profile to get its message across.

Sakya Zhaohui,[12] a nun, founded the Life Conservationist Association in January 1993, along with Wuhong, a Buddhist monk;[13] the Reverend Lu Junyi, a Protestant minister; and Father Wang Jinghong, a Catholic priest.[14] Although LCA is not formally a Buddhist organization, most of its members are Buddhists. Some members are Christians, and others are experts in environmental issues with no connection to any religion. Since its inception LCA has contributed to the cause of environmental protection in a variety of ways. It is trying to push Taiwanese society to change its trends and practices by demanding systemic change of the current system of government regulations. It has also been involved in raising awareness of practices that have implications for environmental and conservation issues in Taiwan.

According to Sakya Zhaohui, there are two key doctrines in Buddhism. One is the law of *yuan qi* (Pali, *paticca samuppada*), or dependent co-arising. Buddhists believe that all beings are dependent on one another and nothing exists by itself. This is the notion of interbeing, wherein all things exist in relation to one another because they are part of an interconnected wholeness.[15] Hence, all beings are equal. The second concept, *hu sheng* (protecting life), is the ultimate spirit of Buddhist ethics. Since all beings are interconnected, if one being is hurt, all beings are affected directly or indirectly. Therefore love and kindness for others should naturally arise in one's heart.[16]

Sakya Zhaohui's *Buddhist Ethics* so popularized the phrase "all beings are equal" (*zhongsheng pingdeng*) that it became an important slogan for many animal rights activists. Zhaohui asserts that there is no sound, rational argument to provide a basis for the claim that an inferior life should serve a superior life. For her this hierarchical consciousness justifies the strong's exploiting the weak, a mind-set that has done tremendous damage to Taiwan's ecology. She has sought to promote the idea that the weaker have an equal right to survival and should not be deprived of their dignity. If this is so, animals' rights should have the same emphasis or focus as human rights.

LCA has three major aims: to educate the public on how to love and protect animals, to pursue legal channels to bring about change through government action, and to prevent activism from causing social or public problems or crises. While Sakya Zhaohui realizes that not everyone will become a vegetarian and that sometimes animals are needed for nutritional or economic benefit, she asserts that we should not console ourselves by thinking that this reality is the "natural" fate of an animal.

> We should feel ashamed and appreciative at the same time while eating animals or using them in medical experimentation or making money from them, because any animal, regardless of its species, would love to be alive. If we cannot make them live anymore at least we do not need to let them die painfully or frivolously.[17]

In 1994 LCA used its connections with more than sixty other social groups, publicizing arguments against horse racing and the issues involved. As a result, people's opinions turned in favor of LCA's initiative and created pressure on legislators to come to terms with its demands. Thus Taiwan became the first country in the region to have laws in support of the animal rights movement.[18] Zhaohui credits her coworkers, activists from other social movements, academics, and the media for these important milestones in LCA's history.[19] Today LCA continues to be a watchdog organization that monitors the implementation of laws for animal protection.

Taiwanese Christian Ecological Center
(Taiwan Ecological Stewardship Association)

Founded in 1992 the Taiwanese Christian Ecological Center was the only Christian organization in Taiwan that prominently sought to "promote the study of land, the pursuit of eco-justice, and the practice of simple life."[20] The center's founder, Chen Cimei, is an educated mother of four with master's degrees in both physics and Christian theology. Her motivation for involvement in the ecological movement stems from concerns she harbored about her family's well-being. These concerns troubled Chen enough for her to want to take concrete action. She started to attend the Homemakers' Union and Foundation's *huanbao* programs.[21] She also sought inspiration and help from the Bible.[22] Then, with the help of some Christian friends who were also active in the Homemakers' Union and support from some academic friends, including a Catholic priest, Luis Gutheniz, S.J., Chen founded the Ecological Center. The original 1992 tenets and those followed today use the organization to create a unified and global ecological ethic, combining Western ecological thought with Taiwan's ancient ecological wisdom.

The ideological starting points for the center's ecological concerns are "seeing" and compassion. Chen encourages members to emulate Jesus and to understand and act on his message to "see" people's pain and suffering, and thus sympathize with them. She further extends it to ecological concerns by saying,

> The Church must practice religious education, preaching, a medical mission through ecological education, bearing witness to ecological action, and healing the sick and the wounded of the earth. When the Center was established, Micah 6:8 became the by-word of belief for us. After all, as the Bible says, "what does the Lord require of you?— To act justly and to love mercy and to walk humbly with your God."[23]

In 1998 the organization changed its name from the Taiwanese Christian Ecological Center to the Taiwan Ecological Stewardship Association (TESA). Chen Cimei served as the center's chair of the board from 1992 to 1999 and has been secretary general since 1999. As Chen told me, "I hope this center can play three roles: thinker, critic, and educator." In other words, TESA aims to occupy the Christian roles of priest, prophet, and minister for environmental protection.[24] The organization has also published a bimonthly newsletter since 1993, with a circulation of about nine hundred people who are able to gain access to current news, details about activities, and new information concerning contributions to the environmental movement in the West.

In recent years TESA has been occupied with searching for and articulating a distinctly Taiwanese environmental ethic. In its view, integrating international activism with local and aboriginal concerns in Taiwan serves as a basis for Taiwanese citizens' interaction with their environment. The organization's well-regarded workshops, educational programs, conferences, and reflective publications intersect to form a campaign that asks Taiwan to come to grips with its relationship with the earth. Creating an environmental ethic, for Chen and the ecological center she founded, requires a fundamental evaluation of human activity and how it is affected by the earth and vice versa.

As noted above, the *Ciji* Foundation and LCA differ greatly in their approaches. While *Ciji* seeks revolution through the gradual changing of individual and collective mind-sets, LCA opts for aggressive, public policy–oriented activism. TESA's methodology is neither as publicly aggressive as LCA's nor as private and personal as that of the *Ciji* Foundation. Chen's leadership and methodologies are characterized by an emphasis on public awareness and dialogue about environmental issues at the community and church level.

New Forms of Dialogue: Of the Hands, the Head, and the Heart

Chinese philosophical and spiritual thought has emphasized that on our beautiful Earth, in every direction, whether toward the macrocosm of astronomy or the microcosm of the atom, we find everywhere evidence that life on Earth is profoundly and cosmically connected. At the foundation of all our perceptions of reality, we find the dialogue between body and spirit, between matter and energy, between electron and proton, between man and woman, between individual and society. The ancient Chinese captured this key insight in their teaching of the dialogue between *yin* and *yang*: each element of creation has an opposite that serves as its complement. Only by recognizing the interdependence between a thing or idea and its complement can both reach their full potential.

This connection between forms of life, in the view of Taiwan's religious organizations, demonstrates the need for a dialogue of perspectives and experiences in creating an environmental ethic. When we speak of interreligious dialogue or cooperation, we typically bring to mind practical forms of cooperation: religious leaders uniting for a cause or in discussion to find common ground on an issue. This form of interreligious dialogue is certainly present among these groups in Taiwan, but their experiences also point to less-obvious incarnations of interreligious dialogue that have shaped the work of each group and also brought forth efforts for a unified environmental ethic in Taiwan, rather than one based on any particular creed. In a broad sense, one can say that the dialogue finds expression in three ways (the three H's): dialogue of the hands, dialogue of the head, and dialogue of the heart. In each of these dialogue forms, different religious traditions have come to understand themselves as self and other, as opposites that have come to recognize themselves as interdependent.

Dialogue of the Hands

Here, in the most common form of interreligious dialogue and cooperation, these groups have joined hands with others to heal the world. They understand that the world all around us is suffering because of environmental degradation. The wounds of the environment and the pathologies of the lifestyle that inflicted them can only be changed when many traditions work together in practical ways to influence society. In this sense, the dialogue can be hands to hands, cooperative activism among disparate religious groups through both teaching tolerance and practicing cooperation.

For example, the *Ciji* Foundation strongly encourages its members to cooperate with other religions to clean the seashore or plant trees.

A specific example of this comes in the rescuing of *Qilan* timber (Taiwanese cypress). On Christmas Eve in 1999, representatives from several religions held a press conference for an emergency rescue of *Qilan* timber in northeastern Taiwan, where the cypress forests were being rapidly depleted by logging and industrialization.[25] The press conference included representatives of the Catholic Justice and Peace Committee, Presbyterians, and Buddhists from the *Xinlong* and *Xiangguang* temples. This cooperation was based on the common feeling of religiosity and compassion in pursuit of both justice and spirituality. The groups called on the government to introduce and enforce environmental ethics through legislation and other forms of social education to stop environmental abuse. Since most people recognize TESA as a major element in the overall Christian effort for environmental protection, they asked Chen Cimei to preside over the meeting, in which numerous religious groups expressed their opinions. The different groups not only joined forces in the cause of rescuing the *Qilan* timber but also provided a common forum to express their views on environmental protection. In this sense they worked together both ideologically and practically.

Sakya Zhaohui has talked about the interreligious cooperation that she and her group, LCA, have undertaken for a public revitalization project. When they joined hands to tackle wildlife crises and endangered species cases, she says, people from different religious faiths all worked together. When LCA opposed a circus in Taiwan, a Catholic priest supported the Buddhists' cause and discouraged his parishioners from buying tickets.[26] In Zhaohui's words,

> Though some religious followers believe that there is a process of self-improvement that is more important than general social projects, every religion needs to participate in social projects as well. It is not important to engage in too much religious debate. All the commentaries and explanations are not as important as doing what is right inside, and of believers agreeing on common goals, and working together. That is when you can really get something done.[27]

Dialogue of the Head

More than practical cooperation, interreligious dialogue of the head involves changing understandings of how we approach the world by learning about others. This sort of dialogue requires that believers be willing to change their self-understandings as a result of understanding the worldviews of others.

This sort of dialogue has been evident in Taiwan since the founding of its environmental movement. When Master Zhengyan started the *Ciji* Foundation, she received great inspiration and stimulation from Catholic nuns. She established and transformed her group by accepting challenges and including other religious perspectives. Some members of *Ciji* are teachers, and they use their occupations to teach their students about all the religions in the world, so that when they grow up, they will have respect for religions other than their own. Similarly, LCA was established when Buddhist temples, the Catholic Church, and Protestant churches all cooperated to build the organization. A mutual understanding permitted them to work together. Among the three groups' similarities, Chen Cimei thinks a simplified life is an important condition for ecological concern and for being a disciple of Jesus. This simplicity certainly mirrors *Ciji*'s sentiments about environmental protection. In *Ciji*, Master Zhengyan has asked members to treat natural resources as a blessing, to treasure them, and to invest in their preservation. The *Ciji* Foundation has even taken up these codes as their slogan, "Knowing our blessings, treasuring our blessings" (*Zhifu, xifu*).

The cooperative actions of these organizations demonstrate their view that the world is far too complicated for any one of us to understand alone. For these activists, how we understand the world determines how we act in the world. For the *Ciji* Foundation, members are encouraged to start from within themselves, to learn simplicity and respect for the earth, and then to teach their families and communities. LCA is founded on the principle that all beings are equal, and it calibrates its activism around trying to realize this principle in law. TESA begins by seeking ecological wisdom from the Bible, then acts to preserve and respect God's creations. Each group promotes not only activism but also worldviews that justify it. When they work together, they seek the mutual promotion of one another's ideas and visions for activism. Their head-to-head dialogue forges mutual environmental concerns between Buddhism and Christianity, changing the orientations of both in the process.

Dialogue of the Heart

When several religions enter into intensive dialogue regarding an issue or set of beliefs, they foster a dialogue of the heart, in which different traditions open to receive the beauty of another. The highest form of this dialogue is creative. Different belief states fuse from their mutual contact, and they create poetry, music, dance, painting, theater, and other arts that express the heart. In arts we find the easiest encounter with the other, the simplest door to dialogue, for everyone loves a thing of beauty, and through the beauty created by the other we most easily enter into the other. The heart-to-heart dialogue among these religious women and the many creative projects it engenders invoke and evoke environmental actions.

The most striking form of this creative dialogue is the development of new rituals, from public protests to mass cleaning of the streets, that generate public interest in *huanbao*. For example, on December 31, 1998, religious groups and nonreligious environmental protection organizations in Taiwan gathered together to push the government to preserve the primal Kuai Mu Forest. This cooperation did not take the form of public protest, but rather, it was an eco-ritual. To preserve these trees, some of which are seven or eight hundred years old, all the environmental organizations in Gaoxiong, southern Taiwan, hosted a forest ceremony to pray for the forests in the city square. In the ritual two dead trees were brought to the gathering as a symbol of the damage done to forests. Candles lit from a common fire were passed along to each person. Some young children read a declaration: "Thank you, forests and trees. Because of you, we can have sweet water and clean air. . . . Our generation would like to make a promise not to cut down trees when we grow up, and to have a promise with everyone to let Taiwan become beautiful again in the next century." High school students performed dramatic skits. Some acted as trees, flowers, butterflies, and birds, and others as businessmen. As the businessmen cut the trees, butterflies and birds disappeared to show the consequences of certain actions. Participants also watched slide shows of the damage done to the forests. At the end, an aboriginal resident singer, Wu Defu, dedicated a song to the gathering entitled "*Dawu* Mountain—My Beautiful Mother."[28]

This eco-ritual, lasting several hours, drew people into both activism and spiritual commitment. Lin Chinxiang, a member of *ciji* and the Mothers Service Team at Gaoxiong, reflected that everyone present was communicating with the forests and attended with respect. City officials and religious and nonreligious groups presented their pledges and made promises to do their best to protect the forests.[29]

These new rituals show the depth of interreligious dialogue with regard to the environment in Taiwan. Like my family's religious mingling, in the name of environmental protection these groups have transcended their traditions to create an inventive ethic that appeals to a whole community.

Taiwanese Lessons in Interreligious Dialogue

While different activist groups in Taiwan often cooperate on environmental projects, there is, of course, occasional friction among groups. One of the most frequent problems is the inequality of financial resources between the larger activist group *Ciji* and smaller groups. Because *Ciji* now has five million members, the majority of financial charity donations go to it while other groups receive little financial support.[30] However, *Ciji* has been working hard for forty years and has earned its reputation as a respected and trustworthy charity organization, and generally, the groups demonstrate respect for one another's special characteristics and achievements.

The distinctive features of this successful interreligious dialogue stem from a Chinese religiocultural tradition that has integrated the philosophies of Confucianism, Buddhism, and Taoism. Since the decline of the Ming dynasty (1368–1644), the concept of three interconnected religions took root in Chinese society, and it still exists as a folk religion today. There is a saying that Confucianism is like rice because it addresses a basic need of all humans for relationships and because Confucianism's main virtue is that of *ren* (benevolent love), which is first cultivated within oneself and then spread outward to the family, community, country, nature, and universe. Buddhism is like medicine because the Buddhists believe that life is suffering, but through the practice of Buddhism, one is able to end suffering and achieve happiness. Taoism is like nature, a blend of sunshine, air, and water.

The philosophies of these three religions together provide spiritual nutrition to people's lives. Rice, medicine, and nature are all required to lead a healthy and happy life.[31] As a common saying goes, "Buddhism is the red flower, Taoism is the green leaf, and Confucianism is the white edible root." Another saying goes, "Red lotus flower, green lotus leaves, and white (edible) lotus roots. Three religions as one family."[32] These religions have "coexisted [in China] through many centuries, not primarily as alternate routes to the same goal, but as complementary. . . . This is one strategy for dealing with religious pluralism. Being Chinese opens one to learning whatever can be incorporated into one's culture."[33] Although people do affiliate themselves with a specific religious practice, great respect for other religions still characterizes contemporary Chinese society. This tradition permits both the mingling of philosophies of my own background and the fluidity of cooperation among several religious groups in the environmental movement.

Since the early 1990s, interreligious dialogue has found its way into the discussion of global ethics, especially among contemporary Western

Christian theologians. Hans Küng and Karl-Josef Kuschel along with Leonard J. Swidler were the first persons to publicly promote interreligious dialogue about global ethics, stressing that uniting different religious communities is a necessary step to uniting nations for the cause of global change. They believe it is the responsibility of all religions to promote global ethics.[34]

Other scholars, such as John B. Cobb Jr. and Paul F. Knitter, have sought to link global ethics with ecological concerns. Cobb suggests that a postmodern Christianity provides an antidote to modern thought and overcomes the hallmarks of modern thinking—anthropocentrism, individualism, and dualism. He affirms the concept of "the integrity of creation," in which attention is directed to the whole of creation rather than only to humanity's dependence on its natural environment. The integrity of creation enables nature to have its own value, with everything intrinsically interrelated. As Cobb notes, this ecological worldview is congruent to the Buddhist idea that every life form is intimately associated with all the others. Positing that Christians should be concerned both with the health of the biosphere and with the suffering of individual creatures, Cobb's ideas, however, leave much room for dialogue with Buddhists' forms of eco-activism, such as LCA.[35]

Knitter agrees with Küng and Swidler that we need global dialogue toward a global ethic in order to carry out our global responsibility. However, Knitter stresses that it will be better if, before working toward developing a global ethic, we heed the warnings of postmodernists and postliberals. They insist that before searching for some kind of common ground, participants should be aware of the diversity of cultural backgrounds. Suggesting that different religions should discuss their various ecological understandings in light of the need of our "one earth," Knitter reminds us that people should show with concrete advice and examples how this kind of dialogue can be practiced.[36] Women scholars, most notably Mary Evelyn Tucker, have brought together scholars from several religious traditions to discuss how religions can better address the devastation of the environment and other ecological concerns.[37]

These Western understandings and hopes for interreligious dialogue are challenged by the Taiwanese case. Interreligious dialogue in Taiwan has taken forms that are unique to the society's religiocultural traditions, and Western understandings of interfaith collaboration can learn a great deal from the Taiwan experience in at least three key ways.

First, in the theory and praxis of interreligious dialogue, we see the distinctions between these Taiwan cases and this current Western scholarship. Many Western groups and individuals emphasize creating common understandings and respecting differences before taking action, but some have started with action, at least as far back as the Life and Work Movement, which Nathan Söderblom, Archbishop of Stockholm, Sweden, launched in 1912.[38] Taiwanese women in the groups discussed above have explicitly promoted action first and understanding later, through cooperation and eco-rituals, in which embodied doing and demonstrating commitment are preludes to, rather than results of, spiritual understanding. This kinetic element of doing is integral for Taiwanese religious women involved in environmental work.

Interreligious dialogue in the West could benefit from the proactive approach of these Taiwanese groups. At a conference of Pacific, Asian, and North American Asian Women in Theology and Ministry in 1997,[39] the Asian American scholar Rita Nakashima Brock, who has for several years studied interreligious dialogue, mentioned to me that the more she studied interreligious dialogue, the more abstract and boring it became to her. I wondered whether, after years of interreligious dialogues seeking common understanding and recognition of diverse backgrounds, the field of interreligious dialogue has changed. My answer, of course, is informed by seeing significant shifts in Western mind-sets away from the absolutism of "I am right, and everyone else is necessarily wrong" to working toward a global ethic, including one aimed at ecological concerns. The experience of Taiwan's religious groups may, however, suggest that negotiating ideological ground prior to action could be more distracting than productive. As Swidler and Paul Mojes, both interreligious scholars, have noted, "Interreligious and inter-ideological dialogue that does not eventuate in action will grow hypocritical, ineffective. Neither can survive singly."[40] Their observation corroborates the importance of doing for these Taiwanese groups and how action has provided and continues to offer ground for ideological and interspiritual understanding.

Master Zhengyan is widely known for expressing this emphasis on doing in the sayings she promotes, such as "Just do it! That's the way"; "Become enlightened while doing things, do things while becoming enlightened"; "If we cultivate ourselves, and take mindful action, there is nothing we cannot achieve."[41] The "Just do it! That's the way" philosophy has been especially popularized among members of *Ciji*. When members first came to *Ciji* doing *huanbao*, they did not know much about religious ideology and were not encouraged to privilege learning over action. After a few years of engaging deeply in *Ciji*'s activities, however, many of these environmental volunteers experienced a deep transformation, and many of them can expound to others why and how the *Ciji* are doing recycling, often in the form of grassroots lectures and education efforts for the public.

TESA provides another example. When Chen Cimei started the organization, her principle work was translating Western theories of environmental protection from English to Chinese, especially the work of Aldo Leopold. Later she turned her focus to promoting a Taiwanese land ethic with coworkers through engaging in grassroots activism and listening to how her fellow citizens understood their relationship to the environment. Like the leader of *Ciji*, Chen sought action first. This is not, of course, to say that groups in Taiwan are unconcerned with theoretical justifications and the theological basis of their work, just that the action remains continuous, even if the ideology is constantly in formation. All of these groups have sought to mobilize their communities first and foremost; their efforts at ideological and theoretical education come through action, not prior to it. The creation of environmental and religious ethics is a process that involves communities in action, rather than simply in learning the ideas of experts and theologians.

Second, the experience of these Taiwanese groups lends credence to the relational model that Western thinkers promote in place of absolutist understandings of truth. More and more Western thinkers, especially feminist theologians, conceive of reality as constituted in mutuality and relationality. To illustrate, Paul Knitter has noted the shift in the model of truth from the exclusively either/or model to the dialogic or relational model. He claims that in the new model truth will no longer be identified by its ability to relate to other expressions of truth and to grow through these relationships. In his words, "Truth is defined not by exclusion but by relation."[42] Truth, by its nature, needs other truth. I argue that when Knitter says "relational model," he means relative, rather than absolute, truths.

Instead of promoting any single, truthful understanding of the relationship between humans and animals, among generations of humans, and among all forms of creation, the ideologies of these three Taiwanese groups permit dialogue, understanding, and even the combination of various perspectives on ecological truth. TESA, for example, has consciously drawn on the experiences and wisdom of Taiwan's aboriginal communities to promote a land ethic that is uniquely Chinese. Here the Christian group also pays respect to other notions of the relationship between humans and ancestors while constructing an earthly ethics in Taiwan. For example, the internationally renowned scholar and adviser for the United Nations Earth Center J. Baird Callicott observes about Taiwan,

The Western idea of transgenerational responsibility and environment seems to be overemphasizing the part of passing assets to coming generations while ignoring the respect for ancestors or exploration and reflection on the lands ancestors left. However, this may be the field where Taiwan, which has always emphasized the tradition of respecting ancestors, can contribute specifically to Western environmental discourse.[43]

This relational model does not, however, entirely describe the work of these Taiwanese groups. They have also engaged a fruitful search for foundations for a common land ethic that resonates with all Taiwanese. Although these groups do not seek to promote an ecological dogma that prescribes how all Taiwanese should interact with the environment, they have not given up the search for an all-encompassing land ethic that can harmonize all the relationships among men and women, successive generations, creation, and animals.

Third, although these activists believe that it is sometimes necessary to highlight the differences in ideology among religions,[44] these dissimilarities have not precluded cooperation in environmental protection work. This work emphasizes harmony in human relations and stresses again the idea that social mobilization and activism are the highest goals: the social movement comes first, and ideological differences can be debated once action begins. Environmental activism has indeed brought many communities close to delving into substantive religious differences, but these discussions are never a precondition for acting toward environmental protection. As Yan Mingru, a Christian, has said,

> I think that people should work together on environmental issues without discussing ideology. I feel that politics, religion, and various movements are easy places for conflicts to arise; so it is better not to talk about beliefs. As long as everyone co-operates on common principles, that is enough. For example, I lived in Switzerland. I was there studying how they handle environmental issues. When I came back [to] Taiwan, I gave a lecture and slideshow on some of my environmental work, and twenty-two Buddhist nuns attended. I feel that even though I am a Catholic, being with those Buddhist nuns and talking about environmentalism felt very natural. I did not feel like there was any reason to dig into any religious differences.[45]

For these activists, then, the motivation for their work also involves a sense of social importance; people need to have an appreciation of connection between the spiritual and social aspects of life. Much of Taiwan's interreligious dialogue has found common ground to propel environmental issues into the hearts and minds of everyday Taiwanese. These groups have actively sought to encompass all traditions equally to "mobilize women from many backgrounds toward a common, concrete, historical project."[46] In this pursuit, differing ideologies and the need for true understanding have taken a backseat to what these activists have identified as the most urgent and pressing need: healing the wounds of Taiwan's natural environment.

Conclusion

As a devout Taiwanese Christian, I know that I can enter into dialogue with other religions and pass down the love of nature and culture I inherited from my ancestors through my generation to the next. For me the real challenge is in upholding my values and ideals while maintaining respect and admiration for the faith and traditions of others.

The stories of three groups of religious women and their involvement in interreligious cooperation inform our studies of interreligious cooperation about different, unexpected forms of dialogue in Taiwan. The religiocultural traditions of Taiwan weave faith perspectives together rather than duel over truth. New forms of cooperation can be of the hands, of the head, or of the heart and can take all of these forms in the environmental movement. These women's environmental movements show that dialogue can achieve mutual understanding and practical cooperation, as well as go further by mingling religious traditions to create new rituals that are relevant to the agenda at hand. This has been and continues to be particularly true with regard to ecological issues. In Taiwan, religious women have been in the forefront in their efforts to establish interfaith dialogue on the status and role of women in diverse situations and the reality of their life experiences.[47] This emphasis on doing and being spiritual while not needing an absolute truth or a religious label is Taiwan's contribution to our understanding of the power of interreligious dialogue and the healing of the earth.

Notes

1. Mary Evelyn Tucker and Duncan Ryuken Williams, eds., *Buddhism and Ecology: The Interconnection of Dharma and Deeds* (Cambridge, MA: Harvard University Press for the Harvard University Center for the Study of World Religions, 1997). Joanna Macy, in her

Mutual Causality in Buddhism and General Systems Theory: The Dharma of Natural Systems (Albany: State University of New York Press, 1991), gives a major theoretical contribution that focuses on the origins of a feminist ecological consciousness. She compares the Buddhist doctrine of dependent co-arising with general systems theory in contemporary Western thought, stressing the complex interdependence in all relationships.

2. Hengching, *Puti daoshang de sannuren* (Wonderful Women in the Bodhisattva's Way) (Taipei: Dongda, 1995), 180.

3. Douglas Shaw, ed., *Ten Thousand Lotus Blossoms of the Heart: Dharma Master Cheng Yen and the Tzu Chi World* (Taipei: Foreign Language Publications Department of Tzu Chi Buddhist Cultural Center, 2002), 12–13.

4. Barry Corbin, John Trites, and Jim Taylor, "Religious Leaders Making a Difference," in *Global Connection: Geography for the Twenty-first Century* (Toronto: Oxford University Press, 1999), 408.

5. Chienyu Julia Huang and Robert Weller, "Merit and Mothering: Women and Social Welfare in Taiwanese Buddhism," *Journal of Asian Studies* 57, no. 2 (1998): 379. Eighty percent of the membership of *Ciji* consists of women, mostly homemakers, who remain at home but are often looking for something meaningful to do with their energy. For further discussion on housewives' activism, see Wan-Li Ho, "Environmental Protection as Religious Action: The Case of Taiwanese Buddhist Women," in *Ecofeminism and Globalization*, ed. Heather Eaton and Lois Ann Lorentzen (Lanham, MD: Rowman & Littlefield, 2003), 123–45.

6. Zhengyan, "Let's Do It Together—Environmental Protection for Mind, Health and the Great Earth," trans. Norman Yuan, *Tzu Chi Quarterly*, Winter 1996, 8.

7. *Ciji 2002 niandu baogao* (Foundation Annual Report 2002), ed. Lin Bizhu (Taipei: Ciji wenhua zhiye zhongxin, 2003), 474.

8. This is a popular slogan among the *Ciji* members. See http://www2.tzuchi.org.tw/tc-env/html/en-pure.htm.

9. Zhang Weian, "Silent Social Reform: The Compassion of Relief Tzu Chi Foundation as a Model for Social Changes," unpublished paper presented at the annual meeting of the American Sociological Association, San Francisco, 1998, 8.

10. *Ciji 2002 niandu baogao* (Foundation Annual Report 2002). Also note that enlisted volunteers sign up one year prior to being classified as *Ciji* volunteers, and they must fulfill a series of requirements, including participation in either eight large recycling events or participation in one *huanbao* event each month.

11. Cheng Qingyuan, director of Gaoxiong Renwu Xiang County Environmental Protection Station, interview by author, December 20, 2003.

12. The founder of this group is Zhaohui. She is often addressed as Sakya (instead of Master) Zhaohui. It refers to the clan or family of the Buddha. According to one interviewee, Zhaohui does not consider herself a master because it implies a greater spiritual role. Similarly other LCA leaders also prefer to be addressed as Sakya as a sign of humility.

13. Wuhong was the secretary general of LCA from 1993 to 1999. In 1999 he founded another organization for protecting animals, Environmental and Animal Society of Taiwan (EAST).

14. Zhaohui, *Niaoru qinyun juan yifei* (Although Tired, Birds Still Fly into the Sky) (Taipei: Fajie, 1996), 75.

15. Bill Devall, "Ecocentric Sangha," in *Dharma Gaia: A Harvest of Essays in Buddhism and Ecology*, ed. Allan Hunt Badiner (Berkeley, CA: Parallax Press, 1990), 162.

16. Zhaohui, *Fojiao lunlixue* (Buddhist Ethics) (Taipei: Fajie, 1995), 62–63.

17. Zhaohui, *Yuantong ruoshao kang qiangquan* (Opposing the Powerful) (Taipei: Fajie, 1994), 22.

18. Sakya Zhaohui, interview by author, June 28, 2000.

19. Zhaohui, *Renjian fojiao shilianchang* (The Testing Ground) (Taipei: Fajie, 1998), 257.

20. Taiwanese Christian Ecological Center brochure, 4.

21. The Homemakers' Union and Foundation has been one of the earliest and largest organizations to combine women's strengths, concern for social needs, and concrete activities for social change. See Zhang Maogui, *Shehui yundong yu zhengzhi zhuanhua* (Social Movement and Political Transitions), 3rd ed. (Taipei: Guojia zhence yanjiu zhongxin, 1991), 64–67.

22. Yang Zhenjuan, *Taiwan jidutu shengtai lingxiu—cong sanwei daibiaoxing renwu tantaozhong zhaochu fangxiang* (Taiwan Christian Ecological Spirituality: Finding Direction from Three Representatives) (master's thesis, Fu Jen University, Taiwan, 1997), 6.

23. Chen Cimei, interview by author, July 16, 2000.

24. Ibid.

25. Chen Yufeng, ed., *Quanguo qiangjiu quilan kuaimulin yundong zhi* (Save the Last National Treasure in Taiwan, Taipei: Qilan guojia gongyuan lianmeng, n.d.).

26. A Catholic priest in Taipei who is actively involved in interreligious dialogue is Rev. Albert Poulet-Mathis.

27. Sakya Zhaohui, interview by author, June 28, 2000.

28. Lin Chunxiang, interview by author, July 4, 2000.

29. Ibid.

30. According to Lu Hui-Xin, "In the beginning, *Ciji* started with a little financial power, but over the forty years of development, it has not only gathered a staggering amount of five million members but has also accumulated sizable donations from its members, while other charity groups or NGOs are receiving less than sufficient financial support. These smaller charity groups might also gain their popularity and financial power over the decades to come (interview by author, July 29, 2000).

31. Lin Anwu, *Xindaojiao yu zhilaoxue* (New Taoism and Therapy) (Taipei: Taiwan Shangwu yinshuguan, 2006), 8.

32. Ibid.

33. John. B. Cobb Jr., "Beyond 'Pluralism,'" in *Christian Uniqueness Reconsidered: The Myth of a Pluralistic Theology of Religions*, ed. Gavin D'Costa (Maryknoll, NY: Orbis Books, 1990), 83, 88.

34. Hans Küng says, "My book *Global Responsibility* appeared in German in 1990. . . . Professor Leonard J. Swidler of the Religion Department of Temple University, Philadelphia, and editor of the *Journal of Ecumenical Studies*, then composed an appeal in which, among other things, he called for the prompt composition of a declaration on a global ethic. I decided to become the first signatory of Swidler's appeal" (Hans Küng and Karl-Josef Kuschel, eds., *A Global Ethic: The Declaration of Parliament of the World's Religion* [New York: Continuum, 1993], 46–47). For further information, see Küng and Kuschel, *Global Ethic*, 72–74; and Leonard J. Swidler, "Toward a Universal Declaration of a Global Ethic," in *For All Life: Toward a Universal Declaration of a Global Ethic: An Interreligious Dialogue*, ed. Leonard J. Swidler (Ashland, OR: White Cloud Press, 1998), 19–23.

35. John B. Cobb Jr., *Sustainability: Economics, Ecology, and Justice* (Maryknoll, NY: Orbis Book, 1992), 82–88.

36. Paul F. Knitter, *One Earth Many Religions: Multifaith Dialogue and Global Responsibility* (Mayknoll, NY: Orbis Book, 1995), 69, 181.

37. Mary Evelyn Tucker and John Grim have edited a series of books regarding relationships between different religions and ecology. For more on Chinese religions, see, for example, Mary Evelyn Tucker and John Berthrong, eds., *Confucianism and Ecology: The Interrelation of Heaven, Earth, and Humans* (Cambridge, MA: Harvard University Press for the Harvard University Center for the Study of World Religions, 1998).

38. Life and Work Movement, September 2006, http://www.interchurch-center.org/content/resources/researchlibrary/pdfs/LIFEWORK.

39. The twelfth Pacific, Asian, and North American Asian Women in Theology and Ministry Conference, Emory University, Atlanta, Georgia, March 14, 1997.

40. Leonard J. Swidler and Paul Mojes, *The Study of Religion in an Age of Global Dialogue* (Philadelphia: Temple University Press, 2000), 171.

41. *Tzu Chi USA Journal* 1, no. 5 (October 2002): 5, 29.

42. Paul F. Knitter, *No Other Name?* (Maryknoll, NY: Orbis, 1984), 219.

43. Lin Yihren, "Shengtai zhilu: huiyu yiwei shanyu qingting yu goutong de zhexuejia" (The Fieldtrip of Eco-history: Meeting a Philosopher Who Is Good at Listening and Dialogue), Report of Taiwan Ecological Center, September 2000, 1–2.

44. For some the hope of engaging in a deeper dialogue to probe bravely into religious differences is a realizable goal. For example, Chen Yuming, a previous member of LCA, wonders, "If we all can get together and talk about the problem of killing animals in different religions, we can create a less harmful alternative. For example, in ceremonies of religious Taoism, people are killing fatted pigs in the past, and now why cannot we just use flour to make a pig to sacrifice to the spirits?" (interview by author, June 27, 2000). It is not entirely inconceivable to think of using pigs made out of flour for sacrifices like these. Muslims, for instance, do not eat pork, and Hindus do not eat beef because of their religious beliefs, which allows different attitudes toward these animals in their respective societies. Asking these kinds of questions can generate a meaningful dialogue.

45. Yan Mingru, interview by author, June 5, 2000.

46. Chung Hyun Kyung, *Struggle to Be the Sun Again: Introducing Asian Women's Theology* (Maryknoll, NY: Orbis Books, 1990), 113.

47. See reports of the two Asian Women's Consultation on Interfaith Dialogue conferences in Malaysia and Sri Lanka in 1989 and 1991, respectively, in Dulci Abraham, Sun Ai Lee Park, and Yvonne Dahlin, eds., *Faith Renewed: A Report on the First Asian Women's Consultation on Interfaith Dialogue* (Hong Kong: Asian Women's Resource Centre for Culture and Theology [AWRC], n.d.); and *Faith Renewed II: A Report on the Second Asian Women's Consultation on Interfaith Dialogue, November 1–7, 1991, Colombo, Sri Lanka* (Seoul: AWRC, n.d.).

Chapter Fourteen

Has Jesus Ever Condemned Divorce?

An Intercultural Interpretation of Jesus' Saying on Divorce

Seung Ai Yang

K im, a forty-four-year-old Korean woman, was filled with joyful expectation and thanksgiving as she and her fiancé entered the office of her church of the past twenty years. After divorcing her abusive husband ten years ago, she had a dreadful life. On top of the economic and emotional turmoil caused by her divorce, she experienced prejudice from her family and church community. "Now it would soon be over," she thought, offering heartfelt thanks for God's mercy and love. The couple had a list of possible dates for their wedding ceremony and went to the church to arrange the service. The staff, however, informed them that they could not have their wedding at the church, because, according to church policy, "it should be the first marriage for both bride and bridegroom. A divorced person cannot have a wedding service here." The staff kindly but firmly explained the nonnegotiable church policy: "For Jesus Christ prohibited divorce." Later they found themselves hearing the same pronouncement from the many other churches they chose as alternatives.

Kim's painful story of doubled marginalization is not something that one hears only from Korean Christians. Since the beginning of Christianity, Christians have assumed that Jesus prohibited divorce. Based on this assumption, many Christian communities have developed an ecclesiastical law or policy that either prohibits divorce absolutely or permits divorce only under certain conditions.[1] Historical-critical scholarship, which has dominated the biblical field in modern times, also endorsed this long-standing assumption. Analyzing the source, form, and redaction of

This chapter draws material from my "Jesus' Saying on Divorce: A Korean Perspective" that appeared in *Bible Today* 35, no. 1 (1997): 49–54.

253

the relevant passages in the New Testament (Matt. 5:31–32; 19:3–9; Mark 10:2–12; Luke 16:18; 1 Cor. 7:10–11), the historical-critical scholarship has produced a twofold general consensus on the "authentic" saying of Jesus. First, Jesus' authentic saying is roughly reconstructed as the following: "Anyone who repudiates his wife and marries another commits adultery."[2] Second, the meaning of Jesus is clear: Jesus prohibits divorce (and remarriage). Whereas I agree with the first part of the consensus, I find the second conclusion problematic. It reflects a considerable inattentiveness to Jesus' context.

This chapter questions the assumption that Jesus prohibited divorce, an assumption that modern scholarship has further reinforced. By means of intercultural dialogue between Jesus' patriarchal context and Korean patriarchal marriage and divorce traditions, I will argue two points. First, the point of Jesus' saying is not the prohibition of divorce but the one-sided repudiation of a woman by her owner/husband. Second, Jesus' saying is not a legal statement that prohibits divorce but a prophetic condemnation of men's tendency to misuse power in patriarchal family organizations.

Jesus' patriarchal context was first-century Palestine, but the nature of the patriarchy in Judaism during this period has been vigorously debated. Jewish feminist scholars have legitimately expressed serious concerns about some Christian feminist scholarship that has underscored Jesus' movement as egalitarian against the negative foil of first-century Palestinian Judaism. Some of them emphasize the importance of the difference between women described in Jewish texts and women in Jewish history. They point out that there were Jewish women who had power in their private lives or leadership in public life, although Jewish texts of the time suggest that such power was reserved only for men.[3] In fact, Hellenistic influences were present in various degrees everywhere in Palestine at that time, and the sociocultural context of Jesus and his audience may well have included some Hellenistic elements. I fundamentally agree that there are problems with Christian bias and with disparities between the text and reality. Diverse practices coexisted in first-century Palestine regarding family, marriage, and its dissolution. The society in general, however, was strongly patriarchal, and women who had power were the privileged few. My major source material for understanding the context of Palestinian Judaism around the turn of the era will be early Jewish postbiblical literature and the New Testament.[4]

By "Korean patriarchal traditions" I mean the patriarchal culture that, under the influence of Confucianism and Neo-Confucianism, has dominated Korea from the Yi (Choson) dynasty (1392–1910) to the present.[5] Again, different customs and practices coexisted in Korea, particularly among royal families and outcasts, but the dominant culture remained patriarchal. Although many aspects of the patriarchal structure have formally disappeared since the mid-twentieth century because of legal changes (de jure), the ethos that used to support the patriarchal system still remains in the minds of most ordinary Koreans and controls their everyday life in various degrees (de facto).[6]

The Point of Jesus' Sayings

Did Jesus talk about "divorce"? Was the theme of these sayings "divorce"? For this question, the key word in the Gospel traditions is the Greek verb *apolyo*. Many English-speaking scholars translate this verb as "to divorce." Others translate it as "to repudiate" or "to put away" or similar words but then simply assume that it means "to divorce." This assumption needs to be challenged.

Growing up in Korea, I often observed two conflicting yet coexisting understandings of the dissolution of marriage that caused confusion and frustration among people. Some seemed to think that the initiation of the dissolution of marriage was reserved only for husbands. Hence wives must always be careful not to make it happen, because the dissolution of marriage meant the total loss of support. Therefore, wives should be grateful to husbands, who "mercifully" keep them. Others, especially educated women, seemed to think of marriage dissolution in the same way as most people think of divorce today. For them, wives and husbands share an equal status relative to the right to initiate the dissolution of marriage. Repudiation and divorce, I have to say, are two different things not only semantically but also institutionally.

"To divorce" as a verb denoting the action of marriage dissolution is a semantically bilateral term. Any party may "divorce" the other. With this verb the distinction between the two parties, one as the subject and the other as the object, is of no importance. Even the subject, that is, the party who initiates the action, may be described with a passive form. For example, the phrase "he is divorced" does not necessarily mean that his wife has divorced him and that he has been divorced by her. In the three phrases, "he is divorced," "she is divorced," and "the couple is divorced," there is no semantic difference in the three passive participles "divorced." In contrast to this bilateral term "to divorce," *apolyo* and its corresponding terms in biblical and postbiblical Jewish literature, such as *shlh*, *grsh*, *trk*, and *shbq* in Hebrew, and *ekballo, exapostello,* and *aphiemi* in Greek, are all unilateral terms, denoting "to repudiate, to abandon, to dismiss, to put away, to banish, or to send away" and the like.[7] The distinction between the subject and the object of the verb is clear. The subject is always the party in power, the husband, and the object under this power, the wife.[8]

Nowhere in the Hebrew Bible do we find an underlying statement about whether or not "repudiation" is in principle something that is permitted or prohibited. All the relevant passages simply assume its practice.[9] Among them, Deuteronomy 24:1–4 is a key text in understanding Jesus' saying, because the frequent discussions in Jesus' time about the repudiation of a wife, including the five New Testament passages mentioned above, are based on this text.[10] It is interesting to note that this Deuteronomy text had a particular meaning in the first century. While it originally addressed the problem of a man's retaking his ex-wife after she married another man, in the first century it was used to support the male privilege of repudiating his wife by giving her a certificate of repudiation. More interesting, both Judaism and Christianity have used this text as the basis for addressing their legal questions about allowing divorce. Most important to my current study, however, is that this text reveals the relationship between husband and wife as understood in Israel's patriarchal society, which seems to have influenced the social ethos of Jesus' time. My translation of the Hebrew text follows:

1a	If a man takes a woman
1b	and owns her as owner/husband (*baal*),[11]
1c	but she does not look good in his eyes,
1d	because he finds in her something unseemly,[12]
1e	he writes her a bill of cutting-off[13]
1f	and hands it to her
1g	and sends her away from his house.
2a	She leaves his house,
2b	and goes off,
2c	and becomes another man's.
3a	The latter man hates[14] her,
3b	and writes her a bill of cutting-off,
3c	and hands it to her,
3d	and sends her away from his house,
3e	or suppose the latter man, who has taken her for himself as his wife, dies.
4a	Her first owner/husband (*baal*), who had sent her away, cannot take her again to be his wife,

4b   because she has been defiled.

4c   For that would be abhorrent to YHWH.

4d   You shall not bring sin to the land which YHWH your God is giving you as a heritage.

The language of this passage presupposes that the relationship between husband and wife is primarily that between the owner and the owned, which regrettably is lost in most modern English Bibles. "Marriage"[15] is expressed by means of terms conveying possession: A man "takes, *lqh*," a woman (v. 1a); he "owns, *baal*," her (v. 1b).[16] She "becomes a man's" (v. 2c).[17] That is, she belongs to him. He becomes her husband as her owner. He is her "owner/husband, *baal*" (v. 4a).[18] The owner keeps his chattel while he likes it, but he puts it away if he does not like it any longer. Similarly, an owner/husband may repudiate his wife when he does not like her any longer, that is, as Deuteronomy says, "when she does not look good in his eyes, because he finds in her something unseemly" (vv. 1cd). The verb for the action of repudiation used in Deuteronomy 24 is the hiphil form of *shlh*, "to send away, to put away" (vv. 1g, 3d).[19]

The relationship between husband and wife is reminiscent of the master-slave relationship. In fact, wife and slave are often dealt with side by side in the Hebrew Bible and postbiblical Jewish literature, apparently due to their close affinity.[20] Then, what is the difference between a wife and a slave? I suggest that one difference is significant for our discussion: in the case of the wife, the husband's ownership is most focused on her sexuality. What is more peculiar is that the husband's ownership of his wife's sexuality is not only limited to the marriage itself but also extends to both her premarital and postmarital life. This concept of exclusive and extensive ownership of the wife by her owner/husband is essential in understanding the patriarchal marriage system of Jesus' context and thus understanding the passages being discussed.[21]

The Husband's Ownership of His Wife's Sexuality in Jesus' Patriarchal Context

Before Marriage

A woman was supposed to keep her virginity until the first night with her owner/husband, but there is no such expectation for him. According to Deuteronomy 22:13–21, a wife whose virginity is not proved on the first night is to be stoned to death. Although this death penalty was no longer in effect at the time of Jesus, the virginity of the wife was such an absolute prerequisite for the marriage that weddings were to be arranged on Wednesday for easy virginity suits at the Thursday court (*m. Ketub.* 1:1). Deuteuronomic law prescribes that a rapist should take the virgin whom he has raped as his wife (Deut. 22:28–29) and that he is not allowed to repudiate her until he dies. This requirement, which is difficult for a modern person to understand, is easily understood in its context: it would be difficult to find a man who was willing to give up his exclusive ownership of his wife's sexuality and marry a woman who had been sexually violated by another man. In both Old Testament times and Jesus' time, an unmarried life was not a matter of choice for a woman. If she were single, it would have been assumed that for some reason no one wanted her.[22] As the rabbis in the Talmud say, "A woman will tolerate an unhappy marriage rather than remain alone" (*b. Yebam.* 113a; *b. Qidd.* 7a).[23] The Deuteronomic regulation regarding a husband who falsely claims that he found his wife not to be a virgin is similar; the husband cannot repudiate her in his lifetime (Deut. 22:13–19). Neither the Hebrew Bible nor rabbinic regulation is concerned about the woman's pain of being forced to live with such a man. The cultural assumption is that marrying her rapist or continuing a marriage with a husband whose false accusation could have led to her execution was beneficial to the woman. That was why the regulation added that these men were permanently deprived of their rights to repudiate these women (Deut. 22:19, 29; *m. Ketub.* 3:4–5).[24] In a society where an unmarried woman had little formal standing, these provisions were legal attempts to decrease the evil of those who had power—men— and to protect the powerless—women.[25]

During Marriage

The concept of the husband's exclusive ownership of his wife lent itself to a unique interpretation of the notion of adultery. In biblical and post-biblical Jewish literature, adultery always means a sexual relationship between a man and a married woman. Whether the involved man is married does not matter at all. What matters is that the woman is married and that the man involved is not her husband. Thus the text specifies that the involved woman is married or that she is a wife of another man, but it is silent about the marital status of the involved man.[26] In other words, the woman is already owned by someone, and the man involved is not her owner. While the unchastity of the husband is not a punishable matter[27] unless it is a relationship with someone else's wife, the unchastity of the wife, including a virgin engaged to be married, deserves death (Deut.

22:22–24; Lev. 20:10). Although the death penalty formally disappeared by the time of Greco-Roman rule, the story of Susanna, who was falsely accused of adultery (in the Greek version, Daniel 13), and the episode of the woman brought in for adultery in the Gospel of John (7:53–8:11) suggest that people still thought that an adulteress deserved death. At the very least a husband was expected to repudiate his adulterous wife. In the New Testament, Joseph is described in such terms when he is called a righteous man who wanted to repudiate his fiancée, Mary, because she was found pregnant before they had their first night together (Matt. 1:18–19).[28]

After He Has Repudiated Her

The text of Deuteronomy 24 prohibits a man's remarriage to his ex-wife who has since married another man, that is, who has been owned by another. This prohibition suggests that her second marriage is regarded as something problematic to her ex-husband. The text specifically names this problem as her being defiled (*tm'*), which is related to adultery or prostitution in the Hebrew Bible. Jeremiah also quotes this Deuteronomy text to make an analogy to Israel's unfaithfulness to YHWH, that is, Israel's playing the whore (Jer. 3:1). Even after repudiation with a bill of cutting-off, a dismissed wife's relationship with another man is identified as something equivalent to a married woman's unchastity. Her marriage tie—the ownership of her sexuality by her husband—is considered still effective even after he has repudiated her. In fact, rabbinic literature reveals that her second marriage was regarded as a kind of adultery in early Judaism. Commenting on Deuteronomy 24:2, which mentions the case of the wife's second deceased husband, rabbis say, "He deserves to die since the one expelled a wicked woman from his house and the other took her into his house." Philo of Alexandria, a Jewish philosopher of the first century who sometimes exhibited a less patriarchal view about women than many voices in rabbinic literature, also expressed a similar view. According to Philo, the woman who married another after she had been repudiated by her husband was the one who had violated her former ties, which she had forgotten, and who had chosen new temptation in place of the old. Regarding the ex-husband who took her back, Philo said that he had deeply stamped on his character two of the greatest of all iniquities: adultery and the employment of a panderer.[29] We can presume that, even in Jesus' time, people thought that the husband's ownership of his wife's sexuality would extend beyond the repudiation.[30]

The Husband's Ownership of His Wife's Sexuality
in Traditional Korean Society

Korean tradition reveals a strikingly similar concept of the husband's ownership of his wife. The husband was called *juin*, which means owner, exactly like *baal* (owner/husband) in Deuteronomy 24. I still vividly remember how perturbed I felt whenever I heard women of my mother's age referring to their husbands as their *juin*. They even grinned at those women of "new ways" who would use the modern, nonhierarchal expression "husband." The influence of the *yin yang* idea elevated the status of the husband even higher. The husband was compared to heaven, and he was to rule over his wife.[31] Unless the husband requested it, the wife was not supposed to discuss what he was doing, even if it was wrong.[32] To make the ownership and rulership of the wife work smoothly, a man was encouraged to find a wife less educated than he and born of a poorer, less-powerful, less-admirable family. It was believed that if the husband (*yang*) did not dominate his wife (*yin*), everything would turn to disorder.

Marriage arrangements were relatively bilateral, only in the sense that the decision was made between the parents or heads of the households of the couple. The dissolution, however, was absolutely unilateral. The husband or the head of the husband's family took the initiative. Traditional Korean society did not have a term corresponding to divorce. It only had the word *sobak*, which denotes "abandonment, repudiation, or expulsion." As in the Hebrew Bible and in first-century Palestine, it was the husband who could expel his wife, and not vice versa. It was not until recently that a new bilateral term, *yihon*, which denotes "divorce," almost entirely replaced the traditional unilateral term *sobak* in Korean society.[33]

As in the Palestinian Judaism of Jesus' time, in traditional Yi Choson society the husband had an exclusive ownership of his wife's sexuality, extending to her premarital and postmarital period.

Before Marriage

Although there was no system equivalent to a Jewish virginity suit, because public discussion of sexual matters was taboo in the Neo-Confucian Choson, virginity was the absolute prerequisite for a bride. A raped woman most often committed suicide or was encouraged to do so by her family unless a marriage arrangement with the rapist could be made. A new marriage arrangement for a young woman once betrothed to someone else was difficult. It did not make much difference if she had never seen her fiancé face-to-face. No one would be willing to take a woman who had been reserved for someone else even by the form of betrothal.[34] Even today it is not a rarity that a bridegroom or fiancé expects the proof of virginity from his partner on their first night, and the lack of proof may result in divorce or breaking off their betrothal. One still hears today of a man's attempt to violate the virginity of his lover so that he can procure the warrant for their marriage.

During Marriage

The concept of chastity was unbalanced between husband and wife in traditional Korean society, as in Jesus' society. A wife's extramarital relationship was unthinkable and believed to be punishable by death in the traditional Choson society. In contrast, a husband's extramarital relationship was not only overlooked but even encouraged unless it was a relationship with someone else's wife. A husband's extramarital relationship was considered an expression of his manliness. A wife's jealousy about her husband's extramarital affairs was taboo; it was one of the seven evils that deserved repudiation. Since the end of the eighteenth century, the influence of Western culture and Christianity has increasingly contributed to the women's liberation movement, which condemns concubinage as well as men's extramarital relationships. This movement, however, has yet to change the deeply rooted male mind-set holding that a faithful husband is not a true man. In fact, even though the Constitution of Korea in 1948 outlawed concubinage, I grew up knowing many girls who had difficult lives because their fathers left home and lived with their concubines.

After He Has Dismissed Her

In traditional Korean society a second marriage was almost impossible for a repudiated woman. Once married, whether repudiated or not, she still belonged to her husband and to his family. The same was true for a widow. The Yi dynasty issued a law that prohibited a second marriage for the widow. Although remarriage has been legally allowed since 1894, it is mostly practiced by those of lower social levels. The misconduct of a repudiated wife or a widow was considered shameful for the former husband's family. Remarriage was considered misconduct for a woman, since she did not remain faithful to her former husband. Even today many, especially in the older generations, are prejudiced against a woman who has married more than once. There are still people who consider "twice-married woman" a shameful title due to the negative connotation it carries. Unfortunately, my family is a typical example. There are three widows in my family who have never considered remarriage an option: my mother (a widow since age 48) and her two daughters-in-law (widows since ages 36 and 49).[35]

The Repudiation and Dissolution of Marriage

In a society where the husband has such an extensive and exclusive ownership of his wife, what would be the situation of a woman repudiated by her husband? When the Deuteronomy text explicitly says, "He sends her away from his house," the house does not simply mean a dwelling place. The house is an overarching term for a whole household or family, including ancestors, descendants, and kindred. The text reflects a patriarchal and patrilinial society, which assumed that with marriage not only the owners of women but also the women's houses changed. The house to which she belonged permanently moved from her father's house to her husband's, or more correctly, to her husband's father's. *Samjongjido* (the rule of three obediences), a woman's rule of conduct in traditional Korea, is also understood in this way. A woman is to follow her father in childhood, her husband during marriage, and her (eldest) son in old age.

In the Deuteronomy text, when the husband sends his wife away from his house, it means the husband has decided that she no longer belongs to his family. The house to which she used to belong does not want to regard her as a member. She is "cut off" from the house. As a sign of this enactment, the husband writes and gives her a "bill of cutting-off," as my translation of Deuteronomy 24 revealed earlier (*spr krtt* in v. 1e and v. 3b). There is abundant usage of the root *krt* in the Hebrew Bible, which refers to the cutting-off of a person from that to which the person used to belong. It denotes the loss of belongingness and related privileges for a person who is judged to have failed to meet the requirement for membership.[36] In short, the Deuteronomy text suggests that when the owner/husband put away his chattel/wife, it was more than dismissal; it was a cutting-off, that is, banishment, expulsion, or repudiation from his house. The Hebrew and Aramaic terms used alongside *shlh* in early rabbinic literature, such as *trk* and *grsh*, also manifest the same environment around Jesus' time.

In traditional Korean society once the husband decided to dismiss his wife, a question arose as to whether she really left the house. Most women could not leave their husbands. First, no house would accept her return.

Her repudiation became a shame not only for her but also for her parents' house, and because of this shame, the parents hesitated to accept their daughter back into their house. Second, once a woman became someone's wife, she was regarded as an outsider to her father's house. The Korean idiom *chulgawein* means "once married, the daughter is an outsider." I still frequently hear this word used in my family's conversations to remind someone, for example, of her "true" belonging, even though we use it rather jokingly these days. Today some parents still instruct their betrothed daughters with the following words: "This is not your house any longer. You belong to your husband's family from now on." "You are that house's ghost, even when you become a ghost" (that is, even after death).

Furthermore, in traditional Korean society a woman repudiated by her husband was suspected of having some physical or moral defect. In a society where it was almost impossible for a woman to make a living by herself, she had now become a woman to be shunned, a woman whom an ordinary person would not take as his wife.[37] In Korean traditional culture it was much better for her not to leave the house and to be shunned by villagers. Instead, she was better off waiting for the time when her owner/husband would change his mind and recall her. Once recalled, she might recover her honor and dignity as a steadfast wife who had endured hardship instead of being disgraced as a repudiated woman, a sinner, or a twice-married woman.

Rabbinic literature suggests a positive correlation between Korean customs and Jesus' society. Mishnah *Eduyyoth* 4:7 reads, "The School of Shammai say: A man may dismiss his wife with an old bill of divorce. And the School of Hillel forbid it. What is an old bill of divorce? If he continued alone with her after he had written it for her [it becomes an 'old' bill of divorce]."[38] This discussion presupposes a situation in which she did not leave the house after the dismissal.[39] It is plausible that a woman in first-century Palestine, after being dismissed by her husband, opted to wait for her recall rather than actually "leaving the house," "going off her own way," and "becoming another man's" (as the language of Deut. 24:2a, 2b, 2c specifies).[40] The frequent rabbinic discussion about the retaking of a wife after her husband has dismissed her supports this conjecture. Especially interesting in our discussion is Mishnah *Gittin* 4:7–8, which lists various rabbinic opinions regarding when a man may or may not take back his repudiated wife.[41] Furthermore, it is noteworthy that this rabbinic discussion in general does not consider the retaking of the wife to be a new marriage. It suggests that for the Jews of the time the retaking was a continuation of a formerly existing marriage, and that the dismissal did not

necessarily mean the wife's permanent expulsion from the house. Therefore, the dismissal could mean both permanent dissolution of marriage
and temporary dissolution. Once the dismissed woman really "left the
house," "went off her own way," and "became another man's," dismissal
became permanent and could mean a legal dissolution of the marriage,
although her second marriage was still regarded as quasi adultery. When
the dismissed woman did not leave the house but waited for her recall, the
dismissal could be either permanent or temporary, depending on the
owner/husband's decision of retaking, and it could also mean a nonlegal
dissolution. The owner/husband's retaking his wife simply meant the continuation of their married life.[42]

The Meaning of Jesus' Sayings

We have seen that in two patriarchal societies the husband's ownership of
his wife's sexuality is exclusive and extensive. The taking, dismissal, and
retaking of a wife were unilaterally powers of the owner/husband. In these
societies we see cultural systems that encourage the repudiation of the
wife in certain cases. Ben Sira advises men about a wife who is not obedient: "If she does not follow as you direct, separate her from yourself" (Sir.
25:26).[43] The Mishnah has a long list of the cases proper for repudiation,
such as no children (*Yebam.* 6:6), idleness (*Ketub.* 5:5), transgression of the
law of Moses or of Jewish custom (*Ketub.* 7:6), and so on.[44] Traditional
Korean society had a list called *chilgojiak*, literally meaning seven evils, as
suitable cause for repudiation.[45] The seven listed evils are improper attitude toward the husband's parents, failure to give birth to a son, unchastity,
jealousy, inherited diseases, talkativeness, and stealing. Even today some
parents of the husband encourage him to divorce his wife if she fails to
bear a son.[46]

In such social structures it is not surprising that the dismissal of a wife
may be subject to the owner/husband's caprice. Between the two famous
rabbinic schools in the first century BCE, the liberal view of Hillel's school
(that a man may dismiss his wife even when she has spoiled a dish for him)
prevailed over the conservative view of Shammai's school (that the repudiation is allowed only in the case of unchastity)[47] (*m. Git.* 9:10).[48] In fact,
Rabbi Akiba goes one step further than Hillel's school in interpreting
Deuteronomy 24:1 and allowing the repudiation of the wife even if he
found another better looking than she (*m. Git.* 9:10).

It is no wonder, then, that throughout biblical and postbiblical Jewish
literature we see various efforts of the society to protect women by limit-

ing men's power. Gradually the bill of cutting-off was understood as a certificate that warrants the woman's freedom to marry anyone.[49] Mishnah *Gittin* 9:3 describes its multivalent aspects:

> The essential format in the divorce certificate (*get*) is: "Behold, you are free to marry any man." R. Judah says: "Let this be from me your bill of cutting-off (*spr krtn*) and writ of dismissal (*'grt shbqn*) and certificate of liberation (*get ptrn*) that you may marry any man you want." The essential format in the certificate of emancipation (*get shtrr*) is: "Behold, you are a freedwoman. You belong to yourself."[50]

The function of the dissolution document changed from the bill of cutting-off to the certificate of liberation and freedom in the midst of societal efforts to protect women from abuses of power in a patriarchal system. It is not surprising that the term used in the Hebrew Bible, "bill of cutting-off," began to disappear gradually and was finally replaced by *get* in Jewish history.

Detailed rabbinic discussions in the Mishnah regarding appropriate form and delivery of a *get* attempt to make the repudiation a less-arbitrary act by the husband's will. Certainly the rule of *ketubah*, which prescribes that the husband should return the bride-price or dowry to his wife when dismissing her, also contributed to making the dismissal something that could not be done just by caprice.[51] Nevertheless, the social structure, which assumed the husband's exclusive and extensive ownership of his wife and thus assumed a double standard of chastity between husband and wife, yielded a mind-set among men that wives were at their disposal.[52] Furthermore, because such a patriarchal society assumed a different role for husbands and wives in the house and attributed all household labor to the wife, the repudiation of a wife meant a new marriage for the husband, often a new marriage to a virgin. While the repudiation meant shame, loss of protection, and even loss of a future for the wife, for the husband it could mean a refreshed life with a new wife, a virgin, who has replaced an old woman.

The meaning of Jesus' saying is clear both in his own context and in terms of Korean patriarchal customs. First, he does not talk about "divorce" but about "repudiation of the wife by her husband." The theme he addresses is not the divorce that people today understand and practice as a bilateral, consensual decision between husband and wife to dissolve their marriage. He addresses a one-sided decision of the owner/husband to banish his wife from his house, denying his responsibility to protect and maintain her by providing "food, clothes, and marital duty" (Exod. 21:10). Jesus exposes the owner/husband's dishonest gesture to grant her emancipation so she can marry any other (Jewish) man she likes. He condemns the exultant expectation of the owner/husband who wants a new life with a virgin, which perceptibly meant a desolate life for the wife. She must wait for a new owner/husband among those in a shallow pool of men who are willing to take a "defiled" woman as their wife and take responsibility for her basic life support.

Second, Jesus' saying is not a legal statement concerning whether divorce is permissible, but instead a prophetic condemnation of patriarchal misuses of power in his society. The frequent debates over whether Jesus has prohibited divorce or prohibited it only if it is followed by remarriage are off the mark. The two issues were not separate in his time, since repudiation in general would be followed by the husband's new marriage. Jesus' saying is prophetic, for he follows the voices of Israel's classical prophets in several ways. From Amos to Malachi, each prophet reproached the "numbness" of his society that takes for granted its structurally oppressive systems of power.[53] Each prophet condemned his compatriots who took advantage of their given, unjust system. According to Amos, people would "buy [as slave] a needy person for a pair of sandals" (8:6). In similar fashion, Jesus reproaches the numbness of his society that takes for granted its patriarchal marriage system. In Jesus' society, a husband/owner could repudiate his wife if she burned a dish, or even when he found another better looking than she was. Jesus condemns his compatriots who take advantage of their power to serve their selfish interests and harm others.

Prophets constantly referred to their community's traditions to remind people of what the God of love and justice had done to teach them and lead them to life. They also used shocking and repulsive concepts or metaphors to describe symbolically the wrongness of the people. Jesus' saying uses both of these prophetic devices. The adultery and the adulterous wife were among the most powerful and frequent metaphors prophets employed to symbolize apostasy from God. Prophets revealed the shame and sin of Israel by feminizing them through the metaphor of an adulterous wife.[54] From the perspective of traditional Palestinian Judaism, neither the husband's repudiation of his wife nor his remarriage can be identified as adultery. Rarely would a sage or a prophet criticize an illicit relationship of a married man.[55] However, it is never called adultery or a punishable sin unless it involves someone else's wife. Jesus literally reveals the evil of patriarchal power by amending the concept of adultery.

When Jesus condemns repudiation and remarriage as adulterous, his condemnation presupposes a prophetic view that the relationship between husband and wife should be reciprocal. According to his prophetic view, not only a married woman's illicit relationship but also a married man's is adultery. Furthermore, according to his view, the conjugal tie, which still remains after the husband's repudiation of his wife, applies not only to the wife but also to the husband. In short, Jesus' saying is a prophetic condemnation of a patriarchal practice that leads to the abuse of marriage; implicitly, it can be read as a prophetic proclamation of the reciprocal responsibilities of the conjugal tie. It is powerful because it is not a simple prohibition of one single action. Instead, it condemns an exploitive system that threatens women's lives, and it condemns those of cold hearts who desire, plan, and execute such exploitation.

My study poses questions about how the church's adaptation of Jesus' saying on patriarchal repudiation can lead to an ecclesial divorce law that respects the powerful, prophetic statement of Jesus. High divorce rates are no longer just a phenomenon of Western societies. According to a 2005 study by the Korea Legal Aid Center for Family Relations, the divorce rate in Korea is among the world's highest.[56] If the surging rate of divorce is related to urbanization, industrialization, and the change of women's status in traditionally patriarchal societies, as the 2005 study suggests, the divorce rate in the two-thirds world also will increase in the near future. Coincidentally, these places are where the Christian population is increasing rapidly these days. The painful situation of Kim's doubled marginalization is not just an isolated episode; sadly, it will be faced by an increasing number of women in the two-thirds world, as well as by women in other places who belong to churches that prohibit divorce. I offer this essay as an invitation to further dialogue for those concerned about people marginalized by their own communities.

Notes

1. Raymond E. Brown, *Introduction to the New Testament* (New York: Doubleday, 1997), 141 n. 37: "The issue is whether this is to be considered as an enduring demand binding Jesus' followers (Roman Catholic position for marriages considered sacramental) or only as an ideal which for all practical purposes can be dispensed from, either relatively easily (many Protestant churches) or for a grave, specific reason such as adultery (Orthodox position, drawing on Matt. 19:9)."

2. Most English Bibles, including RSV and NRSV, use the term "divorces" rather than "repudiates." For a further discussion on the meaning of the corresponding Greek verb, see below. The English translation of the Bible is mine, unless otherwise indicated. For

a comprehensive study of these NT traditions from the historical-critical perspective, see Raymond F. Collins, *Divorce in the New Testament* (Collegeville, MN: Liturgical Press, 1992).

3. Especially important scholars include Tal Ilan, Judith Baskin, Susan Niditch, Ross Kreaemer, and Judith Romney Wegner. Among Christian scholars, Bernadette Brooten has strongly voiced the same concern. See, for example, Tal Ilan, *Integrating Women into Second Temple History* (Peabody, MA: Hendrickson, 2001); idem, *Jewish Women in Greco-Roman Palestine* (Peabody, MA: Hendrickson, 1996, reprinted from Tübingen: J. C. B. Mohr, 1995); idem, "Notes and Observations on a Newly Published Divorce Bill from the Judaean Desert," *Harvard Theological Review* 89 (1996): 195–202; idem, "The Provocative Approach Once Again: A Response to Adiel Schremer," *Harvard Theological Review* 91 (1998): 203–4; Judith Baskin, ed., *Jewish Women in Historical Perspective* (Detroit: Wayne State University Press, 1991); Bernadette Brooten, *Women Leaders in the Ancient Synagogue: Inscriptional Evidence and Background Issues* (Chico, CA: Scholars Press, 1982); idem, "Konnten Frauen im alten Judentum die Scheidung betreiben?" *Evanglishe Theologie* 42 (1982): 65–80; idem, "Zur Debatte über das Scheidungsrechet der jüdischen Frau," *Evanglishe Theologie* 43 (1983): 466–78; and idem, "Early Christian Women and Their Cultural Context: Issues of Method in Historical Reconstruction," in *Feminist Perspectives on Biblical Scholarship*, ed. Adela Yarbro Collins (Chico, CA: Scholars Press, 1985), 65–91. For a helpful summary of the scholarly debate on the interpretation of the Jewish documents from the Persian and Roman eras, which suggest less-patriarchal practices, see John. J. Collins, "Marriage, Divorce, and Family in Second Temple Judaism," in *Families in Ancient Israel*, ed. Leo G. Perdue, Joseph Blenkinsopp, John J. Collins, and Carol Meyers (Louisville, KY: Westminster John Knox Press, 1997), 120–21; and Cecilia Wassen, *Women in the Damascus Document* (Atlanta: Society of Biblical Literature, 2005), 163 n. 103.

4. The postbiblical literature of early Judaism used in this study includes the Apocrypha and Pseudepigrapha, Philo, Josephus, and early rabbinic literature. I use the prefixed *m.* for Mishnah, *b.* for Babylonian Talmud, and *y.* for Jerusalem Talmud, in referring to early rabbinic literature.

5. The Committee for the Compilation of the History of Korean Women, *Women of Korea: A History from Ancient Times to 1945*, ed. and trans. Yung-Chung Kim (Seoul: Ewha Womans University Press, 1976), 83–89; and Sun Ku Lee, "Choson Sidaeui Songni-hakkwa Yosong" (Neo-Confucianism and Women in the Choson Dynasty), in *Uri Yosongui Yoksa* (A History of Korean Women), ed. Hanguk Yosong Yonguso (Seoul: Chungnyunsa, 1999), 163–89.

6. Women generally had an enormously authoritative status in at least one aspect of the traditional, patriarchal society of Korea, that is, as mothers of their children. Children were expected to respect and obey their mothers unconditionally. Both Hebrew Bible and Old Testament Apocrypha also seem to suggest a similar phenomenon (for example, Exod. 20:12; 21:15, 17; Deut. 27:16; Sir. 3:2, 4, 11, 16).

7. Examples of *shlh* are found in Deut. 22:19, 29; 24:1, 3; Isa. 50:1; Jer. 3:1, 8; Mal. 2:16. Examples of *grsh* appear in Lev. 21:7, 14; 22:13; Num. 30:10; Ezek. 44:22; Mic. 2:9; cf. Gen. 21:10. Examples of *trk* are in *Tg. Onq. Lev.* 21:14; 22:13; *Tg. Onq. Num.* 30:10. Examples of *shbq* are found in *Gen. Rab.* 1:17; *Lev. Rab.* 1:34; *y. Ketub.* 11:34b. Examples of *ekballo* are found in LXX of Lev. 21:7, 14; Num. 30:10; Ezek. 44:22; Prov. 19:2; Sir. 7:26. Examples of *exapostello* are found in LXX of Deut. 22:19, 29; 24:3, 5; Isa. 50:1; Jer.

3:1, 8; Mal. 2:16. An example of *aphiemi* is found in 1 Cor. 7:11. Cf. Ezra 10:3, 19, which similarly use the hiphil forms of *yts'* for "to send away, to banish."

8. Elephantine papyri from the fifth century BCE witness the opposite case, in which a wife is the subject of the verb. See J. J. Collins, "Marriage, Divorce, and Family in Second Temple Judaism," 115–16. This Jewish document from Egypt does not warrant that a similar custom was widespread in the Palestinian land. Even the Mishnaic regulation on the extremely rare cases, in which a wife may request the dissolution of marriage, does not conflict with my general description, for what the wife requests the court is still that her husband should abandon her. Certainly the Herodian women's two cases are exceptional: Josephus himself adds that they are not in accordance with Jewish law (*Ant.* 15.7.10; 18.5.4). In this regard, the general consensus of scholarship, which believes that Mark 10:12 (and possibly 1 Cor. 7:10) reflects Roman custom, should be considered correct. Nor would Papyrus Se'elim 13, an Aramaic papyrus from Nahal Hever, necessarily suggest that a woman could generally initiate divorce in Palestine, no matter how one interprets the document regarding the question of whether it is a bill the wife received or she wrote. See Brooten, "Konnten Frauen im alten Judentum die Scheidung betreiben?" and "Zur Debatte über das Scheidungsrechet der jüdischen Frau"; Ilan, "Notes and Observations" and "Provocative Approach Once Again."

9. The prohibition of repudiation in the case of a husband falsely accusing his wife's virginity (Deut. 22:13–19) or in the case of a virgin's rape (Deut. 22:28–29) is no doubt provided on the assumption that repudiation is an unquestioned practice otherwise.

10. According to Joseph Blenkinsopp ("The Family in First Temple Israel," in *Families in Ancient Israel*, ed. Leo G. Perdue, Joseph Blenkinsopp, John J. Collins, and Carol Meyers [Louisville, KY: Westminster John Knox Press, 1997], 65), Jerome (fourth century) is responsible for this phenomenon, because he misunderstood the long sentence in his Vulgate translation of the text.

11. The Hebrew verb used here is *b'l*, and its noun form is used in verse 4a. The verb basically means "to own, to rule over," and the noun means "owner, lord." The noun form also refers to the Canaanite storm and fertility deity, which is generally transliterated as Baal in English Bibles. Other biblical examples of the root *b'l* used to denote husband are found in Gen. 20:3; Exod. 21:3, 22; Deut. 22:22; 24:4; 2 Sam. 11:26; Joel 1:8; Prov. 12:4; 31:11, 23, 28; Esth. 1:17, 20; Hos. 2:18.

12. Literally "(some)thing nakedness." Cf. Deut. 23:15 (23:14 in English Bible), where the same expression is used to refer to human excrement.

13. The term "bill of cutting-off" is found in two other places in the Hebrew Bible: Isa. 50:1 and Jer. 3:8. Both passages describe YHWH's sending away of Israel with a bill of cutting-off. For a discussion of this term, see below.

14. For a suggestion to translate "to hate" as "to repudiate," see J. J. Collins, "Marriage, Divorce, and Family in Second Temple Judaism," 118.

15. The Hebrew Bible as well as early rabbinic literature does not know a word that corresponds to the English words "to marry" and "marriage." The hithpael of *htn*, "to make oneself a daughter's husband (son-in-law)," is used for the meaning "to form marriage-alliance with," that is, "to give a daughter to someone or to take someone's daughter for a son" (Gen. 34:9; Deut. 7:3; Josh. 23:12; 1 Sam. 18:21, 22, 23, 26, 27; 1 Kgs. 3:1; Ezra 9:14; 2 Chron. 18:1). Later rabbinic writings (*Gen. Rab.* 82; *Sipre Deut.* 52) show a development of the use of this verb into the meaning "to marry." The noun form *htnh*, meaning "wedding," is found in the Hebrew Bible only once, in Song 3:11. Alternatively, a

verb *'rs* to mean "to betroth" is used eleven times in the Hebrew Bible (including Exod. 22:15; Deut. 20:7; 22:23, 25, 27, 28; 2 Sam. 3:14; Hos. 2:19, 21, 22). The subject is always a man, and the object is a woman in an active form. The passive participle form is applied only to a woman. Interestingly, in early rabbinic literature, a different term, *qiddushin*, is used for betrothal. According to Tal Ilan, "The use of the word 'consecration (*qiddushin*)' to describe both the talmudic tractate which deals with the taking of a bride and the action itself indicates that betrothal took on, in addition to its technical legal meaning, a spiritual connotation as well" (*Jewish Women in Greco-Roman Palestine*, 89).

16. LXX translates this verb as *synoikeo*, which literally means "to dwell together" but also means "to live within wedlock."

17. Cf. Ezek. 16:8, "I came into a covenant with you, oracle of the Lord YHWH, and you became mine."

18. In Palestinian Jewish society of the first century, as in most Eastern patriarchal society, the power and accompanying responsibility for controlling a woman transferred from her father to her husband when she got married. Mishnah *Ketub.* 4:4 reads, "The father has control over his daughter as touching her betrothal whether it is effected by money, by writ, or by intercourse [whereby betrothal is effected]; and he has the right to aught found by her and to the work of her hands, and [the right] to set aside her vows, and he receives her bill of divorce; but he has not the use of her property during her lifetime. When she is married, the husband exceeds the father in that he has the use of her property during her lifetime; and he is liable for her maintenance and for her ransom and for her burial." The English translation of the Mishnah is from Herbert Danby, *The Mishnah: Translated from the Hebrew with Introduction and Brief Explanatory Notes* (Oxford: Oxford University Press, 1933), unless otherwise indicated.

19. LXX translates it as *exapostello*, which also literally means "to send away, to banish."

20. The two Decalogue versions differ in the order of someone else's belongings including a wife, which one should not covet (Exod. 20:17; Deut. 5:21). This difference reflects different understandings of the wife's status as one's property in comparison with other properties, including a slave. A comparison of wife and slave in the beginning paragraphs in the Mishnah tractate *Qiddushin* is especially intriguing:

> By three means is the woman acquired and by two means she acquires her freedom. She is acquired by money, or by writ, or by intercourse. . . . And she acquires her freedom by a bill of divorce or by the death of her husband. (1:1)
>
> A Hebrew bondman is acquired by money or by writ; and he acquires his freedom by [service lasting six] years or by [the entering in of] the year of Jubilee or by [redeeming himself at] his outstanding value. (1:2)
>
> A Canaanite bondman is acquired by money or by writ or by usucaption; and he acquires his freedom by money paid by others or by a writ [of indebtedness] uttered by himself. (1:3)

As far as the condition of acquisition and that of liberation is concerned, the position of a wife sounds worse than that of a Hebrew slave and rather close to that of a foreign slave.

21. Several scholars have pointed out that a husband owns his wife's sexuality in the Hebrew Bible and rabbinic literature. But to my knowledge, no one has mentioned that his ownership extends to her premarital and postmarital periods. I look forward to continuing this conversation among scholars, especially those who come from a strongly patriarchal background similar to Korean traditional culture. Some scholars point out that in the

Hebrew Bible a woman's sexuality is owned by her father before her marriage. For example, see Tikva Simone Frymer-Kensky, *Reading the Women of the Bible* (New York: Schocken Books, 2002), 59. Ownership, however, is different from controlling power. While ownership includes controlling power over one's possession, one may have controlling power without ownership. With his controlling power, the father is expected to protect his daughter's sexuality and virginity until she is delivered to her owner/husband, for whom her sexuality has been reserved. The husband alone, therefore, has ownership over his wife's sexuality, extending to the periods before and after marriage.

22. Apparently, men could voluntarily choose a single life, and some did (for example, Jesus and the Essenes), as the vigorous rabbinical critique against those people implies. According to a rabbinic criticism, "A man who has no wife lives without joy, without blessing, and without goodness" (*b. Yebam.* 62b), and he "is no proper man" (*b. Yebam.* 63a). The English translation of Talmud is from the Soncino edition, unless otherwise indicated.

23. Sir. 42:9 describes a father's anxiety over his daughter. When she is young, he worries that she may pass her prime time for marriage (before she is taken by a husband). The same is still true for many Korean parents.

24. In dealing with the law of virginity suit, Philo (*Spec. Laws* 3.14.82) makes less-patriarchal comments that the confirmation of marriage is the most distasteful to the falsely accused wife and that the wife has the choice, not the husband, whether to stay or to be freed.

25. Anthony J. Saldarini, in "Absent Women in Matthew's Households" (in *A Feminist Companion to Matthew*, ed. Amy-Jill Levine with Marianne Blickenstaff [Sheffield: Sheffield Academic Press, 2001], 164), interprets the Matthean Jesus in a similar way. Others interpret the Markan Jesus from a similar perspective, while emphasizing the equality of women and men. See Hisako Kinukawa, *Woman and Jesus in Mark: A Japanese Feminist Perspective* (Maryknoll, NY: Orbis Books, 1994), 133; and Joanna Dewey, "The Gospel of Mark," in *Searching the Scriptures*, vol. 2, *A Feminist Commentary*, ed. Elisabeth Schüssler Fiorenza (New York: Crossroad, 1994), 491.

26. For examples, see Lev. 20:10; Jer. 29:23.

27. In the Hebrew Bible, chastity as a virtue for men is rarely mentioned. Criticism is limited to the voluptuous life, and it is never extended close to the point that a man should have a sexual relationship only with his wife. *The Testament of Joseph* (in *Testaments of the Twelve Patriarchs* written in the second century BCE), which praises Joseph's chastity, is not much different.

28. See also Prov. 8:22 LXX: "He that keeps an adulteress is foolish and ungodly." Cf. *b. Yebam.* 63b, which says that if one has a bad wife, it is a meritorious act to repudiate her. For various interpretations of Joseph's motive in relation to his righteousness in Matt. 1:18–19, see W. D. Davies and Dale C. Allison, *A Critical and Exegetical Commentary on the Gospel according to Saint* Matthew, vol. 1 (Edinburgh: T. & T. Clark, 1988), 203–4.

29. Philo, *Spec. Laws* 3.5.30.

30. It seems that the text of Rom. 7:1–3 similarly presupposes the idea that the husband's ownership of his wife's sexuality is effective until his death.

31. Cf. Gen. 3:16; 1 Cor. 14:34; 1 Tim. 2:12.

32. Cf. Sir. 26:14–15; 25:14, which lists "silence" as one of the greatest virtues for the wife.

33. One would still occasionally hear the word *sobak* from conversations among Koreans, but it is used mostly with a tone of sarcasm or joke these days.

34. Cf. Philo, *Spec. Laws* 1.9.107: "And when I say 'virgin' I exclude not only one with whom another man has had intercourse but also one with whom any other has been declared to have an agreement of betrothal, even though her body is that of a maid intact." The translation is from the Loeb Classical Library.

35. For a detailed description of the legal history of a widow's remarriage, see The Committee for the Compilation of The History of Korean Women, *Women of Korea*, 97–99, 267.

36. See, for example, Gen. 9:11; 17:14; Lev. 22:3; Exod. 12:15; Num. 19:20.

37. Rabbinic literature suggests a similar situation in early Judaism, the context of Jesus. See, for example, "What befell their mother that she was put away?" (*m. Ned.* 9:9). To marry an abandoned woman was considered disgraceful, according to *b. Git.* 90b.

38. The tractate continues, "If a man divorced his wife and she then lodged with him in an inn, the School of Shammai say: She does not need another bill of divorce from him. And the School of Hillel say: She needs another bill of divorce from him." The view of the School of Hillel implies that even after she left the house, the owner/husband may retake her, as if she were not dismissed at all.

39. Later interpretation of this text tends to presuppose a situation when a bill of divorce was not delivered to the wife after it had been written. This is plausible, because the text not only says "after he had written" but also is followed by a paragraph that refers to a situation when the couple is together in an inn. However, the text does not necessarily exclude a situation when a bill of divorce was delivered to the wife, and, interestingly, this text and the paragraph that follows are separately preserved in *b. Git.* 8:4 and 8:9, respectively. Either way, this text presupposes a situation when the repudiation is not finalized by her "leaving the house" and "going off her own way."

40. Cf. Jer. 3:1.

41. For further examples from the Mishnah, see also *Sotah* 8:3; *B. Metsi'a.* 1:7; *Mo'ed Qat.* 3:3; *Git.* 4:11; *B. Bat.* 10:9.

42. The analogy of Israel as YHWH's repudiated wife who is recalled (Isa. 54:6) seems to assume the readers' familiarity with this practice.

43. See also the story of Queen Vashti of Persia (Esth. 1:10–22), whose disobedience to her husband resulted in a royal decree that "every man should be master in his own house."

44. In this last case, the husband does not even need to give her *ketubah*.

45. It was codified in the *Ta Ming Lu* of the Chinese Ming dynasty in the fourteenth century and adopted by the Korean Choson (Yi) dynasty.

46. According to a survey of urban families in 1980, 4 percent of the respondents chose to divorce and 6 percent to take a concubine when they had no children. One percent chose to divorce and 5 percent to take a concubine when they had only daughters (Dong-won Lee, "The Changes in the Korean Family and Women," in *Challenges for Women*, ed. Wei-wha Chung [Seoul: Ewha Womans University Press, 1986], 243).

47. The Matthean Jesus shares the view of Shammai's school. The response of Jesus' disciples that "if such is the case of a man with his wife, it is better not to marry" (Matt. 19:10) well reflects its unpopularity.

48. The text is followed by a quotation from R. Akiba, who interprets Deut. 24:1 as allowing the repudiation of the wife "even if he found another fairer than she."

49. I wonder whether this positive implication contributed to the replacement of the term "the bill of cutting-off" by "*get* (bill of divorce)" in postbiblical Jewish literature, which is still used in Jewish society.

50. The translation is mine from the Soncino Classics Collection available as the CD-ROM Judaic Classic Library (Skokie, IL: Dakva Corporation, 1996). An in-depth study of the relationship among these terms would be intriguing, but it is beyond the scope of this chapter.

51. For the financial aspect of repudiation in the second temple period, see J. J. Collins, "Marriage, Divorce, and Family in Second Temple Judaism," 113–19.

52. The repeated advice of Ben Sira that men should keep their "good" or "pleasing" wives may reflect this atmosphere. Similarly, see Mal. 2:14–16; Prov. 18:21 LXX.

53. I owe this significant term "numbness" to Walter Brueggemann, *Prophetic Imagination*, 2nd ed. (Minneapolis: Fortress Press, 2001).

54. For this, see Gale A. Yee's thought-provoking work "'She Is Not My Wife and I Am Not Her Husband': A Materialist Analysis of Hosea 1–2," *Biblical Interpretation* 9 (2001): 345–83. Feminist and womanist scholars have constantly addressed the problem of the sexist metaphors and violent images found in prophetic literature, which might legitimize sexism and domestic violence in our society. See esp. Renita J. Weems, *Battered Love: Marriage, Sex, and Violence in the Hebrew Prophets* (Minneapolis: Fortress Press, 1995).

55. See Prov. 5:15–20; Mal. 2:14–15.

56. My statement is based on the summary of the research that the center has provided on its Korean-language Web site, http://www.lawhome.or.kr/information/information_view.asp?code=bodo&no=102. The research is titled "Research on Divorce Rate III" (in Korean) as a follow-up of the previous two studies published in 1981 and 1987.

Chapter Fifteen

A Story of Its Own Name

Hong Kong's *Tongzhi* Culture and Movement

Rose Wu

The Identity Politics of Hong Kong

Hong Kong has been known as the Pearl of the Orient by the West since its colonization by Britain in 1842. According to Edward W. Said, "The word 'Orient' is not an inert fact of nature. It is not merely there, just as the Occident itself is not just there either. . . . It is an idea that has a history and a tradition of thought, imagery, and vocabulary that have given it reality and presence in and for the West."[1] If we look closely at the history of European colonization, we will see that the relationship between Occident and Orient is a relationship of power, domination, and varying degrees of a complex hegemony between the colonizer and the colonized.

A consequence of this process of colonization has been the construction of an East-West binary in which the West has defined itself in relation to the people of Asia and, by authoring the East as "others," has sought to justify Western imperial domination. Today, although most of the colonies have gained their political independence, we know as we reflect on the present global situation that Western colonialism is still very much alive, except that it is now much more subtle, much more legitimate in the guise of "globalization." For me the East-West binary discourse of colonialism is linked directly to the Western construction of gender, race, class, and sexual differences in our contemporary societies. Thus one major question that concerns me in this chapter is how the Orientalist

This chapter is a revision of the article that first appeared in *Other Voices, Other Worlds: The Global Church Speaks Out on Homosexuality*, ed. Terry Brown (New York: Church Publishing, 2006), 40–57.

relationship between East and West constructs the stereotypical representations of Hong Kong's culture of sexuality—its confrontation between heterosexual and homosexual relationships.

With the end of British colonialism in Hong Kong on July 1, 1997, the community became a Special Administrative Region (SAR) of the People's Republic of China. In contrast to the Chinese government's propaganda, the majority of Hong Kong people do not share its triumphal and optimistic view about the handover and their future. Hong Kong's postcolonial period is marked by double oppression: by the previous British colonial government and by the new Chinese government. As Rey Chow puts it, "Hong Kong's cultural productions are often characterized by a particular kind of negotiation. This is a negotiation in which it must play two aggressors, Britain and China, against each other."[2]

Based on the same polarized logic of West versus East or colonizer Britain versus native China, there is no alternative available for the people other than to acquire another, more positive, identity. What we need is to create a third space between the colonizer and the dominant native culture in which we reclaim our identity. To seek liberation we must move beyond the simplistic dichotomy of West versus East and explore alternative ways of thinking about cross-cultural and cross-boundary perspectives that exceed the dualistic framework of the East-West binary context.

With this in mind, I shall first examine in this chapter the influence of both its Chinese heritage and Western colonialism on the sociopolitical aspects of sexuality in Hong Kong, which has been structured by an unconscious process of domination. I shall then try to capture how Hong Kong's *tongzhi* culture and the Christian movement have acted as a path of negotiation and re-creation between the two aggressors, Britain and China.

Sexuality in the Chinese Tradition

Hong Kong's culture, as a Chinese society, was strongly influenced by Confucian and Taoist teachings. In Chinese culture we do not have an equivalent for the English word "sex."[3] We have *jiaohe*, which means sexual intercourse; *fangshin*, which means things one does in his or her private room; and *se*, which has multiple meanings of erotic and sexual sensation and pleasure. According to Confucius, "Eating and *se* are human nature." Therefore, *se* is not something separated from our daily activities. Research on early Chinese sexuality by the Dutch author Robert Van Gulik, a former ambassador to China, found that traditional Taoist teachings of sexual norms understood sexual relationships to be healthy and neither "repressed" nor "perverted." Furthermore, in ancient Chinese culture, the harmony of sex between husband and wife was thought of as similar to the harmony of heaven (man) and earth (woman).[4]

Sex, however, was not viewed as a private matter until the beginning of the Han dynasty (206 BCE to 220 CE).[5] The earliest study and teaching of *fang chong shu*—the skill we use in our private room—was found in the Han dynasty and was seen as one of the four major skills in practical subjects in ancient Chinese education. In fact, one meaning of Lao-tzu's *Tao* is the womb of the earth; it was seen as a gate to enter all mysteries of life. Both Confucianism and Taoism affirm that human sexual intercourse has two functions, namely, for reproduction and for health.[6] Van Gulik adds that there existed classical literature and picture books in ancient China that could be labeled as pornography according to contemporary Western standards. The restriction of sex was not imposed as a social control until the emergence of Neo-Confucianism in the Song dynasty (960–1275 CE).

However, Charlotte Furth criticizes Van Gulik's notion of the Taoist sexual arts as being too simplistic and without a thorough analysis of its hidden oppression of women. Using a feminist critique, Furth makes the following observation:

> From the very beginning in medieval times, bedchamber arts had been embedded in medical and religious discourses which were not "about" pleasure or women simply as objects of desire, but about what medieval Chinese understood as serious goals of life and death, linking health, spirituality, and social purposes. They were linked to modes of male empowerment which we may define very loosely here as Confucianist or Taoist. The erotic could be seen as a vehicle for social reproduction and the conception of descendants or for individual self-transformation and sagehood. Both of these alternatives require women to serve male goals.[7]

Furth suggests that both Confucian and Taoist constructions of *eros* are better thought of as constituting a historically contingent experience than as either fulfilling or repressing natural instincts. Following Furth's critique, I conclude that the problem of Van Gulik's perspective is that he overlooks the contradiction in the ancient Chinese view regarding sex. First, their attitude toward women was harsh and humiliating, and sexual pleasure was a privilege only for men, particularly the emperors and males of the landed aristocracy. Foot binding and polygamy were the usual practice all over China until the revolution of Sun Yat-sen and the formation of the Chinese Communist Party (CCP) in the twentieth century. In the Chinese feudalistic family system, both women and serfs were treated as the property of men.

In terms of homosexual and transsexual culture, many people think that Chinese society is more repressive than Western society. Some Chinese people even claim that homosexuality was imported from the West. They believe it was never an issue in Chinese culture previously.

Ancient Chinese literature, however, points to a different reality. According to the most representational study, *The History of Homosexuality in China* by Xiaomingxiong, homo-, bi-, and transsexual practices were common phenomena.[8] Many Chinese emperors were fond of male companionship and openly practiced pederasty. Women in the palace also formed couples known as *dui shi*, literally meaning "paired eating."[9] Other popular examples in Chinese history include male homosexuals in Fujian Province and *tzu shu nü* and *chinlan hui* in Shunde in Guangdong Province.[10] Many classical Chinese novels, operas, songs, and poems were full of male-male and female-female romances, such as the stories about Pao Yu, Chin Zhong, Zheng Yuxian, and Xe Bao in *Hong Lou Meng* (The Dream of the Red Chamber).[11]

According to Xiaomingxiong, transvestitism and transsexuality were commonly practiced and accepted in Chinese society, such as in the roles of eunuchs as homosexual lovers or comforters of the emperors and the cross-dressing male actresses.[12] Most transvestites were male actors portraying female characters in Chinese operas. Although they were adored for their feminine roles, in real life they were marginalized like male prostitutes. While traditional Chinese culture was tolerant toward sexual minorities, this open attitude toward homosexuality and transsexual culture was based on the hierarchy of gender and class. Only male elites in society had the privilege to exercise their sexual freedom. Many women and people of lower classes lived under the triple oppression of patriarchalism, heterosexism, and feudalism.

Hong Kong's *Tongzhi* Culture and Movement

How did the colonial discourse on sexuality manifest itself in Hong Kong's legislation? Since the beginning of British colonization, Hong Kong inherited the British common law system, which was deeply influenced by the nineteenth-century Victorian prejudice against male homosexuality. As a result, Hong Kong criminalized homosexual acts between two male adults (over the age of twenty-one) in any public or private place.

The highest penalty was a life sentence. The criminalization of male homosexuality in Hong Kong was not abolished until 1991, after almost ten years of open struggle and resistance.

In 1993 Legislative Councilor Anna Wu urged the Hong Kong government to introduce an Equal Opportunities Bill that would cover many types of discrimination, such as that based on gender, age, sexual orientation, disability, race, political and religious beliefs, union membership, and previous criminal record. Two years later the government was successful in lobbying the legislature to defeat legislative proposals that would have prohibited discrimination on the grounds of sexual orientation, age, and race, but instead it enacted the Sex Discrimination Ordinance and the Disability Discrimination Ordinance. Rather than introduce equal opportunity legislation covering discrimination based on sexual orientation, the government established a special fund to promote equal opportunities for people facing this type of discrimination.

There have been two major struggles since Hong Kong's sexual minorities began their movement in the early 1970s. The first has been its identity of representation; the second, its strategies for resistance and survival. Because the Hong Kong identity has been a contested site for the imperial colonizer Britain and the national regime of China, there is a need to seek Hong Kong's voice and write its own history. Rey Chow writes, "Hong Kong must move beyond not only British but also Chinese habits of historiography, and thus beyond the simplicity of the paradigm 'foreign colonizer versus native colonized.'"[13] How, though, do these two dominant powers affect Hong Kong's *tongzhi* culture and movement in the shaping of its local identity of representation?

In a study that Chou Wah-shan conducted, there was no particular term to identify sexual minorities in Hong Kong before the 1970s. The news media generally associated homosexuality with certain sexual behaviors between male homosexuals and related them to criminal offenses. Female homosexuals were not visible because only male homosexuals were bound by the law and its penalties. Therefore, many people wrongly believed that homosexuality only occurred among men.[14]

Since the mid-1980s the social and political atmosphere has been much more open in Hong Kong. More feminist and human rights groups have been formed, which has affected the public debate on the issue of homosexuality. Moreover, after the decriminalization of male homosexual acts in 1991, many local gay and lesbian groups were registered as nongovernmental organizations (NGOs), such as the 10 Percent Club and Horizons.

Although these changes have opened up more public space for homosexual people in Hong Kong, lesbians have still been treated as second-class members of the homosexual movement. This phenomenon is illustrated by the use of language. For instance, the Chinese word *kei*, the same pronunciation as gay, became popular to identify all homosexuals. However, according to Anson Mak and Mary Ann King, founding members of *Zimei Tongzhi* (Queer Sisters),[15] few female homosexual people would call themselves *kei* because the word delegates women to a subordinate role, as it is usually associated with male homosexuals. Female homosexuals would usually call themselves *tzu kei yar*, meaning "buddies from the same community," or *ngau hai*, meaning "I am," because they refuse to use any label that restricts them to a specific social identity.

The word *tongzhi* first appeared as a word to identify gays and lesbians in the bulletin of a local Lesbian and Gay Film Festival in 1988. After that the word was well received by all sexual minorities in Hong Kong and was commonly used by many gay and lesbian organizations as well as the media. The word *tongzhi* has spread beyond the borders of Hong Kong to China, Taiwan, and other overseas Chinese gay and lesbian communities.

Why was the word *tongzhi* so attractive to the Chinese?

According to Mak and King, *tongzhi* is a word of multiple meanings and possible interpretations.[16] The literal meaning in Chinese of *tongzhi* is "common goals and aspirations." It is also a word of respect meaning "comrade" as used by the Chinese Communists.

Chou explains that there are many good reasons for using *tongzhi* as a word to name the translesbigay identity. First, *tongzhi* is not limited to any fixed identity, such as homosexual, heterosexual, or bisexual. Thus it has the potential to be an inclusive word that embraces all the sexual identities of people. Second, *tongzhi* has meaning beyond simply indicating sexual identity; it points to a respectful ideal of people who share the same goals and aspirations. Third, it breaks the dualistic dichotomies of homosexual versus heterosexual, East versus West, body versus spirit, and so on, therefore allowing flexibility, fluidity, and freedom for movement and change. Last, it is politically a wise choice for Hong Kong's translesbigay movement because it shares the same cultural and ideological heritage with the Chinese Communists.[17]

To me the construction of the *tongzhi* identity marks a significant point in Hong Kong's unique postcolonial discourse. According to queer[18] and postcolonial politics, it fulfills at least two functions. The first is described by Cindy Patton as rhetorical reversal and counter-reversal;[19] for sexual minorities in Hong Kong have reclaimed for themselves the term *tongzhi*, a word that is considered part of the hegemonic vocabulary imposed by China's political regime on Hong Kong, yet it is also a word of respect used to represent Chinese Communists. Thus it functions as a paradoxical political term with both positive and negative meanings in the contexts of Hong Kong and China. Reversing the negative sense of such terms as "homosexuality," "bisexuality," and "transsexuality," *tongzhi* produces a positive and inclusive identity. The second function is the deconstruction of Hong Kong's colonial identity. *Tongzhi* breaks the Western imperialist cultural tradition and transforms it into a Chinese-owned terminology.

This historical review shows how Hong Kong's *tongzhi* movement has sought its own representation by shifting both inside and outside of its relationship to the hegemony of the dominant powers of Britain and China. The construction of this complex identity that crosses gender, cultural, class, and political forces includes the strategies of subordination, resistance, negotiation, and integration.

As for the strategies of resistance and survival, there are some observations that I think are closely related to Hong Kong's postcolonial context. First of all, the choice of the wording *Zimei Tongzhi*, which uses both *tongzhi* and *queer* for their Chinese and English names, is a way to signify their determination to cross borders and boundaries. Instead of importing the Western concept of queer, they have succeeded in contextualizing queer ideology in the Chinese concept of *tongzhi* based on Hong Kong's sociopolitical culture. As a strategy, they have decided not to put sexually subaltern women in the category of female homosexuality. Instead, they have emphasized that women have the right to explore, rethink, and choose how they pursue interconnectedness, heterogeneity, and a multiplicity of sexualities. Furthermore, while challenging the existing male homocentric *tongzhi* communities that often overshadow women and people of different sexualities, Queer Sisters has taken the lead to move beyond sexual rights concerns and has played an active role in different social and political movements in Hong Kong. They have criticized the apolitical stance of many *tongzhi* groups. By avoiding involvement in any political issue, some groups in the *tongzhi* movement have become engaged in social activities merely within *tongzhi* circles.[20]

The second strategy of resistance and survival that Hong Kong's *tongzhi* movement has often emphasized is a conscious move to avoid adopting the coming-out politics of the Western translesbigay movement and to disclaim its use as a universal norm with which to judge other cultural situations.

Instead of choosing to come out as individuals, Queer Sisters has chosen to stand in solidarity with all other marginal people in Hong Kong and to come out as political activists to seek liberation for all people as a strategy of resistance and survival. We should not take "coming out" as a rigid norm for all sexual minorities universally. "Coming out" has a deep spiritual meaning. It is a lifelong challenge for all to pass from one well-defined state of being to another. As Elizabeth Stuart explains, "It implies leaving something behind, 'the closet' of self-hatred, the conspiracy of silence and invisibility, the tomb of self-denial."[21] It is also important to remember that "coming out" is not an individual act; rather, it involves communal participation because we need the support and love of others to help us through the process of moving from the old into the new, just as in the rite of baptism. Many people describe their experience of coming out as a new birth, as resurrection.

The third strategy of the *tongzhi* movement is to return to the Chinese heritage and traditions. Since the handover of Hong Kong, the local *tongzhi* movement has chosen to emphasize the prevalence of homosexuality in Chinese history and the pluralistic sexual culture in ancient China. One example is the decision by local gay activists in June 1999 to hold the first *Tongzhi* Day in Hong Kong during the traditional Chinese Dragon Boat Festival. The festival commemorates Qu Yuan, who has been honored and remembered in Chinese history as a patriot and poet and who was allegedly a lover of his emperor.[22] This strategy was successful in drawing the attention of the media and public to the existence of homosexuality in Chinese history as well as in contemporary society. However, many lesbians and bisexual people criticized the ideological assumption behind *Tongzhi* Day because it unwittingly represented only male homosexuals and excluded other sexual minorities.

Another development is the creation by Chinese translesbigay communities all over the world of a network organized through the Global Chinese *Tongzhi* Annual Conference that has been held every year since 1997. This shift of focus on strengthening the Chinese identity and the promotion of a worldwide Chinese *tongzhi* network indicates that there is an attempt to dismiss homo-, bi-, and transsexual movements as products of Westernization and colonization and to rediscover the cultural roots of homo-, bi-, and transsexuality within Chinese history and traditions. While I agree on the necessity of the Chinese *tongzhi* movement to reclaim its cultural tradition and to deconstruct the colonialist representation of Chinese *tongzhi* history and culture, I also want to emphasize that it is just as problematic to preserve and glorify the Chinese traditions of the past without a critical examination of the particular cultural practices and institutions that I discussed above.[23]

The fourth strategy of Hong Kong's *tongzhi* movement is its willingness to embrace more diversified and marginalized groups by forming coalitions to fight against oppression. One of the incidents that sparked this broad-based coalition was the criticism of the Red Cross guidelines for blood donors that mentioned that all people are welcome to donate their blood except gays, lesbians, sex workers, and AIDS patients. Because of this prohibition, the coalition was successful in bringing together many translesbigay communities, concern groups for sex workers, and AIDS patients and their caregivers to fight against the social stigmatization and discrimination of sexual minorities, sex workers, and AIDS patients.

The efforts of *tongzhi* groups to embrace other marginalized groups and to form coalitions to fight against oppression represent not only a concern for justice but also their view that the *tongzhi* movement can never be separated from the human rights movement. This concern is especially significant in the Hong Kong context in view of the handover. The history of human rights movements has long focused on civil and political rights as well as social and economic rights. There has been neglect, though, of humans as sexual beings in the immense domain of sexualities. Therefore, it is important to modify the strategy of the *tongzhi* movement and to expand its concern and commitment to a wider scope of human rights issues, since the struggle for one's sexual rights is, in fact, a human right and a feminist issue. This echoes Patton's proposal that "we [should] treat identities as a series of rhetorical closures linked with practical strategies, implicit or consciously defined, alliances, and re-alliances that in turn affect the whole system for staging political claims."[24]

An Exodus Community and Its Path of Healing and Liberation

During the public debate on decriminalizing male homosexual acts in the 1980s, the Christian response to homosexual issues was varied. The strongest objections were from a few evangelical church leaders, including ministers from the Baptist Church, Hong Kong Alliance Church, and the Christian organization Breakthrough.[25] They succeeded in lobbying the Hong Kong Chinese Christian Churches Union (HKCCCU), which represents the majority of Chinese congregations across denominational lines, to issue a public statement to object to the government's decriminalizing of male homosexual acts. The Hong Kong Christian Council (HKCC),[26] which represented more liberal views within Hong Kong's Christian community at the time, chose to issue a study report on homosexuality instead of making a statement on their position, in order to avoid direct conflicts with other members of the local Christian community.

Since the 1991 passing of legislation that decriminalizes male homosexual acts, institutional churches in Hong Kong have not been actively involved in any public debate related to homosexual issues. However, one new phenomenon that I have observed recently is the beginning of an antisex and antihomosexual Christian movement in Hong Kong through the formation of the Society for Truth and Light in 1996. Part of their agenda is to monitor the government and the media on issues of sexuality, including homosexuality, based on their perception of Christian moral values of family and fidelity. They opposed the government's legislation to prohibit discrimination on the grounds of sexual orientation as well as the government's special fund for public education to promote equal opportunities for sexual minorities. This approach is similar to the Christian Right campaign in the United States, which asserts that women's rights, gay rights, and sexual rights are threats to their beliefs grounded in "traditional" family values. This reminds me of how Christianity was used as a weapon to colonize the non-Christian world in the past and is used currently as a new ideology in which "Christian family values" are being promoted by the Christian Right as the universal norm, a phenomenon that is, in fact, a contemporary form of colonization.

Owing to the conservative view of homosexuality that many people in Hong Kong hold and the oppressive and heterosexist culture of the Chinese Church, many gay and lesbian Christians find no other alternative but to turn away from the church or to keep silent and figuratively hide themselves in closets. There are incidents in which some gay and lesbian Christians, including seminarians, were forced to leave their church or seminary immediately or were advised to seek counseling and medical help when their sexual identities were exposed so that their homosexual behavior could be "corrected."

However, there was a glimpse of hope when three gay Christians decided in July 1992 to move from being in exile to forming an exodus community[27]—a Christian fellowship under the umbrella of the 10 Percent Club. During the first stage of its development, the fellowship maintained itself as a private gathering at members' homes. A year later, as the membership grew from three to more than thirty, the fellowship began to meet once a month at St. John's Cathedral of the Anglican Diocese of Hong Kong. Their activities included prayers, hymn singing, and Bible studies. During this period the fellowship also began a joint project with the Hong Kong Women Christian Council (HKWCC) to organize theology courses for their members as well as other Christians. These courses sought to provide an alternative interpretation of Christian theology and biblical reflection on homosexuality.

Five years later the fellowship registered with the Hong Kong government as an independent organization named the Hong Kong Blessed Minority Christian Fellowship (HKBMCF). As its name indicates, the group's aim is to witness to the love and blessing of God among sexual minorities. In October 1997 the fellowship was able to rent an apartment for their office and functions. Like a regular church, they meet every Sunday afternoon for worship. They have Sunday school, Bible study, and a choir. Like other churches in Hong Kong, they elect their board members once a year. The only difference is that they are not attached to any denomination. What I see as a major success of HKBMCF is their ability to raise a new breed of young leaders among their members.

Since they became an independent organization, HKBMCF has made a visible Christian witness in Hong Kong. Their constitution lists three objectives: (1) to promote the Christian community's understanding and respect for sexual minorities; (2) to offer support and mutual care for gay and lesbian Christians to worship, pray, and empower one another; and (3) to seek equal rights and dignity in the church and society for all, regardless of one's gender and sexual orientation.

HKBMCF has grown since July 1992 to more than one hundred people. About thirty people have received baptism since this sacrament was introduced in 2001. With the guidance of the Holy Spirit and the devotion of HKBMCF, Selina Sun was ordained as their pastor on October 5, 2004. She explains why she chose to be ordained by HKBMCF:

> It is really God's grace that my encounter with HKBMCF has grown into a loving relationship. My involvement in HKBMCF is also the answer that I have awaited from God over the past five years. When seeking ordination five years ago, I prudently pondered on my vocation to the pastorate, the meaning of becoming a pastor and its role in society as well as in the Church. As such, I came to a definition like this: The mission and role of a pastor should be living among people; a pastor is not someone who lives a life secured by stable incomes or someone who occupies herself with a variety of church chores and yet fails to respond to God's ultimate calling. Hence, I asked God to send me to the flock that is uncared for and to those who linger at the door of his temple and yet feel too ashamed to enter the house of worship.

Upon meditating on the existence of HKBMCF, I believe that HKBMCF should, by all means, be a living testimony to sexual minority groups, society, and even the Church of Christ. She should take on a prophetic role and mission, standing as a bridge of reconciliation in a world of prejudice and discord. Thus, HKBMCF deserves other people's acknowledgement.

Personally speaking, it is not my concern whether outsiders recognize my ordination or not. What is important to me is the meaning behind this vocation, which I believe is God's special kindness to me, the most precious moment in my life and a personal experience of walking with God.[28]

Toward a Liberation Theology of Right Relation

In order to bring liberation to sexual minorities, we must first liberate the church from homophobia and heterosexism and construct a liberation theology that truly reflects the justice and love of God among all of God's people, especially those who are marginalized and excluded because of their different sexual preferences. To do this I propose two alternative interpretations of theology of the triune God and human sexuality that touch on both the doctrine of God and Christian anthropology.

To me the triune God enables us to rediscover the profoundly relational character of the mystery that reaffirms our unity in diversity, our connectedness as a community, and erotic power that is sexual, spiritual, and just. The Brazilian liberation theologian Leonardo Boff points out that because the Trinity is a mystery of relationships existing among divine coequals, a society that is to be a sign and sacrament of the Trinity will be a society that is based on relationships of equality, participation, inclusion, and communion.[29]

The feminist theologian Carter Heyward criticizes the notion of God as controlling power, an attitude that has become the cancerous seed for the growth of sexism and heterosexism in the church and society. To transform this misogynist (woman-hating) and erotophobic (sex-fearing) religion, Heyward chooses *Christa*—a bronze crucifix of a naked female Christ—as a transitional Christian symbol of sacred power. She argues that the power of *Christa* is in the connection she makes between our erotic power and the sacred power in our most profoundly human, most deeply embodied belief of who we are—a relational body of incarnate love.[30] Heyward says that God is justice, and justice is right relation, and right relation is mutual relation. She criticizes the church's efforts to keep

God and sex separate and to imagine God as a male master of the world, a deity who rules nations, families, and women as well as their sexual behavior. These are the root causes of sexism, hierarchicalism, colonialism, neocolonialism, heterosexism, and patriarchalism. The mystery of the Trinity reveals to us that God is not a solitary divine being but a God of communion and solidarity.

Heyward also proposes rejecting the dualistic, hierarchical view of West versus East, spirit versus body, masculinity versus femininity, and heterosexuality versus homosexuality and instead recognizing that spirit and body are one totality of human experience. Through incarnation, God not only participates in human sexual experiences but God also is intrinsically sexual. The doing of God cannot be separated from the being of God; the sexuality of God is the expression of God's spirituality.

Another proposal, in view of the pervasive fear of sex and homosexuality within the church, is for the church to construct a sexual theology that connects sexual relations with justice making. To do this we must transform our ethic of control to an ethic of solidarity. We must transform the binary logic of either/or to a Trinitarian logic of relationship based on freedom, love, and justice. In her book *Saving Jesus from Those Who Are Right: Rethinking What It Means to Be Christian*, Heyward distinguishes between self-righteousness and right relation. Self-righteous Christians are those who claim they have all the right answers and the right to rule and control others. Their ethical theology is based on fear and control. Creating right relation, by contrast, means to seek justice through a dynamic relational commitment with others and God. The ethics of theology is based on Christians' conviction of love, faith, and solidarity in mutuality.[31]

In proposing the ethic of solidarity, I do not mean adopting the assumption that there are no right answers. From a critical feminist perspective, the use of "difference" is unlike the meaning ascribed to "difference" by deconstructionists who seek to interpret the world without any absolutes in life and reality. Both Beverly Harrison and Sharon D. Welch provide some helpful insights to solve this problem.

Harrison proposes that what we need for building a community of solidarity is a critical history that enables us to take the standpoint of "concrete others" who "bear stories of human struggle against domination."[32] The knowledge of sexual minorities is particularly crucial since heterosexual people are the dominant power. However, Welch warns that the logic of standpoint epistemologies entails greater attention to the knowledge of other oppressed voices in order to avoid the tendency to posit a particular standpoint as the only standpoint for our moral discernment.

As Welch explains, "The goal of communicative ethics [or ethics of solidarity] is not merely consensus but mutual critique leading to more adequate understandings of what is just and how particular forms of justice may be achieved."[33]

What is a spirituality of solidarity, however? Put in practical terms, it is a construction of a new kind of "coalitional politics." As Henry Louis Gates Jr. writes, "The challenge is to move from a politics of identity to a politics of identification. . . . A politics of identification doesn't enjoin us to ignore or devalue our collective identities. For it's only by exploring the multiplicity of human life in culture that we can come to terms with the commonalities that cement communities."[34] As a Christian community, we are constantly called to participate in the ministry of loving our neighbors as ourselves. It is a ministry that moves us toward the healing of divisions, toward overcoming brokenness, and ultimately toward achieving wholeness. We as individuals cannot become whole without helping others to become whole. To embrace sexual minorities as equal members of our Christian family is a hospitable act in which our ethics of morality are measured by the whole, the community, and the body of Christ, instead of by individuals. For the church in Hong Kong to become an inclusive Christian community requires us to have faith in the other who is larger than the self. Only through our sense of connecting with "the other"—the larger community, nature, and God—can we grasp a glimpse of hope for life.

Conclusion

As we look at the reality of our world and our church, we must admit that there are brothers and sisters who have sexual orientations different from those of heterosexuals. Because of the mainstream position of the Christian churches that condemn homosexual acts as sin, many sexual minorities continue to hide themselves in the closet, try to change their sexual orientations, leave the church and join other Christian communities-in-exile, or even give up their faith. However, I want to point out that, no matter what positions we take, we are still one family in Christ. As Paul told the Corinthians, "All the members of the body, though many, are one body, so it is with Christ. . . . the members of the body that seem to be weaker are indispensable, and those members of the body that we think less honorable we clothe with greater honor . . . God has so arranged the body, giving the greater honor to the inferior member, that there may be no dissension within the body, but the members may have the same care for one another" (1 Cor. 12:12–25). The purpose of God's creation is not to mold everyone into being the same; rather, God's purpose is to teach us to love and care for one another and to appreciate our differences.

If we embrace our homosexual brothers and sisters as one family and relate to them with genuine care at this stage of Hong Kong's development, we must then ask how we can transform our church into a safe place for all of them even though we may take a different position on homosexuality. Thus I suggest that our church open our space and our heart to allow our brothers and sisters who have other sexual orientations to become a part of our community and to have the same equal rights to participate in all of our religious rituals and activities, including attending worship services and Sunday school, receiving Holy Communion, and accepting lay leadership roles. Moreover, we also have to support sexual minorities to fight for their equal rights in society, such as their rights to employment, education, and housing.

Second, before we condemn homosexuality as sin, we must acknowledge that this stance is not the only or the final and absolute truth. In the past few decades there have been alternative interpretations of the Bible that use a hermeneutical approach and theological reflection about human sexuality and are more inclusive and liberating. We need to change the present top-down approach of moral teaching and transform it into a more inclusive and open dialogical approach of theological reflection. More important, we must respect and include minority voices and experiences as our primary source of theological input in our process of theologizing. The purpose is not to seek absolute authority; rather, it is to explore an inclusive and empowering approach for enhancing our mutual understanding and solidarity among all parties of the Christian community.

Based on the principles of human rights and justice, I personally support same-sex marriages as having the same rights as heterosexual marriages. However, I also understand that there are churches that take the opposite view based on their interpretation of the biblical condemnation of homosexuality; such churches treat homosexuality as a violation of God's purpose of procreation. To me, though, the challenge that God puts to us is not to decide whether homosexuality is a sin, but rather to treat one another the same even though we bear a different image of God.

Notes

1. Edward W. Said, *Orientalism* (New York: Pantheon Books, 1979), 4–5. From 1815 to 1914, the European powers—primarily England and France—expanded their domination from 36.5 percent of the earth's surface to a staggering 85 percent. By "Orientalism," Said means three things: (1) an academic subject; (2) a style of thought based on an

ontological and epistemological distinction between "the Orient" and "the Occident"; and (3) a Western ideology for dominating, restructuring, and having authority over the Orient. Although Said's "Orient" refers mainly to the Middle East, his Orientalism discourse is relevant to other parts of Asia as well.

2. Rey Chow, "Between Colonizers: Hong Kong's Postcolonial Self-Writing in the 1990s," in *Ethics after Idealism: Theory, Culture, Ethnicity, Reading* (Bloomington: Indiana University Press, 1998), 157.

3. In Chinese, the word "sex" is different from the Western meaning of sexual instincts or sexual intercourse. In Chinese, it means human nature.

4. Robert Van Gulik, *Sexual Life in Ancient China: A Preliminary Survey of Chinese Sex and Society from ca. 1500 BC till 1644 AD*, trans. Lee Ling et al. (Shanghai: Shanghai People's Press, 1990), 1–18.

5. Ibid.

6. Ibid., 8.

7. Charlotte Furth, "Rethinking Van Gulik: Sexuality and Reproduction in Traditional Chinese Medicine," in *Engendering China: Women, Culture, and the State*, ed. Christiana K. Gilmartin et al. (Cambridge, MA: Harvard University Press, 1994), 130–31.

8. Xiaomingxiong, *The History of Homosexuality in China* (Hong Kong: Siuming and Rosa Winkel Press, 1997), 4–21.

9. Bret Hinsch, "Lesbianism in Imperial China," in *Passions of the Cut Sleeve: The Male Homosexual Tradition in China* (Berkeley: University of California Press, 1990), 174.

10. Xiaomingxiong, *History of Homosexuality in China*, 302. The *tzu shu nü* in Shunde was a well-known tradition in Qing and contemporary times. Those women who decided to join the community house were called old maids because they had to leave their own family and vowed not to marry as a lifelong covenant. Most of them earned their living through silk production. Their ceremony of receiving new members was like receiving a bride. The woman would be taken to the temple. Her hair would be tied up as a symbol of her special status in society. A cock would be killed, and the woman would drink the blood as a sign of her covenant with the community. Some women would find another woman with whom they wanted to live, and the two would form a couple called *chinlan hui*. After making their vows to each other in the official ceremony, the women were supposed to live together as a married couple and not live apart.

11. *Hong Lou Meng*, one of the world's most well-known Chinese novels, was written by Cao Xueqin in the eighteenth century. The story presents a clear picture of the corruption of Chinese feudal families and society in the Qing period.

12. Xiaomingxiong, *History of Homosexuality in China*, 323–25. According to Chinese tradition, only males were allowed to be trained as opera actors and actresses. Therefore, many men joined the opera school to be trained and later to perform as actresses. Often they were expected to play their female roles even offstage. Many of these male actresses also provided sexual services to the male elites of society.

13. Chow, "Between Colonizers," 153.

14. Chou Wah-shan, *Hou zhimin tongzhi* (Postcolonial *Tongzhi*) (Hong Kong: Xianggang tongzhi yan jiu she, 1997), 348–59.

15. *Zimei Tongzhi* (Queer Sisters) was founded in 1995 as one of the first feminist queer organizations in Hong Kong as well as in Asia. See Anson Mak and Mary Ann King, "Hong Kong's *Tongzhi* Movement: Through the Eyes of Queer Sisters," in *Hong Kong's Social*

Movements: Forces from the Margins, ed. Sophia Woodman (Hong Kong: July 1 Link and Hong Kong Women Christian Council, 1997).

16. Ibid., 100.

17. Chou, Postcolonial *Tongzhi*, 360–69.

18. Eve Kosofsky Sedgwick, *Epistemology of the Closet* (Berkeley: University of California Press, 1990). According to Sedgwick, "The word *queer* comes from the Indo-European root *twerk*, which also yields the German *quer* (transverse), Latin *torquere* (to twist), and English *athwar*." This brief linguistic survey suggests that *queer* has the meaning of "multiply transitive" (xii).

19. Cindy Patton, "Tremble, Hetero Swine!" in *Fear of a Queer Planet: Queer Politics and Social Theory*, ed. Michael Warner (Minneapolis: University of Minneapolis Press, 1993). In her article Patton explains that rhetorical reversal is one of the fundamental principles of the identity discourses of the post–World War II movements. Black, women, and gay liberation movements typically "reclaimed" derogatory terms that were considered part of the hegemonic vocabulary, terms that were symptomatic of pervasive, stereotypical, and negative societal attitudes. They used, for instance, such slogans as Black Is Beautiful and Gay Is Good (146).

20. Mak and King, "Hong Kong's *Tongzhi* Movement," 104–8.

21. Elizabeth Stuart, *Daring to Speak Love's Name: A Gay and Lesbian Prayer Book* (London: Penguin Books, 1992), 81–82.

22. On June 18, 1999, twenty-two *tongzhi* organizations and other support groups organized the first *Tongzhi* Day in Hong Kong. The objective was to educate the public that homosexuality and bisexuality are not only found in the Western world but are also evident in ancient Chinese traditions.

23. I refer here to the fact that the *Tongzhi* Day campaign mainly glorified male homosexual practices between the emperor of the Chu dynasty and Qu Yuan without mentioning the Chinese lesbian tradition and the exploitation of young boys and girls by the royal family and aristocrats.

24. Patton, "Tremble, Hetero Swine!" 147.

25. Breakthrough is a Christian organization formed in the early 1970s to serve as a center for youth counseling and youth education. One of their objectives is to reach out to young people in the community.

26. HKCC was founded in 1954; its membership is denominational and ecumenical.

27. This poetic image was used by Rosemary R. Ruether, in her book *Women-Church: Theology and Practice of Feminist Liturgical Communities* (San Francisco: Harper & Row, 1985), to describe how Women-Church as an excluded community within the patriarchal church is still determined to seek liberation and thus become an exodus community. I find that this theological image reflects the journey of HKBMCF.

28. Selina Sun, "Why I Chose to Be Ordained by BMCF," *Hong Kong Christian Institute Newsletter* 194 (November 2004): 3–4.

29. Leonardo Boff, *Trinity and Society* (Maryknoll, NY: Orbis Books, 1988), 3.

30. Carter Heyward, *Touching Our Strength: The Erotic as Power and the Love of God* (San Francisco: Harper & Row, 1989), 114–18. *Christa* was made by the British sculptor Edwina Sandys. It was displayed in New York's Cathedral of St. John the Divine during the Lenten season in 1984. According to Heyward, this display generated a stir among the Christian community.

31. Carter Heyward, *Saving Jesus from Those Who Are Right: Rethinking What It Means to Be Christian* (Minneapolis: Fortress Press, 1999), 1–30.
32. Quoted in Sharon D. Welch, *A Feminist Ethic of Risk* (Minneapolis: Fortress Press, 1990), 128.
33. Ibid., 129.
34. Henry Louis Gates Jr., "A Liberalism of Heart and Spine," *New York Times*, March 27, 1994, E17.

Chapter Sixteen

Re-creating Our Mothers' Dishes

Asian and Asian North American Women's Pedagogy

Boyung Lee

Searching for Recipes

Many Korean women of my generation went to local colleges and stayed at their parents' homes until their marriage or other significant circumstances of life. I, in contrast, left home right after high school to go to a university in Seoul, the capital city, far from my hometown. Therefore, I hardly had any chance to learn from my mother how to cook. Cookbooks were widely available, but traditional Korean culinary art rarely specifies amounts as measured with cups and spoons; so as a beginner, I found cooking difficult and frustrating. The cookbook instructions left me clueless about the exact procedures and proportions; for instance, "Soak it in salty water until it looks to be ready"; "2 fistfuls of salt"; "1 big spoonful of red pepper powder"; " a little bit of sesame oil." As I read these recipes, I was asking myself questions like, "Is it 2 hours or 3 hours?" "Whose fist size?" "How big is a big spoon?"

Expressing my frustration, I asked my mother how someone like me could ever learn to cook. My mother told me to (1) start with a dish that I had eaten many times before; (2) try to remember the taste; (3) try to create the taste by using ingredients suggested by cookbooks. "Then as I re-create the dish from [my] memory," she continued, "I will create something of my own." Later, when I became a more confident and experienced cook, my mother added one more lesson for cooking that I consider the most significant part of creating a good dish: she said that good food is created by the cook's *sonmat*, which literally means the taste of one's hands. As most Korean dishes are supposed to be made by hands, mixing all the ingredients in an appropriate way during an appropriate time, a cook's hands (more specifically, her or his fingertips) decide the flavor of food. This is the reason that *sonmat* is the key for good food. My mother also said, "Even though you use the best materials to make good food, if your hands do not have right condition, the food will not turn out good. No matter what is going on in your life and the world, don't let the world define who you are and who you should be. When your mind and heart are in peace, your body will be in a calm and peaceful condition, and therefore your hands will have [the] perfect temperature and strength for cooking."

As a more experienced cook now, I find her teaching very true and wise, and I stand and cook in awe of her because the advice comes from a woman who has not had an easy life. My mother lost her parents early in life and was raised by her grandmother, who had been abandoned by her rich and educated husband. As one can imagine, it was extremely challenging for two women to make ends meet and to live safely in patriarchal Confucian Korea without a male protector. Notwithstanding, she persevered and learned one of the most important recipes for life: Do not let the world define who you are and what you can be. Today she gives her recipes to her daughter and others so that they can create their own recipes through re-creating their foremothers' recipes.

This pedagogy of *sonmat* reflects some of the core features of pedagogy as practiced by many Asian and Asian North American women; it is holistic, communal, ontological, and political. It also provides helpful pedagogical strategies for the theological education of Asian and Asian North American women.

Re-creating Our Mothers' Dishes: The Features of Asian North American Women's Pedagogy

For a long time the world of written texts and formal education was the domain of Asian men. Although contemporary Asian and Asian North American communities are known for their esteem of education for sons and daughters, the latter population was largely neglected.[1] For example, in the late 1980s and early 1990s I served as a minister for youth and young adult women at a church located in urban Seoul. The group was composed of young women between the ages of sixteen and twenty-five who worked at transnational textile companies during the day and were simultaneously students in evening high schools provided by their employers. Most of these young women had to give up regular high school educations to support their brothers' education. Although Korean society, like many other Asian societies, puts a high emphasis on children's education, when resources are limited, educational opportunities are primarily limited to sons. In recent years as many Asian countries have developed, they now provide more opportunities for women; however, the primacy of male education continues.

A similar preference for men is also seen in Asian diasporic communities in North America. For example, on June 20, 2003, under the title "Like a Virgin, Young Women Undergo Surgery to 'Restore' Virginity," *20/20* of ABC News reported that every year hundreds of young, scared Asian North American women visit plastic surgeons for hymen restoration before their marriage.[2] Under Asia's (especially its Confucian patriarchal value) system, women's bodies are the property of the family, especially of male members in each household. As the owner of property, the male family members teach women and girls proper behaviors, such as notions about purity and the body. Under this system, women have to live under severe sexual suppression because losing one's virginity brings shame and humiliation to one's family, and thus it hurts the social advancement of male family members.[3] Although Asian North American communities are physically far removed from their homelands, that young North American women of Asian heritage seek hymen restoration surgery straightforwardly suggests patriarchy's hegemony.

This dovetails back to *sonmat*. In sociocultural contexts where patriarchy is a norm and formal education belongs to men, women have cultivated their own stealth pedagogy. The irony here is that from a perspective of educational theory, their creative pedagogy is conceptually and pragmatically more holistic. When I started learning to cook, my mother advised me to remember the taste of the food in my memory and to re-create the taste by using whatever ingredients were available to me. As I followed her advice, I found that remembering the taste of a particular dish not only helped me make the food but also brought me back to the occasion of eating itself—to people around the table, to the atmosphere of the room and its shared stories, and to other events conjured from memory by the dish. In other words, the teaching that I experienced was much broader and deeper than that which I could have learned from a classroom or textbook alone. It was a holistic lesson that involved the stories and experiences of the past, coupled with the present needs and creativity for the future. Moreover, while I was re-creating the dish, I cultivated my own ways of making the same dish, and accordingly I created my own recipes.

This holistic way of teaching and learning as Asian and Asian North American women practice it is faithful to the true meaning of education. The English word "education" comes from the Latin *e*(out)-*ducare*(to lead), "to lead out."[4] The root word for "education" tells us that education is to help people find a truth that is already within them. It is not just a teacher transmitting knowledge to learners, but it is helping learners to remember what they know and to reflect critically on this knowledge in their present life contexts. It is to develop something new for the future. In other words, a good education that integrates the past, the present, and the future helps learners develop their own pedagogy. This holistic integration is exactly what my mother and other Asian and Asian North American women try to teach through their embodied *sonmat* pedagogy.

Many Asian North American women who teach in academic contexts also practice this holistic pedagogy. For example, in 1999 several of the faculty advisers of the Pacific, Asian, and North American Asian Women in Theology and Ministry (PANAAWTM), a grassroots movement of Asian and Pacific North American women in theological education and ministry, developed a communal project that provides materials and strategies for teaching Asian and Asian North American women's theologies in North America.[5] Through critical reflections on their own teaching philosophy and practices and through sharing of teaching materials and syllabi, they identified five characteristics of Asian North American ways of teaching and learning: (1) teaching by example; (2) using dialogue in teaching; (3) teaching without distinction of (socioeconomic) class; (4) teaching according to the potential of the student; and (5) teaching morals and wisdom, not just "knowledge." As number 5 makes plain, these perspectives on and approaches to education are much more than knowledge transmission in school settings, for they involve the teachers' life stories and contexts coupled with critical reflection, praxis, and respect for human dignity and ability.

In this sense the curriculum of Asian and Asian North American women's pedagogy is broad in scope. It is a pedagogy that brings together the past, the present, and the future. Asian and Asian North American women's pedagogy is based on and uses a multidimensional concept of curriculum, one that is esteemed by several educational theorists as a way to achieve holistic education. For example, Elliot W. Eisner, noted curriculum theorist, says that each school offers students three different curricula: the explicit curriculum, one that is the actual content, consciously and intentionally presented as the teachings of the school; the implicit curriculum, one that, through its environment, includes the way teachers teach and interact with students; and the null curriculum, those ideas and subjects in educational programs that are sidestepped. By leaving out options and alternatives, the school narrows students' perspectives and the range of their thoughts and action. Thus the explicit curriculum, which is often regarded as the entire curriculum, is only one facet of teaching. In fact, Eisner points out that the implicit and the null curricula might have more influence over students than does the explicit curriculum.[6]

Whereas Asian and Asian North American cultures have been focused on Eisner's explicit curriculum, highlighting patriarchal values and the education of men, their women have been teaching and learning through implicit and null curricula. Women have been using implicit and null curricula as major resources for their education, thereby transforming kitchens, cooking, and other daily life contexts and activities into holistic classroom and teaching moments. When written texts were only available for men's education, Asian and Asian North American women used their own lived-world experience (for example, Asian women's religiocultural and sociopolitical traditions; Asian myth, folktales, songs, poems, proverbs; and teachings from different Asian religions) for their own and their daughters' education.[7] Maria Harris, a feminist Christian religious educator, thus ventures that everything that a church does—fellowship meetings, informal gatherings, small group meetings, and so on—should be understood as curricula.[8]

The pedagogy of *sonmat* of Asian and Asian North American women is also communal in both its purpose and process. As I said above, while I was remembering the taste of the food, the entire community related to the food came to my mind and heart. In other words, even though I was cooking by myself in my kitchen, I was in communion with many people to whom I was indebted for who I am, and to whom I am accountable. For example, whenever I make a certain Korean pork dish or whenever I see big pots, I ask myself whether my current theological work is contributing to the lessening of the suffering of the marginalized of our society. While I was a graduate student in Korea, I worked with poor Korean women living in huts illegally built on government land in Seoul. On every Sunday between morning and evening services, these women took me to their homes so that I could rest, and they fed me with the most delicious food imaginable. Often the table was set with a big pot of pork and a bowl of rice, which meant that we all ate from the same pot and rice bowl. To me that was the most meaningful experience of communion and theology. Even though I am now physically far removed from that community, I still meet many similar people who provide a community for me, and they challenge me about whether my theological research has much to do with their own daily struggles against racism, sexism, and other oppressions. Therefore, for me, that particular pork dish and its big pot are constant reminders, memories that call me to reflect critically on my accountability to the communities that I serve.

The involvement and presence of community is one of the most integral parts of the pedagogical formation of women of Asian heritages. As explicitly and implicitly reflected in several of the other chapters in this volume, such as those of Rita Nakashima Brock and Anne Joh, Asian and Asian North American women have developed communal personhood. Unlike individualism, which values each person's individuality and independence, the value of the individual in communal Asian societies depends on how well a person adopts communal norms and functions to promote social harmony. Attachments, relatedness, connectedness, unity, and dependency among people are much more important than are independence and individuality. For example, anyone who has paid attention to Korean linguistics can easily find that Koreans rarely use the I-ness words such as "I," "my," and "mine." They instead like to use the word *uri*, meaning we. Almost everything is called "our (something)," instead of "my (something)." For example, when one refers to one's wife, one does not say "my wife"; rather, one says, "*our* wife." We-ness language is a source of comfort for Koreans. They are uncomfortable with I-ness language.[9]

Although the use of what I call *we* linguistics is a unique Korean practice, the importance of community is true for most Asian and Asian North American cultures.[10] In their family-centered communities, Asian and Asian North Americans venture that "our family" means all of the I's melted into one we. Here, "we" does not mean the coexistence of "I" and "you" as independent individual units; rather, it indicates that "you" and "you," and "you" and "I" are the same reality: "I and you exist not as separate units but as a unified one. At the moment when two individuals abandon their own perspective and put themselves in their partner's shoes, they become one, not a separate two."[11] A good example of such communal selfhood is found in Japanese linguistics. The English word "self" is usually translated by the Japanese word *jibun*, and vice versa. However and unlike the English word for "self," *jibun* connotes "one's share of the shared life space";[12] that is, oneself is an inseparable part of ourselves. When two Japanese people exchange greetings by asking how the other party is, the customary way of saying it is "How is *jibun*?" which literally means, "How is ourselves?"[13]

In sum, persons in Asian and Asian North American communal societies can be fully understood only in connection with the larger social whole: others are included within the boundaries of the self.[14] Accordingly, attachments, relatedness, connectedness, oneness, and dependency among people are much more important than independence or individual autonomy. Those who pursue only their own benefit are easily expelled from a community's psyche. In order to create harmony in community life, each member is expected to suppress her or his desires and emotions and to give heed to others' desires and emotions. An individual who attempts to do things in an idiosyncratic way, or who is too ambitious, risks being alienated from the community. Therefore, even though a community member experiences pride, this emotion should not be displayed, and only moderate expressions about one's abilities or accomplishments are tolerated.

In communal cultural contexts Asian and Asian North American women are not full members because the value of harmony and comunity that Asian communal societies emphasize is based on a hierarchical and patriarchal philosophical anthropology. The hierarchy of superior-to-inferior maintains the orderliness and harmony of the cosmos.[15] The superior partners have the rights and duties of educating so-called inferior partners, and inferior partners only have obligations but no rights. In other words, this hierarchy is seen as necessary if the relationships are to work.

Thus the powerless are forced to sacrifice for the value of harmony. For example, contemporary Korean women's social status has greatly improved in terms of opportunities for employment; notwithstanding, in an Organisation for Economic Cooperation and Development report, Korea and Japan had the highest wage gap between men and women.[16] Another example of discrimination against women for the harmony of male-centered community is the skewed sex ratio at birth. The natural sex ratio at birth is estimated to be 105 boys to 100 girls. According to the 2001 Korean census, there are 109.5 boys for every one hundred girls.[17] This skewed sex ratio is mostly due to sex-selective abortion in pursuit of a son.

Although Asian and Asian North American societies promote and emphasize family-knit fellowship and the value of relatedness and harmony, they are based on a hierarchy and patriarchy that force "inferior" members of the group to sacrifice themselves for the sake of those vested with power. In a nutshell, without sacrifice, harmony is not possible; thus harmony, ironically, leavens injustice and social dissonance.

Even though they are not quite full members of communal society, Asian and Asian North American women take communal support for one another very seriously. Rather than abandoning communal personhood based on hierarchical patriarchy and then embracing the Western autonomous self as an alternative personhood, many Asian and Asian North American women seek a communal personhood that respects their being and experiences as women. As many commentators on self-identity, including Western psychologists such as Edward Sampson and M. Brinton Lykes, point out, the autonomous self based on individualistic anthropology is a myth made up for the interests of Westerners during the Enlightenment, one that suppresses the authentic communal mode of human existence.[18]

Therefore, in Asian and Asian North American women's pedagogy, it is critical that their communal personhood is respected, and that knowledge should be generated through a communal process, one that is anchored in a sound community. One of the most important roles of a teacher is to help learners create a learning community together. Thus in the context of learning and teaching, each woman's personal story is equally key to the insights gained through texts and theological discussions. The most commonly used teaching methods are dialogue, storytelling and social analysis, role plays, drama, dance, rituals, and the creation of action plans as a community.[19] One might doubt whether these pedagogical methods could be used in academic and professional theological contexts; however, the present volume has been created by communal discernment processes and learning methods. The authors of this work gathered at Union Theological Seminary in New York City for three days in 2005, telling one another stories. We engaged in communal analysis of the stories that we shared, deepening our conversations over meals and through play, laughter, and rituals. As a result, at the end of the third day, the theme Off the Menu emerged, which inspired more storytelling about food, cooking, and Asian and Asian North American women's ways of knowing.

A similar pedagogical praxis is also found at the annual meetings of PANAAWTM, which bring together about sixty Asian and Asian North American women in theology and ministry. Sharing personal and communal stories and providing intensive mentoring to individuals are as important as the plenary and theological forums. Dance, rituals, movies, and hands-on workshops are opportunities to create learning communities among members. Serious theological debates among members and between participants and faculty advisers are a highlight of the meeting. In sum, knowledge generated through communal discernment is both an explicit and implicit aspect of the meeting. Challenging each other to examine critically the null curriculum of our learning together is always meaningful. As Kwok Pui-lan, a founding member and a faculty adviser often says, we gather together so that "we strive together through supporting each other." In short, remembering and re-creating the taste of the food and creating one's own recipes are a rich collective pursuit.

Another important feature of the pedagogy of *sonmat* of Asian and Asian North American women's pedagogy is its ontological and political nature. Developing one's *sonmat* involves one's entire being and the world around one. Many Asian and Asian North American women have suffered oppressions, such as colonialism, sexism, classism, and racism. They have also been told that they are insignificant. Yet many of us refuse to be defined by others' standards and celebrate our calling and our sense of who we are. As my mother wisely advises, one's perseverance is one's source of *sonmat*. So the pedagogy of *sonmat* of Asian and Asian North American women is clearly an enterprise of epistemology and ontology, one that is concerned with the totality of life.

Sonmat also is a political activity as women pursue peace and justice. Admittedly, many Asian and Asian North American women are now in a much better place than heretofore through education, immigration, and social changes; however, many women and men living in Asia and other parts of the world suffer, so our pedagogy must lead to political transformation. The following statement by Kwok Pui-lan clearly shows the political nature of Asian and Asian North American women's pedagogy:

> For me, the critical test for any theological construction is how much it contributes to lessening human suffering; to building communities that resist oppression within the church, academy, and the society; to furthering the liberation of those among us who are most disadvantaged, primarily the women and the children.[20]

This might be why leading Asian North American feminist theologians, such as Rita Nakashima Brock and Nantawan Boonprasat Lewis, are also social and political activists.

Creating Our Own Recipes: Pedagogical Guidelines for Asian and Asian North American Women's Education

The above features of Asian and Asian North American women's pedagogy also provide important guidelines for the future education of North American women of Asian heritage. First, the holistic, ontological, and political nature of pedagogy that Asian and Asian North American women have practiced should be honored and continued. As stated above, the pedagogy of Asian and Asian North American women is a much bigger and broader concept than mere schooling and classroom teaching. Personal and communal stories and life experiences of Asian and Asian North

American women should be included as resources for theological and educational discourse. Education as character formation, inheritance of wisdom rather than the transmission of knowledge alone, critical thinking and social analysis, honoring Asian cultural traditions and religious practices, and political action plans for social changes are all part of the embodied pedagogy of Asian and Asian North American women.

Second, the communal nature of Asian and Asian North American women's pedagogy should also be honored. However, the communal cultural values of Asian and Asian North American communities need to be revisited and challenged from women's perspectives and experiences. Since communal cultures require individuals to define themselves as part of the group and to subordinate personal goals to group goals, it provides less-rigid ego boundaries.[21] The identification and projection of one person onto another self occurs easily. When a person's ego faces another, especially the authority figure of the community, there is a ready identification with the other so that one takes on similarities and sidesteps differences. This tendency toward the identification with others often perpetuates strong dependency and a lack of self-identity.[22] The powerless, such as women and people from the marginalized classes, easily lose their identities or the value of their existence. Overvaluing relatedness and sacrificing their needs for the needs of others deprive women of the capacity to know themselves; these also contribute to repressed feelings, diffused boundaries, low self-esteem, dependency on others, feelings of shame, deprivation of the right to communicate, ambiguity about themselves and the world, and lack of centeredness.[23] Although communalism affirms the weblike nature of human existence, it can hinder the development of its members, especially women. Asian communal and relational values that sacrifice women for the sake of community, thereby further marginalizing their already marginalized condition, should be challenged by sound pedagogy.

Through a sound pedagogy, Asian and Asian North American women should also be contributing to the transformation of factionalism between in-groups and out-groups, which is another serious pitfall of communal cultural values. According to the research of social psychologists, one of the salient features of communal culture is its in-group favoritism, which in turn creates exclusive and even antagonistic attitudes toward out-group members.[24] To the members of in-groups, such as family, school, region, political party, and the church, people fulfill obligations dutifully. However, in-group members can be cruel to out-group members. Thus there is a premium on belonging to the right group, for unless people cultivate relationships through in-group connections, they have no future. Such in-group favoritism thus promotes classism, regionalism, denominational-ism, and a superiority complex to other religions. Asian and Asian North American women who have experiences of being out-group members within the community should challenge factionalism by emphasizing the responsibility and accountability of each member, thus making the community genuinely inclusive. PANAAWTM is a good example of this approach's success.

For specific pedagogical processes for the education of Asian and Asian North American women in concrete teaching and learning contexts, including both formal classrooms and other educational venues, I suggest the following 5Rs as critical elements: Readying the ground, Remember-ing, Reflecting, Reinterpreting, and Re-searching.[25] I find these 5Rs help-ful processes to follow and frequently use them in my teaching.

Readying the Ground: Gathering Ingredients

Readying the ground occurs when Asian and Asian North American women teachers and learners get to know about each other in a broader sense, especially the social-, political-, and cultural-pedagogical back-ground that they bring to the learning contexts. In other words, it is a process of creating a teaching and learning community together. Through telling and listening to one another's stories and views of the topic to be looked at together, people develop a sense of who they are and what they are about. Without such a sense, it is hard for people to create a commu-nal learning process, an ingredient that is essential to Asian and Asian North American women's epistemology.

In a more formal teaching and learning context, it is also a time for a leader to assess people's different views of the world, texts, and themes, so that she can facilitate the learning process with appropriate information and methods integral to transformation. Every time I offer a new Bible study class, for example, at the first session I usually ask people to share why they are interested in the topic or the book that we are about to study, and what their expectations are of the class. Through this process I remind people that we bring multiple perspectives and backgrounds to the study. I also get a sense of people's various learning styles in order to avoid over-reliance on any one style.[26] The purpose of this process is to help people become aware of their biases and to develop respect for varying view-points, so that they can hear anew old stories and reconsider what it means to venture along the road out to someplace radically different.

Remembering Traditions, Ancestors, and the Community: Cooking

Whether it is formal or informal teaching and learning, remembering is the process when people focus on the subject of learning itself. It is the "cooking" stage, when people identify and name what they already know about the subject. Often it is where individuals voice what they have discovered thus far in the study. For example, several years ago, I observed a group of Korean women leading a campaign to reduce the use of chemical products, such as dishwashing soap, at their church. The church had over five thousand members. Even though it was a time when the Korean church did not have much awareness of environmental issues and ecofeminist discourse, after experiencing different degrees of skin irritation caused by chemical products that they used every day, these women laity decided to do something about it.

At their gatherings women asked one another questions related to the use of dishwashing soap: What had they used before chemical products were readily available? Had they experienced skin problems or other illnesses due to the overuse of these products? What did they know about the ingredients in these chemical products? Their questions generated a lot of storytelling, laughter, and reflection on their lifestyles. In other words, even though the women did not as individuals have much professional knowledge about the products and pollution, by sharing their experiences with each other, they were able to gather knowledge and frame the issue, which are major parts of this process.

In formal educational contexts, such as Scripture studies, participants share with one another what they know about the meaning of a particular text, passage, or theme they study, and what and how their communities have taught about it. They then ask, "How do we now understand the theme?" This process is especially important if the study is introducing a radically different interpretation to participants, instead of the traditional male-centered Western interpretations of the Scripture. At any rate, whether it is a formal or informal educational context, the main "cooking" purpose is to invite people to remember what they know about the topic.

Reflecting: Tasting

Reflection occurs when people are invited to consider different thematic views; it is the time when people hear what and how others, including scholars, think about the topic, and it is when they critically reflect on the ideological background of these views. By comparing views other than those taught by their communities, participants are asked to reflect on the process by which their understanding has developed. Whose ideology shapes these views? Who benefits from them? In other words, this process critically examines one's own and one's community's ideology, and in considering other possible interpretations, it compares one's own worldview with those of others. For example, at the aforementioned meeting of the Korean women, the women who led the gathering introduced detailed information about different types of soap, including all the ins and outs of these products' manufacture. As they did so, women participants weighed in with knowledge that they had. With all the information available, they then reviewed what the manufacturers had told them. Who benefits from the product, and who benefits from this information about the product? Were women harming the environment by using the products? How could we change the situation? By asking these critical questions, women were able to see their own intentional and unintentional contributions to environmental problems.

In a more formal educational context, critical reviews of ideology and its literature are pursued. For example, in a Scripture study class, different interpretations of the same text can be examined and compared: traditional androcentric interpretations, feminist interpretations, and different liberation-theological interpretations. Then the leader invites participants to reflect critically on these different views and to give their impressions. The leader also provides some of the historical background for these various interpretations, the role of traditional interpretations by Western scholarship, and how these have dominated theological discourse in both Asia and Asian North America.

Reinterpreting: Developing Our Own Recipe

In the reinterpreting session, teachers and learners explore new ways to approach an old issue. In the Korean women's gathering, the group collectively made a decision to reduce the use of the soap, with the goal of not using chemical products at all in the future. They explored ways to reduce chemical products by finding organic products and by learning how to make organic dishwashing soaps. In the Scripture class the leader introduces a fresh approach to interpretation. For example, in my biblical pedagogy class, I introduce postcolonial interpretations, using core principles of postcolonial biblical hermeneutics (for example, the power dynamics between the Near Eastern empires and Israel, the internal sociopolitical situations and policies, analyses of character constructions, and the history of interpretations of the text by different empires of the West). Participants are also invited to think critically of ways to apply new interpretations to their own contexts and to those of their community.

Re-searching: Creating an Old but New Dish

In the re-searching process, participants explore different ways of living to implement new meanings and insights that they have gained. What other actions should we take beyond reducing the use of soap? What larger issues should be addressed? What action plans do we need? What does the reinterpretation of the story propose for us? What messages do we readers now find in the story? Asking these questions, I invite participants to research and reflect on meanings that have emerged from new interpretations of the theme. Hereto praxis is coupled with theory: What actions (political, social, cultural, and religious) should we, as individuals and faith communities, take to respond to these issues?

The pedagogy of *sonmat*, a holistic, communal, ontological, and political pedagogy of Asian and Asian North American women, must be far-reaching in scope, spiritually and culturally. Moreover, as an organic pedagogy it should constantly ask about its own null curriculum— "Whose voice is missing?" "What is left out?" "What new issues do we need to address now?" Through asking these questions, Asian and Asian North American women renew their practices by simultaneously inheriting old and developing new recipes for future generations, so that generations to come will ever envision and create a worthwhile world for themselves and their children.

Notes

1. Greer Anne Wenh-In Ng, "Asian Sociocultural Values: Oppressive and Liberating Aspects from a Woman's Perspective," in *People on the Way: Asian North Americans Discovering Christ, Culture, and Community*, ed. David Ng (Valley Forge, PA: Judson Press, 1996), 76.
2. Lynn Sherr, "Like a Virgin, Young Women Undergo Surgery to 'Restore' Virginity," *20/20*, ABC News, June 20, 2003. Transcripts available online at http://www.psurg .com/abcnews-2003–06-20.htm. For a detailed theological reflection on this phenomenon and Asian American sexuality, see my article "Teaching Justice and Living Peace: Body, Sexuality, and Religious Education in Asian American Communities," *Religious Education* 101, no. 3 (2006): 402–19.
3. Chung Hyun Kyung, "'Han-pu-ri': Doing Theology from Korean Women's Perspective," in *We Dare to Dream: Doing Theology as Asian Women*, ed. Virginia Fabella and Sun Ai Lee Park (Maryknoll, NY: Orbis Books, 1989), 140.

4. Thomas Groome, *Christian Religious Education: Sharing Our Story and Vision* (New York: Harper & Row, 1980), 5.

5. Rita Nakashima Brock, Jung Ha Kim, Kwok Pui-lan, Nantawan Boonprasat Lewis, Greer Anne Wenh-In Ng, Seung Ai Yang, and Gale A. Yee, "Developing Teaching Materials and Instructional Strategies for Teaching Asian and Asian American/ Canadian Women's Theologies in North America," The Final Report for a Teaching and Learning in Theological Education Project under the Teaching and Learning Small Grants Program of the Association of Theological Schools and a Teaching Theology and Religion Grant Project of the Wabash Center for Teaching and Learning in Theology and Religion (November 1999), http://www.panaawtm.org/images/final .report.doc.

6. Elliot W. Eisner, *The Educational Imagination: On the Design and Evaluation of School Programs* (New York: Macmillan, 1985), 97.

7. Kwok Pui-lan, *Introducing Asian Feminist Theology* (Cleveland: Pilgrim Press, 2000), 38–50.

8. Maria Harris, *Fashion Me a People: Curriculum in the Church* (Louisville, KY: Westminster John Knox Press, 1989), 63.

9. Sang-Chin Choi and Soo Hyang Choi, "Cheong: The Socio-emotional Grammar of Koreans" (unpublished manuscript, Seoul: Chung Ang University, 1993).

10. According to Geert Hofsteade, who measured the extent of individualism and communalism in sixty-six countries, most Asian countries, such as Korea, China, Taiwan, Japan, and Singapore, are some of the most communal societies (*Cultures and Organizations: Software of the Mind* [London: McGraw Hill, 1991]).

11. Soo-Won Lee, "The Cheong Space: A Zone of Non-exchange in Korean Human Relationships," in *Psychology of the Korean People: Collectivism and Individualism*, ed. Gene Yoon and Sang-Chin Choi (Seoul: Dong-A, 1994), 93–94.

12. Hazel R. Markus and Shinobu Kitayama, "Culture and the Self: Implications for Cognitions, Emotion, and Motivations," *Psychological Review* 98 (1991): 224–53, quotation on 228.

13. I thank the Reverend Mitsuho Okado, a Japanese D.Min. graduate at Pacific School of Religion, for helping me understand the meaning of *jibun*.

14. Markus and Kitayama, "Culture and the Self."

15. Theresa Kelleher, "Confucianism," in *Women in World Religions*, ed. Arvind Sharma (Albany: State University of New York Press, 1987), 138.

16. Organisation for Economic Cooperation and Development (OECD), *Employment Outlook* (Paris 2001): 139.

17. In 1990 the sex ratio at birth was 116.5 boys to 100 girls, and in 1973, it was 104.6 to 100 (Korea National Statistical Office, *2001 Korea Census* [Seoul: Korea National Statistical Office, 2002], http://kosis.nso.go.kr/cgi-bin/sus_888.cgi?ID-DT_18800A& IDTYPE-3&A_LANG-2&FPUB-4&SELITEM-).

18. Edward Sampson, *Celebrating the Other: A Dialogic Account of Human Nature* (Boulder, CO: Westview Press, 1993); and M. Brinton Lykes, "Gender and Individualistic vs. Collectivist Bases for Notions about the Self," *Journal of Personality* 53 (1985): 356–83.

19. Chung Hyun Kyung, *Struggle to Be the Sun Again: Introducing Asian Women's Theology* (Maryknoll, NY: Orbis Books, 1990), 99–114.

20. Kwok Pui-lan, *Discovering the Bible in the Non-biblical World* (Maryknoll, NY: Orbis Books, 1995), 31.

21. Kyung Ja Oh, "Cultural Influences on Child Behavior Problems," in Yoon and Choi, *Psychology of the Korean People*, 143–44.

22. Harry C. Triandis, *Individualism and Collectivism: New Directions in Social Psychology* (Boulder, CO: Westview Press, 1995), 175.

23. Young Ae Kim, "Han: From Brokenness to Wholeness: A Theoretical Analysis of Korean Women's Han and a Contextualized Healing Methodology" (Ph.D. diss., Claremont School of Theology, 1991), 92–98.

24. Harry C. Triandis, "Collectivism vs. Individualism: A Reconceptualization" (unpublished manuscript, University of Illinois), quoted in Seong-Yeul Han and Chang-Yil Ahn, "Collectivism and Individualism in Korea," in Yoon and Choi, *Psychology of the Korean People*, 332.

25. I adapted this 5Rs methodology from Christine Blair, *The Art of Teaching the Bible: A Practical Guide for Adults* (Louisville, KY: Geneva Press, 2001).

26. Brock, et al., "Developing Teaching Materials and Instructional Strategies," 12.

Selected Resources

Books

Abraham, Dulcie, Sun Ai Lee Park, and Yvonne Dahlin, eds. *Faith Renewed: A Report on the First Asian Women's Consultation on Interfaith Dialogue*. Hong Kong: Asian Women's Resource Centre for Culture and Theology (AWRC), n.d.

Abraham, Dulcie, Yvonne Dahlin, Stella M. Faria, Sally Moses, and Sun Ai Lee Park, eds. *Asian Women Doing Theology: Report from the Singapore Conference, November 20–29, 1987*. Hong Kong: AWRC, 1989.

Ahmed, Durre S., ed. *Gendering the Spirit: Women, Religion and the Post-colonial Response*. London: Zed Books, 2002.

Antone, Hope S., and Yong Ting Jin, eds. *Re-living Our Faith Today: A Bible Study Resource Book*. Hong Kong: World Student Christian Federation, Asia-Pacific Region, 1992.

Aoyama, Shundo. *Zen Seeds: Reflections of a Female Priest*. Tokyo: Kosei Publishing Co., 1990.

Arai, Paula Kane Robinson. *Women Living Zen: Japanese Soto Buddhist Nuns*. New York: Oxford University Press, 1999.

AWRC. *Introduction to Asian Feminist Theologies*. Kuala Lumpur: AWRC, 2005.

———, ed. *Faith Renewed II: A Report on the Second Asian Women's Consultation on Interfaith Dialogue, November 1–7, 1991, Colombo, Sri Lanka*. Seoul: AWRC, n.d.

Barton, Mukti. *Scripture as Empowerment for Liberation and Justice: The Experience of Christian and Muslim Women in Bangladesh*. Bristol: Department of Theology and Religious Studies, University of Bristol, 1999.

Brazal, Agnes M., and Andrea Lizares Si, eds. *Body and Sexuality: Theological-Pastoral Perspectives of Women in Asia*. Quezon City, Philippines: Ateneo de Manila University Press, 2007.

Brewer, Carolyn. *Holy Confrontation: Religion, Gender, and Sexuality in the Philippines, 1521–1685*. Manila: St. Scholastica's College, 2001.

Brock, Rita Nakashima. *Journeys by Heart: A Christology of Erotic Power*. New York: Crossroad, 1988.

———, and Susan Brooks Thistlethwaite. *Casting Stones: Prostitution and Liberation in Asia and the United States*. Minneapolis: Fortress Press, 1996.

——, and Rebecca Ann Parker. *Proverbs of Ashes: Violence, Redemptive Suffering, and the Search for What Saves Us.* Boston: Beacon Press, 2001.

——, et al. *Developing Teaching Materials and Instructional Strategies for Teaching Asian and Asian American/Canadian Women's Theologies in North America.* Final Report of a research project, November, 1999. Available online at http://www.panaawtm.org/images/final.report.doc.

Brown, Sid. *Journey of One Buddhist Nun: Even against the Wind.* Albany: State University of New York Press, 2001.

Chen, Carolyn. *Getting Saved in America: Taiwanese Immigration and Religious Experience.* Princeton, NJ: Princeton University Press, forthcoming.

Cho, Wha Soon. *Let the Weak Be Strong: A Woman's Struggle for Justice.* Bloomington, IN: Meyer Stone Books, 1988.

Choi, Hee An. *Korean Women and God: Experiencing God in a Multi-religious Colonial Context.* Maryknoll, NY: Orbis Books, 2005.

Chun, Hyock, Kwang Chun Kim, and Shin Kim. *Koreans in the Windy City: One Hundred Years of Korean Americans in the Chicago Area.* New Haven, CT: Eat Rock Institute, 2005.

Chung, Hyun Kyung. *Struggle to Be the Sun Again: Introducing Asian Women's Theology.* Maryknoll, NY: Orbis Books, 1990.

Chung, Meehyun, ed. *Breaking Silence: Theology from Asian Women.* Delhi: Indian Society for Promoting Christian Knowledge (ISPCK), 2006.

Donaldson, Laura E., and Kwok Pui-lan, eds. *Postcolonialism, Feminism, and Religious Discourse.* New York: Routledge, 2002.

Ecumenical Association of Third World Theologians (EATWOT) Women's Commission, *Proceedings, Asian Women's Consultation, Manila, 21–30 November, 1985.* Manila: EATWOT, n.d.

Fabella, Virginia. *Beyond Bonding: A Third World Women's Theological Journey.* Manila: EATWOT, 1993.

——, and Mercy Amba Oduyoye, eds. *With Passion and Compassion: Third World Women Doing Theology.* Maryknoll, NY: Orbis Books, 1988.

——, and Sun Ai Lee Park, eds. *We Dare to Dream: Doing Theology as Asian Women.* Maryknoll, NY: Orbis Books, 1989.

Foskett, Mary F., and Jeffrey Kah-Jin Kuan, eds. *Ways of Being, Ways of Knowing: Asian American Biblical Interpretation.* St. Louis, MO: Chalice Press, 2006.

Gnanadason, Aruna. *Listen to the Women! Listen to the Earth!* Geneva: World Council of Churches, 2005.

——. *No Longer a Secret: The Church and Violence against Women.* Geneva: World Council of Churches, 1993.

——, ed. *Towards a Theology of Humanhood: Women's Perspectives.* Delhi: ISPCK, 1986.

Gupta, Charu. *Sexuality, Obscenity, Community: Women, Muslims, and the Hindu Public in Colonial India.* New York: Palgrave, 2002.

Gyatso, Janet, and Hanna Havnevik, eds. *Women in Tibet.* New York: Columbia University Press, 2005.

Hertig, Young Lee. *Cultural Tug of War: The Korean Immigrant Family and Culture in Transition.* Nashville: Abingdon Press, 2001.

Iwamura, Jane Naomi, and Paul Spickard, eds. *Revealing the Sacred in Asian and Pacific America.* New York: Routledge, 2003.

Joh, Wonhee Anne. *Heart of the Cross: A Postcolonial Christology*. Louisville, KY: Westminster John Knox Press, 2006.

Joshi, Khyati Y. *New Roots in America's Sacred Ground: Religion, Race, and Ethnicity in Indian America*. New Brunswick, NJ: Rutgers University Press, 2006.

Joy, Elizabeth, ed. *Lived Realities: Faith Reflections on Gender Justice*. Bangalore: CISRS/JWP, 1999.

Kabilsingh, Chatsumarn. *Thai Women in Buddhism*. Berkeley: Parallax Press, 1991.

Katoppo, Marianne. *Compassionate and Free: An Asian Women's Theology*. Geneva: World Council of Churches, 1979.

Kim, Ai Ra. *Women Struggling for a New Life: The Role of Religion in the Cultural Passage from Korea to America*. Albany: State University of New York Press, 1996.

Kim, Elaine H., and Norma Alarcón, eds. *Writing Self, Writing Nation: A Collection of Essays on DICTEE by Theresa Hak Kyung Cha*. Berkeley: Third Woman Press, 1994.

Kim, Elaine H., et al., eds. *Making More Waves: New Writing by Asian American Women*. Boston: Beacon Press, 1997.

Kim, Eunjoo Mary. *Preaching the Presence of God: A Homiletic from an Asian American Perspective*. Valley Forge, PA: Judson Press, 1999.

Kim, Grace Ji-Sun. *The Grace of Sophia: A Korean North American Women's Christology*. Cleveland: Pilgrim Press, 2002.

Kim, Jean. *Woman and Nation: An Intercontextual Reading of the Gospel of John*. Leiden: E. J. Brill, 2004.

Kim, Jung Ha. *Bridge-Makers and Cross-Bearers: Korean American Women and the Church*. Atlanta, GA: Scholars Press, 1997.

———, and Rosetta E. Ross. *The Status of Racial-Ethnic Minority Clergywomen in the United Methodist Church*. Nashville: General Board of Higher Education Press, 2004.

King, Ursula, ed. *Feminist Theology from the Third World*. Maryknoll, NY: Orbis Books, 1994.

Kinukawa, Hisako. *Women and Jesus in Mark: A Japanese Feminist Perspective*. Maryknoll, NY: Orbis Books, 1994.

Kwok, Pui-lan. *Chinese Women and Christianity, 1860–1927*. Atlanta, GA: Scholars Press, 1992.

———. *Discovering the Bible in the Non-biblical World*. Maryknoll, NY: Orbis Books, 1995.

———. *Introducing Asian Feminist Theology*. Cleveland: Pilgrim Press, 2000.

———. *Postcolonial Imagination and Feminist Theology*. Louisville, KY: Westminster John Knox Press, 2005.

Lee, Oo Chung. *In Search for Our Grandmothers' Spirituality*. Seoul: AWRC, 1994.

———, et al., eds. *Women of Courage: Asian Women Reading the Bible*. Seoul: AWRC, 1992.

Lee, Won Sul. *Beyond Ideology: A Christian Response to Sociopolitical Conflict in Asia*. Westchester, IL: Cornerstone Books, 1979.

Lewis, Nantawan Boonprasat, et al., eds. *Sisters Struggling in the Spirit: Women of Color's Theological Anthology*. Louisville, KY: Women's Ministries Program Area and Christian Faith and Life Program Area, Presbyterian Church USA, 1995.

Lozada, Rebecca, and Alison O'Grady, eds. *Creation and Spirituality: Asian Women Expressing Christian Faith through Art*. Hong Kong: Christian Conference of Asia, 1995.

Mananzan, Mary John. *Women, Religion, and Spirituality in Asia*. Manila: St. Scholastica's College, 2004.

———, ed. *Essays on Women*. Rev. ed. Manila: St. Scholastica's College, 1991.

———, ed. *Women and Religion*. Rev. ed. Manila: St. Scholastica's College, 1992.

———, et al., eds. *Women Resisting Violence: Spirituality for Life*. Maryknoll, NY: Orbis Books, 1996.

Min, Pyong Gap, and Jung Ha Kim, eds. *Religions in Asian America: Building Faith Communities*. Walnut Creek, CA: Altamira Press, 2002.

Monteiro, Evelyn, and Antoinette Gutzler, eds. *Ecclesia of Women in Asia: Gathering the Voices of the Silenced*. Delhi: ISPCK, 2005.

Ng, Greer Anne Wenh-In, ed. *Generations Trying to Live Together*. Toronto: United Church of Canada, 1995.

———, ed. *Our Roots, Our Lives: Glimpses of Faith and Life from Black and Asian Canadian Women*. Toronto: United Church Publishing House, 2003.

Orevillo-Montenegro, Muriel. *The Jesus of Asian Women*. Maryknoll, NY: Orbis Books, 2006.

Pachen, Ani. *Sorrow Mountain: The Journey of a Tibetan Warrior Nun*. New York: Kodansha International, 2000.

Pak, Su Yon, Unzu Lee, Jung Ha Kim, and Myung Ji Cho. *Singing the Lord's Song in a New Land: Korean American Practices of Faith*. Louisville, KY: Westminster John Knox Press, 2005.

Ralte, Lalrinawmi, and Evangeline Anderson-Rajkumar, eds. *Feminist Hermeneutics*. Delhi: ISPCK, 2002.

———, et al., eds. *Envisioning a New Heaven and a New Earth*. Delhi: ISPCK, 1998.

Rebera, Ranjini. *A Partnership of Equals: A Resource Guide for Asian Women*. Hong Kong: Christian Conference of Asia, 1995.

———, ed. *We Cannot Dream Alone: A Story of Women in Development*. Geneva: World Council of Churches, 1990.

Ruch, Barbara, ed. *Engendering Faith: Women and Buddhism in Premodern Japan*. Ann Arbor: Center for Japanese Studies, University of Michigan, 2002.

Ruether, Rosemary Radford, ed. *Women Healing Earth: Third-World Women on Ecology, Feminism, and Religion*. Maryknoll, NY: Orbis Books, 1996.

Ruiz-Duremdes, Sharon Rose Joy, and Wendy Koreker, eds. *Dance amid Struggle: Stories and Songs of Hope*. Quezon City: AWIT Publications, 1998.

Russell, Letty M., Kwok Pui-lan, Ada María Isasi-Díaz, and Katie Geneva Cannon, eds. *Inheriting Our Mothers' Gardens: Feminist Theology in Third World Perspective*. Philadelphia: Westminster Press, 1988.

Sharma, Arvind, ed. *Women in Indian Religions*. New Delhi: Oxford University Press, 2002.

Shaw, Miranda Eberle. *Buddhist Goddesses of India*. Princeton, NJ: Princeton University Press, 2006.

———. *Passionate Enlightenment: Women in Tantric Buddhism*. Princeton, NJ: Princeton University Press, 1994.

Slessarev-Jamir, Helene. *A Place of Refuge and Sustenance: How Faith Institutions Strengthen the Families of Poor Asian Immigrants*. Baltimore: Annie E. Casey Foundation, 2003.

Sugirtharajah, Sharada. *Imagining Hinduism: A Postcolonial Perspective*. London: Routledge, 2003.

Suh, Sharon A. *Being Buddhist in a Christian World: Gender and Community in a Korean American Temple*. Seattle: University of Washington Press, 2004.

Tsomo, Karma Lekshe, ed., *Buddhist Women across Cultures: Realizations*. Albany: State University of New York Press, 1999.

———, ed. *Buddhist Women and Social Justice: Ideals, Challenges, and Achievements*. Albany: State University of New York Press, 2004.

————, ed. *Innovative Buddhist Women: Swimming against the Stream*. Richmond, Surrey: Curzon, 2000.

Women's Concerns Unit, Christian Conference of Asia, ed. *Reading the Bible as Asian Women*. Singapore: Christian Conference of Asia, 1986.

Wong, Wai-Ching Angela. *"The Poor Woman": A Critical Analysis of Asian Theology and Contemporary Chinese Fiction by Women*. New York: Peter Lang, 2002.

Wu, Rose. *A Dissenting Church*. Hong Kong: Hong Kong Christian Institute, 2003.

————. *Liberating the Church from Fear: The Story of Hong Kong's Sexual Minorities*. Hong Kong: Hong Kong Women Christian Council, 2000.

Yamaguchi, Satoko. *Mary and Martha: Women in the World of Jesus*. Maryknoll, NY: Orbis Books, 2002.

Yee, Gale A. *Banished Children of Eve: Woman as Evil in the Hebrew Bible*. Minneapolis: Fortress Press, 2003.

Yoo, David, and Ruth Chung. *Mapping Korean American Religions*. New York: New York University Press, forthcoming.

Articles and Chapters

Antone, Hope S. "Asian Women and the Globalization of Labor." *Journal of Theologies and Cultures in Asia* 2 (2003): 97–111.

Asian EATWOT Women, "Towards a New Dawn: Asian Women's Theology and Spirituality." *Voices from the Third World* 26, no. 1 (2003): 136–42.

Baltazar, Stella. "Domestic Violence in Indian Perspective." In *Women Resisting Violence: Spirituality for Life*, edited by Mary John Mananzan et al. Maryknoll, NY: Orbis Books, 1996.

Banawiratma, J. B. "Women's Experience of the Sacred: Between Violence and Life." *Voices from the Third World* 19, no. 1 (1996): 144–58.

Barton, Mukti. "Race, Gender, Class and the Theology of Empowerment: An Indian Perspective." In *Gender, Religion, and Diversity: Cross-Cultural Perspectives*, edited by Ursula King and Tina Beattie. London: Continuum, 2005.

Bong, Sharon A. "The Suffering Christ and the Asian Body." In *Feminism and Theology*, edited by Janet Martin Soskice and Diana Lipton. Oxford: Oxford University Press, 2003.

Brock, Rita Nakashima. "Critical Reflections on Asian American Religious Identity: Response—Clearing the Tangled Vines." *Amerasia Journal* 22, no. 1 (1996): 181–86.

————. "Dusting the Bible on the Floor: A Hermeneutics of Wisdom." In *Searching the Scriptures*. Vol. 1, *Feminist Introduction*, edited by Elisabeth Schüssler Fiorenza. New York: Crossroad, 1993.

————. "Facing Sexual Exploitation: Understanding Prostitution in Asia and the United States." *Journal of Asian and Asian American Theology* 2, no. 1 (1997): 4–20.

————. "Fantastic Coherence." *Journal of Feminist Studies in Religion* 21, no. 1 (2005): 155–73.

————. "Interstitial Integrity: Reflections toward an Asian American Woman's Theology." In *Introduction to Christian Theology*, edited by Roger Badham. Louisville, KY: Westminster John Knox Press, 1998.

————. "On Mirrors, Mists, Murmurs and the Way to an Asian American Theology." In *Weaving the Visions: New Patterns in Feminist Spirituality*, edited by Judith Plaskow and Carol P. Christ. San Francisco: Harper & Row, 1989.

————. "Private, Public, and Somewhere in Between: Lessons from the History of Asian-Pacific American Women." *Journal of Feminist Studies in Religion* 12, no. 1 (1996): 127–32.

———, and Nami Kim. "Asian American Protestant Women: Roles and Contributions in Religion." In *Encyclopedia of Women and Religion in North America*, edited by Rosemary Radford Ruether and Rosemary Keller. Bloomington: Indiana University Press, 2006.

———, Rebecca Ann Parker, David Blumenthal, Traci C. West, Jung Ha Kim, and Marie M. Fortune. "A Witness for/from Life: Writing Feminist Theology as an Act of Resisting Violence—Responses to *Proverbs of Ashes: Violence, Redemptive Suffering, and the Search for What Saves Us*." *Journal of Religion and Abuse* 4, no. 2 (2002): 69–96.

Bundang, Rachel A. R. "Adventures in Baby-Naming: Ministering to the Spiritual but Not Religious." http://www.bustedhalo.com/archive/2003_1work.htm.

———. "Home as Memory, Metaphor, and Promise in Asian American Religious Experience." *Semeia* 90/91 (2002): 87–104.

———. "Scars ARE History: Colonialism, Written on the Body." In *Feminist/Womanist Perspectives on Religion, Colonization, and Sexual Violence*, edited by Nantawan Boonprasat Lewis and Marie M. Fortune. New York: Haworth Pastoral Press, 1999.

———. "Spiritual Brain Drain: A Perspective on the Cost of Denying Women Ordination." http://www.bustedhalo.com/archive/2003_30work.htm.

———. "This Is Not Your Mother's Catholic Church: When Filipino Catholicism Meets American Culture." In *Pinay Power: "Peminist" Critical Theory*, edited by Melinda de Jesús. New York: Routledge, 2005.

———, ed. The special issue on selected proceedings of the 1996 PANAAWTM meeting. *In God's Image* 16, no. 4 (December 1997).

Chai, Alice Yun. "The Struggle of Asian and Asian American Women toward a Total Liberation: A Korean Methodist Woman's Vocational Journey." In *Spirituality and Social Responsibility: Vocational Vision of Women in the United Methodist Tradition*, edited by Rosemary Skinner Keller. Nashville: Abingdon Press, 1993.

Chai, Karen. "Beyond 'Strictness' to Distinctiveness: Generational Transition in Korean Protestant Churches." In *Korean Americans and Their Religions: Pilgrims and Missionaries from a Different Shore*, edited by H. Y. Kwon, K. C. Kim, and R. S. Werner. University Park: Pennsylvania State University Press, 2001.

———. "Competing for the Second Generation: English-Language Ministry at a Korean Protestant Church." In *Gathering in Diaspora: Religious Communities and the New Immigration*, edited by R. Stephen Warner and Judith G. Wittner. Philadelphia: Temple University Press, 1998.

Chakkalakal, Pauline. "Asian Women Reshaping Theology: Challenges and Hopes." *Feminist Theology* 27 (May 2001): 21–36.

———. "Women in Participatory Structures in the Church and Formation of the Laity." *Voices from the Third World* 26, no. 1 (2003): 121–35.

Chen, Hannah. "Circumcision by a Pagan Woman: A Fresh Look at Exodus 4: 24–26." *CTC* (Christian Conference of Asia) *Bulletin* 20, no. 2 (2004): 40–49.

Choi, Man Ja. "Feminine Images of God in Korean Traditional Religion." In *Frontiers in Asian Christian Theology: Emerging Trends*, edited by R. S. Sugirtharajah. Maryknoll, NY: Orbis Books, 1994.

Choi, Young-Sil. "'Prostitutes' and 'Prostitution': What Does John 8:1–11 Say about Them?" *Madang: International Journal of Contextual Theology in East Asia* 1, no. 2 (2004): 81–90.

Chu, Julie Li-Chuan. "Returning Home: The Inspiration of the Role Dedifferentiation in the Book of Ruth for Taiwanese Women." *Semeia* 78 (1997): 47–53.

Chun, Wendy Hui Kyong. "Orienting Orientalism, or How to Map Cyberspace." In *AsianAmerica.Net: Ethnicity, Nationalism, and Cyberspace*, edited by Rachel Lee and Sauling Cynthia Wong. New York: Routledge, 2003.

Chung, Hyun Kyung. "Asian Christologies and People's Religions." *Voices from the Third World* 19, no. 1 (1996): 214–27.

———. "Come, Holy Spirit—Renew the Whole Creation." In *Signs of the Spirit, Official Report, Seventh Assembly*, edited by Michael Kinnamon. Geneva: World Council of Churches, 1991.

———. "Popular Religion and Fullness of Life: An Asian Eco-feminist Reflection." *CTC* (Christian Conference of Asia) *Bulletin* 18, no. 1 (2002): 47–55.

———. "Your Comfort vs. My Death." In *Women Resisting Violence: Spirituality for Life*, edited by Mary John Mananzan et al. Maryknoll, NY: Orbis Books, 1996.

Chung, Mee-Hyun. "Korean Feminist Ecclesiology: A Wholistic Approach." *Madang: International Journal of Contextual Theology in East Asia* 5 (June 2006): 83–104.

Dietrich, Gabriele. "South Asian Feminist Theory and Its Significance for Feminist Theology." In *Feminist Theology in Different Contexts*, edited by Elisabeth Schüssler Fiorenza and M. Shawn Copeland. Concilium 1996, no. 1. Maryknoll, NY: Orbis Books, 1996, 101–15.

———. "Why Does Post-colonial Feminist Theology Need to Relate to People's Movements?" *Asia Journal of Theology* 19, no. 1 (2005): 166–87.

Doi, Joanne. "Tule Lake Pilgrimage: Dissonant Memories, Sacred Journey." In *Revealing the Sacred in Asian and Pacific America*, edited by Jane Naomi Iwamura and Paul Spickard. New York: Routledge, 2003.

Fabella, Virgina. "Christology and Popular Religions." *Voices from the Third World* 18, no. 2 (1995): 22–37.

Gnanadason, Aruna. "Asian Theological Methodology: An Overview." *Voices from the Third World* 18, no. 1 (1995): 83–101.

———. "A Church in Solidarity with Women: Utopia or Symbol of Faithfulness?" In *Feminist Theology in Different Contexts*, edited by Elisabeth Schüssler Fiorenza and M. Shawn Copeland. Concilium 1996, no. 1. Maryknoll, NY: Orbis Books, 1996, 74–80.

———. "Feminist Theology: An Indian Perspective." *Asia Journal of Theology* 2, no. 1 (1988): 109–18.

———. "Jesus and the Asian Woman: A Post-colonial Look at the Syro-Phoenician Woman/Canaanite Woman from an Indian Perspective." *Studies in World Christianity* 7, no. 2 (2001): 162–77.

———. "A Spirituality That Sustains Us in Our Struggles." *International Review of Mission* 80, no. 317 (1991): 29–41.

———. "Yes, Creator God, Transform the Earth! The Earth as God's Body in an Age of Environmental Violence." *Ecumenical Review* 57, no. 2 (2005): 159–70.

Gupta, Lina. "Kali, the Savior." In *After Patriarchy: Feminist Transformations of the World Religions*, edited by Paula M. Cooey, William R. Eakin, and Jay B. McDaniel. Maryknoll, NY: Orbis Books, 1991.

Ho, Wan-Li. "Chinese Religion and Liberation Theology." In *Liberation Theology within World Religions*, edited by Miguel A. De La Torre. Waco, TX: Baylor University Press, forthcoming.

———. "Environmental Protection as Religious Action: The Case of Taiwanese Buddhist Women." *In Ecofeminism and Globalization: Exploring Culture, Context, and Religion*, edited by Heather Eaton and Lois Ann Lorentzen. Lanham, MD: Rowman & Littlefield, 2003.

———. "Respecting Our Ancestors: Christianity and the Confucian Tradition." *Commonweal* 134 (January 14, 2005): 10–11.

In God's Image. Quarterly journal published by AWRC, address: 79 Lorong Anggor, Taman Shanghai, 58100, Kuala Lumpur, Malaysia.

Iwamura, Jane Naomi. "Altared States: Exploring the Legacy of Japanese American Butsudan Practice." *Pacific World: Journal of the Institute of Buddhist Studies* 3, no. 5 (2003): 275–91.

———. "Critical Faith: Japanese Americans and the Birth of a New Civil Religion," *American Quarterly* (forthcoming).

———. "The 'Hidden Manna' That Sustains: Reading Revelation 2:17 in Joy Kogawa's *Obasan*." *Semeia* 90/91 (2002): 161–79.

Joh, Wonhee Anne. "The Transgressive Power of *Jeong*: A Postcolonial Hybridization of Christology." In *Postcolonial Theologies: Divinity and Empire*, edited by Catherine Keller, Michael Nausner, and Mayra Rivera. St. Louis, MO: Chalice Press, 2004.

Kang, Nam-Soon. "Confucian Familism and Its Social/Religious Embodiment in Christianity: Reconsidering the Family Discourse from a Feminist Perspective." *Asia Journal of Theology* 18, no. 1 (2004): 168–89.

———. "Creating 'Dangerous Memory': Challenges for Asian and Korean Feminist Theology." *Ecumenical Review* 47, no. 1 (1995): 21–31.

———. "Who/What Is Asian? A Postcolonial Theological Reading of Orientalism and Neo-Orientalism." In *Postcolonial Theologies: Divinity and Empire*, edited by Catherine Keller, Michael Nausner, and Mayra Rivera. St. Louis, MO: Chalice Press, 2004.

Katoppo, Henriette. "Asian Theology: An Asian Woman's Perspective." In *Asian's Struggle for Full Humanity*, edited by Virginia Fabella. Maryknoll, NY: Orbis Books, 1980.

Kim, Eunjoo Mary. "Hermeneutics and Asian American Preaching." *Semeia* 90/91 (2002): 269–90.

Kim, Grace Ji-Sun. "Weaving a Korean North American Women's Theological Method." *Journal of Asian and Asian American Theology* 5 (Spring 2002): 65–80.

Kim, Jung Ha. "At the Table of an Asian American Banquet." *Semeia* 90/91 (2002): 325–37.

———. "But Who Do You Say That I Am? (Matt 16:15): A Churched Korean American Woman's Autobiographical Inquiry." In *Journey at the Margin: Toward an Autobiographical Theology in American-Asian Perspective*, edited by Peter C. Phan and Jung Young Lee. Collegeville, MN: Liturgical Press, 1999.

———. "The Impact of National Histories on the Politics of Identity." *Journal of Asian and Asian American Theology* 2, no. 1 (1997): 113–18.

———. "The Labor of Compassion: Voices of Churched Korean American Women." In *New Spiritual Homes: Religion and Asian Americans*, edited by David K. Yoo. Honolulu: University of Hawai'i Press, 1999.

———. "The Restoried Lives: The Everyday Theology of Korean American Never-Married Women." In *Mapping Korean American Religions*, edited by David Yoo and Ruth Chung. New York: New York University Press, forthcoming.

———. "Sources Outside of Europe." In *Spirituality and the Secular Quest*, edited by Peter H. Van Ness. New York: Crossroad, 1996.

———. "A Voice from 'the Borderlands': Asian-American Women and the Families." In *Religion, Feminism and the Family*, edited by Anne Carr and Mary Stewart Van Leeuwen. Louisville, KY: Westminster John Knox Press, 1996.

Kim, Nami. "'My/Our' Comfort *Not* at the Expense of 'Somebody Else's': Toward a Critical Global Feminist Theology." *Journal of Feminist Studies in Religion* 21, no. 2 (2005): 75–94.

———. "Response." *Journal of Feminist Studies in Religion* 21, no. 1 (Spring 2005): 137–41.

———. "Women, the Ba-ram Bearers: Asian Feminist Spiritualities." In *In the Power of Wisdom: Feminist Spiritualities for Struggle*, edited by María Pilar Aquino and Elisabeth Schüssler Fiorenza. Concilium 2000, no. 1. London: SCM Press, 2000, 13–22.

Kim, Rebecca Y. "Made in the U.S.A.: Second-Generation Korean American Campus Evangelicals." In *Asian American Youth: Culture, Identity, and Ethnicity*, edited by Jennifer Lee and Min Zhou. New York: Routledge, 2004.

Kim, Seong Hee. "Rupturing the Empire: Reading the Poor Widow as a Postcolonial Female Subject (Mark 12:41–44)." *European Electronic Journal for Feminist Exegesis* 1 (2006). http://www.lectio.unibe.ch/06_1/kim_rupturing.htm.

Kinukawa, Hisako. "'. . . and your God my God': How We Can Nurture Openness to Other Faiths (Ruth 1:1–19 Read from a Feminist Perspective of a Multi-faith Community)." In *Scripture, Community, and Mission: Essays in Honor of D. Preman Niles*. Hong Kong: Christian Conference of Asia, 2003.

———. "Biblical Studies in the Twenty-first Century: A Japanese/Asian Feminist Glimpse." In *Feminist New Testament Studies: Global and Future Perspectives*, edited by Kathleen O'Brien Wicker, Althea Spencer Miller, and Musa W. Dube. New York: Palgrave Macmillan, 2005.

———. "De-colonizing Ourselves as Readers: The Story of the Syro-Phoenician Woman as a Text." In *Distant Voices Drawing Near: Essays in Honor of Antoinette Clark Wire*, edited by Holly E. Hearon. Collegeville, MN: Liturgical Press, 2004.

———. "Looking at the Web: A Political Analysis of Personal Context and Its Relationship to Global Context." *Journal of Asian and Asian American Theology* 2, no. 1 (1997): 51–63.

Kwok, Pui-lan. "Business Ethics in the Economic Development of Asia: A Feminist Analysis." *Asia Journal of Theology* 9, no. 1 (1995): 133–45.

———. "Chinese Women and Protestant Christianity at the Turn of the Twentieth Century." In *Christianity in China*, edited by Daniel H. Bays. Stanford, CA: Stanford University Press, 1996.

———. "Discovering the Bible in the Non-biblical World: The Journey Continues." *Journal of Asian and Asian American Theology* 2, no. 1 (1997): 64–77.

———. "Ecology and Christology." *Feminist Theology* 15 (1997): 113–25.

———. "The Feminist Hermeneutics of Elisabeth Schüssler Fiorenza: An Asian Feminist Response." *East Asia Journal of Theology* 3, no. 2 (1985): 147–53.

———. "Feminist Theology from a Chinese Perspective." In *Towards a Chinese Feminist Theology*, edited by Winnie Ho. Hong Kong: Lutheran Theological Seminary, 1988.

———. "The Future of Feminist Theology: An Asian Perspective." *Voices from the Third World* 15, no. 1 (1992): 141–61.

———. "God Weeps with Our Pain." *East Asia Journal of Theology* 2, no. 2 (1984): 228–32.

———. "Liberation Theology in the Twenty-first Century." In *Opting for the Margins: Postmodernity and Liberation in Christian Theology*, edited by Joerg Rieger. Oxford: Oxford University Press, 2003.

————, and Rachel A. R. Bundang. "PANAAWTM Lives!" *Journal of Feminist Studies in Religion* 21, no. 2 (2005): 147–58.

————, ed. "Asian and Asian American Women's Voices." Special issue, *Journal of Asian and Asian American Theology* 2, no. 1 (1997).

L, Jayachitra. "Deconstructing Christ-Church Model: Enhancing the Dignity of Dalit Women in India." *CTC* (Christian Conference of Asia) *Bulletin* 20, no. 3 (2004): 14–20.

Lee, Boyung. "Brown Women in Need of Salvation from Brown Men? The Myth of Individualism and New Selfhood for Korean Women." *Ewha Journal of Feminist Theology* 4 (Fall 2006): 185–208.

————. "Caring-Self and Women's Self-Esteem: A Feminist's Reflection on Pastoral Care and Religious Education of Korean-American Women." *Pastoral Psychology* 54, no. 4 (March 2006): 337–53.

————. "Challenging *Pax Americana*: A Postcolonial Way of Teaching the Bible." In *Empires in the Bible—The Empire Today*, edited by A. Bieler, K. Butting, G. Minnaard, and L. Schottroff. Wittingen, Germany: Verlag Erev-Rav, 2006.

————. "From a Margin within the Margin: Rethinking the Dynamics of Christianity and Culture from a Postcolonial Feminist Perspective." *Journal of Theologies and Cultures of Asia* 3 (March 2004): 3–23.

————. "Teaching Justice and Living Peace: Body, Sexuality and Religious Education in Asian American Communities." *Religious Education* 101, no. 3 (Summer 2006): 402–19.

————. "When the Text Is the Problem: A Postcolonial Approach to Biblical Pedagogy." *Religious Education* (forthcoming, Winter 2007).

Lee, Kyung Sook, "'God' in Wisdom Literature from the Perspectives of Asian Feminist Theology." *Quest: An Interdisciplinary Journal for Asian Christian Scholars* 3, no. 1 (2004): 61–73.

Lee, Sung-Hee. "Women's Liberation Theology as the Foundation for Asian Theology." *East Asia Journal of Theology* 4, no. 2 (1986): 2–13.

Lewis, Nantawan Boonprasat. "Asian Women's Theology: A Historical and Theological Analysis." *East Asia Journal of Theology* 4, no. 1 (1986): 18–22.

————. "The Connection of Uneven Development, Capitalism, and Patriarchy: A Case of Prostitution in Asia." In *The Power of Naming*, edited by Elisabeth Schüssler Fiorenza. Maryknoll, NY: Orbis Books, 1996.

————. "Human Rights for Asian Women: Toward a Fuller Actualization." In *Human Rights and the Global Mission of the Church*. Boston Theological Institute Annual Series 1. Boston: Boston Theological Institute, 1988.

————. "On Naming Justice: The Spiritual and Political Connection in Violence against Asian Immigrant Women." In *Toward a New Heaven and a New Earth: Essays in Honor of Elisabeth Schüssler Fiorenza*, edited by Fernando F. Segovia. Maryknoll, NY: Orbis Books, 2004.

————. "Reclaiming Liberative Trends: Owning Asian American Women's History of Struggle." In *Revolution of Spirit*, edited by Nantawan Boonprasat Lewis. Grand Rapids: Wm. B. Eerdmans Publishing Co., 1998.

————. "Remembering Conquest: Religion, Colonization and Sexual Violence: A Thai Experience." In *Feminist/Womanist Perspectives on Religion, Colonization, and Sexual Violence*, edited by Nantawan Boonprasat Lewis and Marie M. Fortune. New York: Haworth Pastoral Press, 1999.

————. "Toward an Ethic of Feminist Liberation and Empowerment: A Case Study of Prostitution in Thailand." In *Christian Ethics in Ecumenical Context*, edited by Shin Chiba, George R. Hunsberger, and Lester Edwin J. Ruiz. Grand Rapids: Wm. B. Eerdmans Publishing Co., 1995.

Liew, Tat-siong Benny, ed. "The Bible in Asian America." *Semeia* 90/91 (2002).

Mananzan, Mary John. "Feminist Theology in Asia: A Ten Years' Overview." *Feminist Theology* 10 (1995): 21–32.

————. "Gender Dialogue in EATWOT—An Asian Perspective." *Voices from the Third World* 19, no. 1 (1996): 57–83.

————. "Globalization from the Perspectives of the Victims: Survivors of History." In *Time—Utopia—Eschatology*, Yearbook of European Women in Theological Research, no. 7, edited by Charlotte Methuen. Louvain: Peeters, 1999.

————. "Who Is Jesus Christ?" *Voices from the Third World* 11, no. 2 (1988): 1–16.

"Mapping a Pan-Pacific Feminist Theology." Special issue of *Journal of Women and Religion* 13 (1995).

Moore, Mary Elizabeth, Boyung Lee, Kathleen Turpin, Ralph Casas, Lynn Bridgers, and Veronice Miles. "Realities, Visions and Promises of a Multicultural Future." *Religious Education* 99, no. 3 (2004): 287–315.

Ng, Greer Anne Wenh-In. "Asian Sociocultural Values: Oppressive and Liberating Aspects from a Woman's Perspective." In *People on the Way: Asian North Americans Discovering Christ, Culture, and Community*, edited by David Ng. Valley Forge, PA: Judson Press, 1996.

————. "Crossing Oceans, Crossing Disciplines: Doing Theology as Asians in Diaspora." In *Ecumenism in Asia: Essays in Honor of Feliciano Carino*, edited by K. C. Abraham. Bangalore: Board of Theological Education of the Senate of Serampore College, 1999.

————. "Inclusive Language in Asian North American Churches: Non-issue or Null Curriculum." *Journal of Asian and Asian American Theology* 20, no. 1 (1997): 21–36.

————. "Reading through New Eyes: A Basic Introduction to Reading Scripture from a Feminist, Postcolonial Perspective for Anti-racism Work." *Making Waves* 4, no. 2 (Summer 2004): 27–29.

————. "Toward Gender Justice: Challenges in Human Living from a Confucian-Christian Perspective." *Ching Feng* 41, nos. 3–4 (1998): 345–61.

————. "Toward Wholesome Nurture: Challenges in the Religious Education of Asian North American Female Christians." *Religious Education* 91, no. 2 (1996): 238–54.

Niles, Damayanthi M. A. "Theology and Ecumenical Life in a Global Age: Concerns, Challenges and Coalitions for a New Generation." *Asia Journal of Theology* 18, no. 2 (2004): 310–19.

Ohnuma, Reiko. "Mother Love and Mother Grief: South Asian Buddhist Variations on a Theme." *Journal of Feminist Studies in Religion* 23, no. 1 (2007): 95–116.

————. "Woman, Bodhisattva, and Buddha." *Journal of Feminist Studies in Religion* 17, no. 1 (2001): 63–83.

Orevillo-Montenegro, Muriel. "Shall I Cling to the Old Rugged Cross? Interrogating and Re-thinking the Power of the Cross." *CTC* (Christian Conference of Asia) *Bulletin* 20, no. 3 (2004): 1–13.

PAACCE. Newsletter of Pacific Asian American/Canadian Christian Education Ministries, National Council of Churches USA, New York.

Pacific People. Newsletter of Pacific and Asian American Center for Theology and Strategies, Berkeley, California.

Pak, Young Mi Angela. "Faith as an Autobiographical Strategy: Understanding the Lives of Two Korean Christian Immigrant Women." *Journal of Asian and Asian American Theology* 2, no. 1 (1997): 37–50.

Park, Kyungmi. "A Preview of Challenges for Asian Feminist Theology in the Twenty-first Century." *PTCA Bulletin* 13, nos. 1–2 (2000): 7–15.

Park, Sun Ai Lee. "Envisioning a Future Church as an Asian Women." *Voices from the Third World* 12, no. 1 (1989): 64–94.

———. "Understanding the Bible from Women's Perspective." *Voices form the Third World* 10, no. 2 (1987): 66–75.

Perera, Marlene. "Towards the Twenty-first Century—An Asian Woman's Emerging Perceptions on Mission." *International Review of Mission* 81, no. 322 (1992): 227–36.

Say Pa, Anna May. "Chorus of Voices: Reading the Bible from Many Perspectives." *CTC* (Christian Conference of Asia) *Bulletin* 21, no. 3 (2005): 59–70.

——— (also known as Anna May Chain). "Wives, Warriors and Leaders: Burmese Christian Women's Cultural Reception of the Bible." *SBL Forum.* http://www.sbl-site.org/Article.aspx?ArticleId=455.

Sebastian, Mrinalini. "Reading Archives from a Postcolonial Feminist Perspective: 'Native' Bible Women and the Missionary Zeal." *Journal of Feminist Studies in Religion* 19, no. 1 (2003): 5–25.

Southard, Naomi P. F. "Recovery and Rediscovered Images: Spiritual Resources for Asian American Women." In *Feminist Theology from the Third World*, edited by Ursula King. Maryknoll, NY: Orbis Books, 1994.

Southard, Naomi, and Rita Nakashima Brock. "The Other Half of the Basket: Asian American Women and the Search for a Theological Home." *Journal of Feminist Studies in Religion* 3, no. 2 (1987): 135–49.

Steffi, San Buenaventura. "Filipino Folk Spirituality and Immigration: From Mutual Aid to Religion." *Amerasia Journal* 22, no. 1 (1996): 217–32.

Sugirtharajah, Sharada. "Courtly Text and Courting *Sati*." *Journal of Feminist Studies in Religion* 17, no. 1 (2001): 5–32.

———."Hinduism and Feminism: Some Concerns." *Journal of Feminist Studies in Religion* 18, no. 2 (2002): 97–104.

Tapia, Elizabeth. "Asian Women Doing Theology: The Challenge of Feminism for Theologizing." In *Dance amid Struggle: Stories and Songs of Hope*, edited by Sharon Rose Joy Ruiz-Duremdes and Wendy Kroeker. Quezon City, Philippines: AWIT Publications, 1998.

Tiemeier, Tracy Sayuki. "Retrieving 'Asian Spirituality' in North American Contexts: An Interfaith Proposal." *Spiritus* 6 (2006): 228–33.

Wong, Wai-Ching Angela. "Asian Theologians between East and West: A Postcolonial Self-Understanding." *Jian Dao* 8 (1997): 89–102.

———. "History, Identity and a Community of *Hesed*: A Biblical Reflection on Ruth 1:1–17." *Asia Journal of Theology* 13, no. 1 (1999): 3–13.

———. "Negotiating for a Postcolonial Identity: Theology of 'the Poor Woman' in Asia." *Journal of Feminist Studies in Religion* 18, no. 2 (2002): 5–23.

Wu, Rose. "1997 and the Destiny of the Hong Kong People." *Voices from the Third World* 20, no. 2 (1997): 120–42.

————. "Women on the Boundary: Prostitution, Contemporary and in the Bible." *Feminist Theology* 28 (2001): 69–81.

Xu, Judith Chuan. "Poststructuralist Feminism and the Problem of Femininity in the *Daodejing*." *Journal of Feminist Studies in Religion* 19, no. 1 (2003): 47–64.

Yang, Seung Ai. "Asian Americans." In *Handbook of U.S. Theologies of Liberation*, edited by Miguel A. De La Torre. St. Louis, MO: Chalice Press, 2004.

————. "Jesus' Saying on Divorce: A Korean Perspective." *The Bible Today* 35 (January 1997): 49–54.

Yap, Boon Kiat Natalie. "Religion and Gender Relations, with Special Reference to the Presbyterian Church in Singapore." *Asia Journal of Theology* 11, no. 1 (1997): 45–53.

Yee, Gale A. "The Impact of National Histories on the Politics of Identity." *Journal of Asian and Asian American Theology* 2, no. 1 (1997): 108–12.

————. "'She Stood in Tears amid the Alien Corn': Ruth, the Perpetual Foreigner and Model Minority." In *They Were All Together in One Place? Toward Minority Biblical Criticism*, ed. Randall C. Bailey, Tat-siong Benny Liew, and Fernando F. Segovia. Semeia Studies 57. Atlanta: Society of Biblical Literature, forthcoming.

————. "Yin/Yang Is Not Me: An Exploration into an Asian American Biblical Hermeneutics." In *Ways of Being, Ways of Knowing: Asian American Biblical Interpretation*, edited by Mary F. Foskett and Jeffrey Kah-Jin Kuan. St. Louis, MO: Chalice, 2006.

Yi, Young-Suk. "Saeng-myun Feminism: An Attempt to Localize Eco-feminism." *Madang: International Journal of Contextual Theology in East Asia* 5 (June 2006): 63–82.

Yoo, Yani. "*Han*-Laden Women: Korean 'Comfort Women' and Women in Judges 19–21." *Semeia* 78 (1997): 37–46.

————. "How the Powerful Play Their Bible Game (Numbers 12)." *CTC* (Christian Conference of Asia) *Bulletin* 20, no. 3 (2004): 21–26.

Films and Documentaries

Between the Lines: Asian American Women's Poetry. VHS. New York: Women Make Movies, 2001, 65 min. (Presents poetry readings and interviews with fifteen major Asian Pacific American women poets who speak of personal experiences of immigration and how these events have shaped their writing.)

The Displaced View. VHS. A film by Midi Onodera, 1988, 52 min. (Traces a granddaughter's search for identity within the suppressed history of the Japanese American internment camps in North America.)

Gabriela. VHS. A film by Trix Betlam. New York: Women Make Movies, 1988, 67 min. (Looks at the work of Gabriela, a mass organization of diverse women's groups in the Philippines. Gabriela was founded in 1984 in honor of Gabriela Silans, a Filipina nationalist who fought against the Spanish occupation.)

Japanese American Women: A Sense of Place. VHS. A documentary by Rosanna Yamagiwa Alfaro and Leita Hagemann. New York: Women Make Movies, 1991, 27 min. (Japanese American women describe their experiences of growing up in America and being neither Japanese nor American and their search for a sense of ethnic identification.)

Memory/All Echo. VHS. A film by Yun-ah Hong. New York: Women Make Movies, 1990, 27 min. (Based on the late Korean American writer Theresa Hak Kyung Cha's DICTEE. The film explores cultural identity and displacement through an evocative blend of fiction and autobiography.)

Mitsuye and Nellie: Asian American Poets. VHS. San Francisco: Light-Saraf Films, 1981, 58 min. (This film is about two feminist poets and friends, Mitsuye Yamada and Nellie Wong. They recite their poetry and discuss their upbringing.)

My America, or Honk If You Love Buddha. VHS. Produced by Quynh Thai. Directed by Renee Tajima-Peña. Los Angeles: National Asian American Telecommunications, 1996, 87 min. (The film records the voices and personalities of Asian Americans from China-town, New York, to a debutante hall in Anaheim, California.)

My Journey, My Islam. VHS. A film by Kay Rasool. New York: Women Make Movies, 1999, 56 min. (Through interviews with Muslim women in Australia, India, Pakistan, and Britain, this film documents how they reconcile and interpret the requirements of their faith and the obligations of Western culture.)

Searching for Go-Hyang. VHS. A film by Tammy Tolle, 1998, 32 min. (Traces the return of twin sisters to their native Korea after a fourteen-year absence. Sent away by their par- ents for the promise of a better life in the United States, they instead suffered mental and physical abuse by their adoptive parents.)

Sin City Diary. VHS. Produced, written, and directed by Rachel Rivera. New York: Women Make Movies, 1998, 29 min. (Examines the lives of women prostitutes working near the U.S. Navy base at Subic Bay in the Philippines, before it was closed, and the plight of Amer-Asian children.)

Slaying the Dragon. VHS. Produced and directed by Deborah Gee. San Francisco: Crosscur-rent Media, 1988, 60 min. (This film analyzes the roles and images of Asian women promulgated by the Hollywood film industry and network television over the past fifty years.)

Subrosa. VHS. A film by Helen Lee. New York: Women Make Movies, 2000, 22 min. (Traces a journey to South Korea, the land of a Korean adoptee's birth, to find her birth mother she has never known.)

Surname Viet Given Name Nam. VHS. Directed, written, and translated by Trinh T. Minh-ha. New York: Women Make Movies, 1989, 108 min. (Vietnamese and Vietnamese American women's lives using a pastiche of interviews, still photos, historical film footage, music, and poetry.)

A Tale of Love. VHS. Produced by Trinh T. Minh-ha and Jean-Paul Bourdier. Directed by Trinh T. Minh-ha. Berkeley: Moongift Films, 1995, 108 min. (Inspired by "The Tale of Kieu" and set in America, the film portrays the Vietnamese immigrant experience through the writer Kieu.)

Through Chinese Women's Eyes. VHS. Produced, written, and directed by Mayfair Mei-hui Yang. New York: Women Make Movies, 1997, 53 min. (A survey of the changes in women's lives in Shanghai, China, as Shanghai regains its former status as the com-mercial center of Asia.)

Two Lies. VHS. Produced, written, and directed by Pam Tom. New York: Women Make Movies, 1990, 25 min. (Examines the stressful relationship between two young Chi-nese American girls and their relationship with their mother, who is having plastic surgery performed to alter her oriental features.)

Additional resources can be found on the Pacific, Asian, and North Ameri-can Asian Women in Theology and Ministry Web site, www.panaawtm.org.

Contributors

Rita Nakashima Brock is founding codirector of Faith Voices for the Common Good and Senior Editor in Religion at The New Press. She was a professor for twenty years and directed the Radcliffe Fellowship Program from 1997 to 2001. An award-winning author, she has lectured throughout the world. Her favorite activity at home is dinner parties for friends, for whom she improvises panethnic meals without recipes.

Rachel A. R. Bundang is Bannan Fellow at Santa Clara University's Bannan Institute for Jesuit Educational Mission and the Department of Religious Studies. Trained in Christian ethics, she teaches and writes on feminist ethics and theologies, Catholic moral theology, and Asian Pacific American (APA) religiosity. Her most recent work has appeared in *Semeia*, the *Journal of Feminist Studies in Religion*, and the collection *Pinay Power: "Peminist" Critical Theory*. She is also a consultant on issues such as race and religion, religious pluralism, and liturgy. Her current project proposes disruptive personhood as a corrective to the erased self in APA feminist theoethics.

Anne Dondapati Allen is a doctoral candidate at the University of Denver and Iliff School of Theology in the area of religion and psychological studies in Denver, Colorado. As an Indian Christian woman, she is particularly interested in studying the intersections of faith and gender as they pertain to Christian women in India. An ordained American Baptist minister, she is active in the Justice Commission of the Colorado Council of Churches. A native of South India, Dondapati is partial to the South Indian *Thali*, a platter with an assortment of savory South Indian delights.

Wan-Li Ho received her Ph.D. in religion from Temple University and is currently a lecturer in Chinese and Chinese religion at Emory University. Her research interests include Chinese religion and comparative thought, Asian studies, and comparative ecofeminism; she specializes in Chinese religious women and social activism. She has coauthored *The Tao of Jesus: An Experiment in Inter-religious Understanding* and published numerous articles. She is currently working on a book on environmental activism among religious women in her native Taiwan. She loves yams because they are rich in nutrition and because they are shaped like Taiwan.

Jane Naomi Iwamura is assistant professor of religion and American studies and ethnicity at the University of Southern California. She has published articles on Asian American religions and religious experience, as well as on the representation of Asian religions in American popular culture, in *Semeia*, *Pacific World*, the *Journal of Asian American Studies*, and in the volume *Religion and Popular Culture in America*. She is coeditor of *Revealing the Sacred in Asian and Pacific America* and is currently working on her monograph, "The Oriental Monk in American Popular Culture: Race, Religion, and Representation in the Age of Virtual Orientalism." She is also a cofounder and managing board member of the Asian Pacific Americans and Religion Research Initiative (APARRI) and former cochair of the Asian North American Religions, Culture, and Society Group of the American Academy of Religion.

Wonhee Anne Joh is assistant professor of theology at Phillips Theological Seminary in Tulsa, Oklahoma. Her current research areas include postcolonial theory, poststructuralist psychoanalysis, and violence and nonviolence. She is interested in finding ways to best theorize and theologize violence that occurs within the oppositional relational constructs that are often at the basis of subjectivity, from individuals to social structure to the identity of the nation-state. She is author of *Heart of the Cross: A Postcolonial Christology*. She loves to make dessert her main meal, and she is a recent convert to becoming a lacto-ovo vegetarian.

Jung Ha Kim is a sociologist at Georgia State University and has published in the areas of Asian American religion and spirituality, the Korean American church, women and religion, Asian American women's agency and leadership roles in *Amerasia Journal*, *Voices from the Third World*, *Semeia*, and edited volumes. Her books include *Bridge-*

Makers and Cross-Bearers, Religions in Asian America, and *Singing the Lord's Song in a New Land: Korean American Practices of Faith*. She is cochair of the Women and Religion Section of the American Academy of Religion and works with a grassroots organization, the Center for Pan Asian Community Services, Inc. (CPACS). She is not a "purist"; she enjoys good pan-Asian fusion food.

Nami Kim is assistant professor of religion in the Department of Philosophy and Religious Studies at Spelman College in Atlanta, Georgia. She has published several articles interrogating the unifying category "Asian" in theological discourse. Her current research interests include "megachurch" phenomena on college campuses and a critical global, feminist theology as a resisting voice to the transnational alliance of the Religious Right. Recently she has added deep-fried calamari taco to her long list of favorite foods.

Kwok Pui-lan is William F. Cole Professor of Christian Theology and Spirituality at the Episcopal Divinity School in Cambridge, Massachusetts, and has published extensively in Asian feminist theology, biblical hermeneutics, and postcolonial criticism. Her books include *Postcolonial Imagination and Feminist Theology, Introducing Asian Feminist Theology*, and *Discovering the Bible in the Non-biblical World*. She is cofounder of the Pacific, Asian, and North American Asian Women in Theology and Ministry (PANAAWTM) and is active in the ecumenical movement. She grew up in Hong Kong and loves seafood.

Boyung Lee is assistant professor of educational ministries at Pacific School of Religion at the Graduate Theological Union in Berkeley, California. She has published articles on Asian American cultural, racial, and sexual identities and faith formation, as well as postcolonial biblical pedagogy in *Religious Education, Pastoral Psychology*, and other journals and books. She has led several seminars for Women in Leadership of The Association of Theological Schools of the United States and Canada, and she is the convener of the Pan-Methodist Group of the Association of Religious Education. She loves Korean spicy stew.

Nantawan Boonprasat Lewis is professor of ethnic studies and religious studies and chairs the Ethnic and Religious Studies Department at Metropolitan State University, Minneapolis/St. Paul, Minnesota. She has written numerous articles on the struggles of Asian and Asian American women and has edited *Revolution of Spirit* and coedited *Sisters Struggling in the Spirit: Women of Color's Theological Anthology* and

Remembering Conquest: Feminist/Womanist Perspectives on Religion, Colonialization and Sexual Violence. She has done research for many years on women, religion, sex trafficking, and AIDS in Thailand and neighboring countries. She likes spicy northern Thai food.

Greer Anne Wenh-In Ng is associate professor emerita at Emmanuel College, Victoria University in the University of Toronto; past coordinator of its Centre for Asian Theology; and an ordained minister of The United Church of Canada. A past president of the Association of Professors and Researchers in Religious Education, she has published in the areas of feminist and liberative pedagogies; Asian and Asian North American religious life, worship, and education; and postcolonial approaches to engaging the Scriptures for antiracism work. Her favorite food is bread pudding, which she is still trying to make properly.

Lai Ling Elizabeth Ngan is associate professor of Christian Scriptures at George W. Truett Theological Seminary, Baylor University, in Waco, Texas. She has published articles on biblical interpretation from an Asian American woman's perspective, including an article on Amos in the *Global Bible Commentary*. She is cochair of the Asian and Asian American Hermeneutics Group of the Society of Biblical Literature. Born and raised in Hong Kong, her favorite foods are Ben and Jerry's ice cream and dark chocolate.

Rose Wu was cofounder of the Hong Kong Women Christian Council and is currently director of the Hong Kong Christian Institute. Since the 1980s she has been an active participant in the women's movement and other social and political movements in Hong Kong as well as in the ecumenical movement in Asia. Her education includes theological studies at Chung Chi College at the Chinese University of Hong Kong and a doctor of ministry degree at the Episcopal Divinity School in Cambridge, Massachusetts. Her books include *Liberating the Church from Fear: The Story of Hong Kong's Sexual Minorities* and *A Dissenting Church*. As a Chinese woman, she likes eating steamed fish, which tastes good only when the fish is fresh.

Seung Ai Yang is associate professor of sacred Scripture at the St. Paul Seminary School of Divinity of the University of St. Thomas, St. Paul, Minnesota. She has served on the Committee on Race and Ethnicity of the Association of Theological Schools for six years and as chair during the past two years. Her current research interests include Asian

American biblical hermeneutics, Bible and boundaries, and biblical authority. Her favorite foods are pork and shellfish, which, by coincidence, should be off the menu, according to biblical dietary law.

Gale A. Yee is professor of biblical studies at the Episcopal Divinity School, Cambridge, Massachusetts. She is author of *Poor Banished Children of Eve: Woman as Evil in the Hebrew Bible*; *Jewish Feasts and the Gospel of John*; *Composition and Tradition in the Book of Hosea*; and a commentary, "The Book of Hosea," in *The New Interpreters Bible*, vol. 7. She was editor of *Judges and Method: New Approaches in Biblical Studies*. Her current book project is titled *Class Acts: Marginalization in Ancient Israel* (forthcoming). She is currently general editor of Semeia Studies. Her favorite foods are everything bad for her and lots of it.

Index

CPSIA information can be obtained at www.ICGtesting.com
Printed in the USA
BVOW09s2028250814

364200BV00006B/45/P